CONFESSIONS OF
A PRESIDENTIAL
SPEECHWRITER

CONFESSIONS OF A PRESIDENTIAL SPEECHWRITER

Craig R. Smith

Michigan State University Press
East Lansing

⊚ The paper used in this publication meets the minimum requirements of ANSI/NISO
Z39.48-1992 (R 1997) (Permanence of Paper).

 Michigan State University Press
East Lansing, Michigan 48823-5245

Printed and bound in the United States of America.

20 19 18 17 16 15 14 1 2 3 4 5 6 7 8 9 10

LIBRARY OF CONGRESS CATALOGING-IN-PUBLICATION DATA

Smith, Craig R.
Confessions of a presidential speechwriter / Craig R. Smith.
    pages cm
    Includes bibliographical references and index.
    ISBN 978-1-61186-113-6 (pbk : alk. paper)—ISBN 978-1-60917-403-3 (ebook)
1. Smith, Craig R. 2. Communication in politics—United States. 3. Speechwriting—
United States. 4. Rhetoric—Political aspects—United States. 5. Political oratory—United
States. 6. Freedom of speech—United States. 7. Freedom of the press—United States. 8.
United States—Politics and government—1945–1989. 9. United States—Politics and
government—1989–1993. 10. Speechwriters—United States—Biography. 11. Presidents—
United States—Staff—Biography. I. Title.
    JA85.2.U6S654 2014
    973.92092—dc23
    [B]
    2013022654

Book design by Scribe Inc. (www.scribenet.com)

Cover design by Erin Kirk New
Cover image of the White House is ©iStockphoto.com/Mableen.

g green Michigan State University Press is a member of the Green Press Initiative and
  press   is committed to developing and encouraging ecologically responsible publishing
INITIATIVE practices. For more information about the Green Press Initiative and the use of recycled
paper in book publishing, please visit www.greenpressinitiative.org.

Visit Michigan State University Press at www.msupress.org

For A.P.C.

Contents

Preface

I WAS THE FIRST PERSON WITH A DEGREE IN COMMUNICATION STUD-
ies to be hired as a full-time presidential speechwriter. This memoir explores
the training for that post and its execution. The memoir provides lessons
I have learned that will give the reader an understanding of the nuances
of various structures in our society that touched on my life, from the academic to the news media and the political world. However, there are various
byways along the journey that should also prove interesting to the reader.
The first concerns the American Dream, from the success of immigrants
and cross-cultural integration to the rise of lower-class kids to the top rungs
of American power. The second investigates higher education in America,
shows its value in the '60s, reveals its sometimes corrupt nature, and dis-
cusses how that corruption can be overcome if we simply narrow our focus
to providing an excellent opportunity to mentor students. The third byway
analyzes broadcast news from behind the scenes at CBS. The fourth explores
national politics from my perspective as a presidential speechwriter, a campaign manager, and a deputy director of the National Republican Senatorial
Campaign Committee, while at the same time being in the closet. The final
byway explores my contribution to the fight for freedom of expression in
America.

I believe the early autobiographical material on my parents reveals part
of my training as a writer, and also how some of my political views were
shaped. The root of immigrant stock was grafted to a tree that can be traced
to the first battle of the American Revolution. That heritage played an
important role in the themes I would write about. Furthermore, while my
father taught me what constituted a good argument, my mother taught
me that there was more to a good argument than logic. My education and
experiences provided the skills and practice required to make me into a professional and academic writer.

Acknowledgments

I WANT TO THANK MARTHA BATES AND GABRIEL DOTTO AT MICHI-gan State University Press for guiding this project to completion in a responsible and professional way. My gratitude also goes to Marty Medhurst for recommending the book to MSU Press, and to the anonymous reviewer and Chuck Morris, both of whom provided a reality check and prevented me from running off on paths unrelated to the main highway of this book.

CHAPTER ONE

Meeting Richard Nixon and Robert Kennedy

NINETEEN SIXTY SEVEN WAS ANOTHER MAGICAL YEAR FOR ME. I would complete my master's degree and begin work on my PhD. In March, quite by accident, I would have drinks with Senator Robert F. Kennedy. As fall ended, my request for a meeting with Richard M. Nixon would be granted. When I met with Nixon to present him with a copy of my master's thesis, he had come out of his winter of discontent. He was a rich and comfortable lawyer in New York City, but he still lusted for the presidency that had eluded him. He had lost it to John Kennedy by only 112,000 votes in 1960. Nobly, he did not contest that election. Then he lost the governor's race in California to Pat Brown in 1962, promptly held his "last press conference," and moved to New York to join John Mitchell's law firm.

When I came by his Broad Street office in Manhattan, Nixon was interested in my take on Ronald Reagan, the subject of my thesis. The year before, in 1966, Reagan had become governor of California in a landslide vote. Nixon wanted to know how this actor had done it. My thesis on the speechmaking of Reagan explained how he won, right down to a precinct analysis of the vote.

Reagan wasn't the only Republican winner in 1966. They had scored an incredible comeback from the Goldwater debacle of 1964. Charles Percy of Bell and Howell fame won a Senate seat in Illinois. George Romney of American Motors became governor of Michigan. Nelson Rockefeller was reelected governor of New York. And Reagan, who had given a magnificent television address on behalf of Goldwater in 1964, had become governor of Nixon's home state—a governorship Nixon had lost to the man Reagan beat. However, all was not lost for Nixon, because along with these new names on election night 1966, you also heard the name of Richard

Nixon. He had predicted the results to Walter Cronkite, because he had campaigned all across the country for congressional candidates, and because President Lyndon Johnson had made the mistake of questioning Nixon's patriotism in a televised news conference right before the election. Nixon demanded and got response time just before election night. At the end of his half hour, he excused himself from the public and turned to a second camera to address his closing remarks directly "to the President." It was a brilliant strategy. Pure Nixon. The man was back.

In 1967 I did not know that running into and working for politicians would become my fate. I merely wanted to finish a PhD and become a professor. However, the tension between Nixon and Kennedy would alter my path. The story begins in 1966 when Nixon made his comeback, rising from the ashes of his double defeat. There he was again, the same self-conscious look, the hands held awkwardly in front, a pose assumed for the cover of *Newsweek*, which ironically was owned by his old and future nemesis, the *Washington Post*. There he was again. Yes, Richard Nixon, shaking hands with Katharine Graham, the owner of the *Post*, at the American newspaper publishers' convention. And again, on *Meet the Press* for an unprecedented hour-long interview. Then came a special "Profile" in *Time*, accompanied by a full-page color picture.

How is it that this man was able to make more comebacks than Judy Garland and yet never achieve the adulation of his archrivals, John and Robert Kennedy?

The answer lies deep not only in Nixon's psyche, but in the psyche of the nation. For Americans, myths guide perceptions, and once we elevate people to the level of hero, we tend to forget the reality of their lives. We've done that with John and Robert Kennedy, but never with Nixon. The reason is that Nixon was *perceived* to be a rhetorical man, constantly concerned with the specific audience and the specific issue, while the Kennedys were *perceived* to be more poetic, seeming to look for universal truths and mythic status.[1] They attached themselves to poets, from the Greeks to Robert Frost. They were princes, Nixon was Machiavelli.

While Nixon would go into the '50s remembered for uncovering Alger Hiss, John Kennedy would be remembered for writing *Why England Slept*. While Nixon would go into the '60s remembered for his "Checkers" speech, John Kennedy would be remembered for *Profiles in Courage*. During the first debate between them in 1960, Nixon addressed Kennedy and the specific issues; Kennedy addressed the nation and often ignored the questions he was asked to give the answers he wanted the public to hear. Kennedy went on to reign in Camelot; Nixon lost an election for the first time, then lost again in 1962, and went into exile on Wall Street.

Furthermore, fate seems to have dealt John and then Robert Kennedy mythic lives, particularly if you look at them from Nixon's perspective. Nixon's fate always seemed to be in his own hands. He ordered the Watergate cover-up on June 23, 1972, and for a while it worked. One can see Nixon on election night in 1972, having finally won a landslide, triumphantly uttering, "I told you so!" He carried every state but Massachusetts; it was the sweetest moment of his political career. And it was followed by a blue funk that led him to demand a resignation letter from each of his Cabinet members, allowing him to shuffle it.

Nixon's political suicide was not completed until 1974, but almost every step was his own. He could have gone public numerous times and saved the day. Or as Barry Goldwater suggested, he could have just burned the tapes on the White House lawn, claiming he was protecting state secrets and exerting executive privilege. What motivates such nonstrategic thinking in such a sophisticated mind? Perhaps he believed he was unworthy of the landslide of 1972. Or because of his saintly mother, maybe he never felt right unless he felt guilty. Or, as he claimed, he wanted a documented record with which to refute the inevitable critics he would face after he stepped down from power. As we shall see, that pattern shows up in several of the men for whom I've worked.

Every time I met Nixon in person—once in 1967, once in the summer of 1972, and once in San Clemente after his fall—my feeling of empathy was strong. The rise from poverty, the discovery of Communist infiltrators, the triumph in China, the withdrawal from the war, the electoral losses and victories, etched Nixon into our collective consciousness. In my case, a young man growing up in the subtle seasons of Southern California identified with the debater, the ambitious student, the man who would be president.

But if Nixon is the consummate rhetorical politician, his mythic counterpart was Robert Kennedy. I met him on St. Patrick's Day, 1967, through a strange set of circumstances. I spent most of that day, as did my roommate, working on a master's thesis, the very one I would turn over to Nixon a few months later. That night we went into Manhattan on a double date with a couple of intercollegiate debaters from usc. As Shea Stadium receded into the black depths and the subway sank into Manhattan, the soul I thought had died came back to life.

We met our dates at the Copter Club atop the Pan Am Building. As the escalator delivered us to the plush red lounge, important people at dozens of tables came into sight. The place had a fantastic view, accompanied by the muffled noise of helicopters rising and descending on the roof. In 1967, that sound filled us with dread because it was the sound of Vietnam, and my roommate and I were waiting for the inevitable draft notices.

The "girls" (that's how we talked in those days) had already ordered drinks before we arrived; they worked for Pan Am and were familiar with the lounge. Just as we began to discuss where to eat, I noticed Jesse Unruh, then Speaker of the California Assembly, standing near a phone booth. Penny saw him too and, much to our embarrassment, went to ask him if he would join us.

In those days, Jesse Unruh was physically large; he wasn't called "Big Daddy" for nothing. His big face sagged around his wide, friendly mouth. We were surprised when he accepted Penny's invitation and bought us another round of drinks. He asked us for our "political philosophies." We shocked our dates and they surprised us, not to mention Unruh, when we all admitted to being conservative Republicans. Unruh wanted to know why so many young people were turning to Republicanism. We gave him different judgments, which amounted to "the Democrats got us into a war and the Great Society doesn't reward hard work."

Throughout the ensuing conversation, Unruh periodically left and paced in front of the phone booths. The lines were long, so he would return, defeated. Finally, Mary asked if she could help. He told her he had to call Robert Kennedy and that no one at the phones believed him. What was worse, no one recognized him "even after I told them who I was!" We laughed at his honesty. Mary took Unruh down to her office so he could use her phone.

Unruh returned with a wide, warm grin. He was more comfortable now and began to attack our Republicanism. Finally, he looked at his watch and asked, "How far away is the Waldorf Astoria?"

"Only a few blocks," I chimed in. Would we take him there? We'd be happy to.

When we reached the Bull and Bear Room of the Waldorf, Unruh surprised us by asking us in for another round of drinks. Because it was St. Patrick's Day, the tables all had potatoes wrapped in Irish green ribbons and stuck with white plastic picks. (I still have the ribbon and picks; the potato was last seen growing behind a shabby apartment house in Flushing, New York.)

As we sipped our drinks and talked, we were suddenly stunned into silence. Then we bumped and balanced to our feet. Robert Kennedy had appeared from nowhere. He was dressed in a navy-blue suit and wore a navy-blue and red striped tie. His hair, slightly mussed, characterized the frenzy that was his personality. Unruh introduced us as "student aides"; no one gave him away. Kennedy, in a quiet voice, said, "Hello, how are you?" to each of us, repeatedly taking a swipe at his forelock.

No sooner had we reseated ourselves than a whiskey on the rocks—Old Fitzgerald, we later learned—arrived for Kennedy. He nursed it through the forty-five-minute meeting, which concerned whether or not he should run for president. I have never strained so hard to hear any conversation. Unruh gave him several arguments in favor of running and supported each one with poll data and assurances from other political bosses: Run in '68 or forget '72. . . . If you don't take an ideological stand against Johnson in '68, it will be used against you in '72. . . . Move now, I have California lined up. . . . New York is yours. . . . You can get Daley. . . . The Republicans can all be taken. . . . Romney is shallow. . . . Rockefeller has the same base as you, only they're more loyal to you, and he'll never be nominated after what he did at the 1964 convention. . . . Another Kennedy-Nixon battle would put you in for sure.

Kennedy would not commit. He was worried about splitting the party, about the fact that his own brother had made Johnson vice president, about moderate Republicans winning in '68 and controlling things for the foreseeable future. And he worried about Nixon, who had been so effective in engineering the Republican congressional comeback of 1966.

Unruh skillfully answered each of these concerns. He concluded with a joke about Nixon being from sunny Southern California: "He's a man for no seasons." In the end, neither man left the table satisfied. Kennedy agreed to let Unruh start an organization that would emerge at the opportune moment, but Kennedy was in no mood to tip his hand just yet. Unruh wanted Kennedy to get in the race as soon as possible but settled for the tentative agreement. Suddenly, Kennedy was shaking my hand and saying goodbye. He was shorter than I had expected, his nose more hooked than I had remembered; he looked older than he did on television. He was gone.

Though I have forgotten where we took our dates to dinner, I have never forgotten what it felt like to be near a political pulse like Robert Kennedy's. My dislike for him—arising out of his role in the 1960 campaign, his attorney-generalship, his defeat of the gentle Senator Keating of New York in 1964, and his equivocations—was put aside for the better part of an hour. In those moments, I saw his style and was attracted to it. His opportunism matched Nixon's, but somehow he seemed more alive. Perhaps it was because Kennedy knew tragedy and Nixon only knew melodrama. It is one thing to lose a presidential election and quite another to lose a brother who is president.

A few months later, when I delivered my thesis to Nixon's office at 20 Broad Street, I remembered the meeting with Kennedy. Somehow the warmth of the Bull and Bear Room was as appropriate to Kennedy as the coolness of the Wall Street neighborhood was to Nixon. It was my first face-to-face meeting with the man I had come to admire. Nixon surprised me with his warmth and the enthusiasm he had for what I had written. He was really interested in the concepts and the evidence I had generated for them.

On the first anniversary of my having met Kennedy, he stood in the Senate Cloakroom finally activating the network he and Unruh had discussed. In June, after his assassination, and while watching the Kennedy funeral train, I thought back to St. Patrick's Day in 1967 and the subway ride home that night. My roommate and I just stared out the window of the dirty subway car, dreaming about potentialities. In the summer of 1968, I worked as a graduate intern for CBS at the conventions. In August in Chicago, when I saw Unruh on the floor of the chaotic Democratic Convention, I wanted to remind him of that special night, but couldn't bring myself to break through the huddle of delegates around him. They were singing "The Battle Hymn of the Republic" and crying.

Robert Kennedy was the kind of man who won the crowd over the minute he entered the room. Nixon had to persuade them. Neither was above flouting the rules a little to achieve his aims, but because of who they were, the press, which was pretty liberal in those days, held Nixon to a tougher standard. The press gave the impression that many ideas walking through Nixon's brain had been chewed up by a dark political robot. The same press found Robert Kennedy's mind occupied by a fresh, lush garden blooming in passionate reds, electric blues, and ecstatic oranges against a neon-green mass. But that set of impressions was unrealistic if not dishonest. Robert Kennedy was a public man. Because he extended his imagination, he captured ours. Richard Nixon was a private man. When you penetrated his privacy, the excitement of ideas in conflict came into view: the lust for power, the international plotting, the dreams for a better day, the projections of self.

In the pages that follow, I want to pursue the thesis that the important thing is not the reality, but the myth that allows us to live with and bear the reality. Kennedy's talent made him a myth, and that, for all of his rhetorical talent, Nixon could never be. And so he never tried and was never disappointed. Instead he spent his mind on the pragmatics of reality and in the process did some good things for the nation and the world. Freed of his burdens of power and guilt, he told us valuable things in remarkable speeches, interviews, and books that make us long for the days when such insight was more common among our leaders. For that, despite his sins, he has been welcomed into the pantheon of our political legends.

My meetings with Robert Kennedy and Richard Nixon in 1967 trig-gered something that forced me to test my political abilities. By the summer of the next year, I was a writer for CBS News for convention coverage, and that would allow me to complete valuable research for my dissertation. Eventually, I would become a professor, and a full-time speechwriter for the president of the United States, the president of Chrysler Corporation, and candidates who wanted to be president. I would become a campaign manager for a major United States senator who would eventually be brought down by scandal. I became president of a major foundation that changed the laws that govern the telecommunications industry. It has been a heady life. However, there is one oddity about it: through it all, I remained in the closet at the center of power.

CHAPTER TWO

Geography Lessons

ON A CLEAR NIGHT IN APRIL OF 1775, WILLIAM DAWES AND PAUL Revere rode their steeds from Boston along the road to Lexington and Concord, warning farmers that the British were coming. The next day, April 19, a thousand British redcoats marched on the same road seeking the revolutionary Minutemen and their ammunition depot. On the way the "lobsterbacks" encountered resistance at Lexington Green. Among the ten Minutemen assembled to defend the Green was Isaac John Muzzy, a thirty-one-year-old patriot. He hoped to stall the British on their way to Concord, where a stash of weapons and powder was being removed from a small storage facility. While his father watched, Isaac Muzzy of Lexington arose and fired into the advancing British line. One of the redcoats returned his fire, using the white puff of smoke from Isaac's musket to target him; the ball caught his jacket at heart level and blood rushed out. Isaac Muzzy was the first to die in the first official battle of the Revolutionary War, along with eight other men who were commemorated on the Green in 1799. The British went on to Concord, where they were ambushed by another group of Minutemen. Ralph Waldo Emerson's famous poem about the "shot heard 'round the world" commemorates the event. My father, who would also be something of a war hero, was a direct descendent of the Muzzy clan through his mother. He was a descendant of "Stonewall" Jackson's clan through his father. I will talk a bit more about my father in this and other chapters, because like many fathers of the "greatest generation," he withheld his affection. That in turn made me all the more determined to please him. That desire to win my father over motivated me to work very hard in school, and to form habits that would sustain me through a varied career in and outside of academia.

IMMIGRANT STOCK

On January 22, 1905, a group of workers protesting layoffs marched on the Winter Palace of Nicholas II in St. Petersburg. The Russian army protecting the czar, Nicholas II, brutally dispersed the crowd, killing many of them—their blood turning pink as it dissipated in the snow on "Bloody Sunday." The event led to protests and riots throughout the empire, which were eventually put down. However, hatred for the czar and sympathy for a republican form of government continued to grow.

When he heard about these events from a union organizer, a coal miner named Okrik marched across a rain-drenched wheat field and shared the news with his neighbors in the village square in Sanok, the district capital of Galicia in the foothills of the Carpathian mountains. The city was surrounded by fertile farms and not far from the Dniester River, which runs all the way through the Ukraine to the Black Sea. The area had been ruled by the Poles, the Russians, and now the Austrians. The district was composed mainly of people descended from the Rusyn tribe who considered themselves Ukrainian. They were short of stature, usually blond, flat of face, but long-lived. They were intensely religious, but attuned to political reality. The minority of Sanok's people, about a third, were Jewish. They were the entrepreneurs in the city along the river, and the Christians were either the farmers that tended the countryside in the fertile valley or coal miners like Okrik. The groups existed in an uneasy peace. Okrik discovered that many of these Jews were Zionists who wanted a homeland. He did not discourage their efforts.[1]

Just after the ill-fated 1905 revolt, Okrik decided that the trouble in nearby Russia could spill into his little village. Austria and Russia were threatening each other with war. As a miner, Okrik feared the talk coming from Bolsheviks and Mensheviks that his mine and the local farms should be collectivized should Russia win the war. Thus, he made a painful decision. He would send his oldest daughter, Katherine, to America, the land of dreams.

She was a smart girl, and since she was of age, he believed she could survive the train ride to Hamburg and the steamer across the Atlantic to Ellis Island. Word soon came back from Katherine that America was indeed the land of opportunity. She had been hired to run a boarding house. She claimed that husbands and work awaited in the Rusyn neighborhoods outside of Newark and deep in the Pennsylvania mountains where coal was being mined. In Sanok, Okrik welcomed the news from Katherine and decided to send his teenage second daughter Julia off to America to join her sister. Julia was not a son and, therefore, could not work in the local coal mines. She was another mouth to feed in a poor household.

After trekking her way to Lonczin, Russia, the stepping-off point for

Ukrainians, Julia Okrik made her way to Rotterdam and boarded a steamer for America. For a young woman of thirteen from a landlocked village, the voyage must have been frightening and exciting, particularly when the Statue of Liberty came into view. Scarier still was the walk through the turnstiles at Ellis Island. Julia Okrik claimed on her papers to have been born in 1895, and to be seventeen years of age; however, she was actually born in 1898. Not only was she afraid that her secret would be discovered, Julia almost did not get through processing because she was ill, and no one with any illness was allowed into the country. She was a good enough actress to make it through; she then ran for a restroom, where she threw up. It was not the last time evidence of her pluck would show itself.

Two years earlier on June 28, 1909, my grandfather Mihaljo Postic came to America via Austria and Havre. He quickly adopted the American name Michael and used it when he came to stay at the boarding house of Katherine Okrik and to work in the steel mills nearby. My grandfather was born in Galicia in 1892 and was very religious, but little else is known about his upbringing. He had been drafted, at a young age, into the Austro-Hungarian army and had shot his big toe off in some skirmish. He then deserted the army and fled to America. Katherine Okrik soon made a match between Michael and her younger sister Julia. Born in the hollows of Pennsylvania, my mother, Anna Postic, would be their second child.

Her older sister Mary emerged as the leader of the children until she moved to New York City to find a new life. An event in Catholic school prompted my mother to follow her sister a year later. During a geography lesson, a nun asked my mother where Buffalo was. She told the nun it was on the back of a nickel, since in those days Jefferson's head was on one side and a bison was on the other. The nun rapped my mother's knuckles with a ruler and slapped the back of her head. She fled the classroom and never looked back. The year was 1930 and she was only fifteen years old.

Like her sister, my mother was hired by fairly well-to-do Jewish doctors and dentists in Brooklyn's Park Slope neighborhood, where she absorbed a new culture. My mother was grateful to earn a dollar a day and to have some days off to see the city. She especially liked Coney Island. On top of that, her kind employers wanted her to learn as much as she could about culture. When she was taken to the Verdi opera *Rigoletto*, she witnessed something quite beautiful and sad. She never forgot the moment.

When her sister Mary married a Pole, Thomas Osinski who had joined the Navy, my mother followed her sister to San Diego to help her raise a family. One day my Uncle Tommy brought home a sailor he had befriended. My mom met him on her birthday, December 17, 1937, very shortly after he had received the Good Conduct Medal from the Navy. His name was Ralph Smith and he looked like Dick Powell, the movie star from *Forty-Second Street.* Thus, two divergent streams came together as only they could in America, and they would later inspire words I would write to raise money for the restoration of the Statue of Liberty and Ellis Island.

MY FATHER THE HEATHEN

At my mother's twenty-second birthday party, my father made the mistake of claiming he was brought up without religion by his mother. Born in Augusta, Wisconsin, in 1877, and a trained nurse in Chicago by the time she was eighteen, she became the first woman to claim land as a homesteader in desolate North Dakota. Clementine Ramona Muzzy spent her first winter in a plywood shack, nearly dying of the cold. In the ensuing summer, she married Irwin Ralph "I.R." Smith, the postmaster and owner of the country general store.[2]

Born in West Branch, Iowa, in 1869, my grandfather I.R. was a direct descendent of Judah Jackson, the brother of the famous Civil War general "Stonewall." Clementine swept I.R. off his feet with her strong will, flowing red hair, and survival instincts. She and I.R. had a productive marriage. In 1911, my father was the first born. In high school, he became a good debater, a track star, and an excellent swimmer, one of the few who could make it across Devil's Lake. But things suddenly fell apart for his family. In 1926, my grandfather suffered a stroke and had to be put in a home. Still, my father was able to enter North Dakota State Teachers College (now Minot State University) in 1929, and he started teaching elementary school in the Clear Lake District. During the 1932 election, he campaigned for Senator Gerald P. Nye, a Republican isolationist, and drove him around the district. But in 1933, when wheat dropped to 69 cents a bushel on the open market, the farm was wiped out.

My father left college and joined the Navy to support my grandmother and his siblings. Grandfather I.R. would die in the rest home in 1943. After my father enlisted, he spent a few months in the North Dakota National Guard before shipping out to San Diego for training. In early 1934, he found himself on the USS *Arizona*; luckily he was not on it seven years later when it was sunk at Pearl Harbor. Instead, he moved from ship to ship, learning various skills. On the USS *Tanager*, he helped with a survey of the Aleutian Islands. A few months later he was assigned to the USS *Richmond* and moved up to what would become one of his specialties, fire control operations. In 1935, he participated in the rescue of the crew of the *Macon* and received his first of many commendations. He befriended Thomas Osinski, whose wife, as we have seen, was my mother's sister.

After their first date, it took only two weeks for my father to agree to convert to Catholicism, and in late February of 1938, my parents were married at Our Lady of Angels Catholic Church in San Diego. They had no idea that the marriage would last forever, but somehow it did. My mother usually referred to her status with my father as a "mixed marriage," by which she meant that she was of immigrant stock and that Dad's people were "English." She was ethnic Catholic; his parents were "heathen."

My parents rented a house for $25 a month on 27th Street in San Diego, near the gates to the naval station. After only a month of married life, Dad was shipped off on the *Richmond* for his first trip to Honolulu. My mom moved in with her sister to help her with her children and save on rent until my father returned.

Soon began what would seem like a lifetime of moving as long as Dad was in the service. First, my father was transferred to the USS *Reid* in Norfolk, Virginia, where he brought his new bride. But after only a month, he was ordered to fire control school in Washington, D.C., in October 1939. He was promoted to first class and transferred to Long Island City, New York, for more training in the spring of 1940. My mom showed my father her old haunts, insisting on trips to Coney Island.[3]

PEARL HARBOR

In June 1941, my mom and dad returned to San Diego. But later in the summer of 1941, my father was back in Honolulu assigned to the USS *Shaw*. Because the rest of the world was at war, my father did not allow my mom to travel with him. Japan had invaded Manchuria in 1931, for which it had been censured by the League of Nations. The United States supported the oil embargo of Japan, which only served to increase that country's enmity for the United States. In 1939, Germany signed a non-aggression pact with the Soviet Union and they divided Poland between them. That triggered the Second World War, in which Japan, extending its holdings in China, joined the German-Italian-Soviet Axis. France fell like a ripe plum in June of 1940. My father believed it was inevitable that the United States would enter the war and that it would be fought on two fronts.

On December 4, 1941, he wrote a long letter to my mother that included a premonition of what was to come three days later. Before the letter arrived, Pearl Harbor was attacked. On December 8, 1941, my mom saw the *Shaw's* spectacular explosion on the front page of the *San Diego Union*. It became the signature picture of the Japanese attack on Pearl Harbor. A telegram soon arrived informing Mom that her husband was "missing in action." She believed the worst had happened. Forty-eight hours later she received a call from him. On the fateful Sunday morning, he had been on the back end of the *Shaw* working when the front end was hit, blowing off the bow. He ran to the front as part of the fire control unit. The back of the ship was then hit. My father was blown into the water and, luckily being a good swimmer from his days in the North Dakota lakes, made it to shore.

After America's declaration of war on Japan, Germany declared war on the United States, and Dad was assigned to the USS *Porter*. My mom joined the war effort and became Anna the Riveter on "trim and drill" at Rohr Aircraft in 1942 and 1943.[4] In the meantime, my father returned to the *Shaw* in February 1942 while it was being repaired at Mare Island near San Francisco. My mom joined him. When the *Shaw* was moved to San Diego for further fitting, my parents bought a house on a hill at 929 East 16th Street in National City, immediately south of San Diego; it would become my little paradise. In July 1943, my father was promoted to ensign, and in October he was back in action during the battles to take the Japanese-held islands of New Guinea and New Britain. The next month Dad left the *Shaw* and reported for more training in Norfolk, where my mother joined him.

After the training session, Dad was assigned to the fourth USS *Cushing*, the first three having met their demise in various ways. *Cushing IV*, another destroyer, stayed in Norfolk until May 1944, when Dad sailed off for the Pacific again, but not before my mother told him that she was pregnant. Soon after, Mom flew home to San Diego.[5] I've always believed my love of flying came from the fact that I flew across the country in my mother's womb. She never let me forget that she suffered from morning sickness most of the way across the country, but we both survived.

In August 1944, my father engaged in the battle to take Palau, and then protected carriers for their strikes on Mindinao, Samar, and Cebu in the Philippines, where the *Cushing* came under constant attack but shot down its share of enemy planes. The *Cushing* supported the assault on Angaur in September and screened for carriers at Formosa, Manila, and Luzon while also rescuing downed pilots at sea. As my mother went into labor in mid-October of 1944, my father was helping to prepare the Philippines for its liberation by General MacArthur. I was born on October 13, and my father took part in the important battle of Leyte Gulf on October 24. Soon after, my father was promoted to lieutenant junior grade.

Of course I didn't realize it at the time, but I was born at a turning point in history. War would be more barbaric than ever. For the first time in a major war, more civilians were killed than soldiers. The London Blitz, the destruction of Warsaw, the bombing of German cities including the firebombing of Dresden, the firebombing of Tokyo, and the dropping of the atom bomb on two heavily populated Japanese cities were the price of victory. As the war in the Pacific ended, Dad was promoted to chief gunnery officer. The *Cushing* headed for Bremerton, Washington, where Dad would reunite with Mom and his family and meet me for the first time. He had received the American Defense Medal, the Asiatic Pacific Campaign Award, the Good Conduct Medal, the Philippine Liberation Medal, and the World War II Victory Medal.

MEETING MY FATHER

I met my father at the end of 1945 in Port Orchard, Washington, a lovely island community. When Mom met her prim and proper mother-in-law, my paternal grandmother showed nothing but disdain for "this uneducated Russian." It was one of those many instances in her life when my mother was reminded of her poor upbringing, and each of these wounded her, forcing her to develop ways to cope, which she would pass on to me.

Soon my father was ordered to take the *Cushing* to Long Beach, California. Mom and I returned to the house on 16th Street in National City, and Dad commuted from Long Beach on the weekends, often complaining of the fog along Highway 1. Dad received three pieces of very good news during this time: he was to report to the USS *Leary* in San Diego, he was promoted to full lieutenant, and Mom became pregnant with my sister Avis, who was born a redhead like her father and grandmother. I enjoyed my early years, in which the days were punctuated with naps in the backyard under fruit trees my father had planted.[6] I was dazzled by wind-blown blossoms every spring. The sun turned my hair to California blond.

During late 1948 and early 1949, I watched my mom balloon with another sister. In March Renée was born. I dutifully helped with diaper duty while teaching Avis, who was approaching three, how to speak. I had been an early speaker, and now I wanted my sister to be one too. It was my first fascination with speech and how it worked.

While Dad was on the Navy base during the day, Mom and I worked as a team to keep my sisters fed, bathed, and diapered. We also had plenty of yard time. Then, at the end of the day, I would sit out on the front lawn and watch down 16th Street, waiting for my father to get off the bus. I could see the ships in the bay, beyond which lay the vast Pacific Ocean with its distant horizon. Then he would appear and I would run downhill to him. He would swoop me up and carry me to the house.

The addition of a master bedroom to the little house on 16th Street meant I would have a bedroom of my own. While Dad commuted to Long Beach for additional training, I began kindergarten. School was half-day. So after playing with my pals, I got to play with my sisters and enjoy our home and the company of nearby relatives. It was heaven, and I should have known it could not last.

In this case, paradise was destroyed by the Korean War. Though I was not very conscious of it at the time, there were dark clouds on the international horizon as early as 1946. My father was very cognizant of them, and argued about foreign policy with my Uncle Tommy every time the two got together. I remember sitting on the rug and listening to them in rapt attention, trying to figure out what "nationalism," "capitalism," "containment" and "communism" meant. My Uncle Tommy was a very liberal, pro-union Democrat; my father a conservative Republican. The explosive mix gave me an early political education.

The context for their arguments was very serious. In 1946, Winston Churchill had come to Fulton, Missouri, at the behest of President Truman and declared that "an iron curtain had descended" from the Baltic to the Adriatic. In 1948, Alger Hiss, the undersecretary of state, was embarrassed by a young congressman and former Navy man (my father was quick to point out) named Richard Nixon. By revealing Hiss's former connection to a Communist cell, Nixon instantly became one of my father's favorites.[7] Soon President Truman was requiring all government employees to take a loyalty oath; the practice spread to the states. Hollywood writers who had been Communists, or associated with them, or refused to answer questions before the House Un-American Activities Committee were blacklisted. Professors and teachers who invoked their First and/or Fifth Amendment rights were fired, even if they had tenure.

I remember the 1948 election if for no other reason than that my father predicted that Truman would win. He warned that the Republican nominee, Thomas E. Dewey, the former prosecuting attorney in the Lucky Luciano case and the sitting governor of New York, was too arrogant and overconfident. In fact, my father had not forgiven Dewey for losing to Roosevelt in

1944. My father and I listened to the election-eve speeches of the candidates in November 1948, perhaps my first exposure to American public address. Henry Wallace, the Socialist candidate, gave a plea about helping the poor, which my father disdained. Strom Thurmond, the Dixiecrat candidate, pled for states' rights and segregation, which my father condemned. Then came Truman, who stuck to his "give 'em hell" style, which had first emerged at the Democratic Convention in Philadelphia in the summer. When Truman finished, my father leaned back and said, "Well, at least you know where he stands." Then came Dewey. It sounded as if the Republicans were at a party celebrating victory. My father said, "The bastard will pay for this." The next day my father was vindicated, and the day after that he collected on his bets.[8] As far as I was concerned, my father was a political genius.

In 1949, things went from bad to worse when China fell to the Communists and Russia detonated its first atomic bomb. Then Julius and Ethel Rosenberg were accused of spying for the Soviets and executed. I remember listening to the execution reports live on the radio. In 1950, North Korea invaded its southern neighbor. My father now believed Truman was the worst president the country ever had. Truman had backed down when the Soviets blockaded Berlin; he let Eastern Europe and China slip under the "red tide." His administration was plagued with scandal. He couldn't handle the unions. And now, he was getting us engaged in a United Nations police action in a country that his secretary of state, Dean Acheson, had said was outside our "defense perimeter." The one good thing Truman did, according to my dad, was to appoint General Douglas MacArthur to head the operation.

All of this was too much for the American public; they needed a simple explanation. It came from a demagogue, one of those awful scourges from which democracies too often suffer. A Republican senator from Wisconsin, Joe McCarthy, gave a speech in Wheeling, West Virginia, in 1950 in which he waved his hotel laundry list claiming it contained the names of 205 subversives in the State Department. The claim took the country by storm, and McCarthy—with the support of conservatives, anti-Communist Catholics, and military men like my father, among others—was off on a four-year ride, terrorizing everyone who came into his sights. His story, while a wild exaggeration, was woven from enough facts to give it resonance with the public. There had to be subversives in the government for us to have lost our nuclear edge and for all these countries to have gone over to communism. Besides, McCarthy was supported by some of the most popular commentators in America, including Walter Winchell, who began his popular radio broadcasts with a nod to "Mister and Misses America and all the ships at sea."

THE FORGOTTEN WAR

The headlines from the Korean War were awful. The North Korean army of almost 90,000 soldiers moved south easily against the retreating South Korean army of no more than 40,000 soldiers with inferior equipment. While the U.S.-led UN Police Force was organizing, the North Koreans captured Seoul, the capital of South Korea, and continued pushing south. By August 1, 1950, the South Korean forces were contained inside a 143-mile perimeter around the city of Pusan. However, the UN Police Force poured troops and five hundred badly needed tanks into Pusan, all under the command of General MacArthur, the hero of the Pacific from World War II and also the virtual dictator of the defeated Japanese. Once the Pusan perimeter held, MacArthur ordered a counteroffensive, which turned the tide. On August 18, a major battle raged in which thousands of North Korean troops were killed.

While they were retreating, MacArthur developed an innovative plan. Using the Seventh Fleet, he ordered the softening up of the area in and around Seoul. Then, landing to the west of Seoul at Inchon, MacArthur liberated the South Korean capital, cut the North Korean army in two, and pushed it back into its country and then all the way north across the Yalu River into China. The North Koreans had invaded the South in June of 1950; by November, MacArthur seemed to have won the war.

MacArthur called for the bombing of the bridges across the Yalu, but Truman refused to approve the plan. MacArthur called for the use of tactical nuclear weapons in China, and again Truman refused the plan. On November 26, 1950, the Red Chinese entered the war, crossing the Yalu in droves, just as MacArthur had predicted. Thousands of American troops were captured and many were eventually "brainwashed," turning on their country and even becoming Chinese citizens.[9] MacArthur could not stop the march of the invaders until January 12, 1951, with the Chinese about a quarter of the way into South Korea. In March, MacArthur took the unusual step of writing to Joe Martin, the House Republican leader, claiming "there was no substitute for victory." On April 11, 1951, Truman removed MacArthur for insubordination. If there had been any doubt about my father's politics, they were erased with that one move. My father became an even more avid, militarist Republican cold warrior and would never, so long as he lived, vote for a Democrat.

On a September night in 1951, my father shipped off to Korea; my mom drove us to the Navy docks in San Diego. While my sisters slept, Dad kissed Mom, and then he leaned in through the open car-door window and kissed me. I gave him a hug and rubbed my cheek against his; it felt like sandpaper, but I liked it.

October 9, 1951, found my father launching shells into Wonsan, Korea, and blowing up a huge ammunition depot, while North Korean shore batteries fired back. My father was commended for "extremely accurate fire [that] quickly silenced the enemy shore batteries thus preventing damage to his ship and crew."[10] Two days later his ship, the *Twining*, was strafed by Soviet-made MiGs, but no one was hurt and the *Twining* continued its duty, raiding the Korean coast, rescuing downed pilots along the way. Dad received a commendation from the United Nations for "outstanding service" and was allowed to return home.

When he arrived, Dad told us he would be assigned to Hunter's Point in San Francisco for the summer of 1952. I remember listening to the conventions on the radio. My father favored General Dwight Eisenhower for the Republican nomination because he was a military man, and because he could win and the other Republican candidate, Senator Robert Taft of Ohio, was dull as dishwater. My father was not discouraged by the fact that Dewey supported Eisenhower. "It takes a loser to recognize a winner," he growled. When Everett Dirksen, the gravel-voiced senator from Illinois and supporter of his Senate colleague Taft, condemned Dewey from the podium for "taking us down the road to defeat" in 1948, my father laughed, "So now *you* want to take us down the road to defeat." Eisenhower had not declared his candidacy for the nomination until June. His operatives had to convince the convention to throw Taft's Texas delegates out and replace them with supporters of the general. In an exciting convention, Eisenhower carried the day on the second ballot, and much to my father's delight selected Richard Nixon, by then a senator from California, for vice president.

The Democratic Convention was less interesting. Truman had pulled out after being humiliated in the New Hampshire primary. The Democrats eventually swung to the articulate governor of Illinois, Adlai Stevenson. My father referred to the balding Stevenson as an "egghead." These early sessions with my father, listening to conventions and election night, enhanced my addiction to politics and would serve me well when, eventually, I was covering them for CBS.

Soon after we returned to National City and I started the third grade, General Eisenhower was elected president and Dad was ordered back to Korea. As we read in rapt attention about the slow going in the war, the witch hunts of Senator Joe McCarthy continued. However, because of my father's military status and his support of McCarthy, we never dreamed the paranoia he created could reach us. But it did.

In those days, most families were too poor to afford a single-party phone line. We used multiple-party lines. The technology was so simple that you could listen in on whoever was using the line, or tell them to get off because you had an emergency. To avoid people listening in, my mother and her sister Mary spoke to one another in Ukrainian, thinking nothing of it until one day the FBI came to our door. As a seven-year-old, I sat and watched this man in a fedora enter our house and ask my mother why she was running a Communist cell! She explained the situation about the party-line phone. I couldn't help butting in: "My dad is in Korea fighting the Communists." The FBI man apologized and left.

Eisenhower finally negotiated a truce in Korea that restored the original borders of the two countries. No one had won; thousands of lives were lost, among them more than 54,000 Americans. My father had lost his faith while winning the China Service, United Nations, and Korea Service medals. He said they would be part of a "forgotten war." A story he told me when he returned was quite frightening and woke me up to life's existential condition. One day Dad spotted what he thought was an enemy troop encampment. From the *Twining*, he fired into it and obliterated it. When his superior officer checked the map, he discovered it was a prisoner-of-war camp for Americans. Heartsick, Dad was sent to the brig to await trial. The next day, much to Dad's relief, it was discovered that the North Koreans, in violation of the Geneva Accords, had constructed a fake POW camp to hide a full division of soldiers. Dad was a hero again and got another medal, but he didn't feel he deserved it; he knew he had made a terrible mistake and lucked out. When he returned from the war in early 1953, his bad habits had gotten even worse. He smoked two packs of cigarettes a day and drank a lot more. His mild fits of anger now became legendary tantrums. He put on weight.[11]

At the same time, I was becoming more Catholic, which pleased my mother. I was the star of the catechism class and was learning about an omniscient God who sent his son to redeem us from Adam's original sin. The son was born of a woman who was immaculate (without the stain of Adam's sin) and a virgin inculcated by a holy spirit who had been taken body and soul to heaven when she died. This story appealed to me as a way to transcend the dangers of this world.

MOVING TIME

After the last day of class in the third grade, I came home and saw that Mother had been crying. She said, "Craig, we have to move again, not for just a summer, but perhaps for a lifetime." Dad was promoted to lieutenant commander and we were moving to the Naval Proving Grounds at Dahlgren, Virginia, where he would work on weapons development and—I would later discover—classified missile systems.

So in the summer of 1953, we were off on another journey. I experienced my first bout of depression when my parents sold the house on 16th Street. I had made lots of friends and often played at the Boys Club with my cousin Harvey, four years my senior and a terrific "big brother." He taught me how to fly a kite off the hill behind L Street. He took me into the sewer system of the city, where we chased rats. He knew a cop who let us ride on the back of his motorcycle. He kept me out after dark, much to my mother's horror. When I actually won a plaque at the Boys Club for a model plane I built, I was ecstatic, and Harvey gave me all the credit even though I couldn't have built the plane without his help. Now, I would have to give all this up, particularly the time with my cousin. It was the first time a dark cloud pushed its way across my brain, and it scared me. This wasn't just sadness, it was something much darker and uncontrollable.

The trip to Virginia turned into an odyssey that kept my sisters in awe and distracted me from my depression. First, we drove north to San Francisco to see Aunt Katherine, another of my mother's sisters, who was taking care of my maternal grandfather, and then on to Seattle to visit Grandma Clementine and other members of the extended Smith family. From there it was on to Yellowstone Park, where we watched Old Faithful blow and hiked across fields filled with bubbling mud. Bears came right up to the car. On our way out of Yellowstone, we drove through Craig's Pass, which my mother claimed had been named in my honor. I believed her. We made our way to the Battle of the Little Big Horn, the site of Custer's Last Stand. This side trip required us to go through the Big Horn Mountains. In the summer of 1953, the road up was horribly frightening with its steep drop-offs and narrow hairpin turns. Once you reach the top of the Big Horns, at about 10,000 feet, the road enters a huge meadowland filled with grass and wild flowers, and patches of snow even in the summer. It is quite beautiful and something of a respite from the grueling drive up the mountain range. When you come out of the meadows on the east side of the Big Horns, you can see out over the Great Plains, which is truly breathtaking. I suddenly gained a feeling of infinity as we looked out across America, for the first time understanding how vast it was. Soon we were visiting Dad's home in Fortuna, North Dakota, and his Uncle Ben in Grand Rapids, Minnesota.

Not long after that, an event occurred that also contributed to my knowledge of geography. When Dad took one of his wrong turns, we wound up in Peoria, Illinois, instead of Indiana. When we stopped for directions, I decided to take matters into my own hands. While Dad was in the restroom, I asked the gas station attendant how to read a map. He showed me and I asked Dad to buy it. As we got back in the car, Mom let me ride shotgun, better to navigate for the pilot. This rearrangement also gave her more time to take care of my sisters, a job I was glad to be rid of.

As we drove out of Peoria, I kept my index finger on Highway 24 on the map, and when we crossed other highways, I knew how the map worked. However, Dad began to question my directions. Each minute seemed like an eternity as I prayed for the Indiana border. Dad began talking about turning around, which I could not understand since the sun was behind us right where it belonged if you were going from Illinois to the East. Then, suddenly and much to my relief, we passed a sign that said, "Welcome to Indiana." As reward, Dad pulled into the first motel with a pool.

After over a month on the road, we pulled into the King George Motel in Edgehill, Virginia, on July 29, 1953, and waited for our house on the grounds at Dahlgren to be readied. Right on the Potomac River, the naval base looked like a country club, complete with a private golf course. Our first house was fairly large, with a screened porch and a vegetable garden in the back, where Dad raised tomatoes, corn, and cucumbers. It was magical for me to actually see these vegetables sprout, grow, and produce. It probably explains my sympathy for Jefferson's dream of all citizens having their own plot of land to give them a stake in America and engage them in the creative process of farming. More conservative seeds had been planted in my mind.

None of this prevented me from being reclusive at school and depressed at home. One cure contributed to my education: watching television extensively. *You Are There* on CBS, starring Walter Cronkite, brought history alive and made me into a history buff, and a huge fan of CBS. Little did I know that one day I would go to work at the greatest news network ever created and write words that would come out of the mouth of the most trusted man in America. It all started with the show that ended, "What kind of a day was it? It was a day like all days that alter and illuminate our times. And you were there."

Over the next decade, I would also come close to watching every variety show on television and a few more. From Perry Como to Dinah Shore, from Ed Sullivan to the *Colgate Comedy Hour* (with Dean Martin and Jerry Lewis) to *Your Show of Shows* (with Sid Caesar), it was the golden age of television. We were one of those statistics that knocked Milton Berle from the top of the ratings when we, along with a majority of Americans, switched to watching the theology lessons of Bishop Fulton J. Sheen. He used a blackboard and often claimed that there was an angel sitting on it. Along with my catechism lessons, Bishop Sheen is responsible for deepening my understanding of Catholic theology, something quite different from the church's hierarchy.

Despite the revelations of Bishop Sheen, my depression continued, and it wasn't helped by my father's attitude. I noticed that since our odyssey across the country, my father had become even more distant. Perhaps he perceived something in me he did not like—my navigating, my moping, my obsession with television, my closeness to Mother. Whatever it was, the distance was growing day by day and pushing me further down my black hole.

To cure my woes, my mother made me take lessons to become an altar boy and join the Cub Scouts. I liked the former, hated the latter. I memorized the entire mass in Latin and continued to study for the sacrament of confirmation, taking St. Christopher, Christ's bearer and patron saint of travelers, for my saint. At the beginning of our second year on the base, we moved to a big two-story house that overlooked the Potomac River from a bluff. This meant that Dad was doing very well in his job and had been promoted again.

Continuing my escapism, I began to watch late night television. I was allowed to do this as long as my grades were good. I had no idea at the time, but these programs provided equipment for speechwriting. My fascination with late night television began with Steve Allen, who made me laugh out loud. His improvisational humor revealed a quick mind with an incredible sense of timing. But it would be Jack Paar who really captured me. He was not the best comedian, but he was the most conversational, sophisticated, and self-effacing. He had famous feuds with Walter Winchell and Ed Sullivan. He would walk off his show in a feud with NBC. He would duck an on-the-air swing from an inebriated Mickey Rooney. And Paar would play host to such notables as John Kennedy, Richard Nixon, Clement Freud, and Judy Garland. And I got to see it all *live*. It was another world, one so much more fascinating than my own.

The same thing happened with motion pictures. Mom and I would watch old movies in the late afternoon when I had finished my homework. Even more fun was going to drive-ins or movie theaters to see films. During this time, for example, *Gone with the Wind* was re-released. I was completely captured by the movie and, to my father's disgust, cried at four different times while watching it. More important, during the scene where the starving Scarlett O'Hara pulls a turnip out of the ground and tries to eat it, I became her on the screen. When she spit the turnip out and said, "I'll never be poor again," I repeated the line. Whether it was Vivian Leigh or Montgomery Clift, Elizabeth Taylor or Tyrone Power, I was an equal opportunity employer in terms of creating alter egos. I was also absorbing the dialogue and becoming a different person.

I had the same feeling when I dressed up in my cassock to help a priest with the mass. It was serious showtime in those red or black frocks. The priest who taught me was very good. My favorite piece of advice from him was that if you make a mistake, do it three times and everyone will think it is part of the mass. The candles, the incense, the instruments of communion very much affected me; I assisted the priest as he turned bread and wine into the body and blood of Christ. I was always helping the other boys with their parts on the altar. In school plays I learned that I could memorize everyone's lines and then coach them and cue them, much to the teacher's delight. Once I was on a stage, I had no fear. I was able to take command and perform professionally no matter how nervous I was before the event. I was in control in that space. It was an important lesson to learn at age nine.

Dad was good about taking us on outings to see the historic countryside of Virginia, as long as I read the maps. We visited all the famous places: Mount Vernon, the battlefields, Monticello. I was seduced by my first visit to Washington, D.C., not knowing then what an important role it would play in my life. I most liked visiting the Mall with its monuments. I appreciated the city's low skyline, which made it seem very open. However, my favorite was the Wilderness Battlefield, where our distant relative Stonewall Jackson was shot and killed by his own men when he returned from a reconnaissance. These visits reinforced the history lessons I was getting in school. Living in Virginia made history real.

In the spring of 1955, Dahlgren was finally becoming home to me, and I became less reclusive and made some close friends. My depression had receded. Then one day, Dad came home and over dinner gave us some shocking news: we were moving to Norfolk, Virginia. I left the table, ran to my room, and slammed the door shut.

In Norfolk, my parents rented a house in Algonquin Park, which abutted on a black community just over the high hedge that bordered our backyard; in fact, we lived on Hedgewood Lane. My parents had taken the house because there was an elementary school just up the street. But it turned out that school was for "coloreds" only, a practice I had never heard of before. So my sisters and I had to walk a mile to the all-white Meadowbrook Elementary School.

My teacher was an old maid named Mrs. Henderson. She was very strict and very conservative. One day while talking about history, she said that when he wrote that all men were created equal, Jefferson meant "white men." My hand shot up and she called on me.

"I don't think that is right, Mrs. Henderson."

"Of course it is right. Mr. Jefferson owned slaves and never freed them."

"He did after he died."

"Well, Craig," she intoned, "why don't you explain that to the principal?" She sent me down the hall and my mother was called to come pick me up. I was suspended for the day for "insubordination" in the classroom.

I learned a lot more about Southern culture from our black neighbors. Through the hedge, we could hear them singing, joking, swearing, or arguing. Every day around 5 P.M. they came through our hedge into the white neighborhood with platters of food and pots of coffee. I watched in astonishment as the rich white women of Algonquin Park bought their goods, went inside, put the food on the table, and, according to my mother, claimed they had cooked it for their husbands.

Slowly, I made some friends. But it was becoming more and more apparent that I was different than the other boys. They seemed to have no trouble with baseball or football, but to me, it was all so unnatural. I continued to enjoy playing fantasy games at home with my sisters. This seemed to set my father off. I remember being thrown against a wall, being pulled off a bike and thrown to the ground. What had been indifference was now hostility. My self-esteem suffered another blow when my mother told me to "stop acting like a sissy." So I started to stay after school and tried to play in some football games. Since I didn't mind the physicality, I just threw myself into the games and got accepted as one of the guys. My mother didn't like it when I came home bruised with ripped clothes, but my father gave me a thumbs-up when she wasn't looking.

For the eighth grade, I attended Northside Junior High, which would eventually become infamous when its principal, a Mr. Butler, refused to integrate the place. At the time, however, the all-white school was populated with very good teachers. Ester Swink taught me the basics of grammar and sentence structure in an entertaining way. There was a marvelous teacher of mechanical drawing who took me under his wing and said I would grow up to be an architect. I took Latin and it came easy to me. There was also a sadistic ex-Marine gym teacher who forced us to do clap pushups until we were all bleeding from our chins. But all of this was soon to be left behind.

In January 1958, my dad was shattered when he was told that the Navy was cutting back due to the recession. He was given the option of retiring with twenty-six years of service—with 265 months at sea or on foreign soil—or reverting to the lower rank of chief. His pride would not let him step down to a lower rank. So he accepted the retirement terms. Mom demanded that we return to San Diego, and he had no objection. I was delighted. However, I failed to realize at the time—I was thirteen—that my dad was only forty-seven. He would have to reinvent himself if he were to find work to supplement his pension.[12]

Very soon, however, school was ending and we were packing for another cross-country journey. It seemed to me that every time I had made friends and established myself, the family was moving. However, this time was different; we were returning home. I had kept my idealized version of Southern California in my head. I often traveled to the beaches of San Diego in my dreams. Soon I would see them again for real.

RETURNING TO CALIFORNIA

The trip across the country was another epic trek, with me navigating my hostile father along the highways home. We left Norfolk and traveled down to North Carolina on the first day. We spent the second day touring the Smoky Mountains and stopping at various Native American "outposts." The next day we drove further south into Alabama and Mississippi. Near Oklahoma City, we spotted a large tornado, and instead of getting off the road, much to our horror, my father outran it. The next day it was on through the Panhandle of Texas into New Mexico. We were on Route 66, and all my father had to do was follow it west into the afternoon sun. From Gallup we traveled to Needles, which was insufferably hot. But at last we were back in California. We arrived home to National City, where we rented a house.

In December we moved into our own home, built on 4th Street just down the hill and around the corner from my Aunt Mary, with whom my mother was happy to be reunited. While my sisters suffered through a year of parochial school, I was much luckier. I started the ninth grade at Granger Junior High School. I remember getting our first English test back. I looked the page over and saw that I got 98 out of 100. Then I noted that the two questions that were marked wrong were in fact correct. I waited until the class ended and then privately explained to the teacher that he had not understood what a verb phrase was. I realized that my education in Virginia had moved me quite a bit ahead of the students, not to mention the teachers, in California. Ironically, what was true then of California's educational system is true today.

For the 1959–60 school year, I became a sophomore at Sweetwater High School, which had a reputation for taking lower-middle-class kids and making them into something special. I formed a close circle of friends. I continued to do particularly well in history under the tutelage of Jim Doyle, an inspiring teacher who made historic events come alive for us. His sense of humor was incredibly apt for students. He was the essence of "cool." He also taught after-school choir, which I joined. We did *Glee* way before there was the popular television program. We traveled to competitions and put on shows at the school assemblies.

However, everything wasn't rosy at school. In gym class, I remember taking laps with the boys when one of the bigger guys edged close to me, found a hole in my gym shirt, inserted his finger, and ripped my T-shirt in half. A few weeks later, in the locker room, I got roughed up. I soon figured out I could defuse threatening situations with my sense of humor and an offer to help with homework assignments. Eventually these connections with what we jokingly called the "criminal element" would work to my advantage, but at the time the bullying scared me.

Throughout the spring of 1960, I followed national politics closely. Senator John Kennedy of Massachusetts was the first Catholic to have a shot at the Democratic nomination for president since Governor Al Smith of New York in 1928. Three things attracted me to Kennedy's candidacy: he was charming, he was a naval hero, and he was Catholic. I began to root for him despite my Republican preferences. I couldn't wait for the convention to start, especially since it would be in nearby Los Angeles in the summer. My Dad was less interested in politics in 1960 because, since he had failed as a salesman of new houses and decided to go back to school, he was working toward a teaching credential at San Diego State University. It was tough on him, and he destroyed more than one typewriter in the process. But I was very proud when he got the credential and then a master's degree in biology a year later.

However, before the end of the semester, I was called in by a high school counselor who told me that she was working on my schedule for the fall of 1960, and in the last period of the day, I only had a choice of going into girls' choir or debate. I found this odd, but she explained that because of my college-prep schedule, things had just worked out that way. The college-prep students always went into the debate program. I was furious and immediately complained to Jim Doyle about what had happened. He just laughed and told me to roll with the punch. "Give it a try; you're not doing much in terms of extracurricular activity. And you'll need something to get into a good college."

The fact was that at the time, Sweetwater produced some of the best high school debaters and competitive speakers in the country. They did such individual events as impromptu speaking (after receiving a topic you had two minutes preparation time for a five-minute speech), extemporaneous speaking (45 minutes preparation time and a seven-minute speech on contemporary events), original oratory (ten minutes, memorized, no notes), and dramatic interpretation (ten minutes of a scene, memorized.)

MY JUNIOR YEAR

On the first day of class in the fall of 1960, I arrived in Joe Lagnese's debate class. He asked each of us to walk up on stage and talk about something we felt passionate about. When my turn came, I got on the stage and talked about how I had been railroaded into his class and how unjust and unfair that was. Mr. Lagnese asked me to step outside with him. He took me by the arm and I cringed. Then he said, "If you can speak with that kind of passion and you follow my directions, I promise you, you will be in the state finals this spring. If I am wrong, you need not return to the class in your senior year if you don't want to."

I decided to give it a go. I worked hard, and the training would serve me the rest of my life. Under Joe's patient tutelage, I gathered quality evidence, built strong arguments, made persuasive cases, traveled to tournaments, and maintained good grades the whole time. The training for the individual speaking events was equally rigorous. Because of my knowledge of current events, Joe had me do extemporaneous speaking in addition to debate. I was required to read the newspaper every morning, read *Time* magazine each week, and watch the *CBS Evening News* every evening. Over time, the reading and watching filled me with a pool of knowledge I could tap for speeches. Joe was also insistent on an ethical code of conduct that was very strict. Anyone caught fabricating evidence was kicked off the team. He told us to be "alive, alert, and aggressive" in the debate rounds. We were not to be naive, but neither were we to be deceitful. If we lost, we were to smile through our tears and be proud that we had done all we could to win. Winning was not the most important thing; doing everything right was. And he added, "Never expect anything, and you'll never be disappointed." Talk about a Stoic philosophy.

I befriended a gaggle of brilliant seniors on the squad, who also mentored me. At my first novice tournament, the work paid off: my partner and I tied for first in debate,[13] and I won the extemporaneous speaking event. I was hooked; competitive speaking would be a part of my life from that time on.

All was not roses, however. Because of feelings I had, I began to do research on what it meant to be homosexual. I had never really examined it clinically. So I went to the city library and browsed through some books on psychology. The most complete descriptions, inaccurate as they were, were in books on abnormal psychology. I discovered that homosexuality was considered a mental disorder; some books believed it could be cured with aversion therapy, which scared the hell out of me. I decided it would be best to keep my feelings to myself. I took the first step into the closet. It became a place for intrapersonal communication, a place for conversations in my head about how to cope with living a double life. It became a place in which I would contrive a persona that could survive in a hostile world. In the closet, I would ask: What is appropriate to laugh at? What is the appropriate way to move, to talk, to interact? For most of the rest of my life, I could look, but I could not touch objects of my affection and/or desire. At the time, that situation created a tension that generated an energy that I would channel into my academic career and later my professional life. For the time being in high school, I would also lose myself in national and school politics to distance myself from what were then considered unhealthy distractions.

The next opportunity came with the presidential campaign of 1960, which began with a number of disappointments for me. At his convention, Kennedy put Senator Lyndon Johnson on the ticket, which looked very political. Kennedy gave a lackluster acceptance speech outdoors at the Los Angeles Coliseum. The lead-in was a lot of stupid hoopla, including his sisters, looking like cheerleaders, riding around the track inside the Los Angeles Coliseum in Cadillacs, waving to the crowd.

At the GOP convention a week later in Chicago, Nixon chose the elegant former senator Henry Cabot Lodge Jr., our ambassador to the UN, as his vice-presidential running mate, and also decided to run a clean campaign to make up for his past transgressions. In a marvelous acceptance speech, Nixon promised the "greatest progress in civil rights in the last 100 years." Nixon got me thinking about a lot of things. The Republicans freed the slaves, created the national parks, busted the trusts, and were vastly superior in foreign policy to the Democrats. The Republicans were the party of individualism, freedom, and competition. And there was his biography. Like me, Nixon came from lower-middle-class parents who lived in Southern California. He was a college debater at Whittier. I was warming to him.

Then came the first debate of four between Nixon and Kennedy. It was a disaster for Nixon for many reasons. He had been in the hospital for knee surgery and looked pale. He refused to use makeup because Kennedy, tanned from Palm Beach, refused to use it. Nixon didn't want the Kennedy people claiming that Nixon was a phony who wore makeup. Nixon had lost weight during his hospital stay and so his shirt collars did not fit right. As he exited his car to enter the studio for the debate, he banged his sore knee on the door strut and nearly fainted from the pain. In the studio, the wall behind Nixon had been freshly painted so that the only suit that fit him would stand out in contrast. (Kennedy's dark suit looked sharp against his backdrop.) Throughout the debate, Nixon can be seen sniffing the paint. The hot television lights made him sweat. The cathode tube on the black-and-white cameras penetrated his first layer of skin and revealed his heavy, dark beard. Grumpy and in pain, Nixon looked like a criminal in the dock. As they spoke, I saw that Kennedy addressed the nation, talking about his agenda; Nixon addressed Kennedy, and let the moderator and Kennedy set the agenda. It was a disaster. Worse yet, only half as many people watched the next debates, which Nixon won. It is a miracle that Nixon lost the election by only 112,000 votes, and that margin may have equaled the illegal votes in Illinois and Texas. The only good thing to come out of the election, as far as I was concerned, was that a Catholic was finally president.

CHAPTER THREE

From Student Body President to CBS News

As Joe Lagnese had promised, I made it to the finals of the state tournament in extemporaneous and impromptu speaking, taking third place in each. Back on campus, attention turned to the student body elections for our coming senior year. The only announced candidate for student body president was a very popular cheerleader. He had been elected King of Hearts for the junior prom due to his good looks. He was the odds-on favorite to win the presidency of the student body and was backed by most of the faculty and the counselors. Our gang didn't like the idea of a yes man becoming student body president, and neither did the sitting president and captain of the debate squad.

He urged our gang to put up an alternate candidate. I eliminated myself because I wasn't attractive enough to win. Acne had ravaged my face, which had made me the butt of a lot of cruel jokes. My sense of humor had become acerbic and defensive, which kept my taunters at bay but gave me the reputation of being sharp-tongued. Being handsome, athletic, and smart, our friend Ken was the natural choice to run from our group. Then, he informed us that his family was moving to Denver in the summer and he would finish high school there. I was devastated because I had developed a crush on him, though he was never to know it.

Our next choice was John, my former debate partner. But no sooner had we announced his candidacy than it was discovered he had received a "D" in physics in the fall semester and was not eligible to run, despite high grades in all his other classes. Without much hope, the gang turned to me and asked me to run. I consulted Jim Doyle, and looking on the bright side, he said, "What have you got to lose?" So I declared my candidacy and most of the debate team rallied to my flag, but I was not very well known across the campus. Jim Doyle helped us run a poll to determine where we stood. The cheerleader got 81 percent of the vote in the poll, and I got the rest. I was down in the dumps when a senior debater, who was also a gorgeous cheerleader, came to me and said she would run my campaign for me.

As the campaign began, my opponent's team put up posters showing sexy women endorsing him in little cartoon dialogue bubbles. The students reacted favorably at first to busty models ostensibly endorsing my opponent for student body president. Two days later, beside each of his posters was a picture of a baby endorsing me. Underneath ran the words "Craig will take care of me." The poster battle was followed by a student assembly at which each candidate would speak. My campaign manager told me this was my only shot at winning: "You've got to give the speech of a lifetime." I assured her I would try my best.

At the assembly, my opponent spoke first and was charming. He told a few jokes and gave a speech about his dreams for the school. Then I came forward and told the students that the student body association belonged to the students, not to the teachers or the counselors or the principal. A cheer went up, and I could see the look of shock on the faculty's faces. I told the assembled students that they were not voting for King of Hearts, but for a serious leader to make tough decisions. I continued my demagogic, populist rant through the rest of the speech, which was often interrupted by cheers. I could feel the energy of the audience in me; I channeled my nervousness back to them. The connection was electric and it magnified everything around me. I could see every face; I sensed every move of everyone in the room. It was magical.

On election day around dinnertime, I received a phone call at home from the student body advisor. "Craig, you're the new student body president. You carried 61 percent of the vote. Congratulations." After I calmed down, I realized that rhetoric could be very powerful.

An interesting aspect of the election was the election of other officers. It tells you something about this Southern California school in the days before civil rights, diversity, and gender sensitivity were a big deal. Doreen Hamaguchi was elected student body secretary, and Eisenhower "Ike" Johnson, a black kid, was elected vice president. Of the six candidates for the three offices, one was black, one was Japanese American, one was African American, one was Hispanic, and two were Anglo. Even more interesting, I later learned that three of us were gay. Sadly, Ike would eventually die of AIDS. There were many Asians, blacks, and Latinos at the school and we all mixed together. All the gangs and cliques were integrated; they were not based on race.

MY SENIOR YEAR

As student body president, I was the master of ceremonies at our school assemblies, which gave me a new kind of training. I also announced our home football games. My favorite moment was announcing when our Samoan star, Fafutai Nofutolu, was about to kick a field goal. We won the league championship that year.

At the same time, I had to balance my duties against the forensics program and my advanced placement classes. As I started applying to colleges, I realized there was no choice. I would go to UCSB. In the spring, my decision was confirmed at the state championship there. The Santa Barbara debaters who helped run the tournament had decided to make a full-court press to recruit me. I was flattered and accepted. The tournament was a mixed bag for me. My partner and I failed to make the elimination rounds in debate, but I took second place in extemporaneous and first in impromptu speaking. I couldn't wait to come back in the fall to start college. For now, I had a graduation in the city park to attend, a commencement address to deliver, and a summer to relax into.

I remember vividly the day my father dropped me off at my dorm room in September of 1962, just before the start of my college classes. He helped put my things in my room; the campus was built on a closed base and the dorm was a converted Marine barracks. Other young men were moving in and my assigned roommate arrived soon after I did. After everything was unpacked, I was anxious for Dad to leave. I wanted to be on my own. I watched as his car started down the hill toward Canoga Park in the San Fernando Valley, where he had obtained a teaching position. I had an exhilarating sense of freedom.

Everything seemed to be going well with my classes until my English remediation test came back with a note that I was to be transferred into a "bonehead English class." I was appalled. After all, I had straight A's in high school English. Once I was in the class, Gretchen Wheelwright, the instructor, reviewed my file and said that she believed I was the victim of a reader who didn't like what I wrote. "You're quite the conservative, aren't you?" she commented. She helped me make the most of a bad situation by allowing me to help her teach the course, particularly the lessons in grammar. Nonetheless, I was now one semester behind in the English sequence.

The debate squad was wonderful. The seniors in the program were top-notch, as was our coach, Forbes Hill, who was an expert on Aristotle and got me interested in rhetorical theory.[1] It dovetailed nicely with my history major. I had a good year in debate and individual events under Forbes's direction. I became a close friend of his family, often babysitting for their infant, Harry. Word soon spread through the faculty that I was not only good with infants, but once I put them to bed, I cleaned the kitchen. I began to make a little money, which I badly needed, as a babysitter.

Intercollegiate debate kept us in touch with the domestic and international problems that needed to be solved. The times were full of anxiety about the nuclear age. My worst fears about the Kennedy administration were borne out in two missteps. The first was the tragic miscalculation of encouraging an invasion of Cuba by exiles from the Castro regime. In fairness to Kennedy, the planning for that invasion had begun under Eisenhower, and the CIA gave Kennedy rather bad information regarding the potential success of the operation.

The second crisis was much more of Kennedy's making. He put Jupiter missiles in Turkey and Italy; the Soviets perceived this placement as a threat. They countered by trying to secretly place missiles in Cuba, a ploy that was discovered in October 1962 through various sources by Senator Kenneth Keating (R-NY). Though Kennedy was badly embarrassed, encouraged by his brother he took a belligerent stance, blockading Cuba. As the Soviet ships approached the blockade, the world faced conflagration. Suddenly, the Soviet ships stopped, thanks to Nikita Krushchev, the Soviet premier. He then signed a secret protocol with Kennedy in which Kennedy agreed to remove our missiles from Turkey and Krushchev agreed to remove his from Cuba. The protocol also promised that the United States would not take military action against Cuba.[2]

On the local front, I was delighted with the courses I took at Santa Barbara. In my first year, Bob Kelly taught a course in what he called the history of "big ideas." It was superb. The following year I would take a sequence in ancient history with the comical Samuel Eddy, who regularly brought the house down.[3] He had a national reputation and basically came to Santa Barbara to retire. But his poking fun at the chancellor got him in trouble and he was denied tenure. It would not be the first time a favorite professor of mine would be fired under the arcane rules of academia.

When the next school year began (1963–64), we learned that we were lucky if our grades were above a 2.0, the C average. It turned out that one-third of our freshman class had flunked out of school; some of that was undoubtedly due to the surfing available just 100 yards from the classrooms. Another part of it was the partying that went on; it was not uncommon for a young man to take his date to the beach with nothing more than a blanket and a bottle of rum. Another quarter of the class was on academic probation, and the rest of us made a 2.0 or better. Those statistics somewhat assuaged my feelings of failure, having dropped from a straight A student in high school to a B average student in college.

The most memorable moment of my sophomore year came on November 22, 1963, as I was walking to the debate squad room. I heard the voice of Winston Churchill coming from a student's portable radio. Churchill was saying something about condolences, but I couldn't hear all of his words. When I reached the debate squad room, everyone there was listening to radio reports with rapt attention. "What's going on?" I inquired.

"President Kennedy, he's been shot and killed in Dallas." It is a terrible tragedy when a bullet changes the course of a republic. America would never be the same for my generation. Despite his missteps, Kennedy would be remembered as a martyred saint in our civil religion, a president who created a new Camelot to go with his New Frontier. The world became a much darker place on that day, and as Lyndon Johnson assumed the presidency, some of us believed it would get darker still.

My own romanticizing of the academic world was punctured again when word came that Forbes Hill, our debate coach, had been terminated due to a lack of scholarly publications. We were furious. How could you raise a family, teach your courses, be on the road fifteen weekends a year at intercollegiate tournaments, and be expected to publish research? The University of California had very high standards and they would not bend even for a first-rate debate coach. The rule was simple: no university press book, no tenure. Forbes told us not to protest on his behalf; he would find another job. And he did. He would spend the rest of his career at Queens College of the City University of New York. And he did publish some meaningful works, articles often cited by others.

I realized that I needed more money if I were to survive at college. Luckily, Santa Barbara had a summer high school debate institute. I was able to get hired to run it. Later in the summer, I parlayed my UCSB experience into a similar job at San Diego State, another debate powerhouse. Between the two, I made enough money to pay for my expenses. The high school students I coached were terrific and from all over the country. These were my first teaching experiences and they convinced me that I had a talent for instructing others.

While running the debate institutes, I paid close attention to the presidential campaign. The horn-rim bespectacled Senator Barry Goldwater of Arizona barely defeated Governor Nelson Rockefeller of New York in the California primary in early June, almost assuring Goldwater of the Republican nomination at their convention later in the summer.[4] Former President Dwight Eisenhower was part of a group that tried to block Goldwater by putting forward Governor Bill Scranton of Pennsylvania as an alternative. The movement petered out just as the convention began. Nonetheless, Rockefeller came to the Republican Convention in San Francisco to save the party from its more extreme elements. When a platform battle erupted over civil rights, Rockefeller came forward to defend the record of moderate Republicans and was roundly booed by the Goldwater delegates. When he accepted the nomination, Goldwater sealed his fate with a memorable line: "I would remind you that extremism in the defense of liberty is no vice and that moderation in the pursuit of justice is no virtue." The delegates went wild, and President Johnson, at the peak of popularity, must have licked his lips. He would paint Goldwater as the most extreme conservative ever to run for office, a gun-happy nuclear-weapons advocate.

This conservative-moderate rift in the party could be traced all the way back to 1912 when Theodore Roosevelt tried to take the Republican Party back from his hand-picked successor, 350-pound William Howard Taft. Roosevelt believed that Taft was in the pocket of big business. When he failed to get the Republican nomination, Roosevelt formed the Progressive (Bull Moose) Party, splitting Republicans. Roosevelt came in second to Democrat Woodrow Wilson. Taft came in third. Over time, some candidates have been able to bridge this historic divide in the Republican Party successfully. Calvin Coolidge, Herbert Hoover, and Dwight Eisenhower either kept Republicans loyal or picked up enough independent and Democratic voters to win key elections. Richard Nixon, as we shall see, succeeded only to founder on the rocks of Watergate.

The one bright spot in Goldwater's otherwise ignominious defeat in the general election was a nationally broadcast speech by Ronald Reagan. Reagan used the late October speech to pick up the standard of conservatism and repackage it into an attractive ideology. Two years later he was elected governor of California by over a million votes. And in 1980, he would become another of the Republicans to bridge the divide in the party and transform America.

MY JUNIOR YEAR

The spring of 1964 was very successful for me in debate and individual events. At the start of my junior year, however, I decided to change my individual events lineup. I entered original oratory instead of extemporaneous speaking. Though the coaches had doubts about my ability to succeed in a memorized, self-composed event, I continued to do well and enjoyed the crafting of orations. The Western Tournament at Thanksgiving in 1964 would prove to be the most successful of my career.[5] In my senior year, I would drop impromptu speaking and take up the oral interpretation of poetry. I again surprised the coaches by doing well in the event, which helped me to assimilate the beauty of language.[6]

However, I continued to be afflicted with depression. During these times, nothing seemed any good or meaningful to me. Worse yet, nothing could pull me out of these funks; I had to wait them out, which was very difficult. I tried to focus on past depressions and to remember that they did end. One day I was jolted out of my depression because I witnessed a terrible event. I walked into the dorm shower to find one of the guys sitting naked in a pool of blood, his shower still running. I turned off the shower and helped him up, wiping the blood that was coming from his broken nose. I learned that he had made a pass at another guy earlier in the day, who then caught up with him in the shower. There but for the grace of God go I, I thought to myself and took another step deeper into my closet.

I got on one of the roads to overcoming my depression by accident. On the recommendation of my debate partner, I began to sit in on the class that Fred Hagen taught on Immanuel Kant. Hagen was young, thin, and handsome in a delicate kind of way. He lectured with ease and without any notes. He had no love for God, whom he called a senile sadist. He asked questions that were impossible to answer. He was as witty as they come. So the next semester I signed up for Hagen's class on existentialism. His interpretation of Søren Kierkegaard led me to the conclusion that I was a victim of what the great Dane called "melancholia." Kierkegaard claimed that we exhibited clues of melancholia in demonic acts. Hagen gave an example of this theory by telling us a story of his being in a bar when a homeless person came in off the street and begged people for a drink. When the poor soul got to Hagen, he said, "I'm dying for a drink." Hagen replied, "No, you are living for one." Everyone at the bar laughed at Hagen's line, but he claimed that when he got home, he felt awful about making fun of the bedraggled man. It was a demonic act caused by his depression.[7]

When the blues hit me, I often walked on the beach and meditated. I also self-medicated with liquor. I didn't realize at the time that from the second drink on, alcohol is a depressant. So I was compounding my condition with alcohol.

This is not to say that there weren't a lot of happy periods with good friends. For example, I befriended Paul Bardacke, who like all of us dreamed about running for political office someday. We had become good friends on the debate squad despite the fact that Paul was something of a political radical and lived with a woman, which was unusual at that time. Don't get me wrong. Most guys were having sex before marriage, but very few were living with the women they slept with. Paul was close to Kirk Douglas's son Michael; they were fellow socialists. In fact, Michael lived in a commune in the countryside, and Paul often took me over to Michael's place to party. I remember seeing Michael peeing off one of the balconies into a canyon below. On another occasion, I introduced a Shakespearean play in which Michael acted, with his father in the audience. Michael was so nervous he couldn't get his lines out. Paul, Michael, and I would remain lifelong friends, as we shall see. The Michael everyone came to love in the television series *The Streets of San Francisco* was the Michael we knew in those days at UC Santa Barbara. He was a very kind guy with a great sense of humor, which he has retained to the present.

There was a nice surprise at the end of the spring semester. Earlier, our debate coach asked me to put together a group to enter something called the National Discussion Contest. When I appealed to the seniors on the squad to form a group to record our entry, most of them turned me down. So I put together a group from my cohort. We rehearsed, recorded our session, mailed in the audiotape, and thought nothing more about it. At the year-end debate banquet, we celebrated our victories and gave out humorous awards, such as "hardest person to travel with." However, at the end of the banquet, our debate coach pulled out what looked like an old-fashioned radio microphone covered in gold leaf. He said, "You probably have no idea what this is for, but earlier in the year, I asked Craig to enter the National Discussion Contest." Holding up the microphone he said, "Craig, come on up here, because your group took first place in the nation." That quieted my demons for some time.

MY SENIOR YEAR

In the summer of 1965, I taught the debate institutes again and began to think about graduate school. Thanks to the professors I had at UC Santa Barbara, I had decided that I wanted to teach at the college level. That would mean finding a graduate school and getting a master's degree and then a PhD. In the fall I took the Graduate Record Exam, did well, and began applying to different schools. As I mentioned, Forbes Hill had landed a job at Queens College and he urged me to apply for a graduate assistantship there, which I did. Soon I would be off to New York City.

Before that, I met John Macksoud, a genius who had finished his PhD at UCLA after dropping out of law school. We bonded immediately and he dragooned me into his extracurricular reader's theatre. In the spring, we performed a collection of absurdist pieces culminating with a one-act play called *The Tomatoes Are Falling*. It was an attack on the war in Vietnam and got me thinking that the war might be a horrible mistake. It was my first outing in a serious stage performance. John then guided me through a senior thesis on the public speaking effectiveness of the Anti-Dreyfussards, anti-Semites who wrongly accused a French captain of espionage in the late nineteenth century. The point of the thesis was to make a distinction between being a successful speaker and being an ethical one, and to point out that sustaining a lie was more difficult, and hence required more talent, than sustaining the truth. More important than the thesis was the fact that John got me further into philosophy. He introduced me to the notion of the relativity of language long before deconstructionism and postmodernism became part of the curriculum across the country. I was so taken with him that I doubled into the speech communication major, and then followed that field into graduate school instead of history.

John also did me another favor. The critic and rhetorical theorist Kenneth Burke was visiting our campus at that time. John befriended Burke, a friendship that would last a very long time.[8] I heard one of Burke's campuswide lectures in the fall; it was on the Shakespearean play *Coriolanus*. He concluded a brilliant lecture by observing, "If you have been paying attention, you will have noted that I have made a full circle during this lecture just as Coriolanus makes a full circle in the proper staging of the play which reinforces the full circle he makes in his lifetime." I asked John to request of Burke that I be allowed to sit in on his graduate seminar. Very kind man that he was, Burke agreed, and so I was able to sit at the feet of the master for a semester. What particularly impressed me about Burke was his inductive approach to discourse. He didn't look for the answers he wanted to find. He let questions bring him to original findings. Picking up on what he called a "cue," Burke treated it like the end of a thread that he then followed into the tapestry of words, themes, and arguments. There he found subliminal messages, dialectics, and motives invisible to the naked eye.

LIVING IN NEW YORK

At the end of the summer of 1966, Dad gave me his old 1957 Ford and it began another journey across America. I decided to rent a flat in Flushing, near the Queens campus where I taught the basic public-speaking class, shared debate coaching duties, and took graduate courses.

Russell Windes, the department chair, was a wonderful writer and could teach writing too. He had been an aide to the campaign writers for Adlai Stevenson in the 1956 presidential campaign. He regularly held seminars at his apartment in Manhattan overlooking Central Park and befriended several of his graduate students, including me. He made no secret of his homosexuality, which I found amazing. He directed my master's thesis, which was an analysis of the speaking of Ronald Reagan in his run for governor of California in the fall of 1966. I analyzed a series of his speeches, starting with his speech on behalf of the Goldwater campaign in October of 1964 and concluding with campaign speeches in the fall of 1966. Russ insisted that I back up my assessment of Reagan with a detailed voter analysis. The only place to get one was at CBS's research division; they had the exit-poll data from the election. They were happy to let me use it in the thesis. As we shall see, my connection to CBS's head of the research division, Robert Skedgell, would prove fortunate. Skedgell, who started as a copy boy at CBS, had a soft place in his heart for students.

Forbes had invited me to drive with him to Chicago to attend the annual meeting of the Speech Communication Association, which began on December 27, 1966. He had agreed with me that my progress to the MA was going so well that I should consider a PhD school for the fall of 1967. In his day, Forbes had graduated from the number one school in speech communication, at Cornell. After they lost a political battle at Cornell, that faculty had moved lock, stock, and barrel to Pennsylvania State University in the Nittany Mountains, 90 miles northwest of Harrisburg. At the convention, Forbes introduced to me Carroll Arnold, one of the leading lights at Cornell and subsequently at Penn State. We hit it off and Arnold invited me to apply to their PhD program. In the spring, Penn State offered me a National Defense Education Act fellowship, which meant my tuition and most of my room fees were paid and I wouldn't have teaching duties. I could concentrate on my course work.

Despite all the studying, writing, coaching, and teaching, I did enjoy Manhattan every once in a while. There were dinners at Forbes's and at Russ's place. On the street, I ran into the famous, such as Walter Winchell and Mayor Lindsay. And of course, there was the truly magical moment I mentioned in chapter 1 where Jesse Unruh brought us along as his posse to meet Robert Kennedy. That evening in the Bull and Bear Room at the Waldorf Astoria reinforced my passion for politics and reignited my political ambitions, which meant I had to stay in the closet.

I had to finish my MA thesis and course work during the summer of 1967. So instead of visiting my parents in San Diego, I spent a humid summer in New York City. In the middle of it, a rather odd news story caught my attention. Phil Battaglia, a young rising star in the California Republican Party, had been named executive secretary (really chief of staff) to Ronald Reagan. He had been student body president at USC and worked in the Reagan gubernatorial campaign of 1966. Suddenly, it was announced that he was resigning his position. A few days later, the investigative columnist Drew Pearson told the real story. In an effort to win over the press, Battaglia had bragged that he was smarter than his boss and less conservative. He also was bored by Cabinet meetings and began to skip them. This behavior led Reagan's trusted aide Ed Meese to investigate Battaglia's whereabouts. He discovered that Battaglia was gay, forcing him to resign along with another aide. So this is what happens to people who are outed in Republican administrations, I thought to myself. And I took another step deeper into my closet.

I enjoyed writing my thesis under Russ Windes's guidance. I discovered that Ronald Reagan was one of the most trained public speakers ever to become a governor. Following college, where he led a student revolt to support the faculty, Reagan became a radio broadcaster at WOC in Davenport, Iowa, in 1932. When WOC merged with WHO in Des Moines in 1933, Reagan moved there and developed his impromptu speaking skills, finding that listeners enjoyed the quality of his voice.[9] He learned "how to read so it was natural" while on the air.[10] Reagan also deepened his understanding of politics by debating with H. R. Gross, WHO's news director and resident conservative, who eventually became a well-known congressman. A few years later, while covering the Chicago Cubs spring training on Catalina Island, Reagan took a screen test. In 1937, Reagan launched his acting career with *Love Is on the Air*, the first of fifty-three feature films.

At the behest of his friends George Murphy, who would become a senator in 1964, and Robert Montgomery, who would become a media advisor to Dwight Eisenhower, Reagan not only became head of the Screen Actors Guild, he had moved from liberal Democrat to speaker for Republican candidates. His second marriage, to Nancy Davis, whose father was a conservative Republican, further solidified Reagan's conservatism, as did his speaking for the GE Corporation throughout the fifties. That experience further enhanced his rhetorical technique; he honed his skills at adapting his rhetoric to different audiences during 4,200 hours of speaking before 250,000 GE employees, including assembly line workers, managers, and laboratory scientists.[11] He was soon hosting the eight-year run of CBS's *General*

Electric Theater (1954–1962), a successful television program in whose weekly episodes he often starred.[12] *General Electric Theater* became the third most popular show on television during the 1956–57 season.[13] The twenty-one episodes of *Death Valley Days* (1964–66) was his last stint as a host and star before his run for governor. It, too, served to refine his experience with the medium of television while identifying him with California history.

By the time Reagan gave his televised October 27, 1964, speech on behalf of Senator Barry Goldwater's presidential candidacy, it was clear that the Republicans were going to lose the presidential election, and their minorities in the House and Senate would be further eroded. Nonetheless, the address catapulted Reagan into the political spotlight. It raised more money than any political speech ever delivered on television to that point: $6 million.

In 1965, Reagan saw an opportunity to help the Republican Phoenix rise from its ashes. Political consultants Bill Roberts and Stu Spencer agreed with Reagan because they believed he could project an attractive persona that advanced a conservative agenda in a more palatable way than Goldwater had.[14] In the meeting in which he hired Spencer and Roberts, Reagan agreed to continue to moderate his views and work with "more liberal Republicans" to win the election.[15]

During this time, Assemblyman Charles Conrad coached Reagan about California government. Spencer and Roberts also hired a pair of psychologists to develop a consistent value framework and expand Reagan's literary background, thereby enhancing his ethos on the stump. From the test speeches, poll data, and value framework, Reagan created talking points. In 1965, Reagan traveled the state delivering short speeches followed by question-and-answer periods. I witnessed his performance at UCSB in my senior year and was amazed at how Reagan turned a hostile student audience around. The appeals that proved effective were retained and polished; the appeals that failed were discarded. The test speeches were then destroyed. The result was a carefully worded, modular speech that could be adjusted to different audiences. Evidently, it was mainly constructed by Reagan himself, and then polished by advisors, whom he closely monitored.[16] Obviously, what became known in the campaign as "the speech" was never delivered in its entirety. Instead, modules that were relevant to the immediate audience were pulled from the speech: aerospace in Long Beach, water rights in the Central Valley, and so forth. Thus, by the time Reagan declared his candidacy for governor in 1966, his themes were consistent, polished, and practiced.

My analysis of the 1966 gubernatorial election in California shows that Reagan's speeches appealed to Republicans, independents, and Democrats who had become disaffected with their own party. He easily won the Republican primary and the general gubernatorial election of 1966. I had no idea how important a role my thesis would play in my academic and political careers.

At the end of the summer of 1967, I moved to State College, Pennsylvania, and lived in Atherton Hall, the graduate dorm. I got ready for a whole new world in the forested mountains and valleys of central Pennsylvania. I had never lived in a rural area and never gone to a college that had a big-time football team. Walking to a game in a huge stadium was a whole new thrill. I remember the crisp autumn afternoons, with the beautiful trees on the land-grant campus glowing in various shades of reds, yellows, and oranges. I remember late in November when during a game you could look out to the west and watch a snowstorm march toward the stadium like a vast white sheet. At halftime we would drink hot chocolate under the stands to get warm and avoid the falling snow.

In that fall of 1967, demonstrations against the war in Vietnam were becoming more common. J. Edgar Hoover ordered FBI agents to infiltrate the antiwar movement, which was also linked to the Civil Rights Movement, which already had been infiltrated. In October, demonstrations at the University of Wisconsin turned violent. In the same month, the Pentagon was surrounded by demonstrators who confronted armed soldiers, slipping flowers into their gun barrels. Penn State was not immune to these protests. When demonstrators tried to shut down the administration building, known as Old Main, I joined a group of students who vowed to keep it open. Our grades were being processed at the end of the quarter, and it was the last place that should be closed to protest a war it had nothing to do with. But this was only the beginning of the ways in which the war in Vietnam would touch my life.

CBS NEWS

By the spring of 1968, I decided that I wanted to do my dissertation on the speaking at the upcoming Republican Convention. Earlier, I had delivered a copy of my MA thesis to Richard Nixon at his law firm in New York, as I mentioned in chapter 1. I found Nixon to be thoughtful, witty, and very bright. He was much less self-conscious off camera than on. He seemed natural, and his wonderful baritone voice was much less intimidating in person than it was over the airwaves. I told him that I hoped he would become the

Republican nominee and I wanted to chronicle his acceptance speech. He seemed flattered by that, but took more time questioning me about Reagan and his potential. I sensed that Nixon knew that Reagan was much more a threat to Nixon's nomination than his old nemesis, Nelson Rockefeller.

Back in State College, Carroll Arnold commanded that I go to the Republican Convention and witness the event in person if I was going to analyze the speaking there. I called my friend Ken Khachigian, whom I had helped elect president of the student body at UCSB. He was in law school at Columbia University and working with the Nixon people as aide to Patrick Buchanan. Ken told me that he could get me onto the staff, but it would mean sitting in a hotel room in Miami calling delegates, not the best place to witness speeches.

So I called CBS's research head Robert Skedgell on the chance that I might intern with him in Miami. He told me that all the interns but one had been hired. They still needed a graduate intern. Though the pay was very low, I would be in the CBS newsroom and have access to the floor of the convention. I jumped at the opportunity.

The war in Vietnam took a turn for the worse at the start of 1968. On January 30, the Viet Cong with the support of North Vietnamese launched the Tet Offensive. Some of their soldiers made it all the way into the American Embassy grounds. While the Viet Cong suffered significant losses during the offensive, they scored a public-relations coup. In March, the Democrats of New Hampshire registered their displeasure by voting in droves for Senator Eugene McCarthy (D-MN), who had developed a band of student supporters composed of mainly white middle- and upper-class kids opposed to the war. McCarthy had nearly defeated the sitting President, Lyndon B. Johnson.

In the same primary, Nixon made a stunning political comeback, defeating George Romney, who had claimed to have been "brainwashed" by our generals in Vietnam to explain how he could have supported the war for so long. Few people were ready to vote for someone for president who could be hoodwinked by his own generals. Seeing these events as an opportunity, one year to the day after I met him, on St. Patrick's Day 1968, Senator Robert Kennedy announced his candidacy for president. At the end of the month and at the end of a speech to the nation from the Oval Office, Johnson surprised everyone by withdrawing from the race.

While Governor Nelson Rockefeller still could block the path to the nomination for Nixon, rumors from California indicated that Ronald Reagan, now a popular governor, would also enter the race. It looked like it was going to be an exciting campaign season. However, the national campaign was about to take another dramatic turn.

In early April, I was having dinner at Ken and Meredith Khachigian's apartment in Morningside Heights in New York. I was on spring break; we were celebrating Nixon's success and my good fortune of getting the summer internship at CBS. Then the telephone rang. Ken answered it and turned pale. He put it down and turned on the television set. Martin Luther King Jr. had been shot and killed in Memphis. Rioting was starting in major cities around the country.

I decided I had better get back to Forbes Hills's apartment, where I was staying, before it got too late. Morningside Heights bordered Harlem, and we feared that rioting might break out at any time. Ken walked me to the bus stop and I hopped on the first one to come by for the ride down to 96th Street for the short walk to West End Avenue. As I sat down on the bus, I realized I was the only white person on it. A dozen African Americans stared at me with what I perceived to be enormous hostility, for which I couldn't blame them. After an eternity, I got to Forbes's apartment safe.

When I returned to Penn State to finish my third quarter there, I told my friends that I might not return after the summer. My plan was to leverage my internship at CBS into some kind of job that would take me to Vietnam. I had avoided the draft by taking a student deferment. I didn't believe I would be of much use as a foot soldier. However, I had sent an application to the Foreign Service offering my talents for the war in Southeast Asia. In a few weeks, I received a note turning me down. As we shall see, it was wise of me to keep the note in my files. In the meantime, by late May, Nixon appeared to have eliminated his opponents by winning the Oregon primary. The write-in campaign for Reagan there and in Nebraska had petered out.

On the Democratic side, Vice President Hubert Humphrey was seeking the nomination in LBJ's stead against McCarthy and Kennedy. On the night of King's assassination, Robert Kennedy in Indianapolis had given a heartfelt plea for calm across the country. He reminded the crowd that he had lost a brother to a white assassin's bullet. He quoted from Greek tragedies as if they were holy writ. He won the Indiana primary and the one that followed in Nebraska. However, in Oregon he became the first Kennedy to lose a primary. As a result, Kennedy agreed to debate McCarthy in California before its primary in the first week of June. During that debate, Kennedy supported the American-Israeli alliance in very strong terms. As I watched the election returns come in for the California primary, it appeared that Kennedy had won handily after barnstorming the state, including appearances with Cesar Chavez, the head of the Farm Workers Union. Due to sampling errors, CBS projected an exaggerated Kennedy victory: "KENNEDY 52%, MCCARTHY 38%, OTHERS 10%" flashed across television screens, and most people on the East Coast, including me, went to bed. The final returns would be around 46 percent to 43 percent, a moral victory for McCarthy that no one would remember because of the events that immediately followed Kennedy's "on to Chicago" victory speech in the ballroom of the Ambassador Hotel. Just after 3 A.M. Eastern Time on June 7, I heard a rap on my dorm-room door. I opened it and a fellow graduate student said, "You might want to come down to the TV Room. They've shot Bobby Kennedy." I threw on some clothes and ran to the television in a room just off the graduate dorm lobby. It was packed. It wasn't long before word came that Robert Kennedy had died from wounds inflicted by Sirhan Sirhan, a Palestinian offended by Kennedy's defense of Israel.

TENSION IN MIAMI AND VIOLENCE IN CHICAGO

In late June of 1968, I checked into a fleabag hotel in South Miami Beach. I roomed with three other interns who worked in different divisions for the CBS News Special Events Unit. The next day we were introduced around, depending on where we were to report. I was assigned to work with Beth Fertik and Joan Richman, two thoroughly professional women who taught me a good deal about research. Our pod of interns was to call delegates and create profiles on each one. We had a form that we filled in concerning their age, family, important issues, and candidate preference. The form was then entered into a computer by Warren Mitofsky, the CBS polling genius. I was delighted to be doing this work because it would provide just the audience analysis I needed for my dissertation. All the information the interns gathered would be rewritten into paperback books that CBS floor correspondents would carry with them for live interviews and background information. The other networks had nothing like it.

The week before the convention was platform week. During this week, Walter Cronkite as anchor, Eric Sevareid as commentator, and a host of floor reporters arrived in Miami Beach. The *CBS Evening News* was broadcast from the glass-front CBS anchor booth overlooking the Miami Beach Auditorium where the delegates would soon gather. After a day of calling, we assembled in the newsroom, listened to the *Evening News*, and then went out for hamburgers and beer. CBS had lost the ratings war in 1964 to the team of Chet Huntley and David Brinkley on NBC. CBS wanted the ratings crown back and hoped that Cronkite's team could provide it. Cronkite had already taken the *Evening News* ratings back based on CBS's in-depth coverage of the war and the assassinations.

One day Frank Manitzas, who ran the newsroom, took me to lunch. He told me I was doing a good job. He wanted me to take over supervising the other interns. I was flattered, and in the course of the conversation, I tried to dazzle him with my knowledge of conventions. One of my favorite stories took place at the Democratic Convention of 1956. Joe Kennedy Sr. was trying to get the vice-presidential nomination for his son John. House Speaker and convention chair Sam Rayburn was on board, and Senator Albert Gore Sr. of Tennessee, whom Kennedy had funded, also assured his support. Then Kennedy got what he thought was assurance from the prospective nominee, Adlai Stevenson. But Stevenson threw everything into a cocked hat when he announced that he was turning the nomination of the vice president over to the convention. Joe Kennedy was furious, but took up the challenge, with his large family flooding the floor of the convention seeking delegate votes. Kennedy's rival for the nomination was Senator Estes Kefauver of Tennessee, who had come in second in the Democratic primaries to Stevenson.

On the first ballot, Kennedy led and came within 30 votes of receiving the nomination. At that juncture, various states waved their banners signaling that they were ready to dump their favorite sons and change their votes. Rayburn called Joe Kennedy from the podium and asked for instructions. Kennedy told Rayburn to recognize Gore, Tennessee's favorite son, which he did. The convention hushed as Gore began to speak into his microphone: "I am withdrawing my name from nomination and cast[ing] all of Tennessee's votes for my honorable colleague in the United States Senate [both Kennedy and Kefauver were in the Senate] as the next vice president of the United States, Estes Kefauver." Other states stampeded to Kefauver and he was selected as the nominee. When John Kennedy expressed his anger to his father, the old man said, "Don't get mad, get even."

I could tell that I had impressed Frank. A few days later, Frank took me aside and said he needed me to go over to the Doral Hotel and cover the platform hearings. It turned out that New York City mayor John Lindsay was testifying right after Governor Reagan, who had just declared that he was open to being drafted for the nomination. Frank instructed, "See if you can capture the contrast between a liberal Republican and a conservative one."

Gaudy statuary, looking as if it had been carved from a giant bar of cream cheese, greeted my cab in front of the Doral. But I had little time to contemplate the tackiness of the place. Inside, I flashed my shiny new laminated press credentials, slipped into a seat in the ballroom, and took out my notepad. Mayor Lindsay spoke of moderation and withdrawing from

Vietnam. Reagan, the hawk, would not accept defeat in Vietnam. When they finished their testimony, I rushed back to the newsroom and put my story on the CBS News Division internal wire, known as the CND wire, for the eyes of our reporters only. That night, as I watched the evening news, Frank smiled at me in a funny way. Then it happened: Walter Cronkite was reading my words on the air to 20 million Americans. I couldn't believe it. When the evening news was over, Cronkite came down from the anchor booth and asked to meet everyone in the newsroom. We promptly assembled, and Cronkite asked who wrote the story on Reagan and Lindsay. He seemed grumpy about it, so most people just looked at the floor. I stepped forward and said, "I did, sir."

"Who are you?" Cronkite intoned.

"An intern, sir."

Cronkite said, "You are not in the writers' union. We could get in trouble for that."

Frank intervened, and explained that Florida was a non-union state. Cronkite still didn't like it. "Frank, let's make this guy a writer and pay his union dues for him." Cronkite shook my hand and started to leave. Then he turned around, came back to me, and said, "And by the way, call me Walter."

Frank congratulated me. I was now a researcher/writer for CBS. I would be moved from my little shared hotel room to a suite in the Sheraton Four Ambassadors. Over the next few days, I worked with Frank, who spoke fluent Spanish, to put the delegate handbook together and proofread behind the Cuban printers, who only spoke Spanish. They gave me Cuban coffee to keep me awake for a 36-hour stretch.

By the time the full complement of Republicans arrived for the convention, it looked as if Nixon had the nomination sewed up. However, when I met with Ken Khachigian, he let me know that several hurdles still stood in Nixon's way. First, Reagan began to drain Southern conservative delegates, the old Goldwater crowd, from Nixon. Rockefeller renewed his effort to siphon off liberal Republicans. Nixon's majority was being nibbled away from two sides as an alliance was consummated between the Reagan and Rockefeller teams. We believed a secret deal had been made that if one of them got the nomination, he would name the other as his running mate. That made for an exciting convention.

But the story stayed behind the scenes because Cronkite refused to report it that way.[17] He believed Nixon's spin doctors, most notable among them John Mitchell. Cronkite also believed our own "handbooks," which outlined how to cover the convention. As one of the authors of the handbook, I was surprised that the CBS team would not deviate from the script to report what was really going on; so was political director Marty Plissner, particularly after I reported Ken's assessment to him, and after he began checking around with delegate leaders.

Our version of what was going on was verified when several delegates from New Jersey bolted to Reagan. Then the heavily courted Mississippi delegation—Reagan actually wept while addressing them—said they would go the way Florida went. They chose Florida as the bellwether for several reasons: (1) It had a self-imposed unit rule: however the majority of delegates voted, the rest had to follow; (2) Florida came early in the roll call of delegations; (3) Claude Kirk, the governor of Florida, endorsed Rockefeller and would vote against the unit rule; if a majority joined him, it would free delegates to jump to Reagan; and (4) Florida would cast 34 delegate votes, a hefty number.

Nixon, Rockefeller, and Reagan lobbied Florida heavily. However, Marty and I could not get Cronkite, or anyone else for that matter, to report what was afoot. I was there when the final ballot was taken inside the Florida caucus: Nixon held onto the majority by one vote; Phyllis O'Neill would not desert Nixon. The other states held and Nixon won on the first ballot of the convention by only 25 delegates. What would have happened had Cronkite reported the story accurately? Would other delegates have peeled away? Would Phyllis O'Neill have given way to Reagan's persuasion or home state pressure? If more delegates knew what was going on in the Mississippi, New Jersey, and Florida delegations, would they have found a way of stopping Nixon on the first ballot? And by our calculations, if Nixon did not win the first ballot, his delegate strength would immediately begin to erode because many delegates were pledged to him for only one ballot. How different would history have been if the Republicans had nominated a Reagan-Rockefeller ticket in 1968? We can't know what would have happened with the war in Vietnam. But surely there would not have been a Watergate crisis.

However, Nixon did survive and went about the task of selecting a vice-presidential nominee. The Nixon people decided they wanted Spiro Agnew, the governor of Maryland, on the ticket; he had opposed forced busing, but was a moderate in most other ways. So they devised a complicated scheme of deception to make it happen. They told Southerners that the choice was between Agnew and John Volpe, the more liberal governor of Massachusetts. The Southerners all advised Nixon to take Agnew. He then told Northern leaders that the choice was between Agnew and Senator Strom Thurmond, the right-wing senator from South Carolina. The

Northern leaders all advised Nixon to take Agnew. That was how they achieved consensus around the man who was by his own admission "not a household name."

I gave this story to Mike Wallace, who had become a fan of Nixon. Wallace had followed Nixon into the snows of New Hampshire and become a convert. Among the things that helped Nixon in New Hampshire in 1968 were self-deprecating humor and color television. The new cameras did not penetrate his first layer of skin to reveal his five-o'clock shadow. So it was that Mike Wallace rode Richard Nixon back into the network's ring of top reporters.

I was very unhappy with the choice of Agnew, whom I saw as a bland compromise. But Wallace argued that Agnew was a strategic choice. Agnew would be the attack dog of the campaign. Nixon had run with the distinguished Henry Cabot Lodge in 1960 and had promised a presidency that recalled Lincoln and Theodore Roosevelt. In that race, he played fair and Lodge played statesman. Nixon didn't let Eisenhower campaign for him, because he wanted to win on his own, and because he had been told Eisenhower was too weak with his heart condition to campaign. The choice of Agnew was not the first signal that things would be different in 1968. Nixon arranged to have Eisenhower address the convention from his deathbed. There would be no debates. It was clear Nixon would take no chances in 1968.

The Nixon team looked smart when Agnew's acceptance speech turned out to be a winner. He admitted to not being a household name. He said that he had a script to follow, but was abandoning it. He rolled it up, set it aside, and claimed to speak from his heart about his values. The speech even overcame skepticism in the press. And then Nixon came forward to give his acceptance speech.

As I watched from the floor of the convention, I realized once again that Nixon was a master of rhetoric. He had outlined his speech on yellow legal pads while vacationing at Montauk on Long Island. The staff had then filled in necessary statistics, and issue positions guided by poll data. And this was important because the Nixon campaign polls were innovative. They not only asked voters what they thought the biggest problems America faced were, but they asked what solution the voters preferred. From these "issue positions," a speech was crafted to solidify a majority of voters behind Nixon. It was then stylized by Ray Price, a moderate, pipe-smoking wordsmith of the first order.

The first section of the speech addressed the delegates and united them behind Nixon's candidacy. In this section, he complimented the other candidates and called on their delegates for support. The uniting of the delegates was symbolic of the way Nixon hoped to unite the country. He then lobbed a bomb at his likely opponent, Vice President Hubert Humphrey: "A man who cannot unite his party, cannot unite the country."

The number one issue on everyone's mind at the time of the Republican Convention was the war in Vietnam; however, the public was divided on a solution. Forty-three percent of the public favored escalating the war in Vietnam; Reagan's delegates and some of Nixon's represented this segment at the convention. Forty-two percent of the public favored withdrawing troops from Vietnam; Rockefeller's and some of Nixon's delegates represented this segment at the convention. So when Nixon came to Vietnam, he discussed the Vietnam war and its history. He concluded that America had been failed by its leaders. He then said that while peace negotiations were underway in Paris, he would say nothing to undercut the President. However, he promised that his plan would produce "peace with honor." In this way, he papered over the divisions in his party and the country. "Peace with honor" was vague enough to be embraced by hawks and doves alike.

The next section of the speech addressed crime. Because his poll data showed a strong consensus on the solutions to this problem, Nixon reversed tactics. He quickly summarized the crime statistics, which had been heightened by rioting in April after Martin Luther King Jr.'s death, and went into several solutions, including more funding for law enforcement, a tougher attorney general, and a much more conservative Supreme Court.

The same strategy was used on the rest of the issues of the speech. Quick citation of the problem, and then specific solutions that were embraced by the vast majority of Americans. Thus, even those who had been hostile to Nixon over the years found themselves nodding in agreement with him. All Nixon had to do was cement this argumentative synthesis with a peroration that grabbed his audience emotionally.

Nixon delivered the peroration written by William Gavin, a high school English teacher who had joined the campaign.[18] With his adoring wife and daughters looking on in rapt attention, Nixon began with the story of a young man who grew up in the ghetto and died in the jungles of Vietnam. In sharp contrast, he then told a story of another young man who hears "trains in the night" and dreams of far-off places. He has a football coach who mentors him and a minister who inspires him. He has a saintly mother who opposes his going to war but understands when he does. When he returns from war, first hundreds, then thousands, then millions vote for him: "And tonight, he stands before you nominated for president of the United States." For many in the national television audience, that Nixon was the young man was a surprise, and for many of them, Nixon came to embody the American Dream. The audience at the convention went nuts, cheering Nixon for several long minutes. Nixon came out of the convention with a huge lead over his potential opponents. All he had to do was protect it.

ON TO CHICAGO

Once the Republicans left Miami, we set about writing the handbook for the Democratic National Convention, which was to take place a few weeks later in Chicago. Again, I found myself working with the Cubans in a ghetto in Miami to get the book out.

I was the last CBS newsperson to leave Miami for Chicago. I had been up for 38 hours and arrived at the airport with four boxes of books for the reporters covering the Democratic Convention. Frank Manitzas had bought two first-class tickets for me. One for the books that rode next to me for security reasons, and one for me. I'm afraid my security watch was not very good. Once the plane took off, I had a drink and fell asleep. I did not wake until the stewardess shook me as we were taxiing to the gate at O'Hare Airport. The boxes and I took a cab to the Palmer House, where I was ushered into a wonderful room worthy of a member of the CBS Special Events Unit.

It was at this time that Joan Richman came to me with a proposal. Since she had to be in the broadcast booth next to Cronkite during the convention, would I coordinate the research division in the newsroom when CBS was on the air? "What about Beth?" I asked.

"She's been promoted to producer."

When CBS came on the air for convention coverage in Chicago, I was assigned to my own desk with several phones and a research assistant. Our job was to answer any research questions that came from Cronkite through Joan Richman, or up from the floor from reporters. I learned an important lesson my first night on the job. We had access to wonderful food the entire evening, which was very long. The first time I got hungry, I had some chicken and salad, but because of the tension of having to answer questions or find answers to questions that were going out to 20 million Americans, I could not hold my food down. I never ate again while we were on the air.

During the platform hearing week for the Democrats, it became clear that this convention would be like no other. Democrats were sharply divided between those opposed to the war in Vietnam and those who supported the

President. George McGovern had picked up the fallen standard of Robert Kennedy. Eugene McCarthy led his student group into the city. But these camps were alienated from one another because McCarthy believed Kennedy had ruined his chances for the nomination.

On top of that, protestors were set to come into town on Sunday for convention week. When intelligence sources revealed that the numbers were going to be very large, Mayor Richard Daley called up reserve police officers for crowd-control duty. This step would prove to be Daley's first mistake among many. The reserve officers were usually retired officers who supported the war in Vietnam. Many had sons in the service there; some had lost sons or seen them come home wounded. These officers would have no sympathy for the demonstrators.

On the other side, the demonstrators had no respect for the cops. Aside from blacks' disdain for the police as a results of the riots of April, radical students of all colors despised authority, and these cops represented it in its most repressive form. Controlled by the President's delegates, the platform committee sent its report in support of Johnson's war policy to the convention, which was being held very near the Chicago stockyard where animals were being slaughtered. The press did not overlook the obvious symbolism of this bloody yard.

News soon arrived that Mayor Daley was not allowing members of the press to drive from their hotels to the stockyard convention site. Instead, he would supply school buses to take us to and from the convention. Furthermore, media and delegate access to the convention floor would be through turnstiles that required special security cards. All reporters would be limited to no more than twenty minutes on the convention floor at a time. The news media were thus alienated from Daley and the Democratic leadership. That alienation bled into their reporting.

On the first day of the convention, many of the demonstrators decided to camp in Grant Park along Lake Michigan. In another miscalculation, Daley decided to impose a curfew on the park and clear it at 10 P.M. This meant that the demonstrators were pushed into the streets, causing them to block traffic. When the police pushed them onto the sidewalks, the demonstrators were often forced against department-store and restaurant windows. Some fell through and were badly cut. The police had drawn first blood.

Over the course of the next few days, Yippies, a radical band of violent demonstrators, took advantage of the situation. Getting into the center of a group of peaceful demonstrators, they would throw bags of manure or nail-spiked golf balls at the reserve cops. The cops would then charge into the crowd trying to get at the Yippies. Inevitably this led to more bloodshed.

Daley refused to allow live broadcasts from the streets of Chicago. It wasn't until the film of the violence could be developed that the networks could show what was going on downtown in Chicago. When I saw the first filmed onslaught of police on demonstrators, I was appalled. These poor kids were having their heads bloodied and their bones broken. I had no sympathy for the Yippies and their tactics, but Daley's police were out of control. Later the Walker Report would indicate that the media had done its part to incite violence, often inviting students to trash a building and thereby "make the evening news."[19]

One night, we experienced the street violence firsthand. The badly managed convention had ended after midnight, which it did each night of convention week. I was ushered onto a "CBS Bus," where I sat next to Dan Rather. Cronkite, Sevareid, Harry Reasoner, and several others who were on the same bus. The driver asked us if it would be all right if he took a short-cut to avoid the clogged streets and to get us to the Palmer House quicker. As our leader, Walter gave him the okay. About twenty minutes later, we came barreling down Monroe Street toward the Palmer House. However, a police barricade lay in our path. Just as the bus was slowing down, it was struck by tear gas canisters. We hit the floor, the bus screeched to a stop, and another canister came through the window and spewed its fumes. The driver jumped out and ran to the police, who forced him to the ground. In the meantime, I could not see for the stinging and tears in my eyes. I feared that I had been blinded.

Once it became clear who we were, we were led by the hand into the Palmer House, a block away, and then up to our rooms. But before we got past the lobby, the smell of tear gas gave way to the smell of manure. The demonstrators had covered the interior of the Palmer House with cow manure because part of the hotel was occupied by Humphrey delegates. Once in my room, I stood in the shower trying to wash the tear gas out of my eyes. I had to sleep in a room filled with the stench of the tear gas on my clothes.

The drama in the streets of Chicago was matched by the drama on the floor of the convention. While Mayor Daley sat in the front of the Illinois delegation, which was in the front row of the delegate section, Senator Abraham Ribicoff of Connecticut condemned the mayor for his "Gestapo" tactics. Those watching television could read Daley's lips as he repeatedly shouted back, "Fuck you." It made for great television, and so did the competition between our reporters.

At the Republican Convention, in a year marred by assassinations, Mike Wallace stole his way past Secret Service agents onto the podium. He did a live report from there, much to the delight of Cronkite and the horror of the Secret Service. If Wallace could sneak onto the podium, so could an assassin. At the Democratic Convention in Chicago, with me working as his "floor assistant" on a twenty-minute break from my research duties, Dan Rather refused to leave the floor of the convention at the allotted time. As he was being escorted off the convention floor, I heard Rather yelling for help into his microphone to Cronkite. What I could not hear was Cronkite's furious denunciation of the proceedings and his order to "keep the cameras on Dan." Mayor Daly's goons made the mistake of punching Rather in the stomach and knocking him to the floor. A few minutes later, from off the convention floor while I patched his ripped pant leg with safety pins, Rather did a live interview with Cronkite about the incident.

Mike Wallace was not to be outdone. So he tried to provoke an incident with the Chicago chief of police. When he saw the chief coming, Wallace leapt over a turnstile, thereby violating the security of the convention. The chief grabbed Wallace, who took a swing at the chief. The chief then punched Wallace in the face and he fell to the floor. However, Wallace's cameraman did not get footage of the event because the lighting was bad. Wallace was hustled off to jail. CBS president Richard Salant had to bail him out later that night.

As the convention continued, there was a terribly moving tribute to Robert Kennedy led by his brother Teddy. I came upon Jesse Unruh surrounded by Kennedy loyalists, all of them in tears. The lackluster speeches by McGovern and McCarthy failed to stop the inevitable nomination of Vice President Humphrey, who came before the convention quite late to give his acceptance speech. Besieged and having lost control of his convention, Humphrey tried to put the best face he could on the situation by becoming the "happy warrior," but this was no time for happy talk. Humphrey came out of the convention far behind Nixon, but ahead of candidate George Wallace, who was leading a third-party movement.

Before I left Chicago, I met with Joan Richman and Frank Manitzas, and begged them to get me assigned to coverage of the war in Vietnam. They told me I could be hired as a writer in New York, but that CBS would be reducing its coverage of the war since the new president would surely end the war soon. I didn't want to be a writer in New York when I had a PhD to finish. So I said my goodbyes to the CBS crew and headed back to State College, Pennsylvania. However, I had been irrevocably changed by the experience at the two conventions. Not only was my view of America shaken, I now saw how fragile a democracy could be and how stupid it could behave on the world scene. My view of myself was also changed—I could contribute to the major network in America and I could do it while being in the closet.

FINISHING THE PHD

Back at Penn State for my second and final year, I followed the election in the student lounge, and took breaks from my studies by watching the irreverent *Smothers Brothers Comedy Show*. Soon, I was approached by a tenured professor who had been very kind to me. He told me that he had agreed to write a chapter on Congressman Thaddeus Stevens, the fiery abolitionist, for a book on Pennsylvania orators. However, he did not have time to do the chapter and wondered if he compensated me, if I would write it for him. He paid my expenses to Washington, D.C., to do the research at the Library of Congress and gave me a small stipend when the chapter was done. After it was published, I checked to see what changes had been made in my draft. There were none. And so my second shot at being a ghostwriter had been successful, though of dubious morality.

As I worked to finish my classes, prepare for comprehensives, and write my dissertation, I joined my peers on some nights at a local pub. In those days, there were no word processors; we were lucky to have electronic typewriters. The rule at the bar, the Sword and Shield, was that if you had made progress on your dissertation, you got to order one of their wonderful roast beef sandwiches. The beef was on a spit behind the bar and the smell was intoxicating. The beef was thinly shaved to order and then piled on a fresh German roll. If you had not made progress on your dissertation, you could only drink beer and watch the others wolf down their sandwiches. This incentive system seemed to work, since by mid-semester everyone was ordering the sandwiches when we went to the bar.

I monitored Nixon's campaign on the *CBS Evening News* and through Ken Khachigian, who was finishing at Columbia Law School. Nixon continued to refuse to debate Humphrey, and the sitting vice president scored points by portraying Nixon as a coward.[20] Alabama's George Wallace, the nominee of the American Independent Party, named General Curtis LeMay as his running mate. The man had been head of the Joint Chiefs of Staff during the Cuban Missile Crisis. Later, like Barry Goldwater before him, he had called for the use of tactical nuclear weapons in Vietnam, a war he had supported during the Kennedy administration. Most Americans never quite understood that nuclear weapons could be made with reduced firepower for more precise targeting. Most of them simply saw a mushroom cloud when the word "nuclear" was mentioned. Thus, Wallace and LeMay began to fade from their high of 21 percent in the polls. Since their supporters were mainly Southern Democrats, the leakage went disproportionally to Humphrey, who began to catch up to Nixon in the polls.

In late October of 1968, President Johnson announced a surprise. With less than two weeks left before the election, he stopped all bombing in Vietnam and offered concessions for peace at the Paris Peace Conference. Humphrey was buoyed by this news, and more voters began to return to the Democratic Party. The press continued to dog Nixon about not debating Humphrey. Instead, Nixon relied on town hall meetings, demonstrating his skill at mastering facts and creating spontaneous responses to audience questions. These audiences were screened to provide Nixon with a favorable atmosphere. The only blip occurred in Philadelphia, where a black man challenged Nixon's record on civil rights. It was a blessing in disguise; Nixon handled the moment with aplomb and increased his credibility, though he blasted the staff for letting it happen.

In the meantime, Humphrey imitated Harry Truman's "give 'em hell" 1948 style in an attempt to pull off an upset. On election night, the outcome was unclear; by midnight in the student lounge, I couldn't hold my eyes open any longer. The election seemed to be riding on the outcome of the Illinois vote, much to Nixon's horror. Remember that along with Texas, Illinois had cost him the election in 1960.

In the morning, I came down to the television room to see Nixon standing with his wife and daughters, claiming victory. He had won by only 500,000 votes, and it was very close in several important states. Wallace had taken 13.5 percent of the vote; Humphrey and Nixon basically split the rest. Like Lincoln and Wilson, Nixon would enter the White House with less than a majority of the public having voted for him; however, he had carried 60 percent of the Electoral College. He immediately set about wooing the South to fend off another run by Wallace in 1972. In January 1969, Nixon gave a moving inaugural address in which he appealed in Lincoln's words to "the better angels of our nature." He asked Americans to lower their voices and later called into existence "a silent majority" who he believed supported him and his policies. The public gave him a pass during his first year.

The other appeal to the silent majority came from Vice President Agnew. Not much had been heard from the former governor of Maryland during the first months of the Nixon administration. However, when Patrick

Buchanan came to Nixon with a speech that attacked the news media for distorting presidential rhetoric with "instant analysis," Nixon declined, arguing that it was unpresidential. Nixon suggested that Agnew deliver the speech, which he did in Des Moines after Vic Gold and William Safire refined and intensified Buchanan's prose. The speech was delivered in May 1969, and the reaction was incredible. First, Agnew became well known in America not only for his spot-on critique of the news media, but for his phrasemaking. Second, Agnew succeeded in inoculating the Nixon administration from media attacks. This explains why Nixon survived so long after the Watergate break-in. It took forever for the news media to get through to the public that they weren't out to lynch Nixon unfairly.

In the meantime, Penn State continued to provide me with a remarkable education. Professor Richard Gregg refined my understanding of campaign persuasion and the theories of Kenneth Burke. In my first year, I had taken the three-quarter sequence in American public address from the very scholarly and intimidating Professor Eugene White. Now, in my second year, he allowed me to team-teach the seminar with him. That had never been done before. Nor had the jolly, rotund, bald, and controversial Jerry Philips ever allowed anyone to teach general semantics with him; but there I was, teaching the classical notions of semantics while he dealt with what soon became the "touchy feely" approach to communication studies. He referred to me as the "resident fascist" and I referred to him as "melon head." The students loved it.

I had also become a friend of Professor Richard Kennington. I had taken his class on Aristotle's psychology (*De Anima*) and he was impressed with my paper on Aristotle's notion of potentiality in the soul. He invited me to take his class on Martin Heidegger's dense book *Being and Time* in the winter quarter. When I turned my paper in, he invited me to his home for dinner. I was the only non–philosophy major in the class, and the other students looked at me with envy. I arrived at the snow-covered Kennington home a few days later. He introduced me to his German-born wife and his daughter, who promptly left us alone in the study. After he whipped up some martinis, Kennington pulled out my paper and explained to me that my attacks on Heidegger, while thorough, could all be answered by an even closer reading of the text in its context. He handed the paper, which was full red marks, to me and suggested I rewrite it. After the martinis, we went to the dining room, where his wife served us dinner and departed. As we dined, we continued to talk philosophy. And so it would be over many dinners at Kennington's Tudor-style home in State College. I would eventually publish these papers on Aristotle and Heidegger as scholarly articles. And when I became a professor, I continued the practice of philosophical discussions over dinner with my students.

My formal dissertation advisor was the affable Professor Robert T. Oliver, a Republican to the core. He was the first in our field to delve into intercultural communication. He was a natural for that endeavor since he had served as an advisor to Sigman Rhee, the president of South Korea. Under Oliver's direction, I took a liking to the Chinese philosophers Confucius, Mencius, and Lao Tsu. The latter's philosophy easily merged with my version of existentialism, which took a Zen twist. In the world of free choice, every disadvantage has an advantage and vice versa. Eliminate desire, and you eliminate pain. Talk about helpful advice for a closeted gay man. Zen masters were patient and almost always left the door open to more discovery by answering questions with, "We'll see."

The de facto advisor on my dissertation, however, was Carroll Arnold, one of the most pragmatic minds I had ever met. Like Oliver, he was a Republican, less a rarity in academia then than now. Arnold worked hard to break my bad writing habits, often rewriting whole paragraphs in red ink that were preceded by the phrase "Try it this way." Many years later, in a eulogy to Arnold, I commented that his greatest contribution to the field was not his writing, but his editing of the writing of others. Many of us went on to become scholars because of his untiring efforts.

After I had passed my comprehensive exams in early June of 1969, Arnold worked me through the final draft of my dissertation. The first three chapters went well, but the next two got me in trouble. I wrote too quickly, overconfident that I could finish by the end of June. Arnold put me in my place. He wrote:

> It is 10:30 at night. I grant you I'm tired, for I've been writing all day. This evening was to be for your thesis chapters, but I quit! I've read the first 9 of these pages and I find the whole business so mechanical and so stupidly written that I refuse to go farther. I can think of no reason why I should read stuff where sentences have to be read three times to discover what they may mean, but still more, I don't see why I should read material put together in the way a mechanical man might do it. . . . For God's sake—if you don't care about your own—use your brains.

I've often read this critique to my students when they complain that I'm being too tough on them. Ten days later, I turned in a rewritten chapter 4 to which Arnold responded, "NOW WE'RE GETTING SOME PLACE!" My depression lifted and I completed an acceptable draft by the end of July.

Then in August came the dreaded dissertation committee meeting where I had to defend what I wrote. Oliver led the discussion. Gregg and Arnold asked a few mild questions. Philips passed, saying he didn't know anything about the subject area, and if Oliver and Arnold approved, so did he. I began to think this was going to be a cakewalk. The dissertation argued that Nixon's effectiveness at the 1968 convention in his acceptance speech was due to his ability to adapt to two audiences at the same time—the delegates and the television audience—using his "issue profile analysis." Professor Henry Johnstone, a philosopher who had been looking at the ceiling throughout the proceedings, suddenly said, "May I ask a question?"

My throat tightened as I said, "Yes, sir." I had not taken a class with Johnstone because of schedule conflicts. I had no idea where he would come from, given that he was an ethics philosopher with a national reputation. However, I was required to have an outside member on my committee and Arnold recommended Johnstone, with whom he had recently founded the journal *Philosophy and Rhetoric*, where I served as an editorial assistant.

Still looking at the ceiling, he intoned, "You spend a good deal of time talking about the effectiveness of the speakers you assess in your dissertation. But you don't talk about their ethics at all. Is that correct?"

"Yes," I responded. "Ethics is a different matter than rhetorical effectiveness."

"Yes, that's quite correct," he said to my relief. "I have no further questions."

And with that, it was over. I was now Dr. Craig Smith. It was time to become a professor.

CHAPTER FOUR

First Job Syndrome

IN EARLY 1969, I HAD BEEN WOOED BY SEVERAL UNIVERSITIES. THERE was a shortage of professors at the time, even though many young men were going into teaching because of the war in Vietnam. However, graduate deferments had just been canceled, and unless you were a professor, you were eligible for the draft. Many graduate students defected to Canada; others entered Officer Training School or the National Guard; others feigned homosexuality or maimed themselves. Part of the reason for these actions was that the war was graphically depicted every night on the evening news, with body counts being prominently featured. Stories of the torture of American prisoners of war and "fraggings" of senior officers by mutinying U.S. troops were revealed.

In the job market, the first to approach me was San Diego State University, because the department needed a second debate coach and knew I could do the job since I had run debate workshops for them in the summer when I was an undergraduate. However, Forbes Hill had a friend named Harry Kerr, who taught at Harvard. Kerr tried to convince me to come there to teach public speaking and continue my research. I had never negotiated for a full-time job in my life and so I sought the advice of my best professors. Most, like Forbes Hill and Russell Windes, argued for Harvard. Everyone knew that Harvard was a ticket to a productive career. The man I would be replacing had moved on to Northwestern, which had one of the best communication departments in America. The downside to the Harvard job for me was that I could only teach public speaking, argumentation, or advanced speaking courses, albeit with only a dozen students per class. Furthermore, after rushing to get through the PhD, I was burned out on research. I couldn't get my head around sitting in libraries in Cambridge and then going home to write all night. I was also sick of the eastern winters. When San Diego State told me I could teach whatever courses I wanted, including graduate seminars, the deal was struck.

DEBATE COACH

I found that preparing to teach new classes was a great way to learn new material and hone my skills. In class, student questions and other inter-actions led to more insights. I was happy that full-time teaching was as rewarding as I had hoped. Being a debate coach was time-consuming, and that was fine with me because I had no personal life and no intention of starting one. Just like my high school, San Diego State was known for two extracurricular activities, debate and football. Don Coryell was the football coach who put San Diego State on the map. Watching "Air Coryell," as we dubbed his offense, became a great pastime when we weren't at debate tournaments, which was usually fifteen weekends a year at a minimum. The Western States Tournament still ran at Thanksgiving, and the National Speech Convention and the New Year's Swing Tournaments at USC and UCLA ended any possibility of being home for those holidays. It was a tough life that ruined the marriages of many a debate coach. But I loved it and became very close to the students competing for the school. The forensics team became part of my social life, along with my visits home to see Mom and Dad when I was in town.

In fact, because I was only twenty-four going on twenty-five, I related much more to the students at San Diego State than to the faculty. Because they worked part-time, or had taken time to finish at area community col-leges, the average age of students at San Diego State was twenty-seven. I treated them as adults. I befriended many of them, of both genders and all races; they came over to dinners and parties often. I did not know at that time that the senior faculty considered this inappropriate.

My classes included a graduate seminar in Classic Rhetorical Theory, and three undergraduate courses: American Public Address, Public Speak-ing, and Argumentation. It was a huge workload for a professor; generally no more than three classes a semester is the norm at reputable universities, and even lower in the Ivy League. But the California State University system was different, as I would find out throughout my career. While publishing research was encouraged, it was teaching that was in the center of the road to tenure and promotion. At least, that was what I was told at the time.

It did not take long before I sensed that I was being tested about my sexuality. There were sly references and furtive allusions. But I wasn't taking the bait. In fact, when one of my female graduate students asked me out on a date, I took her up on it. She was twenty-three, and the date was on my twenty-fifth birthday. The date went fine, but what went better was meeting her family. For the next months, I enjoyed coming her to house and helping her and her mother, Ann, make dinner for the brood, which included seven sons and another daughter. Mary, her mom, and I would drink martinis while we cooked, and the younger ones—if they all showed up—ate. They ranged in age from a high school senior to a two-year-old!

Once the kids were taken care of and off to homework or bed, Mary, Ann, and I relaxed over our own dinner. In college I had learned to cook on the cheap. Now I was buying groceries for a family living on welfare and Mary's "salary" as a teaching assistant. Between taking Mary on dinner dates and feeding her family, I managed to save no money over my first full-time year of teaching.

Mary's brothers were all bright, but the fourteen-year-old named Dennis followed me around seeking attention. There was something impish about him. I soon became his big brother; we were only ten years apart in age. He liked kidding around with me and got jealous when I spent time on his older brothers, helping them with their homework or advising them about life. Little did I know he would be a friend for life. My involvement with Mary and her family put the rumors about my sexual preferences to rest. However, I invited Mary into my closet, and she was very good about keeping the secret. It was only fair, since she needed to get on with her life.[1]

THE WAR GOES ON

In November 1969, Nixon consolidated his following by giving an effective speech on the war in Vietnam. The first third of the speech discussed the damage that would be done with a precipitous withdrawal from Vietnam. There was no honor in that, and we would lose our credibility worldwide. In the second third of the speech, Nixon dealt with the problems of continuing to bomb a people into submission, and the need for the South Vietnamese to take over the war effort in a more sustained way. That led to Nixon's program of planned troop reduction over the next three years. The speech won the support of Nixon's silent majority; more important, Nixon never deviated from his plan. He kept his word, which kept the sword at the back of the South Vietnamese and eventually led to a peace settlement. But it would be a long, hard road getting there.

At the beginning of the spring semester in 1970, I was amused to read in the newspaper that students at my alma mater, UC Santa Barbara, had seized the faculty club, disrobed, and jumped in the pool after a campus lecture by William Kunstler, the lawyer for the infamous "Chicago Eight." The eight led the Yippies, who had crossed state lines to foment disruptions at the Democratic Convention in the late summer of 1968, where I witnessed their tactics. Kunstler encouraged the students at UCSB to continue to fight the good fight and resist the powers of capitalism, which included the Bank of America. That bank had, among other sins, opposed the unionization of farm workers who were led by Cesar Chavez.

The faculty-pool seizure was a silly prank that hurt the credibility of the student movement and alienated many faculty who had previously supported it. But a few days later in the little town of Isla Vista, which adjoined the campus, things got out of hand. In the evening, some students broke into the Bank of America and set it on fire. In the ensuing melee, a student was hit and killed by a ricocheting police bullet. Suddenly, the UCSB riots were the most prominent in the nation, and Governor Reagan called in the National Guard to restore order.

At about this time, I had renewed my friendship with John Macksoud, who was fighting for tenure at UCSB. He hated the war and let his students know about it. He also despised the university's administration and some faculty for what he viewed as the hypocrisy of opposing the war but supporting the campus hierarchy. They were pacifists when it came to the war, but autocrats when it came to governing the campus. I visited him in Santa Barbara, where he had developed a student following. John had just won a prestigious award from our association for one of his scholarly articles; however, the university told him to publish a university press book or he would be denied tenure. So he began work on a book that attacked quantitative social science research, revealed the inadequacies of logic in a contingent world, and posited a rhetorical theory to solve these problems. It was an important undertaking that would result in his theory that language was analogy-based and relative. Context often created meaning.[2] I helped him think through his theories, but he was distracted by the student protests. They were about to take another turn for the worse.

However, one of the unforeseen effects of the war soon touched my campus. I attended the annual Student Body Association's budget meeting on April 22, 1970, to make the annual request for funding the debate program. After the agenda and the minutes were approved, the tension rose sharply when the room was suddenly filled with about two dozen Hispanic and African American male students. The black students wore "Black Power" T-shirts that made clear they were from the Black Student Union. The Hispanic group wore red headbands and T-shirts that made clear they were from the Mecha-Maya Student Organization. They surrounded the council table and demanded that the SBA grant $7,500 to the BSU and $23,000 to the MMSO for the 1970–71 academic year. The council turned down the exorbitant requests. In reaction, some of the dissidents blocked the doors, while others circled the table hurling threats at the council. Some female members of the council began to cry. I quickly made my way to the SBA president, who was a former student of mine, and whispered in his ear to grant the request. He told me he wouldn't do it. I told him that nothing he did under duress would be legally binding and we could reconvene under guard later in the week. He nodded assent and then asked for consent to his motion to amend the budget as requested, while I worked the table, whispering instructions to male council members who looked like they might resist. The budget was passed as amended and the meeting was adjourned. The Black Student Union and Mecha-Maya members cheered and marched out.

The council was reconvened two days later under police guard and with media coverage. The council rescinded its previous action, and opened the floor for debate on the budget. Representatives of the Black Student Union and Mecha-Maya apologized for the action of the day before and reduced their requests by 50 percent apiece. Then, and I should have seen this coming, they suggested funds be taken from the debate team's budget. I was furious. These demonstrators were asking the council to punish my debaters, some of whom were African American or Hispanic, because I had helped resist their exorbitant demands. I stood up and defended my actions and asked that in any case the debaters not be punished for something I had done. It was no use. A deal had been cut, and the debate budget was cut from $7,000 to $1,000.

I immediately took the story to the news media and got good coverage, especially from the *San Diego Evening Tribune*, one of the most conservative papers in America.[3] After their reports, it was not difficult for me to raise funds in the community to save the debate program. I created the Robert Taft Forum, named for "Mr. Conservative," the senator from Ohio, and funded the squad for the year. We survived, but I was miffed at the betrayal by the Student Body Association.

KENT STATE

On May 3, 1970, President Nixon announced that intelligence reports had revealed to him that Viet Cong and North Vietnamese troops were using an outpost in Cambodia, in an area called the "Parrot's Beak" (because it poked into South Vietnam), to launch attacks on South Vietnam and retreat to the safe haven of neutral Cambodia. The President announced that an "incursion" was underway into Cambodia to clean out the Communist nest.

The reaction of the news media was quick and condemnatory. Erik Sevareid of CBS, in a stentorian editorial at the end of the evening news, predicted that there would be campus uprisings. Sure enough, the next day there were massive demonstrations across the country opposing the "incursion" into a "neutral" state. The most tragic demonstration occurred at Kent State University in Ohio, where on May 4, students marched on a 28-person unit of the National Guard, stationed to protect the campus against violence. Some say a sniper was spotted on a nearby building, others say it was just a man with a camera with a telephoto lens, but whatever the cause, the National Guard unit felt threatened. Their commander ordered them to fire into the crowd as it marched up a hill toward them. The thirteen seconds of rapid fire from automatic weapons dispersed the panicked crowd, leaving two women and two men dead, eight students wounded, one of whom was permanently paralyzed.

While the demonstrators now had martyrs, I saw in my classes that something had gone out of the student movement. It was no longer a fad; it was no longer fun. As the crisis spread, Governor Reagan declared "a three-day holiday" on the state's campuses. Immediately, many of us organized teach-ins. On day one of the "college holidays," I spoke at Redlands University, a quiet, small liberal arts college 60 miles east of Los Angeles. My job was to explain the history of Vietnam. I began by talking about how China had dominated the region for over a thousand years and then had lost its grip in the nineteenth century. Various nation-states emerged, such as Laos, Cambodia, and Siam (now Thailand). Three other regions reemerged at that time in what we now call Vietnam: Cochin in the south, with its Mekong Delta and rice farms; Annam in the central area, rich with resources such as oil and rubber; Tonkin in the mountainous north, poor, Buddhist, and up against the Chinese border. In 1870 the French saw an opportunity to colonize the area and eventually consolidated it with its other possessions into French Indo-China. Tonkin continued its Buddhist tradition, since it was protected by its jungle-covered valleys and steep mountains. Cochin and Annam, however, were converted to Catholicism and became the jewel of the French holdings in the area. Saigon was dubbed the "Paris of the Orient." From there, my lecture went into the defeat of the French at Dien Bien Phu, the involvement of Americans from advisors with Truman, to economic aid with Eisenhower, to troops with Kennedy. My lecture ended at that point in history, and other professors took over to flesh out what happened next.

Two days later, I was scheduled to give the same lecture at the University of California, Berkeley, a hotbed of opposition since 1964's Free Speech movement. My visit was hosted by a biology professor, who happened to oppose the war. I drove to the professor's house, showered, and left my things since I would be spending the night there. I wasn't into my lecture more than three minutes when the students began shouting at me. I couldn't quite understand what they were saying, but I could tell they didn't like my version of history. In particular, they seemed not to accept the fact that Vietnam had once been three separate regions. If that were true, then the fighting in Vietnam might not be a civil war. And if it was not a civil war, then the United States' involvement to save an ally in the Southeast Asian Treaty Organization might be justified. My job, I reminded the audience, was to give a background history before other speakers dealt with the more pressing situation of the current time. I was booed and then someone threw a tomato at me. Soon all sorts of garbage came flying at the stage: cabbage, lettuce, eggs. The biology professor grabbed me and we retreated to his home, where I put my clothes in his washing machine, showered, and put on fresh garments. I had a restless sleep that night on his couch.

MY RENDEZVOUS WITH REAGAN

After the semester ended, I received a call from Alex Sherriffs, the education advisor to Governor Reagan. He said that he was calling a meeting of professors who had stood up for their rights during the previous semester. He had heard about my lecture at Berkeley and read about what had happened at San Diego State with the Black Student Union. Would I like to come to Sacramento and meet with the governor? "Of course," I said.

On June 10, I arrived at the governor's office in Sacramento, where the selected professors from nine campuses met with Sherriffs before we were to meet with Reagan. I was excited to be sitting in the cabinet room in the state capitol and let Sherriffs know I had written my master's thesis on Reagan's successful campaign of 1966. I was the only assistant professor and by far the youngest person in the group. So here I was, sitting in the governor's cabinet room with his aide, listening to full professors detail their plans to "clean up" their campuses. One professor from UC San Diego said that the campus administration needed to keep dossiers on professors with socialist leanings. I thought to myself that such a practice would lead to a shed full of dossiers, particularly on his campus. UC San Diego was known as the "little red school house on the hill" in La Jolla after it hired the Marxist philosopher Herbert Marcuse from Brandeis. He brought Angela Davis with him, a radical African American who had established ties with Communists in East Germany when she took classes at the University of Frankfurt. Davis was active in Students for a Democratic Society (SDS). After she was hired by UCLA in 1968, the board of regents fired her in 1969 for ineptitude and for using her classroom as a pulpit for Communist propaganda. The courts eventually reinstated her on First Amendment grounds, but in the summer of 1970 she was arrested and accused of being part of a Black Panther conspiracy that led to the abduction and killing of a judge. She was awaiting trial while we were meeting with the governor. Davis would be found innocent in August 1970, but in 1972 she would face the death penalty when a gun registered to her was used in the murder of a judge. Her attorney, Leo Branton Jr., persuaded the jury that she was innocent. She eventually moved to UC Santa Cruz, another hotbed of radical teaching. For years, that campus did not give students grades; all classes were pass or fail.

I was awakened from my reverie on Davis by a professor who called for keeping dossiers on graduate students. "They are the real activists," he asserted. A third professor suggested that conservative students should be hired to spy on liberal professors who were using the classrooms to recruit activists. Before Sherriffs could get to me, Reagan entered the room and we all wobbled to our feet. He jovially shook our hands. At fifty-seven, he was the same tall, rosy-cheeked man I remembered from the 1968 Republican Convention. His friendliness was contagious. One could see why he had such a large following, and why he would easily be reelected governor the following November. We all took our seats, and Reagan began by praising us for our courage. "I even heard that one of you got trashed at Berkeley. Who is Dr. Smith?" I raised my hand, and he looked me in the eye and said, "Thanks for taking one for the team."

Then he asked us to tell him what we would do to improve the climate on California campuses. Out came the dossier proposals and other illegal suggestions such as tapping phones of radicals and the like. Twenty minutes into the meeting, in which I had been marginalized by Sherriffs and the full professors, Reagan's demeanor had changed. I saw a trace of anger run across his face. I recalled that while he had gone after Communists trying to infiltrate his Screen Actors Guild in the late 1940s, he was also a staunch civil libertarian. So I took a deep breath and said, "If I may, Governor Reagan, would you mind hearing from an assistant professor?" The governor nodded and I continued, "Governor, it doesn't matter much what I would do to improve the atmosphere on our campuses. The problem lies in a culture of conspiracy that is just plain nonsense. With all due respect, what these other professors have suggested doesn't just violate academic freedom, it violates civil liberties."

Reagan slapped his hand on the table and stood up. We were all too startled to move. He looked at me and said, "I have never in my life tolerated witch hunts. And I am not going to start one now." Then he looked at the other professors and said, "Gentlemen, you should be ashamed of yourselves." And he walked out of the room.[4]

Meekly, Sherriffs said, "Well, I think we ought to end this meeting." The other professors glared at me as we walked out, and I got away from them as soon as I left the cabinet room.

A few days after the meeting with Reagan, I was shocked by a story by Noel Greenwood and William Tromley, political reporters for the *Los Angeles Times*, about a "secret meeting" between Reagan and professors.[5] Greenwood had been contacted by one of the professors in the meeting who wanted some media time for his ideas. The reporters wrote that the source claimed a "blue ribbon panel" would be established to "investigate" the state's higher education system. Greenwood then quoted Professor Rex Collings of UC Berkeley, who complained about easy grading procedures, and Professor Ronald Berman, who claimed "people attending the meeting were very much interested in restoring the function of the university and that we discussed a number of ways to do it."[6]

Yeah, I thought, a number of illegal ways to do it.

I called Greenwood and told him his story was inaccurate, and I was offended and perhaps libeled by it. I would take no legal action and I would give Greenwood the names of all the professors who attended if he would write a story about what really happened, including that the governor had flatly rejected their plans. Greenwood agreed. On June 16, 1970, his headline read, "UC Faculty Dossiers Urged; Reagan Calls It 'Witch Hunt.'" The article reported, "Smith said the proposal to compile dossiers was made by professors who encouraged the use of undercover agents on the campus and the phasing out of younger faculty members. Smith, a self-described conservative Republican, said the professors offered 'some real wild stuff' and were 'talking about violating civil liberties.'"[7] Greenwood went on to correct the record about the meeting being secret. He quoted me claiming that Reagan wanted order restored on campuses but not at the cost of violating civil liberties. The offending professors were soon sanctioned on their campuses for their suggestions to the governor. Reagan also called me personally and thanked me for straightening Greenwood out.

I had wanted to go to Europe the summer after I finished my PhD. But I couldn't afford it, what with all the spending on Mary's family. So in July of 1970, I took Dennis for a tour of "California, my way." I wanted to interest him in college life and particularly in going away to college. So on our first day, we stopped at UC Santa Barbara, where the ruins of the Bank of America were being replaced by a new, windowless fortress that still serves as the bank there. The next morning I could not find my electric shaver. Dennis confessed that he had removed it from my bag before we left San Diego because he wanted me to grow a beard. "It will look cool," he pleaded.

"It better not itch," I warned. I would keep the beard for the next thirty-five years.

We went on to UC Santa Cruz and saw the student garden plots sitting in the shade of the big redwood trees. We traveled to San Francisco and hiked the city. We crossed the Bay Bridge to UC Berkeley to revisit the spot of my famous trashing, and the campus was eerily threatening the whole time we walked it.

The next morning we drove down past the bright green lettuce fields of Salinas and saw a group marching under red and black banners. I drove closer to see what was going on. The red banners had black eagles, and the group was being led by Cesar Chavez, a modern Gandhi teaching passive resistance on behalf of the United Farm Workers Union. I remembered that when Robert Kennedy was running his ill-fated California primary campaign in June of 1968, he had made a point of taking communion with Chavez, who at the time had been fasting for weeks. I decided that Dennis and I would chase Chavez down and introduce ourselves. When I shook his hand, I noticed that he had the kindest eyes I had ever seen. During our brief conversation, he asked me to make my students aware of the plight of the migratory workers. He calmly and quietly asserted that big corporations, particularly the banks, were backing the farm owners who were cutting corners to make bigger profits. I had seen the CBS television documentary *Harvest of Shame*. Now I could see it in person. The working conditions were atrocious, with workers having to do backbreaking fruit or vegetable picking in the hot Central Valley sun, facing long hours and unsanitary toilet facilities. It was heartbreaking, and I promised Chavez I would say a prayer for his cause. He squeezed my hand and marched on with his people.

SAN DIEGO STATE

During my first year at San Diego State, I had achieved the goals I had set for myself in terms of my student teaching evaluations, my publications, and my service to the department. Now my responsibilities would expand in several ways. First, the faculty asked me to start a mass lecture for the public-speaking classes. Students would come to the mass lecture for two days, and then go to a workshop section for the third hour of the class, where they would give their assigned speeches. There was no classroom big enough for the mass lecture, so I had to give it twice. I had never done mass lecturing before. However, I realized that I could be humorous and relevant if I kept track of day-to-day news and kept my finger on the pulse of popular culture. Each semester the lecture sections grew until I was giving the same lecture three times to two hundred students at a time. I often had serious bouts of déjà vu, thinking, Didn't I already cover this material?

The second expansion of my responsibilities came when the faculty asked me to update the curriculum. So I redesigned it to reflect the new trends in the field. I encountered my first friction with the senior faculty because I was too passionate about what I was doing. I had an idealized view of the academic community; like Plato, I thought the truth would sell itself in the academic world. I was not sensitive to turf battles and special interests. Stupidly, I criticized the textbook we were using in the public-speaking sections, even though it had been written by two members of the department. Talk about naive. The curriculum was updated, but I had made enemies.

The third expansion of my responsibilities came when the codirector of forensics called me in late August to say that he needed to take a leave to finish his PhD. The department told him he could not be promoted without it. I was delighted to be solely in charge of the forensics program because I wanted to make reforms. In the meantime, the team continued to be successful at winning sweepstakes. At the end of the academic year, I was elected the president of the Pacific Southwest College Forensic Association.

By this time, I had befriended a member of senior faculty, John Ackley, who was near retirement. He took me under his wing and often had me over to his home in Point Loma for dinner. His walls were lined with *Cristos*, Mexican crosses of the crucifixion. At our second dinner, I learned that John was gay. He kept a trailer south of the border, loved the culture, and often slept with Mexican men. He guessed that I was gay and told me never to let the other faculty members know. "Keep your private life very private. They only tolerate me," he told me, "because they didn't find out about me until I was tenured and their very successful debate coach." Before he retired from coaching, John had qualified several teams over the years for the National Debate Tournament, and one of his teams had won it. I asked John what was the secret to his success. He said that he saw sainthood in everyone until they proved him wrong. He became a sounding board for me, a wonderful resource for a new and very young professor. When he retired in 1970, the department lost its rudder and I would be one of those who got tossed overboard.

As the 1970–71 school year began, I protested university budget cuts in an editorial in the *Daily Aztec*. I print part of that editorial here because it shows that some things never change at the California State University. The editorial could just as easily have been written in 2012:

> Our educational opportunities . . . are being eroded from two sides. The reason many of you could not get the classes you wanted, or any classes at all, was because the state legislature cut a budget already pared by the governor. Because the necessary faculty could not be hired, classes simply could not be offered. The deterioration of the quality of your education is marked by a library now incapable of meeting your demands, and you are being crowded into larger classes. Since the state legislature overruled the governor [Reagan] and refused to give faculty the 5 per cent raise it granted to all other state employees, we are not at all anxious to overload our classes and schedules when we have been handed a de facto pay cut.[8]

THE NEVER-ENDING WAR

The war continued to haunt our lives in various ways. It was part of the midterm congressional election campaign in which Nixon focused on "law and order" in America. When demonstrators threw stones at him in San Jose during a campaign stop, they played into his hands.[9] Students were drafted, notices about students being killed or wounded in the war were a regular occurrence, and protests continued, though not nearly as forcefully as they had before Kent State. They also had morphed from being against the war to being for women's rights, or Black Power, or Hispanic Power. In late June of 1969, I read about a riot in Greenwich Village at a bar called the Stonewall Inn. When police interrupted the remembrance of Judy Garland's death (she had died a week earlier), the gays fought back, and by 1970 they too were part of the protest movement.[10]

The war haunted me one day in the mass lecture. I was in my second-hour section, lecturing on persuasive speaking and using the war in Vietnam and speeches about it for my examples. Almost halfway through the hour, I noticed a man in Marine fatigues standing at the back doors of the lecture hall. I was in front, standing on the stage, and the students, who were listening to me, could not see the man behind them. As I continued, the man walked down the aisle. I and several students noticed he was carrying a gun. I don't know what came over me, but I heard myself saying, "Aristotle also writes about forensic speaking, by which he meant speaking to the court. As you know, we are a nation of laws and those laws must be respected. Respect means being very careful about life, very careful about life."

By this time, the Marine had made his way to the stage and was just staring up at me. I continued to lecture about care and safety, and the students watched the Marine's gun. Some students in the back began to exit, carefully. And I said, "When people act carefully, as many of you are acting now, they set an example. And everyone should follow that example. And I mean everyone."

The Marine turned around and faced the students, and I feared the worst. I considered jumping him from behind. But only about fifty students had exited at that point and I didn't want any shooting to start. Then the Marine put his hands behind him and pulled himself onto the stage. As I lectured, I edged closer to the Marine as class members kept making for the door. He was looking at his gun and not at them. I put my hand on his head and patted it. He wrapped his right arm, the one without the gun, around my leg and put his head up against my thigh. I continued to comfort him and the classroom emptied completely. I sat beside him, slid the gun from his left hand, and held him until the police arrived. He had escaped from a mental ward on the Marine base. He surrendered gently to the police. A few minutes later, I released my tension by weeping profusely.

The war came after me in another way. On April 14, 1971, I was notified that deferments from the draft for teachers, including professors, had been ended, and my Selective Service number (SS . . . couldn't they have come up with other initials given what the SS stood for in World War II?), 4–140–44–1890, assigned when I turned eighteen, was reclassified 1-A. After some soul-searching, I decided to appeal the classification. Had I been drafted in 1966 when I came out of college, I might have served. But in 1971, it was clear that we would not win this war and boot camp would be a waste of my talents.

When my name was called, I walked into a small room and, all alone, faced five very old men and a stenographer. One of the men was Mr. Fletcher, for whom the hills behind San Diego had been named. He asked me to state the "reason or reasons for which you believe your deferment should be reinstated." I argued that I was an effective teacher and could do more for my country in the classroom than in the fields of Vietnam. I had obtained my PhD in record time on a National Defense Education fellowship, so the government had paid to put me in the classroom. Mr. Fletcher asked if I had a conscientious objection to the war. I told him that I did not object in the technical sense; however, I believed the war had been badly prosecuted from the beginning and we were now bogged down in a war we could not win. I made a point of showing the board my rejected application to the United States Foreign Service. There were no other questions and I was dismissed. I fretted for weeks waiting for the decision, and then the envelope arrived. By a vote of 3 to 2, my deferment was reinstated. I was ready for a vacation.

OFF TO EUROPE

My first trip to Europe led to some realizations that were important in terms of knowing myself and connecting with a sense of spirit. I decided that I would focus on Europe's heart by traveling to London, Amsterdam, Heidelberg, and Paris. In London I stayed a block off Hyde Park, which is gorgeous in the summer, being replete with blossoming flowers and green lawns. On June 30, I traveled to Canterbury to pray at the spot where Henry II's friends struck down Archbishop Thomas Becket during a mass in the cathedral. Becket's conversion from political operative and lover of Henry II to a priest in love with God fascinated me.

From there I traveled to Dover to visit the old castle with its circular steps. I marched over to St. Margaret's Chapel and then to the famous white cliffs. As I clambered along them looking across to France, I was completely absorbed with a view of the English Channel. I suddenly discovered that my path had disappeared and I was on a narrow ledge of white chalk with nowhere to go. I had no idea how I had gotten to that point and began to panic. The beach was straight below me, a good 100 feet down, and on each side of me was sheer cliff. Then I looked up. The top of the cliff was about 15 feet above my head, and there were some plants just above and beyond that I could grab onto. Slowly and carefully, I pulled myself up where tourists were staring down at me in horror. One man finally reached down and gave me a hand. I thanked him as I brushed the white chalk off my shirt and pants. Exhausted, I made my way to the harbor and caught the train back to London.

On July 1, it was time to cross the Channel to the mainland and head for Amsterdam. While I enjoyed the parks, the walks, the ballet and concerts, my most important goal was to see Van Gogh's paintings in person. I had no idea how little justice posters and prints did to his creations. *Starry Night* pulled you into swirls of mystical power representing the magnetic fields at play in the universe. The roots on the trees in his paintings were not painted with brush strokes, but squeezed out of paint tubes like toothpaste, and they were pulsing with existence. Faces were painted in light greens and yellows that captured their moods. It was a stunning experience, and one that would inspire a scholarly article I would write about the relationship between Van Gogh and Gaugin.

Over the next few days, I got lost wandering along the water-filled canals, which curve in ways that fool you. I visited Ann Frank's home and walked in the groves of tall poplars along clear streams in the countryside. I visited the windmills, the Delft blue china plant, and cheese farms. However, there was a dark side to Amsterdam, and I don't mean the houses of prostitution with women sitting in the red-lit windows. I mean the number of drugged-out young American kids in the gutters and on Dam Plaza. I tried talking with some of them, but they were so sleepy or hallucinatory that they made no sense. It was time to move on.

I grabbed a train for Cologne, where I followed the advice of the guidebook: see the magnificent cathedral with its blue stained-glass windows and high arched ceiling, and move on. So after visiting the cathedral, I caught the next train to the ancient city of Koblenz, which means confluence, named so because it is situated where the Rhine and Moselle Rivers meet. I enjoyed the city for a couple of days and then woke up ready to board a Rhine riverboat for a trip that would float by the famous castles and the dock in Rudesheim. As I waited for the boat, I was taken by the sun glinting on the river, and it suddenly struck me that for the first time in my life I was really free. I could do whatever I wanted. I could stay in Europe. I could return home. I could change jobs. I was delirious with freedom. Then the boat arrived and I boarded.

The trip went well at first as I reflected on my discovery. The castles among the hillside vineyards were impressive. But after a while, I began to feel trapped on the boat. Anxiety flared up in my brain. By the time we reached Rudesheim, the dark clouds of depression encased me and I was having trouble breathing. Somehow I found the station where I was to catch the train for Wiesbaden, where I had a room waiting. I stumbled onto the train and into a window seat. Very scared in the hot afternoon, I stared into the red nasturtiums along the train tracks. As I focused on the flowers, something flowed through me. The more I stared into the heart of the red blossoms, the more the anxiety was pulled out of me and soon was replaced by a sense of grace. Tears of gratitude flowed down my face as the train pulled out of the station.

Wiesbaden was a quaint, historically Catholic town with beautiful fountains that comforted anyone who gazed at them. I gave a prayer of thanks in the cathedral before touring the town and moving on to Mainz, which was also a delight. Here in 1456 Johannes Gutenberg invented his printing press and began to turn out the most beautiful Bibles in the world. From there I took the train to Heidelberg, the setting of the famous musical *The Student Prince*, which I had sung in high school. More importantly, it was marked by the *philosopheg* or "philosophers' trail" that runs through the Black Forest and up to the ruins of St. Michael's monastery. The trail had been walked by Hegel, Nietzsche, and most important to me, Heidegger, on whose writing I continued to do research.

On July 11, I caught a train for the long ride to the "City of Light." As the countryside flew by the train window, I tried to meditate and pray. And then a young woman with a dark pageboy haircut sat beside me. She wore a plain, wheat-colored shift that looked like what warriors often wore under their armor. And I thought to myself, she looks just like pictures of Joan of Arc. We struck up a conversation in which she helped me with my rusty grad-school French. As we got closer to Paris, she asked me where I was staying. I told her I had not reserved a place because I was unsure of when I would be arriving, but I knew I could count on those tourist kiosks in the train station to locate a place.

She turned very serious. "That is not going to happen this time. I'd show you a place but I must be on the coast to be a governess to three children, starting today." She reached into her bag and wrote on a scrap of paper. "Here is the phone number for the Hotel Sorbonne. It's a lovely place in a fantastic location and I'm sure they'll have a room for you."

I left the train in Paris not knowing what to think. I went into the station and sure enough, the help kiosk was closed. I exchanged some traveler's checks for francs and change, and called the number she had given me. The woman who answered told me to hurry over because she only had one room left. Amazingly, it turned out to be the nicest room on the whole trip. It had French doors that opened to a courtyard, and a large bed with plenty of room. I did not know at the time that way back in our family's history a group had helped Joan of Arc and she had given them the village of Musé as a reward. The Musés moved to England and became the Muzzys, who moved to America and the rest is history.

On my first night in Paris, I walked to Notre Dame to say a prayer of thanks to Saint Joan. I entered the darkened cathedral in complete awe. Off to one side, I saw a statue of an armed figure who I thought must be Saint Michael, the archangel. There were candles to light in front of the statue. So I dropped some francs in the box, lit a candle, and set it before the statue. It illuminated a sign that revealed the statue was of Joan of Arc.

At Chartres, I studied the cathedral with its two towers, one Romanesque and one Gothic, but it was the stained-glass windows inside that took your soul up to God. One had the likeness of a white dove in the center, and the other, the famous Rosette Window, glowed pink. I also made my way to Versailles with its Hall of Mirrors where the treaty ending the Great War was signed. The manicured lawns were punctuated with elaborate fountains that had been turned on every time Louis XIV entered the gardens.[11]

The best day trip came when I went to Rouen, the site of Joan of Arc's trial and burning at the stake. I prayed at Joan's statue where her face is turned to heaven as flames lick at her smock. I walked over to the cathedral, whose graceful, delicate, lace-like exterior was captured beautifully by Monet. It was a fitting place to end my stay in France.

In London, I trooped through Churchill's World War II headquarters and saw sections of Whitehall open only to academics. Then I went to the House of Commons, where luckily, Conservative prime minister Edward Heath was answering questions. He reminded me why I was a conservative. Edmund Burke, the founder of the movement, explained it this way to the electors of Bristol:

> I did not obey your instructions. No! I conformed to the instructions of truth and nature, and maintained your interests against your opinions, with a constancy that became me. A representative worthy of you ought to be a person of stability. I am to look, indeed, to your opinions, but to such opinions as you and I must have five years hence. I was not to look to the flash of the day. I know that you chose me, in my place, along with others, to be a pillar of state, and not a weathercock on the top of the edifice, exalted for my levity and versatility, and of no use but to indicate the shiftings of every fashionable gale.

Burke saw society as an evolving, living organism that has deep roots in the past, and has retained time-tested policies and principles. It is a grand union of functional parts, which include the church, the community, the courts, and the family, for which one fights. It relies on time-tested institutions such as the constitution and common law to ensure liberty, which provides individualism, competition, and creativity. Individualism should be rewarded after success in competition; creativity contributes to a sense of spirituality and should be encouraged by society. More efficient, hands-on, and inexpensive volunteerism is vastly superior to government intervention. Representative government by people of character is far superior to direct democracy when these representatives govern with prudence. Humans are equal only before God, the law, and the opportunity available to them; they possess souls that allow them to glimpse perfect spirit. Property gives humans the chance to succeed and rewards those who do so while also giving them a stake in their country. Therefore, it must be protected. A law that runs counter to a historic sense of right and wrong, such as natural rights, is no law at all; short of encouraging these goals and providing national security, the government has no role to play in society. Heath represented this philosophy as prime minister and made me proud to be a conservative.

I also visited the Victorian-styled Brompton Oratory to say a few prayers, a practice I've maintained every time I visit London. I took a day tour to Oxford with its incredible library full of ancient documents; to the street in Bainbridge where they burned the three leading Protestant Cardinals Ridgley, Cranmer, and Lattimore in the reign of young Mary Tudor; to the Duke of Marlborough's Blenheim Castle where Churchill was born in the cloakroom (his American mother had been waltzing only minutes before); and to Shakespeare's Stratford-on-Avon for a walkabout and then a performance of *Much Ado About Nothing*.

On my last day in London, I was sweetly sad, simply writing about the philosophical discoveries I had made on my journey. I was now sure there was a God, and I was just as sure that I was not worthy of that God.

BACK TO SCHOOL

In my third year at San Diego State, I felt the national divide in my field between theoretical-history types like myself and the social-science types advocating quantitative studies of the elements of communication, a trend that actually could be traced to James Winans, one of the founders of our discipline in 1915 who opened pathways to psychology. The fight wasn't pretty. However, there was another tension in the department between the younger firebrands like myself, and the old guard, who built the department and had come out of the debate-coaching tradition, but had failed to publish much research. It was a good old boys' network; no females had been hired, nor had any minorities. The untenured, including me, wanted this system changed—not only because of our interest in research, but in terms of adjusting to a campus student body that was becoming more and more diverse.

Our criticism of the old guard was not appreciated, and as leader of the pack, I was singled out. On April 1, I went to my mailbox in the department office and found what I thought was a practical joke. There was a letter informing me that next year, my fourth, would be "terminal." I came out of the mailroom to the department secretary, laughing, only to find her in tears. "Cora," I said, "what is it?"

"I . . . I can't believe they fired you." I suddenly realized the letter was no April fool's joke.

The vote on whether I should be retained was 3 to 2 against retention, based on the charge that I was "divisive." My remarks about the basic course textbook were recounted, as were a few caustic jokes in faculty meetings. Fraternizing with students was also condemned because in their company I made remarks about the department that were disparaging. There's a lesson to be learned in that one.

CONVENTION COVERAGE, 1972

After I filed my grievance and was preparing to leave for CBS to cover the conventions, I noticed a story out of New York City. A gay man named Morty Manford asked his mother Jeanne to march with him in what was called the "Christopher Street Liberation Day Parade." She had formed a group two months earlier encouraging parents to love their gay and lesbian children. The group evolved into Parents, Families and Friends of Lesbians and Gays (PFLAG), which exists to this day. The parade was the forerunner to Gay Pride parades that are now common across the country. It was another step in the growth of a movement that would eventually achieve a good deal more.

As summer started, I hoped coverage of the political conventions for CBS would take my mind off San Diego State. Both parties had agreed to convene their conventions in Miami Beach to help the networks save money. The crew, including Mike Wallace and Dan Rather, remembered me from 1968, and Walter Cronkite insisted I continue to head up the research operation and take care of his questions first. I saw a contrast between the petty bickering at San Diego State and professionalism at CBS.

I began to assemble the research team that would once again help Marty Plissner put together the delegate handbooks for the floor reporters. Our first handbook would be on the Democratic delegates since their convention came first. I wrote the biographies of Eleanor McGovern, Muriel Humphrey, Ted Kennedy, Shirley Chisholm, and many more. I wrote my first piece for Eric Sevareid for the end of the *CBS Evening News*.

And then one afternoon, the Associated Press wire rang five bells. That meant a major, major story was breaking. So I ran to the machine. It reported that a group of men with ties to the CIA had been arrested at the Watergate complex after they had broken into Democratic Party National Headquarters. I called Ken Khachigian, who was still functioning there as an aide to Patrick Buchanan. My worst fears were verified when Ken said, "Don't tell a soul, but this damn thing goes pretty high in the White House."

"Not to the top? Tell me it doesn't go to the top."

"I can't tell you any more because you are at CBS and they would have a field day with this thing." From that moment on, I believed that Nixon was involved in Watergate. The question would be how he would handle the crisis. Eventually the infamous tapes revealed what happened. Nixon told his trusted aides on June 23, 1972, not to disclose his or their involvement in Watergate. Basically, Nixon did not give credence to assurances from his political unit that he would beat McGovern even if he aired out Watergate's dirty linen. His political people had told him he would beat Kennedy, but he lost. They told him he could easily win the California governor's race, but he lost. They told him he would easily beat Humphrey in 1968, and he was up all night until the race was finally decided. Nixon was going to take no chances in 1972. And it would prove his undoing.

The Democrats helped Nixon by running a bad convention and an even worse presidential campaign. McGovern had a majority of the delegates. Nonetheless, the old guard saw the poll numbers and wanted to replace McGovern with someone else. His campaign managers' main challenge was a credentials fight in which the seating of certain McGovern delegates was challenged. The first challenge was to the South Carolina delegation; it was alleged that women had been excluded in the delegate selection process. The night before the challenge, Marty Plissner and I discovered that McGovern's team had decided not to fight that challenge. It didn't amount to that many delegates, and they did not want to get on the wrong side of the women's caucus. The challenge was finally taken up in the early evening of July 10, and though Marty and I had put our story on the CND (CBS News Department) wire, Cronkite began to intone about how the South Carolina vote would be decisive for the McGovern team. I immediately called the anchor booth and told the producer to get the story right. She told me that Cronkite had independent sources that contradicted our story.

The problem was that the other networks followed Cronkite's lead—after all, he was the most trusted man in America.

Just before the voting started, I noticed Gary Hart—at the time, one of McGovern's floor leaders—holding up a blue card, which meant, throw the vote. I again called Cronkite's producer. She could not get through to him, and as the South Carolina vote favored the new delegation and unseated the McGovern delegation, he continued to portray the event as a debacle for McGovern.

Next came a challenge to the huge California delegation. The anti-McGovern forces wanted proportional representation of the primary vote in California, instead of the winner-take-all rule that was in effect at the time. It would have meant that McGovern would lose two-thirds of his California delegates, which would have put his nomination in jeopardy. I knew McGovern must make his stand on this one. Cronkite had dramatized the vote so much that ratings for the evening began to rise. As I looked out across the floor, I saw Gary Hart hold up a yellow card, which meant McGovern would fight the challenge. The McGovern lines held and so there was no change in the California delegation, which would now throw its entire vote to McGovern. In effect, Edmund Muskie, the senator from Maine, and the handful of other candidates lost any chance they had to steal the nomination. The convention was effectively over, and Marty and I had enhanced our credibility with Cronkite since our vote count was within 15 delegates of the final result out of over 2,500 delegate votes cast. Cronkite apologized to everyone in the newsroom for getting the South Carolina story wrong.

The next night, the convention proceeded to nominate McGovern. He then came forward and announced that his choice for vice president was Senator Thomas Eagleton of Missouri. Once nominated, Eagleton gave a peppy, optimistic speech. Ted Kennedy gave one of his convention stem-winders that functioned as a comeback after the horror of Chappaquiddick in the summer of 1969. McGovern did not give his acceptance speech until 3:00 A.M. Eastern Daylight Time, when most people were in bed. Nixon must have been licking his chops.

A few weeks later, the Republican delegates began trickling into Miami Beach. The weather was sweltering that August, but the breezes and the late afternoon showers made it bearable. I got caught in several of these warm showers. The problem was that when you arrived for work or back in your hotel room, the air conditioning would give you chills. You had to keep a towel and a change of clothes at home and at work if you did not want to get pneumonia.

All hell broke loose when it was learned that Senator Eagleton had undergone shock therapy for depression. McGovern said he stood behind Eagleton "1,000 percent." However, on August 1, after only eighteen days on the ticket, Eagleton withdrew his candidacy and McGovern was huddled with his people trying to control the damage—if he couldn't pick a decent VP, how could he run the country? Finally, the McGovern press office announced that he would hold a press conference in Washington, D.C., announcing his nominee in hopes that the Democratic National Committee meeting in emergency session would ratify his choice.

As I shouldered my way through the crowd of reporters in Miami gathering for the live feed of McGovern's press conference, I heard Sam Donaldson tell his ABC anchor desk that he would stake his job on the fact that McGovern was going to name party head Larry O'Brien as his VP. Donaldson was screaming at ABC to break the story and give him the scoop, which they did. McGovern finally appeared and announced that Sargent Shriver, brother-in-law of the Kennedys and the founder of the Peace Corps, would be the nominee for vice president. Sam Donaldson was nowhere to be seen.

In the lead-up to the Republican Convention, antiwar demonstrators got rained on sleeping in the parks. What they did not realize was that Miami Beach was accessible only by bridges, and the police could easily close them to prevent the demonstrators from reaching the convention hall. They would not be a factor at Richard Nixon's coronation.

Neither would the clock. For the first time in history, the Republican Convention was entirely scripted. CBS broke the story when I got a copy of the script from Ken Khachigian. Cronkite was able to make a big deal about it once we came on the air on the first night of the convention. From this point forward, most conventions would be scripted, and the networks began to cut back on how much time they would give the conventions. The primary season had already damaged the conventions because with so many states holding primaries, the delegates were usually signed, sealed, and delivered by the beginning of June. It would be rare for the outcome of a convention to be in doubt as it started, which greatly reduced interest in an institution that could be traced back to 1831. Between 1972 and 2008, there was only one convention that featured a contest on the floor, and I would be a speechwriter for the winning nominee.

In 1972, Nixon's men made sure to get all their best speakers—Ronald Reagan, Spiro Agnew, and Nixon—on in prime time. And as usual, Nixon's acceptance speech, according to the Gallup Poll, was the most remembered event of the convention. However, with a convention so scripted, CBS needed to do something to generate stories. So once the delegate book was done, a grateful Frank Manitzas gave me a cushy assignment. I would work with Charles Kuralt, of "On the Road" fame, to do a story about rich Republicans living on yachts while they attended the convention. By this time, it was clear to me that CBS had a clear liberal, and therefore Democratic, bias. Nonetheless, we had won the ratings war again, and the team of Leslie Stahl, Mike Wallace, Dan Rather, and Roger Mudd on the floor, with Cronkite in the booth, and Sevareid spewing out truisms, and Kuralt and Hughes Rudd doing color stories proved successful.

When I returned to San Diego, the fight to regain my status took a lot of time and energy. I still had to teach, rehearse the debaters, and travel to tournaments. And then in late October it was time to leave for New York City and my first election-night coverage with CBS. Covering lots of elections across the country in one night was very different than covering one convention over a week. In the days leading up to the election, CBS was obsessed with the Watergate scandal. Two days before the election, Frank Manitzas came to me with a proposal. He said he wanted me to write a story on McGovern's dirty tricks in the 1972 primaries to balance CBS's Watergate stories. He had some leads for me to follow. For example, I called a young woman named Rose, who had become a stringer for CBS after she had served as a limousine driver for Edmund Muskie while at the same time being a spy for the McGovern camp. In New Hampshire, where McGovern basically ended Muskie's run for the presidency, the McGovern team knew every move Muskie was going to make. I wrote this and several other similar offenses that I got from Ken Khachigian into a story for the evening news. The night before the election, my story on McGovern's dirty tricks would be balanced by an Eric Sevareid editorial attacking Nixon for Watergate. Frank and I sat with others in the newsroom waiting for my story. It was not in the first segment, and Cronkite broke for a commercial. Then came the second segment, no story. Then came the last segment and not only was there no story, there was no editorial by Sevareid.

Frank and I tracked the evening news producer down. Frank asked "what in the hell" had happened. The producer informed me that "we were used by the White House." "Nixon's guy Chuck Colson" had CBS Corporate assign my story through Frank so the Nixon people could use it as a bargaining chip to shut Sevareid down. "They feared his editorial and were willing to give up your story to stop it. Cronkite is furious that the suits in Black Rock [CBS Corporate Headquarters] would interfere with his show." Wow, I thought, I was a pawn in a national election.[12] It was like being Zelig or Forrest Gump.

On election night, I worked with John Hart on the trend desk. Our job was to see what was going on nationally underneath Nixon's tidal wave. We got some good stories on the air while competing with the anchor desk and regional correspondents' desks, one for each of the directions on the compass. Mike Wallace did the East and Roger Mudd did the South, so they got on early. Dan Rather did the Midwest and Leslie Stahl handled the West.

Nixon won 49 of the 50 states, losing only Massachusetts and the District of Columbia. Nixon's decision to focus on doing his job and then give single-issue speeches proved decisive. It was a lesson I would not forget. Rumors of the peace process moving forward in Vietnam also helped Nixon; Kissinger said, "Peace is at hand." The reasons for such optimism were less than clear at the time. After winning a landslide, Nixon approved the carpet bombing of North Vietnam in "Operation Rolling Thunder," but he soon realized that even without Ho Chi Minh, who died in 1969, the North Vietnamese were not going to "crack." They scored yet another public-relations coup by piling up in the center of Hanoi the remains of B52s they had shot down. They paraded the American pilots they had captured. In March 1973, Henry Kissinger and Lee Duc Tho were nominated for the Nobel Peace Prize for the treaty they negotiated, which was almost identical to what the North Vietnamese had proposed months earlier. Neither side would reveal a secret codicil to the treaty that stated that North Vietnam would not invade South Vietnam as long as Nixon was president. Neither side knew that Nixon's presidency would end far ahead of schedule.

CHAPTER FIVE

Working at
Mr. Jefferson's University

BACK IN SAN DIEGO, I RECEIVED A CALL OUT OF THE BLUE FROM A friend with whom I had gone to graduate school. He had left Penn State to take a job teaching rhetoric and public address at the University of Virginia. He had not completed his PhD and so he was not retained. He called to ask me if I would like to replace him; he would be glad to recommend me to the department. I agreed, and on a cold but clear late November day, I found myself in Charlottesville, Virginia, interviewing for the job of debate coach and teacher of rhetoric and public address.

The vibes at the University of Virginia were positive as I toured the well-groomed, tree-lined grounds. I had a wonderful breakfast with the student committee; each member was articulate and bright. My traditional version of American public address seemed well suited to Mr. Jefferson's University. He had built it and been its first rector. The history department contained professors whose books I had read when doing research on various papers. Unlike San Diego State, this campus could offer PhDs, and there was talk of moving beyond the master's level in the Speech Communication Department. I also felt at home in Charlottesville because of having lived in Virginia as a kid and traveled around the state. I was issued an offer a week later. It raised my salary by 20 percent and promoted me to associate professor, and the dean promised me tenure in one year if the faculty of the department voted for it. I accepted, but asked the officials at Virginia to keep it quiet. I did not want my grievance at San Diego State to become moot.

My grievance finally reached the office of the president at San Diego State in March 1973; it wouldn't be the last time I saw how slowly the wheels of justice turned on a college campus. President Brage Golding, who had a reputation for fairness, called my department chair and me into his office. He told us that he had an agreement drawn up that he wanted us to sign. It overturned my termination; I would be retained and eligible for consideration for tenure in the following year. The agreement forbade the department from ever referring to the "termination" or the circumstances surrounding it. I would agree not to sue the university for any damage to my reputation.

My chair sat stoically through President Golding's instructions and then signed the agreement, as did I. The president thanked us and began to show us to the door. "Before we leave," I interrupted, "I have another document for the two of you." From the look on their faces, I could see they were expecting a subpoena. Instead I handed them copies of my letter of acceptance for the Virginia job, which would start in the fall of 1973.

"But why did you put us through this if you were leaving?" my chair asked.

Now it was Golding's turn to interrupt. "Bob, the lad wanted to clear his name." Then he turned to me. "Congratulations, you're going to love it at Virginia."[1]

While my parents were unhappy that I would be leaving, Dennis was proud of me. I had gotten him into Chico State, where he would have a successful time in the coming years, in fact finding the woman to whom he is still married.

I had talked my new position over with John Macksoud during several visits to Santa Barbara. I returned at the end of the semester to learn that he too would be moving east. Reputable publishers either demanded unacceptable changes to his book, or rejected it outright. So Macksoud decided to publish the book on his own. It is called *Other Illusions* and is not written in the usual academic style. Eventually, I wrote two flattering reviews of the book in major journals, but it never went anywhere. In any case, forced to leave UC Santa Barbara, John landed on his feet, taking a job at the State University of New York campus in Binghamton.

In late August of 1973, I jumped into my 1969 Mustang for the long journey across America to Charlottesville, Virginia. I picked Dennis up in Boise, where he was working on a construction job for his uncle's company. I retraced part of the trip I had taken as a kid in 1953 by driving Dennis up into the Big Horn Mountains, across their beautiful meadows, and down and out across the plains. Dennis and I eventually made our way to Washington, D.C., where I showed him the sights and then put him on a plane home. The next day I drove down to Charlottesville and moved into an apartment on Jefferson Park Avenue that looked out toward Mr. Jefferson's Monticello. It was an easy walk to the little white house on the campus that served as the department office on Dawson's Row. I was given the former kitchen to use as the debate office. It was quaint, but I believed I could make it work.

And work it did. After only two semesters on the campus, my sections of the undergraduate courses expanded to well over a hundred students each, numbers unheard of in the department before that time. The fact that I had worked at CBS News didn't hurt. Soon my courses were cross-listed in American Studies, and students in the Government and History Departments were encouraged to take them. The department's faculty considered me an established scholar who was publishing regularly: eight scholarly articles, two in the prestigious journal *Philosophy and Rhetoric.* I had learned the art of academic titling; one article was dubbed "The Medieval Subjugation and the Existential Elevation of Rhetoric." (Makes you want to run out and get a copy.) My first book, *Ideas in Conflict: The Bases of Argument* was a textbook put out by Bobbs-Merrill in 1972, which I wrote with my former debate partner David Hunsaker, whom I had helped bring to San Diego State after he decided not to become a lawyer. The book did well because it was relevant to students; it used contemporary examples and case studies to illustrate its theories of argumentation. These were drawn from congressional testimony on the war in Vietnam, speeches on the national crime wave, and economic problems. I also completed another textbook, this time on rhetorical criticism, to go along with new articles in American public address on Nixon and Daniel Webster.

However, I enjoyed the teaching more than anything else because the students at Virginia turned out to be very special. At one point, the university had been invited into the Ivy League, but decided not to join those "Yankee schools," which were elitist and private. When I showed up to teach my first class (I had always worn a tie to class at San Diego State, much to the chagrin of the faculty who walked around as if they were in Honolulu), I believed I was well dressed in my sport coat and tie. But as I looked over the class, I realized that almost every male student was better dressed than I was. The next day I went shopping at the "corner," a quaint row of upscale shops near the campus. The one area where I outdid my male students was in footwear. The campus tradition was to wear loafers without socks, which led to many colds among the male students during the winter.

One of the nicest things about the university was that professors called each other "Mister" or "Miss" or "Miz," not "Doctor." It was assumed that if you were on the faculty, you had a doctorate. This tradition somewhat reduced the two-class nature of the tenure system and avoided confusing faculty with the doctors who taught at the medical school.

The school had a football team; the students used its poor record as an excuse to drink. While the rest of America's campuses had fallen into drug use, UVA maintained its tradition of drunkenness. Mint julep–filled Jefferson Cups were ubiquitous. Unlike the football team, the basketball team was a big winner, providing yet another excuse to drink. It was regularly in the top twenty in the United States and won the Atlantic Coast Conference while I was there. Wally Walker, who went on to become an NBA star, took one of my classes.

LASTING FRIENDSHIPS

As at San Diego State, I often had students to my apartment, and later to my house, for dinner. While at San Diego I would find one or two students a year that I wanted to mentor, at Virginia there two or three a semester. Many students of mine went on to careers in the media, including Katie Couric of NBC's *Today Show* and CBS's *Evening News*, and Wyatt Andrews, who eventually became a White House correspondent for CBS News. Wyatt and I provided statewide radio coverage of Virginia's 1975 elections.

The debate team held its own, though I was unable to change the tradition at UVA that no one did individual events. These debaters were all going on to law school. I did advise the on-campus Jefferson Society, which met once a month to discuss some important political or ethical question in parliamentary-style debate. At the end of the evening, the house would divide for or against the question.

Since college, I had always opposed fraternities as aristocratic, anti-educational, and exclusionary. I didn't even go through rush for the eight fraternities at UCSB, fearful of being rejected. However, at Virginia, Zeta Psi focused on helping its members attain better grades, and had a charming mix of young men who became student leaders. After a few meals at the Zeta house as a guest of some of my students, I became a regular and began advising the young men about their lives. Later I even taught a class exclusively for their house. Throughout all of this activity, I remained in the closet, and remarkably, my sexuality was questioned by only one student, who "sensed" that I was gay and came on to me. He was very handsome. But I turned him away and prayed to God not to test me like that again.

THE NATIONAL SCENE

While I vacationed at my folks' back in San Diego for the summer of 1974, the events leading to the inevitable resignation of Richard Nixon occurred. In early August, he spoke from the Oval Office, and it killed me that this man who had come from a lower-class family in Southern California and risen to the top due to his own diligence had thrown everything away by trying to cover up a crime. That night my sister and I joined David Hunsaker and his wife for dinner and the play *Henry IV, Part 2*, by Shakespeare. As I sat in the Old Globe Theatre and heard the words "Uneasy rests the head that wears the crown," I wept. The next day I wept again as Nixon rambled through his farewell to his staff. He spoke of his "sainted mother" and I thought, yes, she was the perfectionist who kept you in a constant state of guilt. It became your comfort; you could not live without it. You were, as Kenneth Burke tells us, "rotten with perfection." And so you committed a crime so that you could feel the guilt again, and in the process you let all of us down.

In November, I returned to New York City to work for CBS for election-night coverage. It was great seeing Mike Wallace, Walter Cronkite, and the other stars at CBS again. My job was to help Marty Plissner put together a context for the election. It was easy; it was all about Watergate. The question was how many seats were the Republicans going to lose in the House and the Senate. I was appalled at how partisan the reporting was. On election night, it was as if Watergate gave the CBS gang an excuse to go rogue liberal. Even though we were live to the nation, every time a member of the House Judiciary Committee who had voted against Nixon's impeachment was defeated, a cheer from the staff went up in the background. Every time a Republican senator lost, another cheer went up. I knew that most of the journalists at CBS were Democrats and liberals—Mike Wallace and Bernard Goldberg being the exceptions—but this was ridiculous.

I again worked with the square-jawed John Hart on the trend desk. We tried to make sense out of the exit polls. The most depressing stories were about how many voters could not name their congressman. Remember, these are people who went into a polling place and cast a vote for someone running for Congress; that's what the midterm election is all about. We found that *only 25 percent of those voters* could name their congressman; the numbers were even lower for state and local officials. So much for Jefferson's essential ingredient to successful democracy—an educated public.

It was a bad night for Republicans. By the end of the evening, they had a net loss of four Senate seats and over forty House seats. They lost the momentum Nixon had given them in the South in 1972. The new president, Gerald Ford, was not helping. He was not a great speaker and had been appointed vice president by Nixon. And now he faced a hostile House and Senate chock full of Democrats seeking revenge for his pardon of Nixon, after which Ford's approval ratings in the Gallup poll dropped from 71 to 49 percent, and would eventually fall to 33 percent as inflation ate away at incomes.

Worse than Watergate was the fall of South Vietnam in the spring semester of 1975. I was furious that the Congress had refused to provide funds to defend the country that was being invaded in what I believed was a violation of the treaty signed in Paris by Henry Kissinger and Le Duc Tho.

My campus life was going much better. I was chosen to give the annual "Honor Speech" to incoming freshmen in the fall of 1975. They were required to read a book of my choosing, which was *Zen and the Art of Motorcycle Maintenance*, a terrific story of a man and his son riding a motorcycle across the country as the man recounts his education and searches for the meaning of "quality." The book is existential and studies rhetoric, so it had become one of my favorites. Over two thousand freshman had to listen to my speech on the university's honor system, which brooks no lying, cheating, or stealing. If you got caught, you were booted off the campus and your name appeared in the student newspaper in a small black box. My Honor Speech began by quoting from Falstaff's remarks in Shakespeare's play about the coming of age of Henry V. Falstaff claims that "honor" is just a word; it can't do anything. In my attempt to prove old Falstaff wrong, I suggested that the honor system ensures "a society in which you can freely find your own potential." I hoped to convince the freshmen that without honor, life is meaningless at best and can be pretty low for those who would trade honor for power, fame, and/ or fortune. It was an easy sell after Watergate.

Members of the administration seemed happy with the address. The dean of students, Ernie Ern, became a fan. Katie Couric did a favorable review for the *Cavalier Daily*. Freshmen flocked to my classes, and I was invited to important parties by various professors, administrators, and clubs. My faculty unanimously recommended me for tenure. In fact, the long letter from the chair on behalf of the committee said the recommendation was made with "great enthusiasm." It continued: "We firmly believe that he amply exceeds all of the standard requirements for a favorable tenure decision." The letter reminded the new dean that his predecessor had wanted to bring me in with tenure, but the department had asked for a probationary year to make sure I could teach effectively in the UVA environment.

Soon after, I received a call from Dean Edwin Floyd, who had just come out of the math department to replace the dean who hired me. He asked me to his office. He was gaunt, thin, and serious-looking in his black suit and thin black tie. He had lost his right hand at some point in his youth and a forked hook had replaced it. Dean Floyd told me that after consultation with the college tenure committee, he wanted to postpone an assessment of my tenure for one year to allow me to "consolidate my research." He could not understand how I could do research on Daniel Webster, who was a nineteenth-century figure, and research on Nixon, who was a twentieth-century figure. I explained that both were politically significant speakers and my work focused on criticism of public address, not biography. He responded that at Virginia, one was expected to be "narrowly focused to develop an expertise, not to be a surveyor who was all over the map." I repeated that my narrow focus was rhetorical criticism of public address, not historical figures; they were simply my case studies. "But," he replied, "you also write about Aristotle."

"With all due respect, sir, I write about Aristotle's theory of rhetoric because it is what I use to perform the analyses I publish." He told me that the committee could not understand this and that I should focus my research in one area. He also told me that working at CBS was a distraction from a serious research focus. "But, Dean Floyd, what I write for the correspondents at CBS goes out to 20 million people. Shouldn't that count for something?"

"It is a service, I suppose. But here at Mr. Jefferson's University, it does not count as scholarly publication. Mr. Jefferson did not even believe that journalism was a fit subject for the students here, so we have never had any courses in that field."

I wanted to say, "Well, screw Jefferson, he owned slaves. Are you going to allow slavery here too? Most of the professors at UVA would have given their right arm to write for Walter Cronkite." But I held my tongue, particularly the part about the right arm. I could see that Dean Floyd was not going to relent. Then he dropped another bombshell. "By the way, it doesn't help that you co-author articles. We only count articles and books which are sole-authored."

"But, Dean Floyd, that makes no sense. I can have my co-authors tell you what I contributed. In some cases, it was out of kindness that I named people co-authors because they played some role in the development of the article or contributed to the research. I've always been generous in that regard, and now you are going punish me for it."

"Well, that's the tradition here and I doubt if you can overturn it." So I shook his left hand and told him I would try to do a better job explaining in my next application what I try to do with my publications. I received a formal letter from the dean saying I would be considered again for tenure during the 1975–76 school year, and if I did not attain it, I would be given a "terminal year" for 1976–77.

The former dean invited me to his house when he learned of Floyd's decision. Because he was a famous professor of the history of Irish immigration and a former dean, Bob Cross lived in one of the "pavilions" on the "lawn" at the center of campus. Jefferson had designed a very beautiful little college. Twelve two-story pavilions, six to each side of the quad, were provided for faculty. They were to teach students in the lower-level living room while they lived in the upper level. Faculty could meet with each other and avoid students by traversing a walkway between the pavilions that was built on top of the small student rooms, which in turn were strung along between the first floors of the pavilions. Still in use, the student rooms have fireplaces but no bathrooms; the location of the bathrooms and showers require that students exit their cubbyholes and go outside. This journey could be quite harrowing in the depths of winter. Only honor students are allowed to occupy the cubbyholes, except for the one that had been occupied by Edgar Allen Poe when he was a student.[2] It is preserved as a tiny museum. Each pavilion has a beautiful backyard planted to match the month that corresponds to its number. For example, the garden of Pavilion Twelve is filled with holly bushes and Scotch pines. The gardens were divided from one another by waving S-shaped walls, which Jefferson had built on a bet that he could not build a wall only one brick thick that would remain standing. The clever inventor came up with curving walls and they stand to this day.

The camellia- and azalea-filled garden behind Bob Cross's pavilion was in full bloom as we sat on his back patio late on a spring afternoon and sipped whiskey. He believed, with the change of deans and a new president, Frank Herford out of the sciences, that the university was turning on the liberal arts and looking for a more scientific orientation. "That's where the government grants are," he informed me. Cross told me to put my publications first on my list of priorities. "That's how you will be remembered in the long run, Craig. Not by your service, not by your students, but by what you publish." I didn't agree with that assessment, but I wasn't going to argue with him. He was trying to help me. As I was leaving, Cross said that even good publications might not be enough.

"Why?" I asked.

"Because Dean Floyd may be trying to get rid of your department."

I was surprised. Yes, the department chair did not fit in on the campus and had taken the department in the wrong direction. I could hear Dean

Floyd saying, "Intercultural communications is not what Mr. Jefferson's University is about." However, I believed the situation could be corrected. Change chairs and refocus the department on its strengths: rhetoric and public address. "Craig," Bob Cross intoned, "it may be too late for that. Just publish your pants off and maybe they'll move you to American Studies."

And that I did. I received a highly competitive faculty research grant that resulted in a publication. That was followed by another article on Webster and then an article on the notion of "rhetorical distance" with David Hunsaker. The problem was that two of these were co-authored and Floyd could use that against me. However, I felt responsible for bringing David first to San Diego State and now to Virginia, and he too needed publications for tenure. Since we were both in the same department, at the same university, Floyd would have to credit the articles to at least one of us. Someone had to write the darn things, I would argue.

Trying to ramp things up and "focus" my research, I applied for and received another research grant in 1975, which resulted in another article, followed by two more. Finally, I received a grant that allowed me to travel to London to study the roots of Puritan rhetoric in America. Hopefully, the dean and his committee would see that I was focusing and I was the single author in several publications.

These achievements did not go unnoticed by Professor Gage Chapel, a colleague at Occidental College in Los Angeles. He wrote reminding me that he too was a Republican and wondered if I would ever be interested in writing speeches for a Republican presidential candidate. I told him that I would, but nothing seemed to come of it except that he had piqued my interest in the possibilities of political speechwriting should my academic career derail.

On December 22, 1975, the department sent another letter in support of my being granted tenure. It also summarized a passel of peer reviews of my work that had come in from leading scholars in the field. The department's letter was seven singled-spaced pages long in making the case for my being tenured, carefully explaining that my research was "focused."

At the beginning of the spring semester, in late January, I took my top debate team to a national tournament at Boston College. They were in competition with eighty other teams, and so I was delighted when, after the eight preliminary rounds, they qualified for the quarterfinals of the tournament. I was off judging one quarterfinal while they were winning theirs. They lost in the semifinal round, but it was a terrific showing, our best of the year, and put the team into the top four in the nation.

When I returned home from the tournament, a letter was waiting for me from my department chair. I was crushed to learn that I had been denied tenure again. I requested a meeting with Dean Floyd, where he told me the decision was irreversible. I told him that my faculty believed I was a valuable member of the campus community. "But," he interrupted, "you are not in a valuable department as far as that community is concerned." Ah, I thought, there it is, just what Bob Cross had told me. They want to get rid of the department and I am the first step.

"I might have to consider legal action given that your predecessor promised me tenure if it were recommended by my department," I threatened.

"That would be unwise. The best lawyers in this state have all graduated from our law school. Besides, we have not violated any procedures. Bob Cross had no right to make you such a promise, if, in fact, he did." I started to protest and he raised his left hand to shush me. "I'll tell you what I would be open to doing. I'll give you a new three-year contract, with the clear understanding that you must leave by the end of that time."

So that's the plan, I thought; they'll shut me up and phase the department out over the next three years. "Can I think about that?"

"Sure," he said, waving his hook in the air. "Take all the time you need."

I concluded that for my own mental health and to set an example for my students, I needed to fight the dean. I had lectured the students on what it meant to be an authentic existentialist. You have to commit to your philosophy; you have to practice what you preach. Now was the time to prove that I was committed to what I had been preaching. Maybe I had seen too many movies, but I believed I could pull off a miracle, as I had at San Diego State, and get this decision reversed.

Without any prompting from me, the school paper took up my cause. The graduate students of my department sent a letter to Provost Shannon expressing their "dismay" over the tenure decision, praising my teaching and the "selfless" way I had mentored them through the thesis process. In a stunning, unprecedented act suggested by Bob Parsley, the Honor Committee president, the student government passed a resolution that I be given tenure. Almost every day there were letters in the school's two newspapers critical of the tenure decision. One particularly touching one came from four female students, one of whom was on the staff of *The Declaration*. "His classes are popular and large numbers of non-speech majors are back for second and third times, as well as those who have heard only good things about his entertaining and inspiring teaching. We feel fortunate to be in one of Mr. Smith's courses. Our only regret is that other University students will not be able to take a course from one of the finest University professors that we have known."

While absorbed in the fight to avoid a terminal year, I ran across an advertisement for a position at the University of Alabama in Birmingham. It had just been given equal status with the famous or infamous University of Alabama in Tuscaloosa, the one at which Governor Wallace had stood in the doorway to block the entrance of the first two black students admitted to the university. Birmingham was looking for a "director" of its new "Division of Communications" that would include speech, print, and broadcast journalism, and public relations. I sent in an application.

Then something happened that reasserted my romanticism. It began with an invitation to the University of North Carolina to give a guest lecture in the spring of 1976. That campus, the oldest public university in America, is beautiful in April, replete with dogwoods, and I was delighted to be there to talk about political communication. It turned out that on this particular day, President Gerald Ford was also visiting the campus to give an address to the Future Homemakers of America. After wins in the Iowa caucuses and the New Hampshire primary, he had lost five primaries in a row to Ronald Reagan, who had given a nationally televised speech to revive his candidacy. The fight for the Republican nomination was on.

So after my 10 A.M. lecture, we all strolled over to hear President Ford at noon. His speech was an embarrassment, and I took a lot of flack from my friends on the UNC faculty for being a Republican. When I got back to Charlottesville, I couldn't sleep. So I wrote a five-page, very polite single-spaced critique of the President's speech, and at 3 A.M. I passed out. The next morning I mailed my screed to "President Gerald Ford, 1600 Pennsylvania Avenue, Washington, D.C. 20501."

Little did I know that a few days before my letter arrived, a White House speechwriter had been fired, the twentieth to leave that embattled writing staff. Since the White House mailroom is a small community full of gossips and people wanting to advance their careers, a mail boy fished my letter out of a stack and sent up to Doug Smith, an assistant to Robert Hartmann, the counselor to the president for speechwriting. Smith showed my letter to Bob Orben, the editor and manager of the speechwriting den. Orben called his friend Gage Chapel at Occidental College and asked Chapel if he had ever heard of me. Luckily, Chapel remembered our exchange from November and recommended me for the job.

When I got the call from Bob Orben, I believed that one of my debaters was playing a practical joke on me. So Orben told me to call the White House switchboard and ask for him. Reluctantly, I did just that and was put through. He asked some questions and then invited me up to the Old Executive Office Building (OEOB) for an interview. I arrived on the 18th of May. I passed through security in awe of the surroundings. The OEOB looked like a giant gray Victorian wedding cake. It had been the State Department for a time and then housed the Department of War before it became the Defense Department. Now it housed various staff, including the Vice President and the speechwriters for the President.

First, I sat down with Doug Smith and handed him a file he had asked me to prepare. I found him to be quite affable. He put me at ease and I was able to talk about what I might do for Ford. Smith was very interested in the fact that I had written my master's thesis on Ronald Reagan, their nemesis at the time. He also liked some of my scholarly work on political rhetoric. "It's the only academic stuff I've ever read that makes any sense," he claimed.

Doug Smith passed me and my file along to Orben, who had been a comedy writer for Red Skelton and Dick Gregory, among others. He was a delightful man, and I would learn he had an eye for perfection. He explained how the writing process worked, and that writers had direct access to the President. I was surprised and delighted. His questioning was much tougher than Doug Smith's. He wanted to know if there was anything in my background that might embarrass the President. "No, I don't believe so," I lied. Orben also wanted to know how I would go about writing a speech. I explained my Aristotelian technique and he seemed impressed. But my heart sank a little when he told me the job came with a 30-day trial period, chiefly because former writers who had been academics had all been abject failures on the job, and I would have to undergo an FBI investigation to get security clearance. Thank God I had been celibate.

As Orben walked me over to the West Wing to see Robert Hartmann, I realized that if I failed any of these interviews, I would be shuffled right out the front door. I also figured that Hartmann would make the call. I was nervous and thrilled at the same time.

Orben introduced me to Hartmann, a fireplug of a man, quite gruff and ruddy of face. Some claimed that was because he started drinking over lunch and rarely stopped until he hit the hay.[3] Leafing through my file, Hartmann suddenly stopped when he got to the material on how Reagan put his speeches together. He began to quote it to Orben and then he said, "This is incredible stuff. Maybe we ought to do something like this here."

Orben agreed and then said, "I'm going to leave the two of you to talk. I have a speech to edit." It was clear to Orben that I had impressed Hartmann. Had I not done so, I'm sure he would have pulled me out of the interview.

Now Hartmann began his questioning. He flicked a page of data at me. "Look at these results from the Texas primary. How do you account for that?" The sheet summarized Ford's bad loss to Reagan.

I wasn't quite sure what Hartmann was getting at. I told him Texas was a very conservative state and very open to Reagan's kind of rhetoric. Hartmann's reply revealed a White House in denial. He said, "I don't agree. It's just magic."

Stunned for a moment, I replied, "Look at the results. Over 400,000 for Reagan; only 136,000 for President Ford. It's not magic; it's enthusiasm."

"What would you do in California? If we could embarrass Reagan there, we could end this fight."

"You can't beat Reagan in California, but if Ford were to make a Trumanesque whistle-stop tour of the Central Valley, he might get enough votes to score a moral victory."

I could tell he didn't like my beard, and he flat out told me that "Every professor we have hired has failed. They try to make the President too eloquent. He's uncomfortable with airy fairy stuff. Worse yet, it takes professors forever to compose a speech. Sometimes a speech has to be written overnight and none of them could ever do that."

"I understand. My training has prepared me to work quickly. I also believe the President should speak the language of the common man."

"Exactly," Hartmann confirmed. "Yes, that's what the President wants. You can dress it up a bit, add a punch line, but keep it simple."

"Like FDR," I conjectured.

"How's that?"

"If you look at FDR's speeches, you'll see that he uses very simple words but uses rhetorical tactics like rhythm and repetition to hold attention. Look at his First Inaugural, 'The only thing we have to fear is fear itself.' Mostly one syllable words and a nice easy rhythm and repetition."

"I never thought about his speeches that way."

"Look at the 'Four Freedoms' address where he ends his appeals four times with the phrase 'everywhere in the world.' Nice alliteration and repetition to drive the point home."

Suddenly, Hartmann stood up. "Can you excuse me for just a minute?"

"Yes, sure."

Hartmann left the room. I sat back and looked at his photos with the President and foreign dignitaries. I thought, this is where I belong. I could do this.

Hartmann returned and asked me to follow him. We joined Doug Smith in the West Wing mess and we continued the conversation. They ate up my theories. When I walked out the front gate of the White House, I was dizzy with enthusiasm. I drove through rain to Pittsburgh, where I was staying with one of my debaters and his family for a few days. That night Ford won his make-or-break primary in Michigan and I waited for a call from the White House. Each time the phone rang, I stood up and listened eagerly for my hosts to summon me. But the call did not come that night, or the next day. But it did come on the third day; Doug Smith called to confirm my appointment and asked me to start the job as soon as possible.

A JOB AT THE WHITE HOUSE

On May 24, 1976, I began as one of President Ford's full-time speechwriters. Hartmann introduced me to the President in the Oval Office and I was overwhelmed by the gravity of the place. There he was: Gerald Ford, thin-haired and puffing on a pipe. I heard Hartmann say, "Pending security clearance, Mr. President, this is Professor Smith. He'll be your newest speechwriter."

The President rose, shook my hand, and then stared at my beard. "Professor Smith, the other professors we've hired work too slowly and try to put big words in my mouth. I want to speak plainly and clearly. Can you do that for me?"

"Why, yes, Mr. President, I believe I can."

"Good. We've got a hell of a climb in front of us. Five primaries tomorrow, then I've got to secure the nomination and overcome a 33 percent gap in the polls to beat a peanut farmer from Georgia."

"I'm up for the fight, sir."

"How old are you? I can't tell with that beard covering your face."

"I'm thirty-one."

"That's a good age. My chief of staff is thirty-four."

"Yes, I know. Mr. Cheney was the youngest presidential chief of staff ever appointed."[4]

"Sounds like you've done your homework. Now let me get back to work. I'll see you when you're assigned your first speech."

I shook his hand. "Thank you, Mr. President." He had a dry, warm hand and a firm grip. I turned to leave him with Hartmann and suddenly realized that I could not see a way out. In my nervousness, I had forgotten how we came into the office, and given its oval shape and that the doors were curved to match the wall, I could not find the exit.

I heard Hartmann over my shoulder as I wandered around the room. "Craig, the door is over there." He pointed and I finally figured out where it was.

"Thank you," and out I went—but imagined the President saying, "Damn professors, can't find their way out of a room with two doors."

A few days later, Hartmann notified me that he was extending my probationary period to 60 days, but he said, "Consider yourself a regular with us." I had to keep convincing myself that I was not dreaming.

The night of May 25th was a nail biter. In the end, Ford won three of the five primaries—Kentucky, Tennessee, and Oregon—all in what the press dubbed "Reagan territory." The next day, after reading all of Ford's testimony from when he was nominated for vice president and reading his most important speeches, I was given a 90-minute briefing late in the afternoon by Doug Smith on the President's preferences. "His range of adaptability is small. We've learned what he likes. You'll want to provide language that makes the President feel comfortable. That will improve his delivery, which, as you may have noticed, needs work." This briefing included a list of words that were never to appear in a Ford speech, since he had learned to pronounce these words incorrectly at a young age. Judgment became "judgahment"; guarantee became "garntee." Jules Witcover later reported:

> Ford's inability to pronounce difficult words, and some not so difficult was immediately seized upon as a measure of his brainpower. . . . In early February [1974], he stumbled an inordinate number of times in a speech on his energy proposals before getting out the word 'geothermal' correctly. A tape of the speech became an overnight box-office hit in the White House press room.[5]

By this time, I could see that too many people wanted to please Ford rather than improve him. Worse, in the competition for the President's ear, there was a good deal of backstabbing going on. And there were relationships to watch for. Cheney was pawn to Rumsfeld's bishop; the same arrangement existed between Brent Scowcroft and Henry Kissinger. William Simon, treasury secretary, and Alan Greenspan, economic advisor, had major domestic-policy influence.

The other members of the writing team included George Denison, a shy man who had come over from *Readers' Digest*; Patrick Butler, a twenty-six-year-old reporter from Tennessee who had become a House staffer; Milt Friedman (not the economist), an aging owl full of wisdom but in no hurry to finish a speech; and David Boorstin, a young liberal who specialized in defense issues, and the son of the famous historian and head of the Library of Congress Daniel Boorstin. David Boorstin and Pat Butler were in league and often ridiculed Hartmann over lunch with me, whom they sought as a new ally. I later learned that before I arrived, Hartmann had once fired

Butler for going over Hartmann's head to the President, but the firing was rescinded by Dick Cheney, who was not a fan of Hartmann's.[6] I observed the interplay from my windowless broom closet of an office.[7]

Gerald Ford's education did not include any extensive training for speaking other than law school. In fact, he lost his campaign for class president in high school, running as a "progressive." At the University of Michigan, he was a football star, not a star orator. At Yale, he learned legal argument and developed a healthy respect for evidence, but did not distinguish himself as a speaker. Nonetheless, his achievement at Yale is impressive when you realize that he coached their football team at the same time he was finishing his law degree in the top third of a very impressive group of students.

Ford served in the U.S. House of Representatives for a quarter of a century and as its minority leader from 1965 to 1974, during which time he gave 530 speeches at Republican fundraisers alone. At such events, speakers often are told their speeches were wonderful, even when they were not. Succumbing to the flattery, Ford was under the impression that he was a good public speaker, when in fact, he was not.

Ironically, in the pre-Reagan era, Ford was probably the most conservative president since Calvin Coolidge, but Reagan's attacks on Ford's moderation, particularly his policy of détente with the Soviets, made him seem more moderate than he was. At heart he was a congressional compromiser, a fiscal conservative with libertarian tendencies who hated government overregulation and believed in a hawkish foreign policy. Like Harry Truman, whom Ford admired, he ascended to the presidency with less preparation for national speechmaking than his predecessor. And like Truman, his speaking style would evolve dramatically while he was president. By the summer of 1976, Ford wanted to pull off the same kind of upset Truman had pulled off over Thomas E. Dewey in 1948.

The UVA student newspapers ran the story of my appointment on the front pages of the papers. When I drove down for the commencement ceremony on the "lawn" a few days later, I sat with my faculty and they congratulated me on my new assignment. When "Pomp and Circumstance" was struck up, the graduates marched through the columns along the lawn. I was shocked and a little embarrassed when I saw that some held signs that read, "Give Smith Tenure."

CHAPTER SIX

Writing for President Ford

Back in d.c., I took a studio apartment on Virginia Avenue in Foggy Bottom, the home of the State Department.[1] I could walk to work, not worry about parking, and sleep a little later in the morning. (I learned that one measure of your clout in the White House was how close to your office you got to park, and how close your office was to the Oval Office of the president.) Our speeches were "staffed" to relevant departments, bureaucrats, and Cabinet secretaries who often went beyond their job of reviewing policy to suggest language that should be inserted.[2] Butler and Boorstin instructed me to ignore these attempts to hijack a speech unless the comments came from someone who had the clout of a Henry Kissinger.

Few people were more influential with President Ford than Hartmann, who traced their friendship back to Michigan in 1966, after Hartmann had served as a reporter for the *Los Angeles Times* for a quarter of a century. Upon the news of Nixon's resignation, Hartmann's first chore was to craft a speech that Ford could deliver after taking the oath of office. Ford told the waiting nation that its "long national nightmare [was] over"; it was time for "a little straight talk among friends."[3] The nation sympathized with Ford's desire to be forthright and forgave his sometimes inarticulate speech. It made him seem more sincere. In the meantime, Hartmann moved into the office next to Ford's that had been used by Nixon's secretary Rosemary Woods, and it gave Hartmann the most immediate access to Ford.

Only a month into Ford's term, Hartmann faced the daunting task of writing the speech that would pardon Nixon. On a Sunday morning after Ford returned from mass at St. John's Episcopal Church, he delivered a national speech in which he granted a pardon to Nixon, who was hospitalized with phlebitis. The situation was highly constrained, most significantly by the fact that Ford's pardon would lead to speculation that a deal had been cut between them before Nixon had stepped aside. Ford overrode the objections of his loyalists, particularly Press Secretary Gerald Terhorst, because the President believed that pardoning Nixon would end the Watergate crisis and Nixon's suffering, would constitute an admission of guilt on Nixon's part, and would clear the way for Nixon to testify against others involved in the Watergate cover-up.

However, the speech Hartmann wrote, as well as its timing, undercut the President's objectives. By delivering it on Sunday morning, Ford opened himself up to charges of trying to slip the pardon under the rug, since the public paid little attention to the news on the Sabbath, September 8, 1974. By failing to delineate the legal thinking behind the speech, Ford missed a major opportunity to justify his action beyond claiming that it was a fair and moral act. It didn't help that his press secretary resigned in protest. Some in the news media claimed that Ford needed the loyalty of Nixon's former employees to help with the governing coalition, and that motivated the pardon. Worse yet, Nixon would not admit guilt until his interviews with David Frost many years later, nor would he testify against his former staff members. For all these reasons, Ford's approval ratings collapsed.

Some changes would be required. Ford replaced CIA director Bill Colby with China ambassador and former congressman George H. W. Bush. Fatefully, during his hearings for the job, Bush was forced to pledge that he would not be a candidate for vice president, a position Ford needed to fill immediately. The CIA director's job was supposed to be nonpartisan. Ford selected former New York Governor Nelson Rockefeller to be his vice president in an effort to unite the Republican Party. Conservatives were not pleased; they still harbored animus for Rockefeller for his attack on them at the 1964 GOP convention. By Halloween of 1975, Ford's administration had a hit low point. More changes needed to be made. Rockefeller led the way, announcing he would not be a candidate for vice president in 1976; Rumsfeld was moved to secretary of defense; Kissinger moved from national security advisor to secretary of state. Cheney became chief of staff and then swept out many of the Nixon loyalists and replaced them with people loyal to Ford. One of the first things Cheney did was move Hartmann out of the office next to Ford's and into the West Wing. Hartmann would never forgive him, and Cheney would always be a bit suspicious of the speechwriting operation.

I stayed out of the fray by reading through Ford's speeches to try to get a sense of his style. I noticed that Ford was giving too many speeches, and that their style was uneven or vastly different depending on who wrote the speech. Despite these observations, I believed that I was precluded from making recommendations until I wrote a successful speech of my own.

Ford inherited and admired the structure of the Nixon speechwriting staff. There was a head speechwriter—in our case Hartmann—who was also a counselor to the President, which gave him direct access to the Oval Office. Then came the five of us who were full-time speechwriters, who reported to Orben as our editor and then to Hartmann. Then came a layer of researchers to check our facts and provide information. These researchers had access to remarkable resources, including the Library of Congress, various executive agencies, and a library in the Old Executive Office Building. In addition, researchers were motivated by the fact that they might, with some luck, be promoted to writers; that's how Pat Buchanan had done it. Researchers were kept abreast of current affairs because they were responsible for compiling the daily summary of news items about the President and relevant to his presidency. And if you were a speechwriter, you counted on these researchers to make you look good.

As I mentioned, Cabinet members or their assistants and undersecretaries would sometimes severely edit or submit entire speeches. Political consultants felt free to alter drafts of speeches once they were on the road with the President and he was out of Hartmann's reach. But by the time I arrived on staff, speechwriters, using their researchers as loyal servants, had gained the upper hand. Hartmann provided dogged protection of the speechwriting operation and guaranteed his writers direct access to the President when they were writing a major speech for him.

However, Hartmann had to deal with a cynical press corps. For example, before my arrival, Ford gave a speech in Kansas making reference to *The Wizard of Oz*. Reporters composed the following ditty based on the song of the Scarecrow from the famous 1939 film:

> I could while away the hours
> Reflecting on my powers,
> As we go down the drain.
> I could spend like Rockefeller,
> I could talk like Walter Heller,
> If I only had a brain.[4]

Up to that point, no one had hit on the strategies that would salvage Ford's rhetorical record: the first was rehearsing speeches; the second was creating a sense of style; the third was overcoming camera fright; the fourth was putting two writers on each speech; and the fifth was giving fewer speeches so each would have more impact. I intended to insist on these strategies once I got some clout.

How speechwriters gain credibility and influence with the president is a matter of luck, timing, effectiveness, and infighting. What makes a writer valuable to a president varies. Some chief executives like applause-getting lines; some like quotations that prove memorable; some want an original approach to issues; others simply like the writer personally. At first, Ford took advice from his speechwriters because of their expertise in writing. If certain strategies proved effective—that is, impressed an audience, the President, or the press—the writer was able to suggest more alterations in argumentation, credibility building, emotional appeals, delivery, style, and arrangement.

THE FIRST SPEECH

My first shot came with the request from the President for an outline of six speeches that he intended to give during the celebration of the bicentennial of the Declaration of Independence. Hartmann recommended putting the speeches together into a booklet with a coherent theme, "The American Adventure." "All drafts should be short, taut, and straightforward. . . . There should be no campaign code words or partisan insinuations whatsoever. . . . Noble and profound thoughts can be expressed in direct and simple words, as Jefferson and Lincoln did." When the speechwriters' outlines were submitted, Hartmann folded in outlines submitted from outsiders and former friends of the President, such as Bryce Harlow and Phil Buchen. Hartmann presented the stack of six-page outlines without the authors' names on them to the President and asked him to choose the one he liked most. My outline began by stating that the purpose the speeches should include lifting the dark cloud of cynicism that had covered the nation because of Vietnam and Watergate. The President picked two of the outlines, one jointly written by Boorstin and Butler, and mine. My influence thereby increased as the three of us coordinated the Bicentennial project. I suggested that two writers be assigned to each major speech and that they write independently of one another during the construction of the first draft. With the President, Hartmann would then decide which was the superior draft. The writer of that draft would then become the primary writer of that speech and incorporate what was valuable from the other writer's work. This process had at least two advantages: it produced a competitive environment that led to better speeches, and it assured better continuity in Ford's style.

However, before I could get to work on the Bicentennial speeches, I was commissioned to write Ford's address to the Southern Baptist Convention meeting in Norfolk, Virginia, on June 15, 1976. No sitting president had ever addressed the convention. I got the assignment because some lines I provided for the President at Arlington National Cemetery for Memorial Day got press; then my talking points for his appearance at an event at Wolf Trap, a concert venue outside the D.C. beltway, impressed Bob Orben.

However, the speech to the Southern Baptist Convention was to be my baptism as a sole writer of a major speech. I was a (gay) Catholic composing a speech for an Episcopalian that would be delivered to Southern Baptists. I consulted with Baptist ministers, revised after the President told me he did not want to say the name Jesus Christ, and produced a speech he accepted.

So this might be a good place to talk about the craft of speechwriting in more detailed ways than I have previously in this book. My training was obvious: high school and college debate and individual events speaking; studying the English language; becoming absorbed in characters and plots in films; studying rhetorical theory and American public address through a PhD program; doing research at CBS and writing it up for reporters; teaching courses in this subject area; and finally publishing scholarly articles on the subject of public persuasion. However, all this theory and practice could become unwieldy if I did not organize it into some coherent set of guidelines for my White House endeavors.

I began by using Aristotle's *Rhetoric* for a foundation and then extended his theories for persuasion with theorists who have provided additional insights.[5] Like his mentor Plato, Aristotle advises that speakers have a thorough knowledge of their subject matter and their audiences because a large part of the art of persuasion is at least appearing knowledgeable and adapting to a specific audience. For President Ford's speech in Norfolk, the audience was a fairly homogeneous, conservative, Southern religious group, making my job easier. I also received reports from White House advance people about what these people wanted to hear. But the whole issue of venue is even more important than that. You should not let your clients be put into a venue in which they perform badly or are uncomfortable.

Let me give you some examples. Ronald Reagan would become the master of the State of the Union Address. He seemed to come alive before the Senate and the House, his Cabinet, the Supreme Court members, and the gallery listening to him in the House Chamber in the Capitol. He was also the first president to single out a hero in the gallery when he asked Lenny Skutnik to stand up; he was the man who jumped into the icy Potomac River to save the lives of people who survived the crash of an airplane into the Fourteenth Street Bridge in Washington, D.C. Bill Clinton also seemed to gain energy from an audience—the larger the better. His worst speech was delivered from the Map Room of the White House, with no audience, when he defended himself to the nation during the Monica Lewinsky affair.

Richard Nixon was terrific at press conferences. Even during the Watergate crisis, his poll numbers went up after each press conference. His weakest venue was speaking from the Oval Office behind his desk into a camera. Contrariwise, Ronald Reagan's worst venue was a press conference; often, he or his press secretary later had to claim he "misspoke" when answering a question. For Ford, we finally got to the point where he was very good with a script if he rehearsed.

President Ford would need to be introduced in Norfolk, and I would write that little speech to enhance the prior reputation of the President and to allay any hostility toward him that might exist. Think of this introduction as an audience warm-up.

Theorists after Aristotle expanded on what speakers should accomplish in the introduction of a speech. The speaker needs to gain the attention of the audience at the outset, perhaps with a quotation, a story, a topical joke, or a local reference. The speaker needs to acknowledge those of importance on the dais and in the audience, and then set out a theme for the speech, which frames the persuasion that is to follow. Speakers should tell the specific audience why it is important that they understand what the speaker is talking about, and then provide a preview of how the speech will proceed. This organizational step is crucial because speeches are basically invisible—they are vibrations in the air—and audiences need guidance through them. Furthermore, the more the audience witnesses that the speaker is in control of the speaking situation, the more they trust the speaker. Think of your favorite waiters: they know what they are talking about, they don't need notes to remember your order, they are sure of what they are doing. A speaker's use of organizational language—transitions, for example—helps him or her assert control over the situation, enhancing his or her credibility.

The body of speech can be organized in myriad ways: advantages of a proposal versus disadvantages; causes for a problem versus its effects; past, present, future; local, state, national, international. It is important to select the organizational format that suits the topic and the audience. Each division of the speech should be marked by an internal summary and transition to the next point, again providing guidance for the audience, which needs to feel secure in the speaker's hands. The arguments of the speech (see below) need to have evidence that will impress the audience and be drawn from sources the specific audience respects.

The conclusion of the speech should briefly summarize what has been covered in terms of the main points the speaker wants the audience to take home. The speaker should then draw out a major conclusion and reinforce it with an emotional tone that moves the audience into the proper state of mind for the action the speaker seeks. An exit line should be provided that either ties back to the opening of the speech or provides a new quotation, a historic example, or the like that matches the mood sought and the conclusion endorsed. The properly crafted exit line signals the audience that it is time for applause.

That's the basic outline, but Aristotle provides further guidelines for the form of a speech when he argues that public speeches fall into three categories depending on their intent. Deliberative addresses endorse legislative proposals for the future and seek to show that these proposals will result in an expedient end, or provide more contentment for the public. The audience for such speeches functions as a legislative body. The State of the Union Address is a good example of a deliberative speech. The ceremonial speech seeks to reinforce certain values while praising or blaming various figures or events that illustrate such values. Its aim is honor or dishonor, and it can be a speech of display in terms of the speaker's talents and virtues, and/or it can endorse and exemplify virtues the speaker wants the audience to embrace. The audience sits as observers for such speeches. The Inaugural Address is a good example of a ceremonial speech. The forensic speech concerns a past act and is directed at an audience that acts as a judge or jury, listens to a prosecution or defense, and seeks justice or injustice. Nixon's press conferences on Watergate, or Clinton's self-defense during his impeachment serve as examples of this genre. Cleverly, Aristotle recognized that these overarching forms might not be discrete. A ceremonial speech might hide forensic judgments inside. A deliberative speech might use an endorsement of certain values to advance its cause. So a campaign speech is usually a mix of a deliberative agenda, a forensic condemnation of the sins of the opposition, and a ceremonial celebration of certain American values—usually freedom, individualism, competition, order, and patriotism for Republican audiences.

The general form of the speech can then be filled in with arguments and evidence that make a case. Several principles guided me through this phase of the writing process. First, should the arguments be inductive, that is, moving from specific examples and/or statistics to a general conclusion? Or should the arguments be deductive, that is, applying a generally accepted rule to a specific case? Inductive arguments are more suited to hostile or divided audiences because if you start with your conclusion, they will be turned off. You need to guide them inductively to the conclusion, keeping them open to your ideas. Deductive arguments are more suited to friendly audiences where you are trying to reinforce values, attitudes, and opinions that are already in place. Second, what is the quality of the evidence? Is there enough of it to make the point with *this particular audience*? Third, what is the quality of the sources for the evidence and are they compatible with *this particular audience*? Fourth, are the arguments clear and understandable? Have they been adjusted to the level of understanding of the audience? How much background must the speaker supply to ensure that the audience understands the point being made? Fifth, can any of the arguments be summarized with a telling example that will bring the argument home to *this particular audience*? Ronald Reagan was exceptional at this tactic and used it well in 1976 when running against Ford. In one of his popular speeches, Reagan ran through a list of welfare abuses and then summed it up with the telling example of the "welfare queen," a woman indicted in Chicago for drawing many welfare checks using various aliases and driving a Cadillac.[6]

The telling example can also be expanded into a narrative that is compelling. There is nothing like a good story that is coherent to get your point across. More sophisticated still is the use of a historical story to make a point about the present or the future. I used this tactic in the Bicentennial speeches because we were under instructions to keep the speeches looking into America's third century as a nation while still celebrating the past. Whether it is Pericles's funeral oration or Lincoln at Gettysburg, speakers celebrate the sacrifice of those who went before us to rededicate ourselves to preserving our values into the future.

Once I had composed what I believed to be the necessary arguments, whether based on statistics, testimony, examples, or narratives, I sought to determine how to enliven them by bringing them close to the audience in terms of emotions. While sound argumentation results in long-lasting persuasion, emotional appeals can open the audience to this argumentation immediately. As Aristotle makes clear, speakers need to determine to what state of mind they want to move the audience, and then determine what causes that state of mind in this particular audience.[7] Those causes then need to be brought close to the audience in terms of time and space, using picture language that makes the causes tangible. For example, if I want to move an audience into a state of fear so that they will support my defense budget, I might call the Soviet Union an "evil empire" and then show that their missiles can reach the United States in only fifteen minutes. Thus, what was once remote becomes something near and fearful. Once an emotional state is accomplished—and this is crucial—it needs to be directed toward some goal. When Reagan created his "evil empire," he manifested fear of the Soviet Union in the audience, which he then directed toward support of his massive increase in defense spending.

Aristotle argues that the most potent weapon in a speaker's arsenal is credibility. If speakers are believable, it is easier for them to get their arguments accepted; for example, they can get by with less evidence. However, if a speaker is not credible, he or she has no chance of persuading an audience. There are many ways for a speaker to achieve credibility. First, there is the prior reputation of the speaker. Past deeds can work to the advantage of a popular president who has made good decisions. The prior reputation, as we have seen, can be enhanced with a good introduction from a master of ceremonies. Second, credibility flows from the fact that speakers demonstrate that they know what they are talking about. The arguments and evidence used to make the case play a large part in this strategy. But so does the proper pronunciation of words and the ease with which difficult policy matters are discussed. President Clinton was a genius at this strategy. Third, speakers should show that they have the best interests of the audience at heart. Aristotle called this goodwill; Freud called it taking care of others. The trick is to find out what those audience interests are. A group of educators has different interests than a group of engineers, though both groups may have overarching interests in terms of income, survival, and justice. Fourth, speakers need to align themselves with the values of the audience by showing that they are virtuous in ways *this particular audience* admires. What has the speaker done that displays the virtues this audience embraces? Courage is defined differently by the Veterans of Foreign Wars and the American Pacifist Society. Finally, what are the ways in which the speaker can identify with the individual audience members? And I mean "identify" in the Freudian sense in terms of becoming one with the audience. This important step can be achieved by talking about shared goals, shared experiences, shared values, and shared material desires. More than that, identification is often achieved by projecting a persona with which audience members can identify. However, since audience members have different identificational needs, speakers often seek to project different personas at different moments in the speech to sweep as many audience members as possible into their persuasive net. Some of us identify with leaders; some identify with caregivers.

Freud tells us we all have a narcissistic side; that is, we identify with a perfect past, perfect present, or perfect future vision of ourselves. If a speaker can become that vision, he or she is more likely to bond with us. Some speakers use nostalgia to conjure up a perfect past with which an audience identifies and bond with them that way, taking them back to a simpler, more uncomplicated America. Some speakers appeal to hope and change to identify with a perfect future and bond with audience members who identify with those utopian visions. To achieve identification, speechwriters need to tap into images that are part of the collective unconscious as outlined as far back as Giambatista Vico and as refined by Carl Jung. Some phrases have become what Michael McGee called "ideographs," links to ideology that bring an audience together.[8] Through ideographs one can invoke the civil religion of America as a chosen land—Puritan leader John Winthrop's and much later President Ronald Reagan's "shining city set on a hill"—populated with a "chosen people," who are on a mission to be an example for the rest of the world. Politicians often claim that America is a chosen place born of an "errand into the wilderness," whether that errand be to settle the West and bring culture to the indigenous population, or to fulfill America's "manifest destiny"[9] or its "rendezvous with destiny."[10] Americans like to hear that they are exceptional, even though objective history might portray them otherwise.

One of the more difficult things to achieve, and one that is vastly underrated as a persuasive tool, is stylistic tone. There are times when a simple, undecorated style is appropriate. Let the statistics speak for themselves. However, as I explained with regard to appeals to emotion, there are times when speakers need to paint pictures with words to achieve their ends. Introductions and conclusions, because they tend to be less substantive, need more eloquence to hold attention. Striking metaphors can convey meaning more efficiently and effectively than drawing on literal comparisons. Style was always the last thing I checked for when writing a speech because it had to be adjusted to the content that was in place, and it can provide much-needed moments of beauty that break up the traditional rhetoric of political speaking. And sometimes when you hit on a solid metaphor, you go back through the speech and make sure the other metaphors, similes, and other tropes and figures are compatible with it.[11] Furthermore, word choice and phrasing create a rhythm in the speech. It can be periodic, "of the people, by the people, for the people," a style preferred by President Obama; or it can be loose and running, a conversational style preferred by President Clinton. Or you can mix these styles to achieve variety and hold attention, as did President Reagan.

The style then leads to the question of delivery. What style best suits the president in terms of his comfort level with delivery? If the speaker is dull, or even monotonous, a well-turned phrase can overcome the problem, as Vice President Spiro Agnew demonstrated time and again. What's not to like about dubbing the press "nattering nabobs of negativism"? However, good speakers know that they can control, and therefore vary, the rate at which words come out of their mouth; that is, they can speak rapidly to get through statistics and slowly for emphasis on a conclusion of an argument. They can control pitch, the highs and lows of the voice, for dramatic effect. And they can control volume, making something loud for emphasis or softer to draw attention. In this way, a talented speaker achieves vocal variety that holds the audience's attention.

It is important that writers determine the best type of delivery for their clients. Barack Obama likes a cadenced or periodic delivery, as we have seen. He needs a teleprompter to keep the rhythm right. Bill Clinton likes a conversational delivery; he often wanders off his scripts, does riffs on a theme, and instructs the audience with such phrases as "Now listen to this," or "This is important."

Finally, I want to make it very clear that *the art of speechwriting is rewriting.* The speech needs to sit overnight and then be edited carefully again and again. Once big problems are solved, such as the order of the arguments, then little ones emerge that also have to be corrected. Franklin Roosevelt's major speeches went through at least ten drafts; in the Ford administration in more modern times, we were lucky if we had time for six. However, the "tinkering" is important and can provide a consistency of style that carries the speech.

Once the speech is done, it must be rehearsed and mastered. That is the hardest thing to get a president to do because of his busy schedule. But a good speechwriter knows, and this was particularly true with Ford, that a great speech can be ruined by poor delivery.

In Norfolk, at the Southern Baptist Convention, it all came together for Ford and me. Early in the speech to the assembled ministers, the President was interrupted by applause. He was taken aback and lost his place. When he recovered, he got used to the fact that a line could draw applause from an audience if he delivered it properly. He was interrupted 15 more times in the twenty-minute speech. My credibility with him was further strengthened when the speech received a strong review in the *Washington Star*, a rare event in Ford's prior rhetorical history. The headline read "Ford . . . Wows Baptists."[12] I was promptly moved out of the broom closet and into a huge office with 20-foot-high ceilings, a classic federalist desk, and three television sets so I could watch each network at once.[13] Three tall windows, arched roundly at the top, provided a view down G Street through the drawn-back royal-blue velvet curtains. I could order anything on the menu of the White House Mess and have it delivered, or I could walk over to the West Wing and eat in "the mess" watching the likes of David Gergen, director of communications, and Ron Nessen, press secretary, sitting a few tables away. These two were of particular interest to me because they attempted to place the speechwriters under Gergen's control just after I arrived at the White House. Hartmann forced Nessen not only to retract the proposal, but to apologize personally to the speechwriters. I suspected Cheney was behind the attempted power grab.

To celebrate my success, I took off for Nag's Head with a friend and spent a wonderful 48 hours swimming, drinking, laughing, eating, and sleeping soundly. But our trip was cut short when my pager went off and I was recalled to Washington, D.C., because of a crisis in Lebanon. All non-military American personnel would be withdrawn. The Lebanese civil war had flared up and the Marionite Christian forces were in a state of near collapse. Syria, which had for most of history run the place, moved in and stabilized the coalition government.

Despite becoming more influential as a presidential writer, I was dogged by two conflicting conditions at the White House: boredom and paranoia. The boredom arose from the fact that I had rarely in my life been in a 9-to-5 job, though this one was often 7 A.M. to 10 P.M. when we had to be on call. Because of the long hours and my ability to write speeches quickly,[14] I was often sitting in my office with nothing to do.

The paranoia arose from my fear that the FBI would discover that I was a homosexual, celibate though I was, or had smoked pot once with students at San Diego State or written nasty editorials about Vietnam policy in the student newspapers at UVA. What's more, I could be out of a job in November through no fault of my own. Ford was well behind Carter in the polls; Reagan had not gone away. In fact, the race for the Republican nomination continued to seesaw. Even if Ford won the nomination, he would be wounded for the general election.

The incessant gossiping also got to me. In the speechwriting shop, people were putting one another down behind their backs, attributing horrible motives to one another, and generally acting in uncivil ways. I tried as best I could to avoid it. But, as one might expect, the further down the totem pole you are, the worse the gossip is to which you are subjected. During this time, I talked to Ken Khachigian a few times while he worked in the Department of Agriculture, where he had been exiled after Watergate. He told me that in the Nixon White House, Erlichman and Haldeman ruled with such iron fists that no one dared go around them. In reaction, Ford was so open and accessible, very often the last person to get to him was the one that carried the day with an idea. So competition was fierce to get in to see Ford, and a sense of disorganization had pervaded the White House until Dick Cheney took over as chief of staff.

So I made an appointment to see Cheney and discussed some of my concerns. He was very accommodating, particularly about laying down the law regarding access to the President—"You come through your counselor and your counselor comes through me." To his credit, he also tried to put a damper on the gossiping, but that was a more difficult nut to crack. So here I was writing speeches for the most powerful man in the world, and I was plagued with misgivings.

In the midst of all this angst, I received a call from Alan Perlis, the chair of the English Department at the University of Alabama in Birmingham. He was the head of the search committee for the director of the new Division of Communications; he invited me down to Birmingham for an interview. Figuring I had nothing lose, I took him up on the offer. When the plane landed in late June amidst deep green tree-covered ridges, I turned to a woman sitting next to me and said, "I didn't know this plane stopped before going on to Birmingham. Are we in North Carolina?"

She laughed, "No, young man, this is Bu-min-ham. Isn't it beautiful? It was founded in 1872, *after* the Civil War, by steel barons from Pittsburgh."

"Wow. I thought it would be flat and surrounded by rice paddies."

"That's Montgomery. Dreadful place. Never go there."

Alan Perlis met the plane and drove me to campus. My first stop was to meet the dean, Tom Hearn. We instantly hit it off. He liked my ideas for creating a new communication division. He loved tennis and so did I. Then it was on to the student committee. Not one of them had ever met anyone who worked in the White House. The faculty committee was tougher; they were, in fact, suspicious of people who worked in the White House. Furthermore, faculty in the liberal arts tend to be very liberal, so my Republicanism was not pleasing to them. However, I presented a clear plan about how to build a program and what role new faculty would play in the project. "I am not a one man band," I assured them.

Alan and his wife Paula insisted that I stay with them instead of a hotel, which was fine with me. They lived on the second ridge behind the city. We watched the sun go down on their back patio, sipping wine and chatting. The orange sunset was framed by pink-purple thunderclouds that had moved through in the late summer afternoon. Now the air was fresh and clean, and you could see ridge after ridge on the northwestern horizon. After dinner, a lime-green luna moth landed on the outdoor lantern. Then the night lit up with a thousand fireflies; everything twinkled.

The next day, after a few more meetings with administrators, I flew back to Washington, D.C. The day after that, one of the White House operators put through a call from Tom Hearn, the dean in Birmingham. He offered me the job and we settled on generous terms. The only holdup was my request that I come in with tenure. He said that would be appropriate given that I was to direct a whole division, a rank above department chair; but tenure would have to be approved by the faculty of the English Department. I told him that was fair, half-hoping they'd vote me down so I wouldn't have to make the hard decision about leaving the White House before the election.

One thing I did know. I was not going back to UVA. I wrote my letter of resignation on White House stationery and addressed it to my colleagues in the department, Dean Floyd, Provost Shannon, and President Herford, with a copy to Bob Cross.

Back at the White House, I attended the President's reception for the Republican National Committee where Senator Barry Goldwater, "Mr. Conservative," endorsed Ford for president. This was a blow to the Reagan camp especially given what Reagan had done for Goldwater in the 1964 campaign. Adding irony to the event was the presence of Nelson Rockefeller. It was Goldwater's victory in the 1964 California primary that gave him the nomination over Rockefeller. By this time in the campaign, Rockefeller had announced he would not be a candidate for vice president so that Ford could appease conservatives, if he needed to, by selecting one of them for the ticket. Rockefeller had a very large head, but was short. No one knew that unless they saw him in person because he made a point of never having his picture taken with taller people around, or if they were around, the picture would be taken with everyone sitting down.[15]

Ford thanked Goldwater profusely and then began to wander off topic into his history with the Republican Party. George Dennison leaned over to me and said, "He's off my script, damn it." I could see members of the crowd heading for the open bar. The President tried to wrap his remarks up, but it was clear he couldn't locate a punch line to do it. Finally, Rockefeller jumped to his feet, clapped his hands, and yelled, "Let's hear it for the President." The crowd got the message and applauded loudly. The President headed off to give his first Bicentennial speech, which was set for Williamsburg in what had been Virginia's House of Burgesses.

THE BICENTENNIAL

Because of the ceremonial nature of the Bicentennial speeches, Hartmann allowed us considerable stylistic latitude, as long as there was no "whiff of pomposity or pretentious elegance." I was the primary writer for the speech at the "Washington Gala" on July 3, the "Spirit of Washington" address delivered at Valley Forge the Fourth of July, and the minor speech at the opening of the Centennial Safe of 1876 from the Grant administration. My backup drafts for Independence Hall and Monticello were popular enough with the President that portions were included in the final drafts.[16]

On July 1, Butler and Boorstin's speech for the President at the Air and Space Museum went very well, but the *Washington Star* reported that staff members had made fun of the speech in the back of the hall.[17] The President was infuriated. A few heads rolled and that was a good thing. I didn't want any second-guessing or carping when the President got to my speeches a few days later.

For this set of speeches, I had argued for vivid imagery, interspersed cadenced phrasing, and *decorum*, that is, meeting audience expectations by using appropriate tropes and figures. These were ceremonial speeches that could ascend into the grand style recommended by Cicero, senator of Rome and noted rhetorical theorist. I told the writers this was an opportunity to write some high-minded thoughts and paint some literate portraits. For example, on July 3, delivering my speech at Valley Forge, Ford said:

> They came here in the snows of winter over a trail marked with the blood of their rag-bound feet. The iron forge which gave this place its name had been destroyed by the British when General Washington and his ragged Continental Army encamped here—exhausted, outnumbered, and short of everything except faith. . . . Yet, their courage and suffering—those who survived as well as those who fell—were no less meaningful than the sacrifices of those who manned the battlements of Boston and scaled the parapets of Yorktown.

After the speech, Ford signed a bill making Valley Forge a national historic site. The speech made headlines across the country, as did the one that followed at Independence Hall. In both speeches, we followed Hartmann's directive to reach "for the future while retaining a reverence for the past." For example, at Independence Hall the President said, "Each generation of Americans, indeed of all humanity, must strive to achieve anew. Liberty is a flame to be fed, not ashes to be revered even in a Bicentennial year."

During this period, there were still small speeches to write for the President. For example, on July 2, Ford was to accept a replica of the Pioneer Monument in Salt Lake City from a group of Mormons. Everything any president says is scripted. The president may decide not to use your script, but you do have to provide one just to be safe. So I arrived in the Oval

Office with the speech written out on cards. On this occasion, the President looked at the speech cards and handed them back to me. When we arrived in the Rose Garden, which was in full bloom under the hot summer sun, I pulled the cards out just in case he wanted them. He looked around and then took the cards from me. After the Mormons made the presentation, Ford read from the cards, stumbling several times.

On August 4, I wrote a speech for the President to deliver to representatives of Boys and Girls Nation, again in the Rose Garden. When I arrived at his office, the President looked the cards over, handed them back to me, and we headed for the Rose Garden. Once we were there, the President received a plaque and I held out the cards. He waved them off and gave a perfect speech. I was impressed.

On the pathway back to the Oval Office, I revved up my courage: "Mr. President, with all due respect, may I ask a question?"

"Shoot."

"Well, sir, a while back, you kind of stumbled with the remarks to the Mormons and now you were right on with your remarks today. What was the difference?"

"There were cameras at the Mormon ceremony; they were filming me. It makes me nervous." Here was a man who had given countless speeches, had plenty of aides, consultants, and advisors, and not one of them had discovered that he was camera shy.

"Mr. President, we are going to fix that."

I reported my discovery to Hartmann, and he said, "So what are you going to do about it?"

"Rehearse him in front of live cameras, that's what." And from that point on, we did, and the President got much better.

More importantly, the moment led to a personal connection between me and the President; he began to ask for personal advice. One such occasion concerned one of his sons. I was not unfamiliar with his children. By some odd coincidence, I had seen his daughter Susan at a fraternity party at UVA a year earlier. Around 10 P.M. at the party, some frat boy bet another one that he couldn't kiss Susan Ford on the butt. When the guy tried, he was immediately pounced upon by the Secret Service agents and hauled away.

I had read that the President's second son, Jack, was carrying on with the likes of Bianca Jagger and Andy Warhol. Along with White House photographer David Hume Kennerly, Jack could be seen exiting clubs in Manhattan at late hours of the night. He even admitted to smoking pot, embarrassing his father.

Then one day the President called me in to discuss his son Steven, who was enrolled at Utah State University. The President told me his son was not very happy there, and could I give him any advice on a place that might be more suitable? I was flattered that the President would ask. "What's he interested in?" I enquired.

"He likes to be outdoors. Loves horses. Maybe animal husbandry."

"Well, I suggest he go to Cal Poly San Luis Obispo. They have a great program in the veterinary fields as I recall." Sure enough, Steven transferred to Cal Poly, SLO and graduated successfully.

On the Fourth of July, halfway through the Bicentennial speeches, we were all invited to the White House back lawn to watch fireworks that would explode over the Tidal Basin. I took Diane Debuck, a former student from UVA, as my date. At UVA and after, Diane and I had had wonderful dinners together where we talked about literature and philosophy. She was an excellent writer and proved it on several freelance assignments for local outlets in Alexandria, where she had moved after graduating. She became one of many women in my life that I felt perfectly comfortable around; I shared everything with her, except my sexual preference. In a letter dated January of 1976, Diane had written, "Thank you for the encouraging words. I assure you I will not soon forget the line tossed to the drowning." She continued that she didn't want to be considered a "student to my professor. Why oh why do you have to be away for mid-winters, I was hoping to do some hell-raising with you back at the U."

On the Fourth, after we had some of the available cuisine, I spread my coat on the lawn and Diane and I sat back and watched the fireworks. Just as they began, the President came out onto the Truman balcony and waved to everyone.

The rest of the Bicentennial speeches went well, helping to move Ford ahead of Reagan in the race for the nomination and close the gap in the polls with Carter. For example, the *New York Times* of July 5, 1976, read, NATION AND MILLIONS IN CITY JOYOUSLY HAIL BICENTENNIAL. The subhead read, "President Talks: Philadelphia Throngs Told U.S. Is Leader." A second story on the front page led with a large picture of Ford traveling and quoted more material from his speeches. The *Times* reported favorable comments on the speeches from persons in the crowd.

After the Bicentennial speeches, the President rewarded the speechwriting staff by giving us the presidential yacht *Sequoia* for an evening. As we arrived at the gangplank, the yacht's teak rails and brass fittings shone in the late afternoon sunshine. Bought by the Navy in 1933, the yacht served many presidents. On a beautiful summer night in July, we were piped aboard the same yacht on which Franklin Roosevelt had supped with Winston Churchill. It had been a favorite hiding place of Nixon's. The walls were covered with historic pictures of presidents entertaining potentates. Before I could read the first caption, however, a white-uniformed Filipino waiter put a martini in my hand. As I thanked him, I saw Hartmann over his shoulder; the old man gave me a wink and raised his martini toward me.[18]

We motored down the Potomac to Mount Vernon, and as the sun set, a bugler played the national anthem and tears ran down my face. The *Sequoia* then turned back toward Washington, and the President came on the speakers from the White House thanking us for the Bicentennial addresses. Then we sat down to a sumptuous dinner. Afterward I stood besotted on the deck, holding tight to the rail, as our boat motored upriver to the city. The monuments were lit and looked stunningly white against the night sky. It was the high point of my life.

The next day the formal job offer arrived from Birmingham. I got everything I wanted. After a fitful night of sleep, I accepted the offer. I didn't believe Ford could win the election, and I finally wanted to close the book on tenure. I would start in the fall, leaving the White House before the election. Now I had to screw up my courage to tell Hartmann.

On July 13, late in the afternoon, I found myself meeting with the President, Orben, and Hartmann to discuss my draft of talking points for Ford's address to the subcabinet officers. The President told me that I might want to start thinking about working for the political wing of the administration. I was surprised, and so it seems was Hartmann. Back in Hartmann's office, he asked me to review a draft of a speech that Butler had written. He told me he would hold anything I said in confidence, but he wanted my candid opinion. I pointed out the weaknesses as objectively as I could. "Rework it for me, will you? And think about what the President said." That pushed me back to indecision about going to Birmingham.

The Democrats held their convention in mid-July, and Carter made the mistake of trying to hold his big tent party together by giving a vacuous speech in which he promised never to lie to the American public. Oh please, I thought, who in the hell are you kidding? I began to hatch a strategy for the President's fall campaign that would open with his acceptance speech. He would challenge Carter to debates, the first since the infamous Nixon-Kennedy confrontations of 1960. The debates would force Carter to take stands on the issues, come down from the clouds, and thereby reveal his duplicity or naiveté. For example, you can't be in favor of busing and hold the South in line; you can't favor affirmative action quotas and hold labor in line.

With nothing to lose, I felt confident enough to write a memo calling for an integrated approach to issues for the ensuing fall campaign and a limited number of set speeches. I laid out four issue-position speeches in the memo and added that Ford should stay in the White House being president for as much of the time as possible. Hartmann resisted strongly, but nonetheless took the memo to the President, who read it, approved it, signed it, and sent it to Jim Cannon, his campaign coordinator, who was more than a little annoyed at my interference. Cannon dubbed the advice "the Rose Garden strategy." However, Stu Spencer,[19] the President's most trusted political advisor, accepted my recommendations. Hartmann confided that Ford had told him that I should be promoted to "issue coordinator" for the coming campaign. My life was suddenly a good deal more complicated.

THE ACCEPTANCE SPEECH

At the end of the primary season, Ford had won fifteen and Reagan had won twelve. Neither had secured the nomination. On July 26, Reagan tried to knock everything into a cocked hat by announcing that his choice for the vice-presidential nomination was Senator Richard Schweiker of Pennsylvania. No candidate in modern times had ever named his vice-presidential choice before securing the nomination. Because the Pennsylvania delegation to the Republican Convention was in play, Reagan's move was clever. It wed him to a moderate from a state with delegates Reagan badly needed. Reagan then challenged Ford to name his vice-presidential nominee.

As that drama unfolded, work began on Ford's acceptance address. Suggestions from friends poured in, and Hartmann filed away statements and phrases he believed might prove useful at the Kansas City Convention. We crafted a version of the acceptance speech containing more stylistic devices than Ford had ever used. Earlier successes with them in the Bicentennial speeches seemed to have eased his mind about employing them in the acceptance speech. Hartmann insisted that the speech needed to make a headline in its first few lines, and a challenge to debate Carter would achieve that end.

August twelfth was fretful. New York Senator James Buckley, the brother of William F., said that he would allow his name to be put in nomination at the convention. The strategy was obvious: he was working with Reagan to chip away New York delegates from Ford. When I met with Hartmann, he was in a bad mood. After we went over some material for the acceptance speech, he asked me who I'd pick for Ford's vice-presidential nominee. I told him that former Pennsylvania Governor Bill Scranton would be my choice. Scranton had been in Ford's law class at Yale. He was a bright, articulate moderate who could deliver Pennsylvania to Ford at the convention and in the general election. And if they got Pennsylvania, they would win. Hartmann said I was not alone in my recommendation, but there was also a strong contingent for Senate Minority Leader Howard Baker of Tennessee, since he could cut into Carter's Southern base. "He would be my second choice," I told Hartmann.

Since Hartmann was leaving for the convention the next day, I believed it was time to tell him I was planning on leaving the White House to take the Birmingham job. I nervously stumbled through my rationale for leaving, hoping I was not hurting his feelings and praising him for being a wonderful mentor to me. He said he could understand that, but urged me to stay and take a promotion. I told him I would rather work as an outside consultant, particularly with regard to giving advice to him for the President on how to debate Carter. He was again understanding and told me he would look into how that might work. "You are trying to have the best of both worlds," he correctly surmised.

When Hartmann arrived in Kansas City for the Republican Convention, he found that the Reagan people were playing their last card. They proposed Rule 16C, which would require all potential nominees of the convention to name their vice-presidential choice before the balloting began. As we have seen, Reagan already had named Senator Schweiker as his choice, so he had nothing to lose. However, if Ford named a vice-presidential choice, he might offend just enough delegates to prevent him from getting the nomination. So the test of strength for the nomination would come down to which side would win the fight over Rule 16C. Ford carried the day when the delegates defeated Rule 16C. The battle for the nomination appeared over.

But then Senator Jesse Helms offered an amendment to the platform that could only be read as criticism of Ford foreign policy. Almost everyone on the Ford team, except Henry Kissinger, advised Ford to let it pass. They did not want another fight, this time on an ideological issue where they were more vulnerable. Conservatives don't like changing the rules, so they voted against Reagan on 16C. But they are susceptible to ideological appeals. Spencer asked Ford, "Who would care about a single plank in an unread platform?" Kissinger was appalled and threatened to resign.[20] Ford overruled him and the convention approved Helms's amendment. This moment would come back to haunt Ford right after the second debate with Carter, as we shall see. At the time, however, Ford had dodged a bullet.

On Wednesday night, as the roll call began, you could feel the tension in the convention hall. For several minutes, there were no breakthroughs by either side. In fact, some states were coming in closer than Ford's team had anticipated. In the end, Ford won the nomination on Wednesday night with only 117 votes to spare out of 2,257 cast.

Because of the closeness of the race and the need to unify the party, Ford's team considered accepting Ronald Reagan as his vice-presidential running mate. Stu Spencer, who had helped elect Reagan governor, was strongly in favor of the idea. But Ford remained cool to the notion. He needn't have worried. The deal was ruined by Reagan's press man, Lyn Nofziger, who did not want Reagan on what he saw as a losing ticket. Nofziger wanted Reagan to run for president in 1980. So he lied to the Ford team by telling them that at the agreed-upon post-nomination meeting between Ford and Reagan, Ford must not ask Reagan to run with him. Reagan would be insulted by such a gesture. Instead, Ford should ask Reagan's advice about those on Ford's short list for vice president. The Ford campaign staff believed what Nofziger told them. It would change history.

When he arrived at Reagan's hotel room, Ford showed six names to Reagan. Among them were Governor Scranton and Senator Baker. Coached by Nofziger, Reagan said that only Senator Robert Dole of Kansas was acceptable from those on the list. Ford had known Dole a long time and was comfortable with him. So Ford added Reagan's advice to his own preferences to overrule his advisors and put Dole on the ticket. In my opinion, Dole brought nothing to the ticket but his grumpy nature, which showed up in his debate with Walter Mondale during the fall campaign. As for Reagan, he didn't do nearly as much as he could have for Ford in the ensuing campaign, and many years later reported that he was unhappy Ford had not asked him to be his running mate.[21]

Ford's acceptance speech the next night followed Dole's. Ford made clear what many Republicans knew: he was in fact more conservative than Nixon. This was an important point to drive home since from the beginning of the primary season, Carter also had portrayed himself as a conservative. To win the election, particularly in crucial Southern swing states, Ford had to bring back into the Republican fold the conservative Democrats Nixon had so carefully courted.

Ford rehearsed his speech not once, but five times before live television cameras in the convention hall in Kansas City, with the help of media advisor Don Penny, a former comedian who had become a delivery specialist. When he opened his speech at the convention, Ford grabbed the headlines by challenging Carter to debates because "the issues are on our side." The well-delivered speech earned applause 65 times in forty minutes. *Newsday's* assessment was typical: "Far and away the best stroke at the convention was Jerry Ford's personal accomplishment at the podium Thursday night. . . . It was the finest oratory heard by a party that had summoned all its best campaigners to Kansas City." The speech contained more memorable lines than most of his political speeches. For example, Ford encapsulated his service to the nation in phrases marked by alliteration and internal rhyming: "We will build on performance, not promises; experience, not expedience. . . . My record is one of specifics, not smiles. . . . To me, the presidency and vice presidency were not prizes to be won, but a duty to be done." The speech's impact in terms of poll data was striking. He now trailed Carter by only 10 points.[22]

CHAPTER SEVEN

Writing for President George H. W. Bush

HAVING LIVED IN VIRGINIA AS A CHILD AND THEN AS A PROFESSOR, I suffered under the impression that the South was homogeneous. Anyone who spends some time traveling in the South quickly realizes that it has very diverse pockets of culture within other pockets of culture. Inside the colorful Miami environs lie Cuban, African American, Haitian, and Jewish enclaves, to name but four. Atlanta sports a large Jewish community, a thriving city center, and a remarkable number of suburbs, each unique unto itself. When I arrived in Birmingham in the fall of 1976, it was a thriving city with special places like Five Points, where shops and restaurants sit on the conjunction of several streets. Tuscaloosa lies 30 miles to the west, while Atlanta, looking a lot like Oz as you come upon it, lies 150 miles to the east. Four hours south is the Gulf Coast with its beautiful white sandy beaches lapped by turquoise water. In six hours you can drive to New Orleans and enjoy the mysterious streets of the French Quarter. In less than four hours, you can be in Memphis for blues and barbeque. Nashville's country music is a quick two hours up Interstate 65.

Because the steel magnates of the North had formed the city during the Reconstruction period when carpetbaggers found iron in its red hills, Birmingham never knew the Civil War; but it did know the Great Depression. It was one of the worst-hit cities because its steel mills closed when production collapsed across the nation. Nonetheless, the population leaned toward the Republican Party, a fact that separated it from the rest of the state. George Wallace, the Democratic populist governor, ran so poorly in Birmingham that he refused to complete the interstate freeways through the city. When I lived there, Interstate 20 stopped outside the west side of the city at Bessemer, so that drivers had to endure myriad traffic lights to cross through to the other side of the city, where they could pick up Interstate 20 at Irondale on their way east. Interstate 65 stopped on the north side of the city at Fultondale, and you could not pick it up again until you reached Hoover, south of the city. Even when you were on the interstate, you might find yourself going 25 miles an hour behind a tractor in the left lane because Wallace had told the farmers he had built the interstates for them.

The charm of Birmingham came from its people and the fact that it was built at the tail end of the Appalachian Mountains, hence the lovely ridges distinguishing it from the flatlands of the rest of the state. Birmingham did have its problems, not the least of which was overcoming the stains of racial prejudice. Sheriff Bull Connor had used German shepherds and water guns to control demonstrations in the 1960s. It was from the Birmingham jail that Martin Luther King Jr. had penned his famous letter. However, by the time I arrived in Birmingham, it was working hard to overcome the negative image. The University of Alabama at Birmingham played a large role in that mission.

The university housed the medical school, famous for its world-renowned heart surgeons. It was a commuter school that embraced its community and facilitated the enrollment of at-risk youth. Unlike the staid, traditional university branch at Tuscaloosa, Birmingham's branch had no football team, nor any fraternities or sororities. It did have new buildings and many vibrant programs, particularly in the arts.

I followed the presidential election closely and sent memos to Hartmann about how Ford should handle Carter in the impending presidential debates. In the first debate, Ford benefited greatly from low expectations. The press was sure the "brilliant" Jimmy Carter with the degree in nuclear engineering would tear the bumbling Ford apart. Ford held his own, scored more points than Carter, and forced him to reveal specific positions that surprised Southern conservatives. After the first debate, the polls closed to a dead heat. I began to wonder if I should have stayed at the White House.

That speculation ended with the second debate in San Francisco at the Palace of the Arts on October 6, where Ford made a mistake. In answering a question from Max Frankel, a reporter from the *New York Times*, in defense of his policy of détente, he said, "There is no Soviet domination of Eastern Europe, and there never will be under a Ford Administration." Ford pointed out that Yugoslavia was free of the Soviets, and Romania and Poland had similar tendencies in mind. When Frankel asked a follow-up about whether Ford had said Poland was free of Soviet dominance, Ford said, "The United States does not concede that those countries are under the domination of the Soviet Union."

Immediately following the debate, Stu Spencer advised the President to clarify the answer he had given. Ford did not believe he had misspoken, perhaps remembering the first part of his answer to Frankel instead of his answer to the follow-up question. Spencer pressed him again: Didn't the President mean that in their hearts and minds the Poles were not dominated by the Soviet Union? At some point Kissinger joined the conversation and supported Ford's decision not to retract. Remember that Kissinger was humiliated in Kansas City when his advice on the Helms amendment undercutting détente was rejected. Now he pushed his point again, defending his policy of détente. Did the President want to insult the Soviets and hence endanger Kissinger's negotiations to get Anatole Sharansky out of the Soviet Union? This time Ford went with Kissinger, and the decision proved fatal.

Carter's team and the national media had a field day with Ford's gaffe. The mistake allowed the nation to recall Ford's other mistakes and bumbling. (After Ford had slipped coming down the rain-soaked stairs of a plane in Salzburg and fallen to the tarmac, Chevy Chase had made a career out of characterizing Ford as a slapstick president on the popular *Saturday Night Live* television program.) Several days after the debate, Ford bowed to pressure, and in California, on the campaign trail, said that he meant the Poles in their hearts and minds were not dominated by the Soviet Union. It was too late.

Ford fell back in the polls. The third debate was a virtual tie, with both candidates speaking so carefully that the television ratings plummeted with each passing minute. Over the last weeks of the campaign, it didn't help when the President said he would be rooting for his alma mater, the University of Michigan, in a key football game with Ohio State. It was crucial for Ford to carry Ohio if he were retain the presidency.

On election night, though Ford lost by about two million votes, the electoral college vote was much closer than predicted and could have been won had Ford carried Mississippi and Ohio. The race was close in both states. However, when the votes came from the southern Ohio counties, the Ford team knew that the Nixon-Ford era was over. The country looked forward to a new beginning, and I turned my attention to my new job.

As usual, I befriended students and had them over for dinner. However, my main time was occupied with building the new program, which I named the Communication Arts Division. There were some part-time faculty in place who could teach broadcasting or public speaking. Some faculty were moved over from the English Department, where they had been teaching courses in journalism. But basically, the division was mine to build, so I set about recruiting young PhDs to populate the program. After a year, we had a strong foundation for the diverse program. I had hired Martha Martin, John Wright, and Larry Hosman for the fall. They proved very able teachers who loved their students and who could publish at the same time. Though they eventually moved on, they were the foundation of what became and remains to this day a strong department.

POT LIQUOR

I also began to reach out to the community in different ways. One of my African American students had invited me to his home for dinner, if I didn't mind "poor folks' food." He lived with his parents in a rundown part of town in a row house. I was reminded of the poor black community that was just over the tall hedge behind my house in Norfolk when I was growing up. Sitting on a stoop in Birmingham, I had a beer with the student and his father before dinner. Inside the house, as it cooled in the evening breeze, we shared a meal that consisted of ham, collard greens, and corn bread, which one was expected to dip in "pot liquor," the drippings from the vegetables. These dinners were regularly replicated throughout my stay in Birmingham.

After the first dinner, it occurred to me that African American students came out of an oral culture and therefore might be better served by the university if they took the basic public-speaking course before they took the basic English course, which was more alien to them. So I put in for a federal grant to try my theory out. Fifty at-risk entrants to the university were placed into two public-speaking classes, 25 students each, in their first quarter, and two basic English courses, 25 each, in their second quarter. Fifty more at-risk students did exactly the reverse. I taught one of the fall sections of the public-speaking classes and another one of them in the winter quarter. Ninety-nine of these students were African American.

The results were stunning. The at-risk students who took the public-speaking course first had a much higher retention rate in the university and also had higher grades than those who started with basic English. The reason was not difficult to discern. Because public speaking was oral, and these students came from oral cultures, it was easier for them to assimilate tools for critical thinking, such as the evaluation of evidence, organizational skills, and grammar, in the public-speaking environment than in the basic English composition class.

Since the Tuscaloosa branch of the university was not far away, and since I knew their former debate coach and now chair, Annabel Hagood, and their current coach, Cully Clark, I often came to Tuscaloosa to visit with them and guest-lecture. Annabel was quite good at putting on a dinner; the liquor flowed as freely as the conversation. I soon became one of her favorite guests, and because of the drinking would stay in her guest room rather than drive back to Birmingham in the middle of the night. One night after the other guests had left, Annabel asked me if I missed coaching debate. "No," I responded, "I loved it while I did it, but once you are out of it and look back, you ask yourself, how did I do that for all those years?"

"I know what you mean," she said as she sipped some brandy. "Weekend after weekend, holidays, the whole nine yards. You just never think about it while you are doing it."

"But you do love the debaters. They are the most talented kids I ever knew."

HYDE AND HEIDEGGER

In my second year, Annabel added Michael Hyde to her faculty, a bright young man who had just finished his PhD at Purdue. We immediately hit it off. In fact, he had applied for an opening I had at UAB, but I had discarded his resumé, believing he would never come to my department since I assumed he wanted to be at a flagship institution. "Oh, no," he informed me at our first dinner at Annabel's, "I wanted to come to UAB to work with you." I was flattered and we began to collaborate on research. My work with Michael encouraged me to delve deeper into Heidegger's thinking, where I found a link to the spiritual world. Heidegger argued that by rejecting the common herd and its prattle, one could meditate on and stand in hearkening attunement to the spiritual. Such meditation, I argued, increased intuitive powers. However, I explained that intuition was a tricky term that had been defined in different ways. For Plato, it meant turning into the soul and questioning back to pure truths found in the noumenal world, the non-material world of perfect forms. For John Locke, it meant truth that was readily apparent to the senses; we intuit the heat of the burner through our sense of touch. For Zen masters, intuition often meant enlightened clarity resulting from intense meditation and realizing that desire was the root of pain. For Heidegger and for me, it meant spiritual insight into hidden and transcendent meaning—the intuition of something others don't know or see, but that you know is absolutely true. Once you reach that kind of intuition, you are a more creative person, and often your art calls others to spirit. And you are a more sensitive person in that you begin to read others better; you sense their neuroses or their spirituality more quickly and more accurately. It would take a while to get that theory published. In fact, no journal in my field would touch it.

Then Michael got me into an international phenomenology conference at Purdue, where things got interesting. I was put on a panel where I was supposed to react to the paper of another professor who was talking about Heidegger's view of science. I would be given enough time to insert my own views on Heidegger in my response. As I listened to the other professor's paper, I realized that I sharply disagreed with his interpretation of Heidegger. I began my report by pointing out the difficulties in his reading of Heidegger. Note the use of academic politeness in my rhetoric:

> Professor Stewart's paper seems to me to be a careful analysis of Heidegger's view of natural science. . . . I would point out, however, that Heidegger separates himself from the tradition of Kant and Husserl more radically than Professor Stewart would have us believe. The ways in which Heidegger rejects the explicative powers of natural science are far more radical than the ways in which Kant performs this function. Furthermore, I have some difficulty understanding how Professor Stewart can argue that Heidegger evolves from Kant and is at the same time compatible with Wittgenstein. Perhaps this is a result of Professor Stewart's tendency to define and use major terms, such as *Dasein*, to suit his own purposes.

I then moved on to my own agenda:

> Sophists, like Protagoras, found no easy access to the "truth." Instead, they decided to build the "better illusion" through rhetoric. . . . The twists and turns of philosophy since that time provide a road map of rhetorical theory. Existential thinkers, for example, have forced a reevaluation of rhetoric. . . . Different existentialists have different descriptions of rhetoric. But whether this rhetoric be "edifying," "willful," or "authentic," it is derived from how it functions to create an existential situation. In Martin Heidegger, we find a philosopher who completes a careful study of rhetoric taking it back to Heraclitus and forward to individual existence and transcendence.

The paper focused on a Heideggerian theory of rhetoric, eventually comparing authentic rhetoric (discovery of self, understanding, taking responsibility) with inauthentic rhetoric (ambiguous, curious, chatter). Uncovering truth, I argued, was the key to understanding, which could create a state of hearkening attunement, a readiness to hear the voice of God. Once heard, that voice could be reconstituted into a rhetoric that would bring others to a state of hearkening attunement, eventually expanding the realm of spirituality in the world.

As I finished the paper, there was some whispering and buzzing in the room. Then the moderator recognized a wizened old woman who rose to her full five feet in stature. She spoke in loud and harsh German; she seemed to be very angry. She pointed at me and then at Professor Stewart. All I could translate was the phrase "*hounded drek.*" It means "dog shit." Good Lord, I thought, is she saying my theory is dog shit? I leaned over to Michael Hyde, who was on the panel beside me, and whispered, "Am I in trouble or what?" He wrote a quick note to me that read, "No. She says you reduced his paper to dog shit."

The woman was Anna-Teresa Tymienicka from the World Institute for Advanced Phenomenological Research. More importantly, she was the coeditor of *Analectica Husserliana*, the leading journal of phenomenology.[1] At the end of the session she came to me, and with Michael's help as a translator, she invited me to rewrite my remarks into an article for her journal. So my article on Heidegger appeared in an international philosophy journal, and only then was my thinking on this subject accepted in America in my field. I would continue down this path for many years, inviting other scholars in my field to follow. After all, rhetoric was a field studied by Plato and advanced by Aristotle. No field has better academic roots than that.

GIVING UP TENURE

During this time, John Macksoud decided that tenure was immoral and told his department at SUNY Binghamton that he would not accept tenure if they offered it to him. They told him that if he refused tenure, he would have to leave, because if they didn't give him tenure, it would get them in trouble with the American Association of University Professors (AAUP). John resigned and took a terminal year. He moved into an apartment in Binghamton and began saving what he could.

John convinced me that he was right about tenure, and he encouraged me to resign mine. The main argument came in the form of a poem he entitled "Outlaw Wine (To CRS)" and it reads:

It is vain my friends to pretend that a saint
Having tasted outlaw wine could fail
To discern that lawful drink is as pale
As spit. What else could it be? It must sit
And stay in the bellies of Christians whose intimate
Traffic with courage extends to its
Spelling.
But Jesus the outlaw stands large in the mind.
He who said he was lawful while Pharisees tried
Him. Whatever he said it is certain he died
As an outlaw, was judged so and suffered the fate
Of an outlaw whose passion was feared in the states.
Who knowingly drinks his blood partakes
of outlaw wine.

I wanted to become an outlaw, but I didn't believe John had been properly informed about the AAUP. So I went to my university and told them I wanted to be stripped of tenure and evaluated the way assistant professors were evaluated. I hated the two-class caste system under which we were suffering: the tenured aristocrats versus the untenured slaves. The power relationship is contradictory to academic freedom of the ideals of university life. Untenured professors are often afraid to advance controversial ideas, let alone confront or even vote against tenured professors. By the time they get tenure, they have been compromised into the hegemonic thinking of their tenured associates. And at the time I made this an issue, post-tenure reviews had no teeth, and in too many cases tenure was protecting laziness. At least today some schools are trying to correct that problem.

None of this would be necessary if we just went to a contract system. Professors might start with a three-year contract; if they did well, it could be increased to a five-year contract. If they continued to do well, extend them a seven-year contract. If professors did poorly in terms of teaching or publishing, then give them a shorter contract and a final terminal year when you wanted to let them go. But in no case is a lifetime contract justified. After a legal wrangle, I got the university lawyers to draw up a contract under which I gave up all my rights to appeal any decision to terminate me. The AAUP begged me not to do it, but they said they would not censure the university if the contract went into effect. The day I signed it, I felt terribly liberated, a desperado. And according to the AAUP the only department chair ever to give up tenure. It would not be the last time I caught the attention of the AAUP.

REVIVING REPUBLICANISM IN ALABAMA

When I read in the paper that the Republican Party had elected a new, young state chairman, Bill Harris, I decided to give him a call and offer my services. Our first meeting was over lunch on January 27, 1977. At the time, no more than 10 percent of the voters in Alabama called themselves Republicans, and most of them were in Birmingham. Alabama was deep Confederate territory that had voted for George Wallace for president in 1968. Those who ran the Republican Party treated it like a country club. They had no interest in making it into a viable entity. Bill Harris was different; he saw that though Alabamans called themselves Democrats, they had long since embraced the conservative principles housed in the Republican Party. Barry Goldwater had carried the state in 1964; Nixon carried it in 1972, and was making significant inroads when Watergate stopped Republican momentum. In 1976, the election of Jimmy Carter, a former Southern governor, was another setback. But soon the Carter administration was unraveling. As he began his administration, he gave a two-part speech on energy in which he sounded like a minister chastising his flock. Rather incongruously, he did this while sitting in a rocking chair wearing a sweater. Massive inflation would follow, and then our embassy in Iran would be seized by radical Islamists who came to power because Carter had insisted that the shah of Iran make certain reforms or lose U.S. aid. The shah's secret police were a terror. However, when the shah made some reforms—for example, liberating women—he was overthrown and replaced by a right-wing ayatollah.

That came a few years after Bill Harris and I set out to make Alabama a Republican state. We hit it off immediately. He put me on the Republican steering committee, and we began to give speeches across the state to recruit young entrepreneurs, farmers, and executives into the party. We told them our party was the land of opportunity in terms of political advancement as opposed to the crowded Democratic Party, which was impossible to break into. I also agreed to work with potential candidates as a kind of media consultant. In May of 1977, that led to a tough lesson. I wrote a speech for Guy Hunt, our presumptive candidate for governor, then traveled to hear Hunt give the speech. It went well, but in the Q&A that followed, Hunt made a racist remark. I wrote him that I would never work with him again, and that he'd better clean up his act if he ever wanted to become governor.[2]

Before the situation could be turned around from the doldrums of 1976 and 1977, Bill and I also needed to raise money. The quickest way to do that was to host a dinner for a big-name speaker. Most of them demanded a huge fee unless they planned to run for president in 1980. So we put together a request letter in May 1977 that went to likely presidential candidates. We quickly learned that of the big guns, like Reagan and Connally, none would come to Alabama because the state was seen as a waste of time. We found one exception: George H. W. Bush, the former head of the CIA when I was at the White House, and before that ambassador to China and the UN, head of the Republican Party, congressman, entrepreneur, and war hero. We immediately began to plan a dinner at which he would speak.

I had always liked George Bush, a bright, sensitive man whom you would like to have as a brother or a best friend. So I looked forward to his speech. The event, in the new Birmingham Civic Center on October 28, 1977, was well attended. I was seated with a lively group, including a blond young man who was something of a political nerd. Since I was a speech professor and former presidential speechwriter, he goaded me into agreeing to give a critique of Bush's speech when it was over; so as he spoke, I wrote notes on a napkin. When Bush finished, I delivered my assessment to our table. Basically, it amounted to nice guy, terrible speech. It had no sense of style; it was disjointed and often cryptic; his delivery was neither fluent nor energetic. The nerd told me he was traveling with Bush. They were looking for a speechwriter and had heard from former President Ford that I was in Birmingham. The nerd was Karl Rove, who had set me up and I loved it. Would I like to meet Ambassador Bush after the dinner? You bet.

When I met Bush at the intimate post-dinner gathering, I told him that I remembered the great job he did in reviving spirits at the CIA after he took over after the Watergate crisis. Bush asked me what I thought of his speech. I told him I would send him a full critique. A few days later I sent the critique to his staff leader. It included these passages:

> Ambassador Bush conveys credibility by exuding character, expertise, goodwill, and, at times, spontaneity. These factors should be enhanced in the future. His prior reputation works to his advantage and those who introduce him should be scripted to highlight that he was the youngest Navy pilot in World War II, that he was shot down over the Pacific, rescued by a submarine and won the Distinguished Flying Cross, and three other medals, that he is a self-made businessman, that he won his congressional seat in a heavily Democratic district in 1966 and then was unopposed for reelection, that he served with distinction as our party chairman during its worst crisis, that he served as ambassador to China and the U.N., and that he revived the flagging CIA after Watergate. . . . A sense of style must be developed. There were many missed opportunities for

parallel structure, alliteration, balances, and the like. . . . Ambassador Bush needs to let his audience know where he is going. Ideas need to be grouped and structured. (Castro was mentioned twice in the speech, but the mentions were ten minutes apart.) Why wasn't all the energy material grouped together into a deep structured unit? . . . Only in a few places in the foreign policy sections did the speech develop enough emotion to excite the audience. This gives the audience the impression that the ambassador has a passion for foreign policy but not for domestic policy.

I then offered to fly over to Houston to work on a campaign speech for Bush.

On November 11, 1977, Bush wrote me a personal letter inviting me to Houston in January for an interview. I told him I would be in Houston as soon as I got back from London, where I would spend Christmas with friends. I then received a two-page letter from Karl Rove detailing what would happen when I came to Houston. Then came a transcript of a speech that Bush gave in Albuquerque. I sent a critique back that was very detailed and outlined a longer speech that Bush could use for most occasions by picking and choosing the issues to be covered for the immediate audience. This was the same technique Reagan had used when he ran for governor of California and about which I had written my master's thesis.

A letter was waiting for me when I arrived at my friend's place in London. Bush told me to visit with Jennifer Fitzgerald, who was working as Ambassador Kingman Brewster's chief of protocol at the American Embassy. Jennifer had been a loyal Nixon Republican who met Bush while he was chairman of the party. She had been with the Bush team ever since. Because Bush was a Yale graduate, when the Republicans fell from power in 1976, he was able to get Jennifer on with Brewster, who had been president of Yale. Bush's letter to me concluded, "I am deeply touched that you want to help me. I am deadly serious. I know it is a Long March but I'm up for it. Happy Christmas over there." Jennifer Fitzgerald and I met at the Embassy and were simpatico; she okayed me to Bush.[3]

When I went to Houston in early January to meet with Bush, I was put up at the ritzy Galleria Hotel. All dressed up in my best three-piece suit, I was driven to Bush's home in the River Oaks neighborhood on a Sunday morning. Bush, in a red Izod polo shirt and slacks, greeted me at a side door. "If you'll take off that silly vest," he laughed, "I'll cook you breakfast." First, he gave me a tour of the hacienda, and then asked me to sit at the kitchen bar while he cooked up some eggs, bacon, and toast for me. He asked if I wanted coffee and I said I did. He filled a cup with coffee, handed it to me, and slapped some bacon into a hot pan.[4] Just then Mrs. Bush entered the kitchen in a housecoat and stared me up and down.

"George, this young man is drinking coffee without a saucer. The Chinese delegation is coming tonight and I don't want a spot anywhere."

Summoning up courage from God knows where, I responded, "Mrs. Bush, I came to your door in a three-piece suit. If you think I'm going to spill one drop of this coffee, you don't know who you are dealing with."

Both Barbara and George laughed. "George," she said, "I like this young man."

For the next few hours, Bush and I went over a speech I had written for him. He liked it and added examples and some figures he had in his head on national defense. Then we retreated into the den, where Barbara joined us and we listened to his speech before Washington's Gridiron Club, an off-the-record night among the press and major players in Washington. Bush was genuinely funny in front of educated people. His humor was dry and offbeat. The more I knew him, the more I liked him.

The important thing was to get Bush on the road to the 1980 nomination. Our first tour began in February of 1978 with a speech to Texas Bear County Republicans in Houston. It went well. The chairman gave Barbara a bouquet of yellow roses and Bush the Texas state flag. As our Saberliner took off through a snowstorm for Tulsa, Karl Rove read a book and I tried to break the tension by saying how beautiful the roses were. Barbara replied, "I would rather have had the damn flag." This woman could be tough. Later Karl told me that he was afraid of her and that I should always be positive in my criticism of George Bush. "She's very protective, Craig. I've learned that the hard way." Bush then handed me a few changes for the speech in Tulsa the following night. After we landed and I got into my room at the Hilton, I worked until 3 A.M. on the final version of the speech.

The speech in Tulsa was the real test. There were plenty of Republicans there to hear it, but they leaned toward the candidacy of John Connally. By this point in time, Connally's speeches were legendary. In one section, the former Democratic governor of Texas attacked the Japanese for illegal trade practices and said his policies would leave them sitting in their Toyotas on their docks with no place to go. The line always got a cheer.

Karl and I had decided that Bush couldn't out-Connally Connally. Bush needed to be his own man. That meant starting each speech with some humor that was created on the spot, then adapting the opening to the local audience, and then getting very serious about the issues, displaying his knowledge of foreign policy. Throughout the Tulsa speech, you could hear a pin drop. No applause interrupted the speech, but the audience was attentive. When it ended, Bush got a long, standing ovation. People near me said exactly what I wanted to hear: "Now, that was presidential." We were betting that Bush's issue orientation would in the long run overcome the passion and flash of Connally. In those days, making a cowboy president was unthinkable.

Bush came over to me after the speech and I held my breath. "Craig, I thought it went very well. I felt very comfortable with that speech. And, you know, Barbara really liked it too." Barbara winked at me as we left the hotel ballroom. At 6:30 A.M. she flew home and I traveled on with Bush and Rove. I suggested some minor tweaks for the speech and he approved them. We landed in Chicago for a day crazy with activity. There were two breakfasts, a pre-lunch cocktail hour with donors, a lunch featuring my speech on the economy at a commercial club, more meetings, another cocktail hour with donors before dinner, then a dinner and a modified version of my campaign speech. It was a tough life, with very little down time for a candidate, and this was almost two years before the election. God, I thought, what is it going to be like during the primary season?

The next day we arrived at Beloit College, a very small, 1,000-student liberal arts campus in southern Wisconsin. We were the guests of the president of the college, Martha Peterson, who looked something like Margaret Mead. She had scheduled a press conference for noon on the steps of her presidential mansion, where we each had been given a room. The news media was hostile to Bush, but he parried the questions well. He knew that he would be questioned about his role as national party chairman during Watergate, and then head of the CIA. I admired his diplomatic tenacity.

After freshening up, Bush and I went for a walk through the campus, which was gleaming white in the sunshine after a snowfall. It was wonderful to be alone with him and just talk like friends about nothing in particular. He liked me to take his mind off the campaign and into academic subjects. Eventually we found our way to a hall where Bush was to lecture on China. The place was packed by the time President Peterson introduced Bush. As I stood offstage holding his overcoat, I felt very protective of him. I was proud that his lecture was quite good. He needed no notes and the students listened in rapt attention. Then came time for questions. Several were hostile. But again, he parried the questions well and won the crowd over.

President Peterson had arranged a dinner in the evening for some local fat cats and politicos; we were not far from Chicago, Des Moines, Milwaukee, and Madison. When she offered us all a round of drinks, Bush demurred, saying he'd given up alcohol for Lent, "but" (pointing to me) he said, "you can count on beardo over there to have a gin martini!" From then on, I was "beardo" on the Bush team.

During the dinner, the fat cats asked a lot of pushy questions and made a lot of demands, but Bush handled them with finesse and dignity. I would have thrown my plate at them. It is one of the reasons I could never run for public office. Even educated, well-to-do people suppose that politicians should do their bidding. After Bush and Rove retired, I stayed up until 2 A.M. talking with Martha Peterson about the sad state of education in America.

After a good night's sleep and hearty breakfast, we were off to Rockford for a press conference and then a fundraising luncheon. Karl had scheduled me to leave the entourage at O'Hare Airport and return to Birmingham. Since this was my first road trip with the team, I suspected that Karl didn't want to book me on for too long in case my chemistry with Bush was bad. Bush was to go on to Akron to deliver "the speech" again. Karl hadn't told Bush that I'd be leaving. He was surprised and seemed sad to see me go. I said I was sorry but I had to get back to my duties in Birmingham. "I thought Karl let you know."

"Well, no he didn't. We'll miss you."

"Good luck, Ambassador. Knock 'em dead in Akron."

"They're already dead in Akron," he quipped. When I got back to Alabama, Karl called to say the speech in Akron went very well.

Soon Adam Clymer of the *New York Times* wrote that Bush had become a "hot property on the G.O.P. dinner circuit. . . . He draws his experience into his speeches, which are well-spoken, with effectively timed punch lines."[5] Later in the year, *Newsweek* wrote, "Bush is toning up his once flat style of speaking—and increasingly his speeches seem to catch fire."[6] A few weeks after I got home, Bush sent a private letter in which he promised "to work on the speech you sent me, and I'll do what you suggest and let you know how it goes."[7] I continued to send versions of "the speech" to Bush, who regularly sent back notes expressing his gratitude.

"The speech" was not to run over thirty minutes, not counting opening remarks and local adaptations, but had enough material to run ninety minutes. The object was to take the most appropriate thirty minutes for the local audience. I regularly updated the speech, especially in terms of new evidence and current events. But the main themes were set, the major issues engaged. And that made my job a little easier. It also gave me a chance to put some of my existential beliefs into Bush's mouth. Here's a passage from Bush's call to the Republican Party to return to its roots by creating our own identity and building our own home in the American political system. This Party was born out of a struggle for principle and if it is to survive and flourish, to principle it must return. . . . Nothing creative, nothing worth while exists that does not come from the individual or from cooperation among individuals. It is not society that provides us with inventions, but individuals. It is not society that creates art, but single individuals. The individual in freedom is the productive force of this greatest of all cultures.

After a discussion of such other core values as "security," "responsibility," and "freedom," Bush moved to the meat and potatoes of his speech, beginning with an attack on the Carter administration:

It seeks compromise at almost any cost. It would not only surrender the Panama Canal but pay the Panamanians to take it. It would not only renegotiate the SALT agreement, but would rewrite it to our disadvantage. . . . First, we must maintain a credible force: This means we must not only develop the B-1 Bomber and the MX and Cruise missiles, but any other weapon that proves us credible. . . . We cannot on the one hand surrender Angola to Cuba, and on the other maintain credibility in Latin America.

The transition to domestic issues was a natural for Bush, given his strong record on civil rights:

We must guarantee human rights at home before we can advocate them abroad. . . . Reducing unemployment among our minorities will give credibility to our call for human rights abroad. . . . Let's provide incentives not only for energy exploration but for economic growth. Let's plan on steady development, not with hit or miss programs, but with a full range of research and development options including solar, wind, geothermal, oil shale, and nuclear. And let's assess our environmental needs not with passion and prejudice, but with objectivity and optimism.

The speech holds up pretty well over thirty years later.

Because Bush came to Alabama, and news was spreading about the work of Bill Harris and me to rebuild the party there, more speakers came. In the spring, I was delighted to welcome former President Ford to the university, which further enhanced my credibility there. Afterward, I treated myself to a solo trip down to Fort Walton Beach on the Florida Gulf Coast. The sand was white and clean; the water was warm, aquamarine, and clear. The trip gave me time to meditate on my life and pray for spiritual growth in the midst of all the political activity. It was important to keep the inner spiritual core strong if I was to remain creative and at peace in the closet.

When I returned to Birmingham, I continued my spiritual quest over dinners with Michael Hyde. I kept in physical shape by playing a lot of tennis. I kept in mental shape by teaching my classes and publishing my research. The University of Alabama, Birmingham was getting a reputation as a good place for young professors to begin a career, which was fine with me. I wanted new PhDs so I didn't have to break any bad habits that were formed by professors coming from other departments.

In March 1978, Bush asked me to consider moving to Houston for the summer to work on his campaign. I told him I wasn't interested in doing the job full-time. I could fly over from Birmingham whenever he needed me. At the end of the spring, Bush gave several commencement addresses, which gave me a chance to nudge him a little further down the road to a "kinder, gentler nation" with spiritual values. At Phillips Exeter Academy in Andover, from which he graduated before attending Yale, Bush told the students:

> I believe the pursuit of happiness should be a spiritual quest, not a material game. The real rewards in life are personal, not public; they are moral, not monetary; they are of the heart, not of the intellect. . . . This spirit of sacrifice would direct us toward magnanimity, to helping, to sharing. It would direct us away from self seeking, self satisfaction, and self indulgence. . . . The role of the private citizen in a democracy is to assure that the political and economic foundations remain strong, to work for the spiritual values that hold the nation together, and to demonstrate beyond a doubt the power of individual action in a mass society. If our citizens will accept this challenge, we can restore faith where cynicism now prevails. We can bring hope where despair now prevails. We can continue the struggle for individual freedom where collectivism now prevails.

The summer became rather hectic. I had speeches to give in Alabama and I enjoyed getting to know the state better. There were trips to Houston to work on speeches, meet with the political team headed by Jim Baker, and get to know Bush better. One day he asked me to sit in on a meeting in his office. Bush's son George W. was running for Congress from the district in west Texas that centered on the city of Midland. There was some talk that the rowdy younger Bush would be challenged in the primary by a member of the Christian Right. So his father decided to meet with a leading clergyman from Midland in an effort to gain support for his son and to dissuade the Christian Right from fielding a candidate. I would serve as a witness to the conversation so that the minister could not make false claims about it later. The Christian Right rejected Bush's advice, and though his son won the primary, he lost the general election in part because the Republicans had been divided by the primary fight. This lesson was not lost on George W. or his father. Unfortunately, it made them, in my opinion, much too deferential to the Christian Right.

MURDER IN MOBILE

Back in Birmingham that summer, news arrived that Alabama Democratic Senator "Big Jim" Allen, a master of Senate parliamentary procedure, had died. Bill Harris and I decided this presented us with an opportunity to test the revitalized Republican Party. We recruited a former Republican congressman from Birmingham, Jim Martin, to run for the newly open seat. The Democrats nominated Don McDonald, a liberal labor lawyer. Martin and I hit it off and he asked me to write his speeches and coach him through the campaign. I told him we could do to McDonald what Ford did to Carter: force him into debates and then reveal to the public what a liberal he was. Martin agreed with the strategy; the problem was that McDonald was smart, way ahead in the polls, and knew that the debates would give exposure to Martin's underfunded campaign. I told Martin to keep hammering for a debate. "Call the man a coward if you have to."

Martin was a quick study when it came to speeches, and I quickly adapted his policies to the Alabama electorate. We were short on funds for the campaign, so we took advantage of every possible event to get Jim free airtime. He flipped more pancakes than Aunt Jemima. Slowly, our poll numbers improved. Soon the National Republican Senatorial Campaign Committee (NRSCC) took notice of our race and sent a consultant, let's call him Sean, down in October. We struck up a fast friendship; he was witty, a devotee of Theodore Roosevelt—he had even developed a Roosevelt accent. On his second visit, he revealed to me that he was a closeted gay man with a wife and child. He sensed that I was gay and I allowed as I was. It was such a relief to have someone to talk to who was in a similar situation to mine. However, the fact that he was deep into the cover-up with a wife and child was troubling. We exchanged views on what it is like to be in the closet in the Republican Party and became loyal but unromantic friends.

At Sean's suggestion, the NRSCC pumped some money into the campaign. That gave us another boost when we put all of that money into television and radio commercials, some of which continued the drumbeat for a debate. Soon the news media was hammering McDonald about not debating with Martin. Finally, McDonald caved and agreed to one debate in late October. I negotiated the tedious details with his staff. Because they were all labor lawyers, the final agreement took some time to work out. My mantra became, "If you insist on that rule, I have to go to the news media and explain how unfair you are being." However, I got the debate into the 6 P.M. dinner slot when most Alabamans could watch it on television when they got home from work.

A few days before it was to take place, we flew to Mobile on a private plane with Martin's campaign manager and the brother of the late Senator Allen. In Mobile, Martin and I worked on debate strategy. At a fund-raising dinner, Allen's brother and the senator's widow endorsed Martin for the Senate seat, opening the door to crossover Democratic voters. Our timing was perfect; the newspapers went crazy with the story. The next morning, Martin appeared with Senator Barry Goldwater on a destroyer in Mobile Bay to push defense issues. That afternoon, we were scheduled to fly back to Birmingham on the private plane and continue to ready Jim for the big debate. However, after the press event with Goldwater, Jim told his campaign manager that he wanted to stay in Mobile an extra day with me, away from distractions. Jim's campaign manager and Allen's brother were to take the private plane back to Birmingham; we would follow on a commercial jet the next morning. Allen's widow planned to stay with friends in Mobile for a few days.

Just as we were finishing rehearsing Jim for the debate, the phone in his hotel room rang. Jim picked it up and suddenly turned ashen. He almost fell over the bed trying to seat himself. He ended the phone conversation with, "I understand. I understand. Of course, make all the necessary arrangements." The private plane carrying our campaign manager and Allen's brother had crashed. No one survived.

The debate was canceled, the funerals were held, and suddenly it was election day. Throughout the day, Bill Harris and I got news of different kinds of election fraud across the state, which we promptly reported to election officials and the FBI. In many rural districts, the lever next to Martin's name had been removed from voting machines. In the cities in the evening, Democrats loaded school buses with poor people, handed them what is called "walking around money," and had them vote in place of people who had not shown up at the polls. Despite these tactics, Jim Martin carried every major city in the state of Alabama. But it was not enough. McDonald carried rural precincts by huge margins, sometimes ten to one. In the end, Martin got 45 percent of the vote to McDonald's 55 percent.

A few weeks later, the report on the plane crash was completed by the FAA and the FBI. They ruled that the plane had been sabotaged; its fuel lines were cut. The perpetrators of the crime were never found. I never forgot how close Jim and I came to being killed along with the others on our staff. Then another event reinforced my feelings of mortality. I had followed Harvey Milk's career with interest. He was a gay activist who got elected to the San Francisco Board of Supervisors, the first openly gay person elected to public office in America. Another member of the board, Dan White, couldn't deal with Milk's positions, nor those of Mayor Moscone, and on November 27, 1978, White killed them. He would get off on an insanity plea, claiming he had become deranged by eating too many sweets.

All of this was too much for me. I accepted an invitation to be a guest professor at Northwestern University in Evanston, Illinois, for the winter quarter. I wanted some away time to consider what to do with my life and whether now was the time to come out. However, I was about to become deeply embedded in the machinery of the national Republican Party.

CHAPTER EIGHT

Working for the United States Senate

ON JANUARY 5, 1979, I RECEIVED A LETTER FROM GEORGE BUSH informing me that he had put together the "George Bush for President Committee." Jim Baker was named committee chair. Then Bush added, "Needless to say, I want and need your help in this. . . . It would be great to have you involved."[1]

While Jim Martin had lost his Senate race, he had made a strong showing; in other states, the Republicans had done quite well, picking up enough seats to make the chairman of the National Republican Senatorial Campaign Committee into a hero. His name was Bob Packwood, former boy wonder from Oregon. Because he would be up for reelection to the Senate in 1980, he had to give up his post as chairman of the NRSCC and accepted the post of chairman of the Republican Senate Conference, at that point a largely ceremonial post for the Republican caucus. Packwood decided he wanted to energize the Conference. If he could make it into something worthwhile, it would be a step toward him becoming minority or majority leader.

He sat down with his staff in February 1979 to plot the ways in which he could serve his fellow Republican senators and thereby make them beholden to him. Packwood named Sean, who had come to Birmingham to assess the Martin campaign, executive director of the Republican Conference. Sean suggested to Packwood that the Conference staff be composed of people who could provide media services, including speech and editorial writing, and commercial and public service announcements, back to the senators' home states. Sean suggested me for the speech and editorial writing operation. Packwood approved the concept and I was invited to Washington, D.C., for an interview with Mimi Weyforth Dawson, Packwood's chief of staff.

I met with Mimi in the spring of 1979 after returning from my stint at Northwestern University. Her desk sat in the middle of the suite of offices the Senator occupied. She was surrounded by secretaries and legislative assistants because she wanted "to keep an eye on them." Her desk was littered with Coke cans; she had an addiction to Coca-Cola, reinforced by her efforts to stop smoking. She also had a weight problem at the time I arrived, which meant her physical presence matched her psychological power. Both were large.

She was impressed with my speechwriting expertise at the presidential level, my managerial skills at the academic level, and my political knowledge from the Ford, Bush, and Martin campaigns. I returned to Birmingham believing that I was going to get a job offer. However, I was asked to return to D.C. in May for two days of interviews with other Republican senators' administrative assistants (in reality chiefs of staff). I met with nine of them, and again the interviews went well. On June 2, I was offered the position of director of Senate Services for the Republican Conference of the United States Senate. I began to add up all the pluses and minuses of my current position and a return to Washington. Could I do more good on the porches of Birmingham and in my classrooms than I could do back in Washington, D.C.? But that was not the right question. The existential question was could I live with myself for the rest of my life knowing I passed up a chance to get back into politics and serve at the national level? The bottom line was that while I loved living in Birmingham, and while I was proud of the job I had done at the university, I hadn't gotten Washington out of my system. I had Potomac fever and needed to be where my potential would take me.[2] I was confident that I could always return to the academic world.

In the meantime, the Bushes came to Birmingham in the spring, with azaleas and white and pink dogwoods blooming all over the place. Barbara wowed the campus with a lecture about her experiences in China. George spoke in the evening downtown, and instead of giving the stump speech, he spoke off the cuff and it did not go well. I wrote to Jim Baker that the speech, if you want to call it that, failed because Bush "took no stands on the issues. Worse, the speech had no punch lines. He wandered all over the place. I really wish I could come over, work through his speech again, and rehearse him, rehearse him, rehearse him."

On May 4, Bush returned to Alabama to raise money. One item of note on his schedule was a speech in rural Clanton, a tough sell to the redneck crowd. However, they were just the kind of people that could help Bush win the primary a year later. Barbara accompanied her husband on this trip, and after a buffet-style dinner in a gymnasium, Bush was introduced by the local

GOP chairman, who used my introduction. Well-rehearsed, Bush used the speech I wrote for the occasion. When he finished to a standing ovation, I turned to Barbara and asked, "What did you think of the speech?"

She looked me straight in the eye and responded, "It's not important what I think, Craig. It is important what you think."

"He did very well. Have you been making him rehearse?"

"Yes." She looked away. "But he hates it. He thinks it is unmanly to rehearse a speech."

"That's silly. All the great speakers rehearse."

"Why don't *you* tell him that?"

Luckily, CBS News covered the speech and gave it solid reviews. They were impressed with the organization of a raft of facts that demonstrated Bush's command of the issues. Bill Harris told me, "Tonight, for the first time I saw the possibility of a Bush victory in Alabama."

Events took another turn when Dean Hearn got promoted to vice president for academic affairs. I had missed what was going on in terms of campus politics while teaching at Northwestern. I came by to congratulate Tom on his appointment and he surprised me with a new possibility. "Craig," he said, "you've done a great job as director of the Communication Arts Division. While the other department chairs have various talents, none of them can match your administrative skills. I'd like you to consider becoming interim dean of the College of Humanities."

"Wow, I never expected that."

"It would set you up to be the permanent dean. During your interim year, we do have to run a national search for the position, but I can't imagine that we'd attract anyone as talented as you."

"Can I think about it?"

"What's to think about? It's a promotion and much higher salary."

"Well, Tom, I have another offer in hand." I confessed that I'd been to Washington for an interview and I would have to weigh that offer against his.

While I could be making more as a dean, at thirty-four, I wasn't ready to devote the rest of my career to academia in the Deep South. An offer like the one I received from Packwood might never come again. I accepted the job in Washington, D.C. I felt like I was heading home. Any guilt about leaving was assuaged when Cully Clark agreed to come over from Tuscaloosa to take my place as director of the Communication Arts Division.

However, there was one more event that took place in Birmingham that provided a fitting farewell. Though I had little admiration for the man's past actions, I put in a request to ex-governor George Wallace to come to campus, because he was a historic figure. I also knew that he began his career as a populist fighting for the little guy, but lost his first election to a race-baiter. That would never happen to Wallace again. However, some believed that in his heart, he really wasn't a racist. Wallace agreed to give a lecture to students in our summer session on June 24, 1979. Wallace was wheelchair-bound because of the assassination attempt on his life in the 1972 Maryland primary. The Wallace entourage arrived replete with highway patrol guards. He was in a three-piece suit and sitting in a wheelchair. I introduced him to the assembled students. He said he wanted to talk "for a bit to you all here in Buh-min-ham" and then he would take questions from the students.

What followed was an impressive display of knowledge about effective political communication. Wallace said that in the political world, "You must learn to oversimplify to be successful. Shorthand rendition of the facts in a shorter period of time is more attractive to people."[3] In the question and answer period, when Wallace was asked which papers he read, he included the *New York Times*, which in campaigns he had ridiculed as full of "pointy headed liberals." When a student asked him why he read the *Times*, he replied, "Because I need to know what the enemy is thinking." In terms of his own style, Wallace said it was partly derived from Harry Truman and Billy Graham. Then came a question about Martin Luther King Jr. Wallace replied, "He was a very good speaker. You know he was effective when buildings, streets, and days were named after him." He was then asked in light of his being shot, whether he had changed his mind about gun control. He responded, "No, I was shot in a state with gun control. Four people were shot. We were all shot in a gun control state." Then Wallace suddenly cut off the session, said his goodbyes, and headed out of the building. Had the question offended him? I wondered.

Though the ending seemed a little abrupt to me, I was impressed with Wallace's facility with language. That night while I was cooking for a few friends, the phone rang:

"Hello," I said.

"Is this Dr. Smith from UAB?"

"Yes, it is. How can I help you?"

"Do you have a moment to speak with Governor Wallace?"

"Why, yes, of course?"

Wallace was put on the line. "Dr. Smith, I owe you an apology."

"Governor, please call me Craig, and why would you owe me an apology?"

"Well, my damned hearing aids went out, and I couldn't hear the questions anymore, so I had to cut off the interview session. And I was having such a good time. I just wanted to apologize and thank you for your hospitality."

"Governor, you are most welcome. I don't think the students realized that anything was amiss."

"I'm glad to hear that. And by the way, Cornelia and I would love you to join us for dinner sometime soon." Cornelia, his second wife,[4] had been a Miss Alabama.

"That would be wonderful, Governor."

"Good. My staff will be in touch."

"Thank you, and have a good evening."

"You too, Craig."

I never did get down to Montgomery before I left for Washington, D.C. But I remember Wallace for his honesty and the way he related to the students that hot June day in "Buh-min-ham."

SERVING A SENATOR

As a new employee, I came to Senator Packwood's office to introduce myself. He was only a dozen years older than I, having started his U.S. Senate career in the year I started teaching at San Diego State. He wasn't much for small talk. He quickly made clear that he wanted to return the Republican Conference of the U.S. Senate to its pre–World War II glory days as a propaganda machine for Republican ideas, by which he meant moderate senators' ideas. He liked the idea of me writing editorials and speeches for his colleagues, knowing full well the value of IOUs on Capitol Hill. However, like President Ford, he was leery of professors; he told me they were too theoretical and absent-minded to survive on Capitol Hill. The only good one he ever had was Mark Hatfield at Willamette University in Salem, Oregon, and Hatfield left academia to become the most beloved governor and then senator in Oregon's history. Packwood, the junior senator to Hatfield's senior, would let me prove myself because of my White House experience, but he had his doubts about my ability to tough it out in Washington.

I noted the similarities between myself and Packwood. He and I had been high school and college orators and debaters. We both loved history, particularly European history. We often slipped into arcane discussions of historic moments that excluded the rest of his staff and made me feel close to him. We both grew up in lower-middle-class families. Like me, Packwood had no need of speechwriters, though he was not averse to accepting suggestions for a well-turned phrase. Because he had cataract problems, he had to memorize large sections of his speeches for delivery, and writing them out helped him in the memorization process. We were both environmentalists and fiscal conservatives. We favored a strong military and opposed protracted wars. And I would eventually convert him to favoring gun-control legislation, though he needed the NRA to win elections in Oregon. There were differences. While my voice is fine, it has a nasal quality that is sometimes marked by a lisp. His baritone was more audience- and media-friendly. He was an agnostic who favored a woman's right to an abortion; I'm a Catholic who does not. He abjured the spiritual world; I embraced it.

One of my advantages in terms of building a relationship with Packwood was that my stories about writing for President Ford and operating in the White House fascinated him. I could see that Packwood had ambitions beyond being a senator; like many men of his generation, he had not given up on the dream of becoming president of the United States.

I soon learned that the Senate was different than the White House. It was separated into the famous chamber in the Capitol and offices of senators in the Russell, Dirksen, and Hart Buildings. Since it was more elegant and a quicker walk from the Capitol, the Russell Building was the preferred office location. Every two years after the national election, some senators would not be returning, and seniority determined who got their offices. When there is a change in which party has the majority, wholesale office swapping occurs. Though we were the minority party, the office of the Republican Conference was in a beautiful room in the Russell Building with ancient globes of light with stars etched in them; the globes hung from the ornate wood-carved ceiling. We shared the large space with the Republican Senate Policy Committee, run by Senator John Tower of Texas, and all of us had separate desks. I particularly liked the fact that we were not in separate offices or cubicles where it was easy to get bored, as I had learned in the Old Executive Office Building while a presidential speechwriter. The senators were accessible to us. When I got my first haircut in the basement of the Hart Building, Senator Edmund Muskie of Maine sat in the chair right next to me and was perfectly happy to chat.

I soon learned that Senate staff could be as territorial as White House staff. My proposals to upgrade the Conference came under immediate attack from Packwood's loyalists. I found that neither Mimi nor Sean had laid the groundwork for my arrival. Packwood encouraged competition among his staff, so they went after my memo laying out a plan of action. I was depressed by the attacks, but figured out that I needed to fight back if I were to survive in my new position. My debate training stood me in good stead; I refuted their objections one by one. I also took a course at the Library of Congress to master parliamentary procedure in the Senate; the procedures are quite arcane and take on a language of their own. That is why senators try to operate by "unanimous consent." Once someone objects to a motion, the Senate falls into parliamentary hell, often run by the oldest members of the Senate and their staff because they are the only ones who can figure out what is going on. These rules include the anti-democratic filibuster, which ostensibly protects the minority party or a minority faction. The filibuster was enshrined in American civil religion by Frank Capra's film *Mr. Smith Goes to Washington.* The real truth about the filibuster is that it is horribly anti-democratic and was used to bottle up civil rights legislation for years. When I came to the Senate, 60 votes were required to shut down a filibuster. Since neither party had 60 votes, some senators needed to cross the aisle for a filibuster to be stopped. The knowledge I gained in Senate parliamentary procedure was one more asset I could offer to Packwood's colleagues.

It didn't take long before senators were calling Packwood, thanking him for speeches and editorials I wrote for them. I conducted writing seminars for their staffs, which proved popular. A typical letter from Packwood to a senator read this way: "Dear Sam [Hayakawa]: I am, of course, delighted to make Dr. Craig Smith available to you to conduct a writing seminar for your staff, and I understand he has already started. He told me that about 23 of your staff participated in the first session earlier this week."[5] These seminars were a win-win. The staff members learned a valuable skill and then were able to take the writing burden off of me. I made reports at the weekly meetings of the Republican senators' chiefs of staff.

My position was not assured until late July, when Packwood's staff went on a retreat in Culpepper, Virginia, some thirty miles down the road from the Capitol in the countryside filled with Civil War battlefields. Each unit of the Packwood empire was to give a report and answer questions from the Senator, which often took on a prosecutorial tone. On the first night after arrival and dinner, Mimi rehearsed us to make sure she knew what we were going to say. Packwood did not like surprises. After the rehearsals, Packwood led us in his favorite game: charades. My team barely beat his team, when my team guessed the movie title I was assigned in 30 seconds. Ironically, the title was *Thirty Seconds over Tokyo.* Over martinis, Packwood expressed his admiration for my quick study: "You know, I think charades is the best way to determine the quality of a person. We play it at every social event I host for the staff. Benjamin Disraeli, the prime minister of England, played the game at parties at his estate in the late nineteenth century."

The next day, Mimi led off and some of the staff gave supporting reports on legislative initiatives. Mary Hasenfus reported on the preparations for Packwood's impending 1980 reelection campaign. Bill Diefendorfer reported as the staff director for the Minority Staff of the Committee on Commerce,

Science, and Transportation, on which Packwood was ranking minority member. Finally came Sean with a report on the Conference, which I would supplement. Packwood was scheduled to wrap up right after I finished. I was infuriated as I waited to give my report because Sean was over time and way off script. I could see that Packwood was fidgeting and Mimi was glowering. Finally, Sean introduced me. As I began my report, Mimi looked at me and pulled her thumb across her throat. I transformed myself into a college debater, speaking at about 300 words a minute. Packwood literally fell out of his chair laughing.[6] He then got up and thanked me "for that imitation of Noel Coward,"[7] and gave his speech. We all got drunk that night, and Packwood and I could be seen in private conversation often.

I came up for air and reestablished my ties with friends, mostly former Virginia students in the area. I had rented a rooftop, 13th floor pillbox that was the only apartment on the top of Jefferson Building in the Arlington Towers complex on the Potomac River.[8] The previous occupant of my little box was the famous political cartoonist Herb Block of the *Washington Post*, who had always caricatured Nixon with a five o'clock shadow. I could see why Block loved the apartment. The two-story loft contained a bedroom that sat over the kitchen looking into the two-story living room, which had a 180-degree view of the Potomac that started at the Francis Scott Key Bridge into Georgetown, swept past the monuments on the Mall, and finished looking down to the Pentagon. The one drawback was that planes landing at National Airport, now Reagan Airport, flew right over the place. I believed I could touch their bellies at times. Luckily, National had an 11 P.M. curfew.

THE RISE OF PACKWOOD

Since I became a leader in the Packwood organization and was involved with it for many years, it is important that the reader understand who Packwood was and how he rose to such prominence. His story tells us a lot about American politics. In 1964, as a thirty-two-year-old member of the Oregon State House of Representatives, Bob Packwood developed some new ways of campaigning that included extensive use of volunteers. Packwood and his wife Georgie mapped out routes on detailed city maps to make sure every citizen in high-turnout voting areas was contacted in some way. The maps were the most efficient routes through these neighborhoods and were carried by pairs of volunteers. If they received no answer when they knocked on a door, they left literature and marked the address down so they could return on another day. If the door opened, the neighbor was given literature and asked if he or she would allow the team to put up a lawn sign for Packwood in the weeks leading up to the election. The lawn signs, which suddenly seemed to spontaneously spring up everywhere, were maintained by the volunteers, who removed them the day after the election. Backing the entire volunteer operation were phone banks used to gather more volunteers, more household locations, and to turn out the vote on election day.

Packwood not only developed this highly detailed system, he sold it to his Republican colleagues in Oregon. In the face of Democrat Lyndon Johnson's overwhelming presidential landslide in 1964, Packwood's machine actually succeeded in winning a Republican majority in the Oregon House. That made Packwood the Republican whiz kid. He was brought to Washington, D.C., to explain just how he had done it. He continued to organize in Oregon despite the news media's position that the Republican Party could never recover from the Goldwater defeat.

The media had been wrong on this point before and would be proved wrong again. By 1966, Lyndon Johnson's Great Society was a mess. Inflation was increasing. In 1965 serious race riots in the Watts district of Los Angeles frightened the nation. The war in Vietnam continued to escalate, with continuing body counts on the evening news. In November of 1966, the Republican Phoenix rose from its ashes to score impressive comebacks in the midterm elections. The Grand Old Party reestablished working minorities in the House and Senate. As I mentioned in chapter 1, Ronald Reagan became governor of California; George Romney became governor of Michigan; Nelson Rockefeller was reelected governor of New York. And, of course, Richard Nixon, who had helped so many candidates over the years, was once again mentioned as a candidate for president. The Republican field would be crowded in 1968; the scent of victory was in the air just four short years after the Goldwater debacle.

In Oregon, when no other Republican would challenge the redoubtable Democratic senator from Oregon, Wayne Morse, Packwood saw a chance to take a giant step forward. Morse had been elected as a Republican years before, but had become increasing liberal. He became an independent in the early '60s and was one of only two senators who opposed the Gulf of Tonkin Resolution in 1964, which authorized Lyndon Johnson to escalate the war in Vietnam. Morse became a Democrat and continued to be one of the war's most vociferous critics. With the Tet Offensive of early 1968, the election became a referendum on the war. Viet Cong troops had penetrated the American Embassy grounds, and though they had suffered tremendous losses, the Cong had punched a psychological hole in the American ego. The country divided sharply as to how to conduct the war. With over 400,000 troops committed, President Johnson was not backing down. Eventually, three times as many bombs as we dropped in all of World War II were dropped on Vietnam.

Packwood was a hawk on the war, though he had never served in the military because of his eyes. In the 1968 campaign, Packwood consistently tried to force Morse into a debate. Morse refused, and Packwood remained far behind in the polls. Then fortune struck. At the national level, Nixon had refused to debate Humphrey, who had replaced Johnson when the president took himself out of the race. Then one day, Humphrey came to Oregon to campaign with Morse. With Morse beside him on the platform, Humphrey said Nixon was a coward for not debating him. Packwood jumped on the opportunity and forced Morse into a debate. A few days before the debate, Morse's press secretary and close friend died. During the debate, Morse seemed off balance; Packwood was young and aggressive. When asked what he would do about war protesters, he said he would "throw those kooks in jail." The debate was televised statewide from the Portland City Club, which was filled with a conservative audience. Encouraged by the audience's cheers and guided by his own talent, Packwood won the debate easily. The victory fired up Packwood's huge grassroots effort. Lawn signs sprang up like tulips. Packwood made up ground in the polls. Fundraising took off, especially when businessman Bill DeWiess put together $300,000 for a new round of commercials. On election day, the Oregon returns showed a dead heat. After several recounts and court rulings, Packwood was declared the winner and became the youngest member of the 1969 Senate.

Packwood's Senate campaign set the model for his next four successful reelections, which also included a hugely successful fundraising operation. There was one other thing that would become a Packwood campaign trademark and ultimately come to haunt him. Packwood was particularly taken by how detail-oriented women were in campaigns. His wife Georgie had always served as second-in-command, and his mother Mindy worked with volunteers.[9] So women were prominent in Packwood campaigns. For the 1968 campaign, for example, Anne Elias was campaign manager.

However, rumors spread that Packwood, after drinking, came on to women. In 1992 Julie Williamson would allege that late one day in 1969 in his office, Packwood accosted her. She claimed that he pinned her to the wall, stepped on her toes, and tried to remove her girdle. She fought him off. The odd thing about Williamson's story is that by her own account, on the same day as the alleged attack, she came back to Packwood's office. Then she drove him home as was her custom; he could not drive because of his bad eyes. Evidently trying to prove that truth is stranger than fiction, she claimed that she bawled Packwood out in the car and that he never bothered her again.[10]

When Packwood began to work on his reelection campaign for 1974, his chief of staff told him that he needed to dress like a senator, not a mismatched college freshman. Packwood's poor eyesight included a lack of ability to see certain colors. Furthermore, Packwood did not believe that clothes make the person, and cared little for style. His wife had tried to overcome his careless attitude, to no avail. So he often went to the office wearing uncoordinated ties, jackets, socks, shoes, and pants. His chief of staff came up with the idea of tagging all of his dress clothes and shoes either A, B, or C. All of the items marked A went together; all of the items marked B went together; and all of the items marked C were also coordinated. That way, Packwood would no longer be a fashion embarrassment on Capitol Hill.

Senator Packwood made two crucial decisions as the 1974 campaign began in the midst of the Watergate crisis: first, he would raise as much money as possible; second, he would appeal to what he called "unnatural constituencies for a Republican." These included feminists, union members, and ecologists. By 1974, when Packwood was renominated for the Senate, he had the support of such noted women as feminist Gloria Steinem. He had won over the building and trade unions. And he had become a champion of saving the whales. In fact, he gave secret information regarding the location of the Soviet whaling fleet to Greenpeace. This allowed Greenpeace to harass the Russians and make national headlines.[11]

As expected, the Democrats renominated ex-senator Wayne Morse. This was the first election after the great Watergate scandal. Once again, the media was writing the obituary of the Republican Party. Republicans around the country who had defended Nixon would go down in droves. But in Oregon in the summer of 1974, Morse died of a heart attack. The Democrats scrambled to find someone to put up against Packwood. They nominated state legislator Betty Roberts, trying to regain the women's vote. Roberts was no match for Packwood, particularly in debates. He won overwhelmingly.

Packwood had assembled a first-rate staff, which burnished his image as a brilliant senator, a tough taskmaster, and a perfectionist. He had remarkable control over, and concern for, details. An apocryphal story greeted each new addition to the staff. Sean told the story to me. "The Senator pays us to think. It's our job. If you wrote a news release claiming that the Senator wanted the United States to invade Mexico, the Senator would defend your judgment. 'I pay Craig to think,' he'd claim. But if you'd misspelled Mexico, he'd fire your ass!" I got the point, while Sean chuckled.

Here's a passage from a typical Packwood memo on formatting a briefing page for him:

> Occasionally staff puts into the briefing book material that runs horizontally across an 8½ x 11 page rather than vertically. While I prefer it vertically, it's not always possible. I would prefer, however, if when material is prepared horizontally that the holes be punched at the top of the page rather than at the bottom.

Packwood was an Anglophile who, as I mentioned, loved European history.[12] Once when we were traveling on the Metroliner to New York City for a speech to the NBC board and other important figures, Packwood and I got into an argument over who first owned the duchy of Schleswig-Holstein near Denmark. When we returned to Washington, Packwood demanded I prove my point since the Library of Congress study on the matter that he had ordered supported his view. Thank God for my high school history teacher, Jim Doyle. I proved the Library of Congress wrong.

By now, I was as happy and as secure as one can be in the Washington environment. For example, in the fall of 1979, Jim Fallows, who wrote speeches early in the Carter administration, and I put on a bipartisan talk on the art of speechwriting. I met Frank Gannon, the former Nixon staffer who was now the chief of staff for Senator John Heinz, the handsome heir to the company fortune. I met Heinz and his wife Theresa on several occasions. Packwood was jealous of Heinz's fortune, natural grace, and good looks. He didn't like it one bit that many people were talking about Heinz as a potential presidential contender.[13] It was as if Packwood was playing Nixon to Heinz's Republican version of John Kennedy.

When my friends came to my place, over drinks, we would look down the Potomac as the monuments lit up. Each day I was awed by the fact that I was driving to the Capitol to work for a leading senator. At lunchtime, I would walk among the monuments or visit the museums on the Mall or be taken to lunch by a lobbyist, friend, or colleague. On the weekends, I could travel to the Chesapeake or up to Binghamton to see John Macksoud, who now lived in a small apartment. John kept me thoroughly grounded. Philosophical discussions were rigorous. Every assumption was questioned; every move that hindered a spiritual connection was condemned. Then everything was reassembled.

During one of these sessions, John told me that my worst enemies were boredom and loneliness. "Why?" I asked him.

"Because to escape either one, you will sometimes do desperate things. Try to embrace them, turn them into opportunities for meditation," he wisely advised. Every time I left those meetings, I came away more sure of my values and goals.

ADVISING BUSH

While all of that was going on, I kept writing speeches and editorials for senators and kept in touch with George Bush, who was now running full bore for president. The Republican field was crowded, but he thought he had a good shot. He believed that Reagan was too old to win the nomination, having failed to gain it in 1968 and 1976. Howard Baker, the minority leader from Tennessee, reminded people of Carter, though Baker might make a nice vice-presidential nominee to sew up the South. Bob Dole, senator from Kansas, had been on the losing 1976 ticket, and his performance in the vice-presidential debate with Mondale was seen, rightly or wrongly, as one cause for the loss to Carter. Jim Thompson, the governor of Illinois, posed a bigger threat, but he was not a great speaker. And then there was John Connally, who was tearing things up with his rough and ready rhetorical style. The bet was that the race would come down to Bush and Connally in the Texas primary.

I continued to counsel Bush. For example, after the Iowa debate of leading candidates, I sent Bush a long memo evaluating his performance. I made the following points:[14]

1. Use all of your time. You had a tendency to answer quickly and cryptically. In an oral situation, people retain only about a third of what they hear. Give them an introduction, organized data, and a conclusion. Your answer on the agricultural questions—your first full one and number six in the format—was severely weakened by a lack of direction. 2. Stay on your turf. Begin and end with your position and make it sound positive. Sandwich attacks and refutations in between. Your energy answer was a good one but could have been more powerful if handled as follows: "Since 1968, when I was on the House Ways and Means Committee, I have advocated the decontrol of oil prices along with sensible windfall profits' taxes. Decontrol makes conservation a natural product of market forces. Decontrol encourages exploration. Decontrol makes alternate energy fuels competitive. Those who would tax or ration fuel impose artificial government regulation on the free market system. It hasn't worked in the past

and it won't work in the future. That's why I have always favored decontrol and natural market forces to help us become energy independent." 3. Watch out for missing premises. You are so bright and knowledgeable that you assume a good deal when you answer a question. Unfortunately, the public is not as knowledgeable and so they don't understand elliptical answers. 4. If you use an anecdote or aphorism, don't go back and use it again. You give the appearance of having a limited stock of material and of being programmed. 5. There may not be much difference between the candidates on issues, but there are some real differences in personality. I want a talented, compassionate, sensitive, bright man in the White House. So be yourself and you'll be president. You don't need to feign strength; television catches that kind of insincerity.[15]

Bush responded in his own hand, "Keep the ideas coming on how to deal with Reagan."[16]

When Bush won the Iowa caucuses in early 1980,[17] it made him the front-runner. But once he won Iowa, he claimed he had the "big mo," meaning momentum. That was a mistake. It is unpresidential to talk about politics as if it were a football game. Besides, he needed to stay on message, and for him that meant sticking to the issues that people cared about most. He would pay for this shift in tone and set up what I would call the battle between the good guys (me and Barbara Bush, among others) and the bad guys (Lee Atwater and Vic Gold, among others) on his staff.

Matters first came to a head in New Hampshire in March when Bush got sandbagged at a debate set up by the Reagan staff. They agreed to pay for a debate in New Hampshire, and Bush agreed to participate as long as it was one-on-one between the two leading candidates. Someone should have smelled a rat. Once Bush arrived at the venue, the other Republican candidates showed up and Reagan said they should be allowed into the debate. While the various staffs wrangled over what would happen next, Bush stayed onstage and bantered with the audience. Finally, Reagan came back to explain what had been agreed upon. He and Bush would debate after the other Republican candidates were allowed to make a short statement. When the local publisher who was sponsoring the debate tried to cut Reagan off, he yelled, "I paid for this microphone, Mr. Green," echoing a line from the Spencer Tracy film *State of the Union*. Reagan's angry one-liner showed he had real blood in his veins, and it was played on all the news shows the next day. Very little coverage was given to Bush and Reagan's debate. Reagan went on to win in New Hampshire and became the major obstacle to Bush getting the nomination.

TIDEWATER

The best event that Senator Packwood organized during those halcyon days was the Tidewater Conference, which took place at the quaint Tidewater Inn in Easton, Maryland, in early February. Years before, Packwood had put together a Dorchester Conference in Oregon for state Republicans where they would plot strategy, discuss issues, and have some fun putting on skits at a closing banquet. Packwood had decided that as the out party, the Republicans needed a national version of Dorchester. Over two days, statewide elected Republicans (governors, attorney generals, secretaries of state, etc.) and Republicans elected to the U.S. Senate and House would gather and debate five legislative resolutions.

The third Tidewater Conference was my first. These conferences were a success for a number of reasons. First, Packwood planned them efficiently; he saw to every detail, including the invitations to be mailed, the rules of conduct, and the resolutions to be debated. Second, Packwood supplied the staff for the conferences, and attendees were allowed to bring only spouses. Spouses were allowed to participate in the debates, but not to vote on the resolutions. At the third and subsequent Tidewater Conferences, I served as parliamentarian, and prominent Republicans were selected as chairs of each session. Thus, I functioned as the keeper of order for such notables as Congressman Jack Kemp and Senator Alan Simpson. I was able to renew my acquaintance with Dick Cheney, now a congressman. As far as Senator Packwood was concerned, no task was beneath any staff member's dignity. It would not be unusual for Packwood to call a staff member and tell them to head back to Washington, D.C., to pick up a lost bag at Dulles Airport for a visiting dignitary.

One night I was assigned the task of awaiting the arrival of Senator John Warner and his wife Elizabeth Taylor to make sure all was in order at the Tidewater Inn. Taylor had helped Warner to the Republican nomination and eventual election as one of Virginia's senators. It was during that campaign that Taylor choked on a piece of chicken, was saved by the Heimlich maneuver, and then made fun of on *Saturday Night Live*. The Warners arrived at 2 A.M. and were moved by the fact that, though sleepy-eyed, I had waited in the lobby to greet them. My favorite moment came the next day when Liz agreed to have her picture taken with me. In the ensuing conversation, I found her to be very bright and concerned about the issues, but it was hard to listen when I was being captivated by those incredible violet eyes. She later autographed the picture, "To Craig, who kept our debate in order, Elizabeth Taylor Warner."

The third reason for the conferences' success was that they were a lot of fun. No ties. Lots of late drinking and a great banquet at the end. Fourth, the press was invited and it gave great coverage of the events. For example, when Taylor and Warner got into a debate over whether women should serve in combat units in the armed forces, the argument made the front page of the *Washington Post* on February 3, 1980. At one point, Warner had said, "Now, Liz, hold on here."

And she replied, "Don't you steady me with that all-domineering hand of yours."

"I'm sorry, but you don't have a vote on this issue."

"Well, you invited me here."

This exchange took place at the "table debate" phase of the meeting, which kept me hopping to make sure everyone stayed on schedule and on topic.

We then convened the general session and debated the resolution and its proposed amendments. The last event of the second conference on its last day before dinner was a straw poll that was taken to determine preferences for the Republican nomination for president. I was delighted when Bush beat out Reagan.

THE PACKWOOD REELECTION CAMPAIGN

Mimi's choice to manage Packwood's reelection campaign turned out to be a dud. I never met the poor guy. The first I heard about the trouble was from Sean, who was angling for the position. He told me that I would replace him as executive director of the Republican Conference, while he went off to run Packwood's reelection campaign. He saw it as a big step up on his career path. But Sean's over-the-top demands included naming his wife press secretary for the campaign. Mimi was not only appalled by these demands, she suspected that Sean's machinations were a bid to undercut her authority. So she sought an alternative. Ricky Silberman, Packwood's press secretary and the wife of the former ambassador to Yugoslavia, Laurence Silberman, had taken a shine to me. She suggested to Mimi that I be named the new campaign manager.

Mimi was convinced I wouldn't take the job, but she and Packwood did not want it to go to Sean, who was the only other available choice. She called me in and asked me what I would do if the job was offered to me. I told her I would have to think about it. I would be in Oregon from

February through November, with several chances to return to Washington. I quickly and quietly met with Sean and filled him in on what was going on. I told him that I owed him for bringing me back to Washington. So if he didn't want me to take the campaign manager job, I would understand. Sean was very supportive. He claimed it was a great opportunity for me, though he would miss me while I was gone.

In the midst of writing Lincoln Day speeches for a raft of senators, I met with Packwood on a very cold day in February to accept the offer to become his campaign manager for his 1980 run. Packwood sat shuffling through some papers on his desk as Mimi ushered me into his office. It was a private trophy room. Plaques and pictures of the famous hung on the walls; the mantel over the fireplace was covered with awards; the coffee table was cluttered with ceremonial gavels and autographed books. The walls were lined with bookcases filled mostly with histories, biographies, and first editions.

Packwood began the conversation. "I've always wondered why you gave up being a professor. My father taught before he became a lobbyist. He loved being a teacher and hated being a lobbyist." He gestured for me to take a seat.

"Academia is a small world with lots of hypocrisy, I'm afraid."

Packwood was surprised. "Hypocrisy? And you came to politics?"

"Honestly, Senator, I find people a lot more open in the political world than in the academic. There's a lot of insecurity among some professors. And it gets translated into a lot of backbiting and passive aggressive behavior. In the political world, at least the rules are clear."

"There's a lot of insecurity here too. You'll find that out soon enough," the Senator intoned. "So why do you want to manage my campaign?"

"You have the reputation of being a fine legislator. You've been a lifelong Republican who has worked hard for the party. You are the ranking minority member of two important committees. *And*, since I've never managed a campaign, I thought this would be a good one to learn on."

"What about Martin's campaign in Alabama?"

"I became second-in-command there."

"I heard from Sean that you were the de facto manager. But never mind. Do you agree with all the positions I've taken?"

"I disagree with you on some. But your positions on defense, the economy, the Middle East, and most everything else are virtually the same as mine."

"How much does my *pro-choice* position bother you?"

"Having looked into your speeches, I'm convinced that you came to that position conscientiously. It certainly wasn't taken for political gain."

"You can say that again!" He laughed. "The last time I was in Portland, the Catholics spit on me. You're a Catholic, aren't you?"

"Yes, sir."

"Devout?"

"I suppose you could call me devout. I don't spend as much time in front of statues and candles as my mother does, but I'm there on Sundays, and even better, on some late afternoons."

Packwood was confused. "Late afternoons?"

"I feel closer to God in an empty church, and most afternoons they're empty."

"I admire that, even though I've never had such a feeling. Do you think your religion might get in the way?"

"My religion is a personal thing. I really can't imagine how it could have any impact on a political campaign."

"Are you sure?" he asked.

"The only way it could get in the way is if you did something in your personal life that violated a sense of character."

Packwood leaned back. "So you've heard the rumors."

"Yeah. But I believe a man to be innocent until proven guilty."

"You know in 1968 we put a tail on Wayne Morse. I was sure he was having an affair. We never got a thing on him."

"I hope you'll remember that in this campaign. Your opponent is a union man. They can follow you anywhere. Hotel maids are often unionized in Oregon."

Packwood looked me in the eye. "Don't worry. Getting reelected is much more important to me than getting a little action."

He then told me that Mimi was in charge of the big picture; I would be in charge of day-to-day operations. I said that was fine, not realizing what I had agreed to, and still reeling a bit from his last remark.

Senator Packwood had only minor primary opposition and led his likely challenger from the other party in the polls. Furthermore, there would be little problem in raising money for a powerful incumbent senator who sat on important committees. Yet I did have second thoughts. What if Packwood lost? My political career would be ruined along with his. In fact, if we won this election, everyone would say, given the situation, that the Senator would have won anyway. But if we lost it, I could become the scapegoat. I would be seen as the manager who lost a sure thing. "It's a classic no-win situation," I told John Macksoud over the phone. He calmed me down. He reminded me of a few of my talents, and that my interest in politics and my ambition would help me survive. "You need to get through this experience," he said, "not back off from it. Frankly, I want it out of your system."

First of all, that meant learning what an Oregon campaign was all about. Watergate had changed the face of campaigns, with all kinds of restrictions on fundraising. At first, I was overwhelmed by the complexity, but remembered a good deal from the 1978 campaign in Alabama. Fundraising ran from direct-mail appeals, through breakfasts, lunches, intimate cocktail times, dinners, and post-dinner drinks for big donors only. The campaign needed to also raise money by soliciting political action committees (PACs) (set up ostensibly by employees inside companies or unions, but generally run by the corporate or union political director). Then there were in-kind contributions of time and equipment. In our campaign, we would have the support of the National Rifle Association's members working for us in the field, while the Building and Trades Union built our lawn signs.

Then came the complicated question of how you get media coverage. Unpaid media included the coverage of news events (saving the whales), rallies (How many people can you turn out in Salem?), and pancake flipping (Do it in a small town to get local paper coverage). Paid media was expensive advertising. Television was the most expensive because it covered a larger area and had a larger audience; but you needed to target various audiences by picking the programs during which the ads were run. Reruns of the *Lawrence Welk Show* guaranteed a senior-citizen audience, so the ad on Social Security would run there. Radio was also good for targeting because radio stations are required to keep records of their demographics. Punk-rock station KPOT would provide an entrée to young voters. Newspapers would carry ads, but more important was their editorial endorsement. Then came the creation and distribution of door hangers, flyers, and lawn signs. And finally, there were phone banks to run to locate who our voters were and if they needed absentee ballots, then to obtain lawn-sign placement permission, and finally to turn out our vote on election day. (We didn't have to worry about the Internet or social media in those days.)

The advertising required research both in terms of the Senator's strengths and patching over his weaknesses. It also required opposition research into our opponent's record, and I was an expert at that kind of thing. Poll data was part of the research operation. It showed us where Packwood was strong, so we would want to turn that area out in terms of voting. It showed us where he was weak, so we could target advertising into those areas to try to repair the damage. Poll data also provided useful information we could share with donors, making them feel like campaign insiders.

To run this operation, I needed a press secretary who could double as a scheduler. I needed an office manager, a research aide, a financial officer, and a director of volunteers. I needed to contract out our advertising, our polling, our direct-mail operation, and some of our other fundraising operations, while keeping a tight rein on all of them. For example, no direct-mail solicitation could go out without my approval and the Senator's.

I soon discovered that despite all of the exposure to his constituents over the years, Packwood remained something of a mystery to them. A poll showed that fewer than 50 percent of the voters knew that he was married. Only 41 percent could name a legislative accomplishment. As I read the poll data comparing Packwood to his former teacher and now fellow senator, Mark O. Hatfield, it was clear that Hatfield had the hearts of the voters. He was sort of a saintly father figure. Packwood had their minds; he was seen as a political manipulator able to deliver the goods. It is interesting to note that Hatfield, a World War II veteran, became advisor to the Young Republicans while he taught at Willamette University. Packwood, who was 4-F because of his eyes, became one of Hatfield's favorite students, as I have mentioned. They sat together in the school cafeteria, Packwood quietly listening to Hatfield hold forth. Packwood then went off to New York University Law School, where his life was changed in two ways. First, he was elected class president, indicating a popularity he had not known before. Second, he came under the influence of a fellow student named Paul Berger, who took him to Israel to see that democracy at work. Packwood became a lifelong supporter of Israel.

After law school, Packwood returned to Oregon, very much ready to get into politics. The natural thing for Packwood to do would have been to support Hatfield's run for governor. Instead, Packwood supported Hatfield's primary opponent. Hatfield went on to win. I have no idea why Packwood did this, but it indicates a certain opportunism that would surface again and again in his career. When Hatfield entered the Senate, he established his moderate Republicanism inside his evangelical Christianity. He claimed his religion led him to oppose the war in Vietnam. Packwood broke with Hatfield again, supporting the war when he ran for Senate in 1968 as we have seen.

To overcome his negatives in 1980, we tried to position Packwood as a family man and political leader. His adopted children were incorporated into television commercials, and his wife appeared in one in which she bragged about his accomplishments. We also tried to position him as a statesman, particularly when it came to foreign affairs. Finally, we would argue that his seniority was important to Oregon; it gave Packwood "clout" in the nation's capital.

Before I left on my first Oregon trip, I went to the staff gallery of the Senate and watched Packwood stride to the center aisle and deliver a speech. As each minute passed, more and more senators entered and paid attention to the junior senator from Oregon. When the speech ended, nearly half of the senators had arrived, an unusually high number. If you have visited the Senate, you know that its business is usually run by a handful of senators, and they hardly ever listen to one another speak.

I noticed that few senators questioned Packwood's positions, and that those who did were extremely courteous, even more courteous than Senate decorum demanded. The flowery preludes to their questions—"I want to say first how much I admire the esteemed Senator's breadth of knowledge and depth of research"—revealed a kind of homage. Packwood commanded the floor of the Senate with his probity, sagacity, and élan. He would be a great minority or majority leader, I thought to myself.

In three weeks, Mimi and I produced a campaign budget, a management plan, and a grassroots organization plan—each meticulously pieced together and carefully proofread before being given to the Senator for review. He initialed each document without making a single change. In a show of further confidence in me, Senator Packwood selected my design for the lawn signs over other staff and consultant suggestions. I began to realize that political consultants, particularly those from advertising firms, were all hat and no cattle, as they say in Texas. At best they relied on "common wisdom," which they rarely adapted to individual campaigns. For example, one consultant suggested the lawn-sign slogan "Packwood Again," to reinforce the incumbency theme. I reminded him that if our opponents simply added a question mark to the slogan, it could be read sarcastically: "Packwood Again?" After that meeting, Packwood wrote the following memo to everyone involved in the campaign: "My comments are only meant as suggestions to be considered. Commands come from Craig Smith."

CHAPTER NINE

Running a Senate Campaign

I flew to Portland to open a campaign headquarters. By the time my plane landed, I had dissolved the last remaining doubts about taking the job. It was an existential plunge. This job would both advance my career and expand my mind. As long as I was learning something new, anything could be tolerated—even defeat.

The day after I landed in Portland, the Senator sent me a memo "re: headquarters." My first task was to locate a proper "storefront" to rent as a campaign headquarters. Satellite offices would open later in Eugene, Medford, Salem, Baker, Pendleton, and other cities where volunteers could be found to operate them. What followed in the memo was a list of specifications. Some were reasonable: "3. A parking lot for volunteers." And some were not: "16. Rent must not exceed $1,600 a month." And some were troubling: "27. The building must have two entrances, one exclusively for my use, which must be hidden so that I may enter and leave without being seen."

The headquarters I finally located cost $2,000 a month plus utilities. I memoed the Senator that it was the only one in Portland's downtown area that met all of the other specifications. I never heard another word on the subject. Mimi explained, "That's good. That means he's satisfied with what you've done. Enjoy the silence; he only speaks to criticize."

From the day I signed the lease, I had two weeks to finish hiring the staff, set up the "grand opening," and establish myself with the press. Reporters would be crucial since a favorable story or editorial endorsement was worth far more than any political commercial. This was particularly true of the *Portland Oregonian*, which was basically the only newspaper serving the three counties that overlapped the biggest city in the state. Before we could move into the headquarters on March 1, we had to work on Dorchester xvi, the Oregonian Republican conference that was the predecessor to

Tidewater. Packwood wanted me there. We took the campaign van to Astoria, playing Hearts along the way. After we arrived at the Pacific Ocean, we played charades in the van and then retired to our hotel rooms around 12:30 A.M.

The next morning Packwood and I walked along the beach and discussed the speech he would give at the conference. We had hired Roger Ailes as our campaign consultant. He and I became allies and good friends. Ailes, who had produced the *Mike Douglas Show*, one of the first daytime talk shows to succeed, had lost a small fortune in his first divorce. He reinvented himself by becoming a campaign consultant, and was one of the few that was authentic; he knew what he was doing. He did not believe one size fits all. He filmed Packwood's speech at Dorchester and edited it into commercials. We also did a sunset shoot with the Senator heading down the beach.

The address at Dorchester went well, with some of my suggested lines showing up. But the best line was written by the campaign press secretary. The context of the line was the failure of the Carter administration. By this time, Carter was funneling secret aid to the Taliban in Afghanistan to overthrow Soviet's puppet regime there; Carter's interference prompted the Soviet Union to invade the country. Carter then announced that the United States would not participate in the Olympics in Moscow in 1980. He then increased the defense budget from $115 billion to $180 billion at the behest of his hawkish secretary of state Zbigniew Brzezinski. Because Carter had protected the dying shah by allowing him to be treated in the United States, the American Embassy staff had been taken hostage in Iran, and President Carter seemed wholly incapable of handling the situation. However, the USA hockey team had just beaten the Soviets at the Winter Olympics in Lake Placid and won the gold medal. As he discussed national defense, Packwood said, "The time for seconds and silver is over." The line brought down the house and made for a great commercial.

The Senator would commence the primary "fight" on the evening of March 10 at the headquarters. The staff had been told that I had ultimate hiring and firing authority, and that all members of the staff hired by my predecessor would have to reapply. I rehired them because, thank God, they were all competent. Among them was Elaine Franklin, who became the Portland volunteer coordinator in exchange for the campaign paying for daycare for her children. Elaine was a British citizen who refused to become an American, even though her husband had made the conversion years before. I enjoyed her accent and bluntness, as did Packwood.

The Senator arrived at the gala opening of his headquarters to find two hundred volunteers, miles of bunting, four kegs of beer, ten jugs of wine, twenty pounds of cheese, and enough crackers to fill the Columbia Gorge. He was introduced by Jack Faust, the campaign chairman and a prominent Portland lawyer. Jack and his wife Alice were not only the savviest, but the kindest people I met during the campaign.

As Packwood spoke to the crowd, I watched Georgie as she dutifully watched her husband. She was one of the new breed of political wives who tried to model themselves after Jackie Kennedy. They were pretty in a hard, cool, sophisticated way—not a hair out of place, not a bead of sweat on their pale, angular faces. They never laughed; they only smiled as if they had heard each joke before and still enjoyed it. They exercised in private clubs and health spas. They never drank anything stronger than white wine. They could nurse one glass through a seven-course meal.

As he spoke, Georgie studied her husband's graying temples and wrinkled neck. She never took her eyes off him, probably imagining him as he looked during the 1968 campaign. "In conclusion," Packwood was saying, "our opponent can't win the election, *we* can only lose it. If we fight, this Senate victory, our third together, will be the greatest of them all." The crowd applauded enthusiastically and the Senator said, "Now, let's get back to the beer." Everyone laughed and moved in to shake his hand.

The next day, the Senator, his campaign press secretary, and I traveled to radio and television stations along the road to Astoria and back to Portland. While traveling in the Senator's large white van, we played Hearts again. The Senator insisted on keeping score and playing for a nickel a point. "I'll collect at the end of the trip—it's a tradition on my campaign swings." There is a lot of luck in Hearts, and one bad move can prove disastrous. The key was to play conservatively and wait for an opportunity to strike. At the end of the two-day tour, the Senator was more than 400 points behind me. His press secretary was dead last. "All right, I'm going to save your ass," the Senator said to his press secretary. "I'm paying off all our debts to Craig by taking him to dinner."

The next night, I picked the Senator up at the Red Lion Inn in Portland, his favorite hotel, though it was nonunion. He gave me instructions on how to drive to Chuck's, a restaurant that had brought Packwood luck in past campaigns. "I've been coming here for twenty years." The Senator seemed uneasy. "Every campaign."[1]

I sensed that I needed to get the Senator to his table and a drink as quickly as possible. Packwood was a private man who was surprisingly nervous about social affairs. The maitre d' emerged from the dining room, but did not recognize the Senator, an oversight that heightened the tension. Once we were seated in a cushy red booth, the cocktail waitress rescued the situation and salved Packwood's ego when she said, "Senator, can I get you a drink?" She wore a short, tight, black outfit that revealed long legs covered with mesh stockings.

"Uh, yes, two beers for me. Uh, Craig, what do you drink?"

"Everything. But tonight I'll have a martini, very dry and up, Tanqueray."

"Stirred or shaken?" She smiled and the Senator did too. I couldn't tell if she was being sarcastic.

"Shaken, please." The waitress vanished and returned before we could exchange four sentences.

"Thank you," the Senator said as he eyed her stockings. I looked at the ceiling.

"You're welcome, Senator. Just wave when you need another beer."

Packwood wasn't finished with her. "Why don't *you* keep an eye on *us*?" He gestured at our drinks.

"Sure. Sure." She winked and wiggled off, feeling the Senator's glance on the back of her thighs.

"I wish I could have what you're drinking," he said to me. "Tanqueray's my favorite."

"Well, why don't you?"

"Oh, Mimi hasn't filled you in?"

"About what?" I asked.

"I tend to drink a little too much. So Mimi has ordered me to drink only beer."

"You can get drunk on beer, you know."

"Yes. But it takes a long time and I have a small bladder. I hate getting up and running to the bathroom every five minutes. Worse, with my vision, I can miss steps at night, so I have to be walked to the restroom. It's a pain in the ass and Mimi knows it."

"Can I ask why you sometimes drink too much?"

"I never get hangovers. I'm a freak of nature, I guess." When the waitress returned with a new martini for me, the Senator requested one for himself. "What the hell. I'm just flying back to D.C. in the morning," he rationalized.

Over dinner we discussed history, politics, and Packwood's political future. He confided a split desire: he couldn't decide whether he wanted to become majority leader soon or run for president later. I told him his shot at the presidency was contingent on two factors: he needed to beat his opponents in the primary debates, and he needed to be the only liberal Republican in the group. While his opponents divided up the mainline conservatives, he could win primaries with only 20 to 25 percent of the vote. "You could pull a reverse Jimmy Carter," I told him.

"What do you mean?"

"Carter claimed to be the only legitimate conservative in the Democratic field in 1976. He came into the primary as 'Jimmy who?' He won New Hampshire with a bare 25 percent of the vote because the other Democrats split the rest of the vote running as standard liberals."

Back at the hotel, the Senator made my day. "Craig, you're good. If you carry the campaign off well, I'll find you a nice fat committee to run."

"Thank you, Senator. But there is no need to—"

"I said, '*If* you carry this campaign off well,' remember that!"

Soon after, I was recalled to D.C. for a strategy meeting, and would use the occasion to pick up my car to drive it back to Oregon. The strategy session went well. At the end of it, the Senator threw an arm around me and said he wanted to have another one of our meaningful dinners when he came to Portland. I was very surprised at the show of affection and I could see that Mimi was too.

The day after a farewell dinner in D.C. with friends, I started across the country. When I arrived in Portland, I put the primary campaign into high gear. For example, we thought it would be good public relations to participate as a team unit in the 12.5-kilometer March of Dimes fundraiser walk in our "Packwood 80" T-shirts. Near the end of the event, anti-abortion activists spit on us. They had saved their venom for the hated Packwood campaign while allowing other pro-choice groups to march on by unmolested.

A few days later, Mimi told me she had made a mistake in hiring a local advertising firm to make our commercials for the primary. The Senator reviewed their product and found it to be disastrously out of touch with the reality of the recession. Their first commercial showed Packwood and his family sitting around a dinner table loaded with expensive cuisine. Roger Ailes's work from the Dorchester conference was much better. So he would make the commercials as well as advise the campaign. "Your job," she told me, "is to fire the local firm and make sure they don't invoke their 30-day release clause. The Senator doesn't want to pay them for another second, let alone another 30 days."

I met with Ailes over lunch and told him I was upset about being put in an awkward position. "I didn't hire that damn firm, and now I have to fire them and get them to eat their exit money from the contract."

Roger told me not to worry. "Take me with you when you meet with them. I'll handle the tough part."

The next day at the emergency meeting with the advertising firm, I filled them in on what had happened. Their plush offices were on the tenth floor of a downtown high-rise. Their feel-good ads about the Packwood family were out of touch with the current economic situation, and their purported cost overruns were ridiculous. In light of that, I was terminating their contract immediately. The head of the agency said that was unfair and unfeasible. After a little more give-and-take over the 30-day release clause, Roger interrupted him. "Can you fly?"

"What?" the executive replied.

"Can you fly?"

"What is that supposed to mean?"

Roger explained. "It means that if you don't agree to terminate the contract immediately, I'm going to throw you out that f—king window." The executive backed down, signed the appropriate papers, and Roger and I left the building.

For the next two months, I worked 70 to 80 hours a week, hoping to produce the large victory expected in the primary. I tried to build consensus by ferreting out the causes of problems before offering solutions. It was often difficult to know when to lead and when to be silent, but I made sure I worked on each and every project. However, hard work wasn't the only thing sustaining me. Since high school I had had to role-play. No one could know who I really was. I was a survivor because I was an effective communicator. All of those skills were honed in college and in the jobs that followed. It is one of the benefits of learning to live in the closet, empty though the darn thing was. Now I became a campaign manager, invoking a persona gleaned from political movies, working with Stu Spencer at the White House, and witnessing the Alabama campaign as second-in-command.

The next big event was the erection of the infamous lawn signs. Packwood's supporters in the building and trade unions came to headquarters to assemble them. The stacks of stakes and wax-coated signs (to fend off the Oregon rain) were massive. Packwood wanted 15,000 lawn signs set up and maintained in the primary, and 30,000 in the general election. If we did that we would break all records (and destroy the forests of Oregon). The numbers were way too high. Packwood was no longer a young grassroots candidate; lawn signs were no longer a new innovation. Getting people to take them was not difficult, but getting volunteers to maintain them was. Soon I realized that the Louis XIV strategy would be needed. Louis insisted that the fountains of Versailles always run. However, doing that drained the water in the area from the local farms. So Louis's gardener was given a signal each time Louis was about to enter his gardens. The gardener then turned on the fountains. As far as Louis was concerned, they were on all the time.

In the 1980 campaign, we made sure we knew Packwood's travel plans in detail. Lawn signs were to spring up on May first across the state for the late May primary. The streets and highways where Packwood traveled were given priority. Extrapolating from what he saw, Packwood assumed other streets and highways were as densely populated with lawn signs as the ones he traveled. No one gave the plot away.

BUSH STRUGGLES

Despite the fact that John Connally had faltered, getting only one delegate after spending $12 million, news from the Bush campaign was not good. On March 12, he sent me a handwritten note that read, "Good luck out there. Took it in the gut in S.C., Fla., Ala. too. Now on to Ill. Thanks Pal." I was particularly upset by the loss in Alabama; we had worked so hard to set it up for him.

However, Bush losses disappeared from the news cycle because the media was all abuzz about the Iran rescue mission that had been aborted because of sandstorms. Carter's administration was in even more trouble. But I couldn't be distracted by the presidential campaign; I had my own campaign to keep on track. Packwood's fundraising operation was massive and as detailed as everything else he did. He kept cards on everyone he ever met. The gigantic card file in his office became a resource for contributors in every campaign and could be used to personalize the appeals. Here are some samples:

William Milfred Batten: Batten is Chairman of the Board at J.C. Penny Co. He received the Americanism Award at the Anti-Defamation League's Award banquet at which Packwood spoke on Wednesday night, October 24, 1973. Packwood chatted at length with Batten. Batten was selected as Chairman of the New York Stock Exchange in April of 1976 and Packwood dropped him a note of congratulations.

Donald B. Stott: Stott is a Senior Partner with Wagner, Stott and Company in New York. Packwood first met him at a breakfast hosted by Lester Pollack at the Regency Hotel in New York on Thursday, March 31, 1977. Stott has attended briefings and dinners on June 9, August 2 and October 13, as well as co-chairing the meeting of July 13, 1977. He had lunch with Packwood on June 9 and August 2, 1977, bringing Al Gordon to the August 2 luncheon with him. The Senatorial Committee [which Packwood ran at the time] set up an appointment for him, Bunny, Gordon and Whitehead in Senator Baker's office on October

13, 1977, concerning rule 390. Senators Baker, Packwood, Schmitt, Tower and Javits attended the meeting. [Senators] Heinz, Lugar and Brooke met separately with the group. Stott attended the March 31, 1978, [Senatorial] Trust function; he has also given an additional $5,000 and sent a check to the Senatorial Committee from his father, Robert L. Stott, for $5,000 on January 23, 1978. Don Stott attended a dinner for Packwood hosted by Lester Pollack at the Regency Hotel in New York on Wednesday evening, April 19, 1978.

As you can see, the cards are unusually candid; they were maintained by Cathy Wagner Cormack, who also transcribed Packwood's diaries each morning in Washington, D.C. Cathy had a heart of gold, and more than once I confided my troubles to her. She was war-weary, the kind of woman who had seen it all in the political world and yet stayed on out of loyalty. She was Packwood's Rosemary Woods. And as we shall see, the tapes and the secretary were not the only parallels between Packwood and Nixon.

While we were assembling our final push for the primary, Bush's campaign continued to vacillate between the issue-analysis strategy endorsed by Barbara Bush, Jim Baker, and me, and the political talk pushed by his press secretary, Pete Teely, and Vic Gold. In fact, I had revised Bush's stump speech for the Pennsylvania primary on April 16, but the speech was remembered for one line that Teely inserted in Philadelphia in which Bush referred to Reagan's fiscal program as "voodoo economics." Bush won the primary with 54 percent of the vote on April 22.

From Portland, I immediately redesigned the set speech. I called the new version of the speech "A Different Kind of President," and again stressed his intelligent and compassionate persona: "And so tonight, I challenge you to think, to reason, to act with a serious sense of responsibility." Filled with parallel structure, the speech examined America's past, present, and future. The past set up values we need to reembrace; the present analyzed the problems we face; the future outlined Bush's solutions. That last section began with a barely veiled alliterative attack on Reagan: "Americans, it is time we stopped falling for single-sentence solutions to complicated problems. If you want a president who gives you cosmetic answers to complicated questions, don't vote for me." In that section of the address is also a prophetic line: "In the Middle East, there is no reason why the United States should be the enemy of Islamic nations."

One of the funniest moments in the Oregon campaign came at Easter, April 6 that year. I had continually tried to get Catholic staff to attend church, particularly those who had fallen away over the abortion issue. For Easter, Mimi came out with Packwood to check up on things. She had lost some weight, enhancing her good looks, which reminded me of Anne

Bancroft. She, like many Packwood staffers, was a Catholic. During Lent, she went to mass every day. She was glad to help me push staff into attending mass on Easter Sunday. The night before Easter Sunday, Mimi and I attended a vigil service where a Jesuit priest got carried away and gave a long sermon on eschatology and existentialism. We thought it would never end. The next morning we picked up Mary Hasenfus and took her to mass. To Mimi's and my horror, the same Jesuit mounted the pulpit and gave the same sermon. Mary vowed never to attend mass again. And from that time on, whenever I started talking about "spirit" or anything religious, she would threaten to leave the room.

By this time, I was designated as the only person who could speak in Packwood's place on the campaign trail. It was easy for me to praise the man. On April 23, for example, I spoke at a meeting of the Washington County Republicans. We got a big crowd because one of the other speakers was Jeb Bush, who came to praise his father. We had a great time together talking about his "poppy."[2] For me, from there it was on to the Calaroga Terrace Seniors' Home. It was clear this group cared only about Social Security, which I found rather depressing. Then I met with the Multnomah Republican Central Committee to cement their endorsement in the primary over the right-wing challengers the Senator faced. Since I was a conservative Republican, I could defend Packwood against critics who thought he was too liberal.

With foreign policy in the forefront on the national scene, Bush's candidacy was revived. He came much closer to winning the Texas primary than people had expected. Reagan got 52 percent of the vote; Bush got 47 percent. But still, he had lost in his home state. To that point in the campaign, those of us on what I call the right side of the issues had carried the day with Bush; he would provide a complicated tax-incentive program, oppose the Panama Canal Treaty as drafted, oppose legalized abortion, portray himself as reasonable and sensitive, take the fight to Reagan in California, and focus on issues instead of political strategy. Nonetheless, by mid-May, Reagan was within 200 delegates of the nomination. Bush sent me a handwritten note from Michigan on May 17: "Sorry to miss you in Oregon. [He had done a joint fundraiser with Packwood while I was traveling in another part of the state.] . . . I've been using a lot of [your] speech." If Bush could carry Oregon and Michigan on May 20, he could take the nomination fight to the floor of the convention. Packwood publicly endorsed Bush, and privately criticized Reagan as a "tired old lightweight."

In our campaign, twenty volunteers worked on the phone bank every day from May first to the primary to turn out the vote. During the last week before the primary, newspapers, television, and radio ads saturated the voters with the Senator's name, accomplishments, image, and positions on the issues. I believed privately that the Senator's public prediction of 65 percent of the vote was conservative, and he did too. We were hoping for about 80 percent of the vote in the primary against a split field of right-wing, born-again candidates. However, we had not figured an act of God into our calculations.

MT. ST. HELENS

One May morning while Roger Ailes and I were driving across a bridge in Portland, we came upon a strange scene. People had abandoned their cars and were looking at a mushroom cloud off to the north. We climbed out of my car and joined them. The giant gray plume looked like an atom bomb had gone off. However, we soon learned that it was an eruption of Mount St. Helens, located in the southwest corner of Washington State. At first the westerly wind blew the ash toward Boise. Then the volcano erupted several more times over the next few days and the wind change brought ash down to Portland and Salem. In some places, the ash fell at a rate of six inches a day. While coastal areas were spared, valley and inland areas were preoccupied with it. Lives had been lost; salmon bled to death in the rivers as the volcanic silt slit their gills. Fruit and vegetable crops were ruined. Nature had supplanted politics as the major concern of the citizens of Oregon. Every night on the national news, their towns, their neighbors, their words were carried to America. It was impossible for candidates to travel, let alone draw crowds in the ash-covered towns. When we ventured outdoors, we wore surgical masks. One night I got caught in the rain and falling ash. My windshield wipers clogged and stopped working. It took me hours to get home, and by that time I was covered with muck.

I was depressed all through the primary voting that followed the eruptions of the volcano because I suspected turnout would be low. By the time the Senator arrived at the headquarters with his wife for the party late that evening, he had been declared the winner, but with only 64 percent of the vote. Worse, just as Packwood finished his acceptance speech at our headquarters, the campaign manager for his Democratic opponent walked up to him in front of the media and challenged him to debate his opponent seven times across the state. Packwood was furious that he had crashed our party and angrier still when the moment was played on the news later that night. Our opponent would be state senator Ted Kulongoski, a good-looking labor-liberal.

There were other ups and downs that night. Bush lost the Oregon primary, but won in Michigan. The press wrote him off, and finally Jim Baker prevailed on Bush to withdraw gracefully from the race. Reagan would be the Republican nominee for president. All we could do in the Bush camp was pray that he got selected for vice president. In the meantime, in the other party, Carter had put down the challenge of Teddy Kennedy.

The next day I provided rationalizations about the vote turnout. Our opponents in the primary were unknowns; but their supporters, whether zealous "Right-to-Lifers" or severe critics of government, had fought through the ash, rain, gray goo, or deadly dust to vote for the Christian Right candidates in our primary, which also helped Reagan in Oregon's presidential primary. Many of the Senator's supporters, sure of his victory and fearing for their lungs, had stayed home, and that in turn hurt Bush. Furthermore, we had cut back on media advertising to save money in the closing week of the campaign. I waited anxiously for the Senator's response. It was nonresponsive and read as follows:

> I noted that the Libertarian Party candidate wants in on the debates. It strikes me as a good idea because that will confuse the debates and drain voters from Kulongoski. Since she's a woman and I support women's rights, why not invite her in. What do you think?

I replied in caps immediately:

> I HAVE NO DOUBT THAT YOU WILL WIN THE DEBATES. ADDING A THIRD CANDIDATE WILL GIVE THIS LIBERTARIAN WOMAN EXPOSURE THAT MIGHT TAKE VOTES FROM US. THE LIBERTARIAN WILL ATTACK YOU, NOT YOUR OPPONENT. I OPPOSE THIS STRATEGY STRONGLY.

As the summer began, the debate over the debates continued. I was named chief negotiator for our side and tried to argue the opposition down to three debates. At first I got nowhere, especially when the flurry of activity surrounding the primary soon melted into a languid June in which Packwood told the press he wanted all of the debates to take place before Labor Day due to his Senate schedule. The opposition turned us down. Mimi then told me to delay debate negotiations until after Labor Day. "The press won't push until then and the Senator wants Kulongoski to squirm for a while."

I sighed, "Again the Machiavellian side."

"This ain't a sock hop," she responded.

As the summer progressed, I got to know Georgie Packwood better. She was much less secure than I had imagined; her insecurity motivated her constant involvement in the campaign. It also made her hypercritical of others, especially her husband. In one case, when he finished a speech to a standing ovation, he came to her for approval. She quickly pointed out that his tie was "a little crooked" and that had ruined the speech for her. Packwood was crushed. But I got the feeling that he sometimes lived for that kind of punishment.

Like Nixon, Packwood had a wonderful and saintly mother, Mindy, who gave her all for his campaigns despite her age. I'll never forget walking into headquarters one morning and seeing a group of Republican women—the "blue hairs," as opposed to the young, pro-choice gang of women who were Democrats for Packwood—addressing and stamping envelopes. There among them, working the hardest, was Mindy. It would be difficult for a son to live up to her standards.

INTERREGNUM

The days following the primary were slow. Though I made acquaintances in Portland, I was close to none of them. I knew my stay was temporary, so I was reluctant to make permanent attachments and didn't have time for them in any case. Though I traveled the state widely, speaking on behalf of the Senator, I had no one of interest to return to. The lull in the campaign did allow me to take a few trips up to Seattle to visit Dennis where he now lived with his wife and two children.[3] I also visited my sister Renée in Yreka near the California-Oregon border, where I could relax with my nephews and go fishing with my brother-in-law.

In late June, the campaign staff focused on the meeting of the state's AFL-CIO in Portland. They were expected to make an endorsement, and even though he was a Republican, Packwood wanted it. He was on good terms with Lane Kirkland, the national head of the union. But the local Oregon leaders were beholden to Kulongoski. The first step was a motion of the board of directors. Mimi, a devout unionist, would address them. She asked me to help her with her speech. Panic set in when Mimi was informed that the board leaned toward Kulongoski. We worked late into the night to equip Mimi with arguments that would turn the situation around. The next day she appeared before the board and was followed by Kulongoski's representative. She considered it a major victory when the board voted to remain neutral in the race. However, Kulongoski appealed the decision to the floor of the convention that night. Then Kulongoski's people announced that they had discovered that while Senator Packwood had registered at the Hilton, a union hotel, he was really staying at the Red Lion, a non-union hotel. The local AFL-CIO then endorsed Ted Kulongoski for senator.

If that weren't bad enough, Packwood decided to invite the Libertarian candidate, a woman named Toni Nathan, into the debates with Kulongoski. I was furious. I had seen *The Empire Strikes Back* just a few days earlier and argued that Packwood would pay for going over to the dark side on this issue. Nathan would get much more publicity than she normally would have received; she would then pull some female voters and Libertarian Republicans from Packwood.

A few days later, I entered the room in the Holiday Inn in Portland to begin the meeting with Kulongoski's people on the debate format, knowing I wouldn't get everything I wanted. My opposite number was a labor lawyer who believed that no issue should be agreed upon until *all* issues were settled. This approach caused the negotiations to go on for days while each and every final detail was discussed. Senator Packwood and Mimi had insisted that I try to seal the agreement on the third day. After handshakes and coffee, I sat down across from Kulongoski's representative.

"George," I began authoritatively, "let's start on the items where we've reached consensus."

"That's fine with me as long as you understand that we have no final deal until all points have been settled. Of course, that Libertarian woman will do whatever we tell her." He laughed.

I sighed, "Fine. First, there will be a lectern for each of the three candidates, set 9 feet apart and facing the audience." The Senator looked better standing and speaking than sitting and talking. If this point were lost, I had been instructed to break off negotiations.

"That's fine with us."

"Second, tickets will be divided 40 percent each for our campaigns, 20 percent for the Libertarian." I knew this would prevent Kulongoski's side from packing the place with enthusiastic supporters, a much easier task for a labor Democrat than a moderate Republican.

"Fine. We have no problem with that."

"Third,"—and here I used reverse psychology—"and I know this one is a little difficult for you, answer periods are to be three minutes long with no follow-up questions and no rebuttals."

Kulongoski's man took the bait. He demanded shorter answer periods and follow-ups. After feigning disappointment, I gave in. Packwood wanted the shorter answer periods and the follow-ups because of his debate skills and his normally cryptic responses to questions. He did not want longer periods in which Kulongoski could orate.

The last issue was over where the debates would take place and who would host them. That the final debate would be in Portland at the Jewish Community Center was non-negotiable. So George insisted on a debate in Salem at a place of their choosing, to which I agreed. Then I pushed for the first debate to be in Coos Bay, which they didn't like. I didn't blame them; it was on the coast and quite remote. "Why not Medford?" George asked.

"We promised the fishing industry we would do one on the coast, and we need something in the south of the state. You can pick the venue, if you like."

"Oh, all right."

I was happy when I returned to the office to report to Mimi. "We got everything we wanted!"

"Fantastic!" she drawled out in Missourian. "I could just kiss you." And she did.

The Republican Convention provided a respite from the campaign. It was now clear that former congressman John Anderson had done to George Bush in the primaries what Bush hoped John Connally would do to Reagan: Anderson subtracted just enough votes from Bush in crucial primaries to ensure Reagan's plurality. I recalled that in 1978 Bush had helped Anderson retain his seat in Congress, once giving a speech I had written at an Anderson fundraiser in Rockford, Illinois. Anderson had promised to endorse Bush if he ran for president. Some gratitude, I thought. So Reagan was crowned with the Republican nomination, and Anderson was running as an independent, ready to drain off Jimmy Carter's votes in the general election. The ego-driven Anderson was spoiler all the way around.

The drama at the convention was all about Reagan's running mate. Behind the scenes, Kissinger tried to broker a deal in which former President Ford would be selected. Kissinger wanted to be secretary of state again. Though I was fond of Ford, I believed it was a very bad idea for him to take the vice-presidency. It would be the biggest step down in a career since John Quincy Adams returned to the House of Representatives after losing the presidency. My former boss Walter Cronkite came to the rescue. During a live interview from the CBS anchor booth, he asked Ford what would happen if he disagreed with Reagan on some policy. Ford said that they would work things out because it would be like a "co-presidency." When he heard that word, Reagan hit the roof and dropped Ford from contention.

In the meantime, on Wednesday night at the convention, Bush gave an excellent speech that roused the crowd and called for unity among the delegates. Reagan was watching, and to the consternation of some of the conservatives on his team, he put Bush on the ticket. I was happy that Bush was selected; if the Reagan-Bush ticket won, I might have an appointment waiting for me in Washington after the campaign.

During the next week, Packwood asked me to speak on his behalf to the Oregon Republican Party Convention. The speech went well; several officials even asked me if I would be interested in running for public office in Oregon. I was very flattered. On August 13, a new poll came out showing Packwood with a huge lead: 59 percent to 28 percent. It looked as if we were doing all the right things. When the opposition report on Kulongoski's record was completed by the staff researcher, I rewrote it into attack commercials just to be on the safe side.

At the Democratic National Convention, Teddy Kennedy treated President Carter like a leper. After a disastrous interview with Roger Mudd before the primaries began, after terrible goofs all though the primaries, Kennedy had seemed to be a man who did not want to win. Then, on the night of Carter's renomination, Kennedy came forward and gave the best speech of his career. As the cameras panned the crowd, I could almost hear the delegates saying: "My God, where was *this* Kennedy for the last six months? We've nominated the wrong man."

On August 17, Henry Kissinger came to Portland to give a speech at a fundraiser for us. We set a record for the state by selling out the 825 seats. While he was waiting to head out to the head table, I had a few minutes alone with Kissinger, whose accent was much less pronounced in regular conversation than in his speeches. Kissinger remembered that I had been one of Ford's speechwriters and autographed a copy of his memoirs for me.

Packwood gave an excellent introduction for Kissinger, who kept everyone in awe for 50 minutes. It was a lucid, witty, brilliant performance. He began by saying, "I'm glad you finally stopped applauding and sat down. I have trouble looking humble for more than 60 seconds. [*Laughter*] And thank you for inviting me to a $200 a plate dinner. There is only one problem, someone took the $200 that was under my plate." [*Heavy laughter*]

After Labor Day, the campaign picked up and I was speaking all over the place. For example, I spoke in Bend on September 2nd, and on the 11th, flew to Baker, Oregon, in a single-engine plane to attend a Republican rally. The flight back down the Columbia Gorge that night with the full moon glinting off the river was spectacular. That same night, Bush was campaigning for his ticket and speaking on behalf of Packwood in Medford.

CAMPAIGN DEBATES

As the summer drew to a close, polls showed our race getting closer, as we knew it would. Almost any candidate can expect to get at least 40 percent of the vote because of the support of his or her party. By September 15, ten days before the first debate, the Senator had 51 percent of the vote, his opponent 38 percent. Packwood was particularly worried; his dreams were built on his attaining a landslide. It helped that the *Oregonian* endorsed Packwood on the 26th of September and his poll numbers went up to 54 percent versus 33 percent. However, I noticed that the poll did not include Toni Nathan, the Libertarian.

October was debate month. The Coos Bay debate would not be well attended by the media, nor would it be broadcast. Nonetheless, Packwood prepared extensively for it. He had a huge briefing book outlining his position and votes on every imaginable issue. The day before the debate in Coos Bay, Senator Packwood arrived at campaign headquarters in Portland in a tense mood. He was ushered into his private office without so much as greeting me. Surprised, I sat in my office fumbling through a series of three-by-five cards, each of which contained a unique idea for the debate; after all, I had been a debate coach and helped the Ford team for their debates with Carter. I stared out the window at the passing traffic, then reached into my coat pocket and pulled out my wallet. I flipped it to a picture of my mother. The phone buzzer startled me back to reality.

"Craig," said the Senator, "get your ass in here." I entered the Senator's office, cards in hand. "Mimi says you have some ideas for the debate. Let's hear them."

"Certainly. Senator, these things are a matter of attitude and drama. If you have the right attitude, and know how to seize a dramatic moment, it will go well—"

"Provided you've done your homework," Mimi interrupted.

"Of course."

"Craig,"—the Senator glowered at me—"this drama business. Do you mean something like what Reagan did to Bush in New Hampshire?"

"Yes, sir. By getting mad and grabbing the microphone, he solved his biggest problem. He proved he had real blood coursing through his ancient veins."

"And you think that I should do that?"

"No, sir. Your problem is not age."

"Thank God for that!" Mimi laughed.

"Senator, your problem is that you are seen as a part of the big-government machinery in an anti-incumbency year. What I propose is to convert that liability into an asset during the debate."

"Like what?"

"Like a strong national leader. Someone who is responsible on all the controversial issues, speaks for his state, but more important, also speaks for his nation."

"Why?"

"Because your record shows that you don't dodge controversial issues, and that you have been sensible both on economic questions and on foreign policy. More important, your opponent is fifteen years, almost a generation, younger than you are. Senator, every time you treat him like an inexperienced upstart, he will seem less qualified and his attacks on you will seem more insolent. At the same time, this tactic will play to the chauvinistic pride of the voters and will likely bring home the right-wing Christians."

The Senator's face lit up. "I like it." Mimi nodded approval. "I do like it," he continued. "Sit down and let's see what else you have on those little cards."

In the "opponent's briefing book," I included every possible bit of information one could get on Ted Kulongoski. I underlined one fact that could be used to devastating effect. Since the Oregon Senate kept track of each committee meeting, we could see when Kulongoski arrived and how long he stayed. On average he arrived forty-five minutes late for committees. "Why don't you dub him 'Tardy Ted' if you get the chance?"

"That's ingenious," Packwood crooned.

By all accounts, Packwood won in Coos Bay. The "Tardy Ted" line got a big laugh. However, Packwood was not happy about the debate. Kulongoski had more people turn out on his behalf, and he was the aggressor in the debate, referring to Packwood as "Mr. Abortion." Toni Nathan heckled both of them, but singled Packwood out on Republican issues, just as I had predicted.

A week later at 11:30 A.M. I found myself standing in front of a large restaurant in Salem, waiting for the doors to open so I could get inside with our volunteers and set up for the second debate of the campaign. Gena Hutton, one of our county chairs, had brought a busload up from Eugene to supplement the Salem group. Where, I wondered, were the Kulongoski people? This was his turf. When the doors were opened, the mystery was solved. The room was covered with Kulongoski signs, and his supporters filled the front two-thirds of the room. They had arrived at 10:30 A.M. and been let in by a union sympathizer on the restaurant's staff.

The League of Women Voters, which was co-hosting the debate with the Salem Chamber of Commerce, refused to take any action, though Kulongoski's people had clearly violated the rules. It was not the first time, nor would it be the last, that I saw the Democratic bias of the League. The Chamber ordered the signs taken down, but managed to clear only one table up front for Mrs. Packwood, Jack and Alice Faust, and myself. When Packwood finally came into the room, I could see he was angry. He was booed by the Kulongoski crowd; they were clearly trying to throw him off his stride. The Libertarian candidate, Toni Nathan, seemed bemused by it all.

By any objective standard, Packwood won the debate. But in closing he attempted to tell a joke, flubbed the punch line, and was laughed at by the Kulongoski people. He departed the debate with Georgie, Jack, and Alice. And after doing my job as a spin doctor with the news media, I made my way to the white van, where Packwood sat slumped and depressed. The minute I came through the door, Georgie went after me. She said the staff had let the Senator down, and in turn was the cause of him making a fool of himself. She was going to have it both ways. She would be her husband's protector while at the same time reducing his confidence further. She knew he was a perfectionist, so the closing gaffe was all he remembered of the debate. I tried to assure her that the debate had gone well and that the press would portray it that way. She would have none of it. She stunned me when she unleashed what must have been a pent-up peeve: "You need to be less loved and more feared by the staff." At that point, Alice Faust came to my defense. That seemed to quiet Georgie. I apologized to the Senator for the snafu, explaining that the restaurant was union, and that a waitress had let all of the Kulongoski people in early. He looked up at me and I saw the face of scared, small child. Mimi pulled me out of the van and gave me some advice: "You might want to make yourself a little scarce around campaign headquarters for a few days."

When I got a chance, I called Gena Hutton. "Could we have dinner tomorrow night?"

"Of course," she replied.

When I arrived at the restaurant in Eugene, Gena looked more beautiful than ever. She knew I was seeking solace for the events in Salem. Through a couple of cocktails, she tried to revive my spirits. The conversation shifted from the campaign to Packwood himself as a light dinner arrived. "Gena, I'm not sure anyone knows him. He's a very private person."

"Well, I guess with all the publicity you'd be driven to privacy," she said, looking out the window at the Willamette River flowing by. I decided not to interrupt her reverie. I simply watched the candlelight dance over her face and hair. "How is Kulongoski doing?" she asked, turning to me. "In the polls, I mean."

"Don't tell anyone, but our latest survey gives him only 41 percent of the vote. Almost any Democrat should get at least 40 percent."

"Why don't you release it?"

"Because," I said, sipping my wine in mid-sentence for effect, "the press wouldn't believe it, and it would make your job tougher. How many volunteers do you think you would get if we released a poll like that? They would think they were no longer needed."

Gena's brow furrowed. "I never thought of that. It would probably shut down contributions too."

"Wrong again. Donors like to go with a winner. So Jack Faust will show the poll data to the appropriate people." I smiled.

"Now I know why you're the manager and I'm the field worker."

"Your day will come. Just remember that only a few years ago I was a professor in the South with no knowledge whatsoever about how to run a campaign. But let's not talk shop, let's get back to the world of spirituality." In the candlelight, her tan face was golden. Her New Age, romantic ideas were refreshing. My loneliness and depression forced my hand to reach across the table and take hers.

The final debate at Portland Jewish Community Center was to be televised statewide. The day before, I visited the site to see if there was some way I could get our troops in early and turn the tables on Kulongoski. I found an ancient guard who thought the world of Packwood. I talked him into opening a side door the next night, two hours before the debate was scheduled to start. The debate rules forbade signs, so I got our volunteers to hide PACKWOOD 80 signs under their shirts and blouses. When Packwood walked on stage, the place erupted in cheers. He then devastated Kulongoski in the debate, partly because Kulongoski kept stumbling. At one point he said, "As the only person on the stage to have served in the military . . ." and before he could finish, there were loud boos from the audience. Toni Nathan laughed, Packwood shook his head in mock disgust. I looked over at Mrs. Kulongoski and saw the pain in her face. At another point, Kulongoski accused Packwood of manipulating the legislative process for his own gain: "Don't you think it is odd that Senator Packwood with a snap of his fingers got this timber reforestation bill passed just before this election?"

Packwood responded, "If my state had a senator who could pass legislation with the snap of his fingers, I'd sure keep him in the Senate." The place went nuts. In his concluding remarks, Packwood then told his favorite story about writing a speech late at night and needing to look on the globe for the name of the capital of a country. He snuck into his son's room where the globe was stationed. He lifted the globe and began to leave the room, but his son woke up and said, "Dad, where are you going with my world?" "My friends," Packwood concluded, "that's a question I face every day." His supporters rose to their feet and shouted and clapped. Packwood 80 signs appeared everywhere and were carried statewide over television.

We held a post-debate celebration at the Fausts' house. Standing on a chair, Packwood thanked everyone for their help. Then he turned to me and said, "I'm particularly grateful for what you've done. It was important for me to have the audience on my side."

A few nights later, I took Packwood's place at a "candidates' fair" in Northwest Portland. It started with candidates for lower offices and hours later finally arrived at Senate candidates. I deferred to Toni Nathan's surrogate and then began to speak on behalf of Packwood when low and behold, Ted Kulongoski walked through the door. I finished my remarks and felt obligated to introduce Kulongoski. As he began he said, "I hate to speak in opposition to Bob Packwood tonight because I like Craig, and my staff respects him. He knows how this game is played."

ELECTION TIME

From there to election night, it was travel, speak, sleep, travel, speak, and keep the office in line. On the national scene, two major events turned things toward a major Reagan victory. First, when Carter refused to debate him, Reagan debated Anderson. Reagan didn't do all that well in the debate, but he revealed Anderson for the liberal he was. That meant many moderate Republicans returned to the party and supported Reagan. With that boost in the polls, he closed on Carter. So Carter agreed to debate Reagan in late October, hoping to finish him off. However, Reagan clearly won the debate with Carter. Reagan was not only wittier ("there you go again"), warmer, and more charming than Carter, he used more evidence and had better arguments. At one point, trying to become more human, Carter talked about discussing nuclear proliferation with his eight-year-old daughter Amy. Television revealed the inauthenticity of the claim and the audience giggled. The five liberal university debate coaches that assessed the debate for the Associated Press voted 4 to 1 that Reagan had won.[4] A huge swing in the undecided vote occurred as a result of Reagan's performance.

Oregon is three hours behind the East Coast, so we began to get information about what was happening on election day quite early. We had sources all over the place, and it was becoming clear that Reagan was going to win by a landslide. At 4 P.M. our time, Dan Quayle defeated the incumbent Senator Burch Bayh in Indiana, then Senator McGovern lost in South Dakota. I wished I could be at CBS to watch the reaction; but of course, due to their exit polls, they already knew what was going to happen. By the end of the evening, the astonishing net gain of twelve seats would put the Senate in the hands of the Republicans for the first time since 1954, and Packwood would be a prime beneficiary.

But my satisfaction was to be brief. Packwood was disappointed by his election returns. He received 52 percent of the vote, to 44 percent for Kulongoski, to 4 percent for the Libertarian. Exit polls revealed that the Libertarian vote would have gone to Packwood. Toni Nathan had robbed him of his big victory. He was depressed by the results, believing they hurt his presidential chances. This despite the fact that Reagan had won an overwhelming victory and Packwood couldn't figure on a run for many years. Packwood would now head the Commerce Committee and be selected to return as head of the National Republican Senatorial Campaign Committee. However, the blame game started in his office back in D.C. while I took time to wrap things up in Portland, visit my relatives in California, and drive back across the country.

CHAPTER TEN

The National Republican Senatorial Campaign Committee

A FEW DAYS AFTER THE ELECTION, MARY HASENFUS AND I WROTE A report on the important tri-county Portland vote. We concluded that we had turned out as much of our vote as possible, that Libertarian Toni Nathan had cut into the Packwood vote, and that despite our advertising efforts, the voters did not have an emotional connection with Packwood.[1] Instead, they admired his smarts and his clout in the Senate. After we sent the report to Packwood, I took a month off to drive across the country, visiting friends and family along the way in the hope of restoring my soul. At one point, I took Highway 168 out of Monterey over to Salinas, where I caught Highway 101, El Camino Real, the mother route of California. I drove south while the full moon came over the mountains lining the east side of the valley.

I had been through the Salinas Valley many times, had in fact traveled Highway 101 since childhood. And now, beneath a gleaming white moon, I sped down it again, feeling at home in the clear, cool night air. I saw the silver sides of mountains, the slivers of water in wide washes, the fertile fields squeezing into the narrow arroyos, the bunched blotches of dark green leaves of the eucalyptus trees dripping with dew along the highway. Something was here that the materialist could not capture, something beyond nature, inspired by a moonbeam on a shiny live oak leaf.

Just outside San Luis Obispo, the fog began to roll in from the ocean. Breaking through the pass from the valley out to the sea at Shell Beach always thrilled me. And tonight was no different. The fog patches sped by, covering and uncovering the stars and moon. Suddenly, the road opened onto a beach, and the image swept my soul across the metallic surface of the ocean out onto the horizon. I pulled the car over and watched the moon appear and disappear through the fog. I looked across the silver-veiled sea and floated into a deep sleep.

I woke around 6 A.M. and drove to breakfast in Pismo Beach while the clouds burned off in the morning sun. An hour and a half later, on the UCSB campus on the coast at Isla Vista, I saw the tan, blond students walking to the beach with their surfboards and was taken back to the same beach where for the first half of the 1960s I studied history, thought about existentialism, and prayed for good grades. I saw the buildings I learned in, the dorm I lived in, and the grassy hollows I wished I had made love in.

The place simply had not changed. At 75 degrees under a perfectly blue sky, with mild winds blowing across the beach, the campus seemed timeless and as beautiful as the students who populated it. It was as calm and comfortable as its little algae-edged green lagoon. How, I wondered, did anyone get anything done here? How had I ever managed to graduate from this place? I walked through the campus under the coral trees, and along the rolling lawns. The nostalgia was overpowering. It was all too much. I hurried to my car and drove south into Los Angeles.

There I visited relatives and friends, and then it was on to San Diego and some time with my parents. While there, I called Sean to see when he needed me back at the conference to get ready for the Senate Republican Caucus elections. He told me to move my tail east as soon as possible. Mimi was bad-mouthing me to the Senator's staff, and it was clear that she was not going to provide a place for me in the reorganization of the staff. I drove to Washington as quickly as I could, stopping at friends' homes along the way only for an overnight stay. And then I was back in Arlington.

FINDING A PLACE

When the newly elected and returning Republican senators convened in December of 1980, they gave Packwood his second term as the head of the National Republican Senatorial Campaign Committee, a vastly larger operation than the Republican Conference. Vice President Bush found a good job for me as chief of staff for Ray Donovan, the new secretary of labor. I turned it down because I wasn't up on, or interested in, labor issues; I didn't think much of Donovan; and I thought I could get a more interesting job from Packwood if I could just get by Mimi. That would be difficult because I reminded Packwood of his election, which was unpleasant for him given his expectations of a bigger victory. However, Mimi soon got an appointment to the Federal Communications Commission and lost her influence over the Senator. When I finally got a meeting with Packwood, I explained to him that had he listened to me with regard to including the Libertarian candidate in the debates, he would have had his landslide. To his credit, he conceded the point. Then he moved on to say that my most valuable function for him in the campaign had been in research. When he assumed his post in January of 1981, he would make me research director of the National Republican Senatorial Campaign Committee. And by the way, he continued, "Why don't you come to the inaugural and the ball as my guest. I have a box."

In 1981, the inaugural balls were classy; not an expense was spared. I sat in the Senator's box with Lane Kirkland, Ricky and Laurence Silberman, and Georgie Packwood, who seemed to have mellowed toward me. The champagne never stopped flowing, and when the Reagans arrived and did a turn on the dance floor, the room filled with magic.

As I moved into my new job, for diversions I kept up my campus lectures, my writing, and my visits with John Macksoud who had moved into a house we had restored in Madera, Pennsylvania.[2] It was deep in the woods, about 35 miles from Pennsylvania State University. So I could visit John and also my former professors on the same trip. I was now deep into the inner sanctum of Republican politics and discovering some odd oxymorons. I found out over a lunch that a right-wing Republican fundraiser was gay. He confessed that he could never become part of a staff or a campaign. He was trying to draw me out. I felt sorry for him, but I wasn't going to tell him that I was gay, because I knew he was right.

A few months later a friend told me that a born-again Christian, moderate Republican senator was gay and the model for the senator who is outed and commits suicide in Alan Drury's wonderful novel *Advise and Consent*. I checked the story out with Packwood, who said, "Oh yes, it is well known. In fact his lover is his chief of staff, who works for a dollar a day since he is heir to a fortune." The senator had one of those arranged marriages with his wife, who also worked as a realtor. Her job would eventually lead to charges of a conflict of interest when she was paid huge sums to find housing for Arabian diplomats who then sought favors from her husband, the ranking member on an important Senate committee. The worst case was a payment of $55,000 from a Greek financier while he was seeking approval of his company's bid to build an oil pipeline in Africa. She badly tarnished her husband's otherwise stellar reputation.

Later still, I learned that Terry Dolan, the head of the National Conservative Political Action Committee and the brother of Reagan speechwriter Tony Dolan, was gay. He would eventually die of AIDS, which in 1981 was barely on the nation's radar. It had certainly caught my attention by the end of that year, and I talked to Packwood about what he could do about it.[3] It was not until 1982 that the Center for Disease Control named the malady AIDS; the reaction of the Reagan administration was even slower.

AT THE SENATORIAL COMMITTEE

My various jobs at the Senatorial Committee gave me lots of opportunities to reestablish myself with Senate staffs and campaign operatives. As 1981 began, my research team provided every Republican senator running for election in 1982 with a book that detailed his or her voting record, and showed how it could provide the grist for campaign speeches, commercials, and debates. The books also looked at "vulnerabilities" so that our incumbents knew what negative advertising could be done against them. Wherever possible we also did opposition research on likely opponents of the incumbents to provide them with attack ads.

In states where Democrats would be running for reelection, we wrote books on them for use by the eventual Republican nominees. Relying on my experience in debate, my goal was to make these sets of books the most thorough and most accurate in political history. Unlike irresponsible groups such as the National Conservative Political Action Committee, which often used isolated votes to distort an incumbent's record, we made sure that the votes were typical and accurate. The operation was so credible that it was imitated by other Republican and Democratic committees two years later.[4]

Once our operation was up and running, Packwood also used it to chase pesky challengers to Republican incumbents from their races. A classic case occurred with Connecticut Senator Lowell Weicker, easily the most liberal Republican in the Senate. When rumors spread that Democratic Representative Toby Moffett might challenge him, I was unleashed to do my thing. Miles Benson of the Newhouse News Service interviewed me and then related what would happen if Moffett got in the race:

> Craig Smith, director of the research division of the [NRSCC], will swing into action. "First, we'd do a key vote analysis of Moffett's record based on 150 key votes cast in the House since he was elected in 1974," Smith explains. "Then we'd do an overview to compare those votes to poll data that came in from

Connecticut and see if he is out of sync with voters—as I'm sure he is on busing, abortion, budget and tax cuts. The second step would be to look at all votes Moffett cast, with an eye to vulnerability, and divide those votes into 21 issue categories—labor, regulation, taxes—and report our analysis to the Weicker campaign."[5]

Moffett got the message and dropped out of the race. Packwood was very pleased.

The Senator worked with Rod Smith, our finance director, to construct a fundraising campaign second to none. It relied heavily on Packwood's new love for direct-mail solicitation. This strategy was born of one of those small coincidences that always amaze me. In our 1980 Senate campaign, we hired a consultant named Paul Newman, who just happened to be an ex–college debate coach of mine.[6] I was delighted to work with him and watch him work his magic with direct-mail solicitation, which he had invented in the aftermath of Watergate. The Democrats hadn't even started it by 1981, the year Paul made sure the Republicans were the party of the small donor. Paul's method was rhetorical; that is, each letter that was sent out was adapted to receivers based on their zip code and party affiliation. Six percent was considered a good rate of return; it not only paid for the mailing, but you could put half the money received into the bank. You also created a "house file" from each contribution so that you could go back to those people later in the campaign. Invariably, the return from mailings to the "house file" was much higher than 6 percent.

Packwood also set about to recruit the best and the brightest of local politicians to run against vulnerable Democrats so that the Republicans would retain their majority in the midterm elections of 1982. One such candidate was Judge Mitch McConnell of Louisville, Kentucky. McConnell would eventually win a Senate seat and become majority leader in the Senate.

As part of the leadership team at the Senatorial Committee, I monitored the races in several states. Since the NRSCC had lots of money to distribute, I was treated as royalty when I arrived on the scene. In Tennessee, we hoped to run Congressman Robin Beard against Democrat James Sasser. My job was to get field reports and try to find a way to keep Beard from putting his foot in his mouth. I failed in the latter task. The man had a terrible temper and regularly it flared up at reporters. Even in rehearsals with me playing the hostile reporter, I could get under Beard's skin. I knew then he'd never make it.

In Washington State, I advised a whole series of potential Republican candidates on how to run. But beating redoubtable Senator Scoop Jackson would prove impossible. At least I got to visit with Dennis in Seattle every time I came to the state. It was wonderful to catch up on him and his ever growing family.

I was delighted to take on North Dakota, because my dad came from there and I still had relatives there. The North Dakota Republicans were very suspicious of outsiders. But when I spoke at the state committee meeting at an outdoor barbeque in Medora, I talked about how my grandmother Clementine Muzzy was the first female homesteader in the state. I talked about my grandfather's general store in Fortuna. And I talked about Teddy Roosevelt and the life he had led in and around Medora. I became a favorite son of the state.

With my roots and credibility established, I tried to seduce state senator Earl "the Pearl" Strinden to run for the U.S. Senate. I believed he would win, but he did not believe he could defeat the sitting Democrat Quentin Burdick, who, poll data showed, most people in North Dakota believed was a Republican. After the dust settled, the state party went with a native son who had spent most of his life in D.C. His name, Gene Knorr, made for some great negative advertisements because the Republican running for Congress was named John Nething. So the Democrats ran on the slogan of NEITHER NETHING NOR KNORR. You can't make stuff like this up. The Republicans went down to defeat.

However, the most fun and frustration I had was working in California. First, we had to get Republican incumbent senator Sam Hayakawa out of the race. I genuinely liked the man. An internationally known semanticist, he had been president of San Francisco State University and—wearing his trademark Tam o' Shanter—kept demonstrators in their place during the troubled early '70s. That led to his election to the U.S. Senate. Once there, he asked me to teach his staff how to write letters[7] of response to constituents and speeches for him. However, Senator Hayakawa was narcoleptic and often appeared to pass out during meetings and meals. While in one of his "states," he could hear what was being said. I remember being at a lunch with a lobbyist and the senator when he appeared to nod off. The lobbyist started making fun of Hayakawa despite my pleas and hand gestures to knock it off. Soon Hayakawa awoke, repeated what the lobbyist had said, and told him to leave the table. Hayakawa and I then enjoyed a lovely lunch together, discussing rhetorical theory.

However, the press was unforgiving to Hayakawa. Most of them were dying to get even for his iron-fisted response to demonstrations at San Francisco State during the Vietnam War, which had converted him into a Republican darling in 1970. In 1981, I looked at the poll data and saw that there was no way he could win reelection. Furthermore, I could see the campaign that would be run against him. So I put together some mock campaign ads and took them over to his office with the leadership team of the Committee. The ad showed newsreel film of him asleep as the Senate conducted business, as he sat at committee meetings, and as he met with constituents. The ad concluded, "Sam Hayakawa, asleep at the switch." When he saw the ad, he began to weep. Then he raised his hands and said he would not run again. We all felt terrible as we left the room, but for his well-being and the sake of the party, it had to be done.

Since California was the BIG ONE and lots of people were running, all of us on the leadership team visited the state. On these trips, I would always find time to stop to see former students, relatives, and various sites. One day I stopped by the cathedral on the campus of the University of San Francisco. It's beautiful inside. On this particular day, I noticed that the green light over the confessional was on. So I took advantage of the opportunity to purge my soul. I entered the dark booth, and the priest slid back the panel on his side of the little window between us.

I began with the usual opening: "Bless me, father, for I have sinned. It has been three months since my last confession."

"Are you a student here?"

"No, father, I'm visiting from Washington, D.C."

"All right. Tell me your sins." I promptly confessed among other things that I had sexual thoughts that the Church condemned as sinful, and explained that I was homosexual.

"Do you act on these thoughts?" he asked.

"No, father."

"Do you ever have sex with another man?"

"No, father."

"I really don't think you have much to confess," he told me. "You should hear what I have to listen to, especially here in San Francisco. By the way, did you say you were from Washington, D.C.?"

"Yes, father. Why?"

"By any chance, would you have access to President Reagan?"

"Not really, but I do have access to Vice President Bush."

"Can you please get them to do something about AIDS awareness?"

"I can talk to the Vice President about it. I'm sure he'd be understanding."

"That would be wonderful."

"And father, what about my absolution?"

"Your sins will be absolved when you talk to the Vice President."

"Thank you, father."

He shut the little window as he said, "Take care of yourself."

In Washington, D.C., as the HIV/AIDS crisis accelerated, I met with the Vice President as promised. He told me that the President was considering the matter but was caught in the crossfire of conflicting advice. Nancy Reagan had many gay friends. His son Ronnie, who was active in the ballet community, and Surgeon General Koop wanted Reagan to make America more aware of the disease—for example, explaining that it was not just afflicting gay males. However, his Christian right conservative advisors, such as Secretary of Education Bill Bennett, opposed the President getting involved. Tragically, Reagan developed a blind spot on the issue. His secretary of health and human services, Margaret Heckler, did pay attention to Dr. Gallo's claim that he had discovered the cause of AIDS. However, Reagan would not speak publicly about it until 1985; he may have been awakened by the death of Rock Hudson from the disease in the same year. However, Koop's report was not released until 1986. Reagan finally authorized the Watkins Commission to study the epidemic in 1987. Worse yet, in 1986, the Supreme Court in *Bowers v. Hardwick* upheld a Georgia law prohibiting homosexuals "from engaging in sodomy." In other words, the U.S. Constitution contained no protection for consenting adult homosexuals having sex. This dreadful decision kept many people in the closet and was not overturned until the summer of 2003 in *Lawrence v. Texas*. Leaving no doubt about the intent of the Court, Justice Anthony Kennedy in his majority opinion wrote that *Bowers v. Hardwick* "now is overruled."

THE WASHINGTON ROLLER COASTER

George Bush was never able to get a position for me that was better than the one I had. When it came to the ones I would take, I made the final three, but never got the final offer. For example, I was among the final three for assistant secretary of education. However, given the high-level political work, and the access to the Senate chambers and various White House events, I was happy where I was. I even turned Roger Ailes down when he offered me a job in New York City to join his media firm.

Had a bullet moved a bit to the left, Bush could have become president and my life would have changed on March 30, 1981. But as it turned out, Ronald Reagan's luck held when an assassin's bullet failed to do him in. The event moved Reagan closer to sainthood. So anyone challenging him was taking on a dangerous mission. Bob Packwood would make that mistake.

Problems started when Packwood decided to proceed with Tidewater IV against my advice. We were no longer the out party playing loyal opposition. We had won the Senate and the White House. Holding a policy conference could lead to trouble. Packwood decided to move ahead anyway, and to me his motives were obvious: he wanted to be majority leader eventually and the Tidewater Conference was a great way to show off his talent.

The 1981 conference took place May 15–17 and attracted so many members of the electronic media that we blew out Easton's electric generator. A record 117 politicians attended the event, including 13 senators, 74 congressmen, and 8 governors. House members Jack Kemp, Dick Cheney, and Millicent Fenwick rubbed elbows with Senators Ted Stevens and Alan Simpson. Things began to go awry when *People* magazine, on the day before the conference, ran a story on Packwood in which he was critical of President Reagan. Packwood's criticism was motivated by several factors. First, he questioned Reagan's intellectual depth. Next, Packwood supported abortion rights; Reagan did not. Then, as a die-hard supporter of Israel, Packwood opposed Reagan's plan to sell AWACS surveillance planes to Saudi Arabia.[8]

Ed Rollins, a dark eminence and a political advisor to the President, attended Tidewater to monitor Packwood's actions, though staff had been forbidden to attend. He had nothing good to say about my boss when the two of us had drinks. Rollins warned me that Packwood's "ass was grass." That worried me until I read David Broder's flattering column in the *Washington Post* entitled "High Tide for Republicans." It ran the day after the conference, which had run smoothly. I hoped now everyone could get back to work and forget about the nonbinding resolutions of the conference.

The summer began with the annual retreat of the Packwood empire. My small role would be to report on the progress of the research division of the NRSCC, so I could relax and enjoy myself. I was surprised when after my report, Packwood announced that I would be moved up to deputy director of the NRSCC. My salary went up, and my responsibilities expanded to include providing media help to incumbent senators up for election. On June 7, I prepared a memo under Packwood's name to President Reagan that would go through Ed Rollins. It summarized 33 statewide polls we had taken for the upcoming Senate races. Complimenting the President on his high approval ratings, the report then detailed appropriate ways by which he could help us keep control of the Senate in the midterm elections. The key was that we be able to use Reagan's signature on fundraising letters. Permission was eventually, grudgingly granted.

The summer was filled with wonderful events. For example, thanks to Vice President Bush, I was invited to sit in on a secret briefing by President Reagan to Republican senators at the White House. He told them that it was his intention "to spend the Soviets into the ground." It was the beginning of the end of what he would refer to as "the evil empire," cleverly picking up on the popular culture of the day.[9] The lynchpin of the President's plan was the Strategic Defense Initiative, an anti-missile system that the press promptly dubbed "Star Wars" in response to Reagan's line about "the force is with us." I was later a guest at several White House functions. And I found someone new on whom to focus my mentoring, one of my research interns, John. I met him at a cocktail party because he was interning for a congressman; we retired to a couch where we instantly fell into lively conversation. I hired him to work as a part-timer in the research division at NRSCC. He did good work, so I moved him up to full-time. And we became close friends.

On September 16, 1981, I served as a go-between for the Vice President and Packwood. Packwood had met with Reagan confidentially on the AWACS issue, and Reagan had slipped by making public part of their private conversation, violating protocol. I did the best I could to patch things up. But Packwood wanted Bush to know that Reagan owed him one.

That night I was attending a White House dinner with a date from my staff. We had drinks downstairs and then were led through the Vermillion Room and Library to the reception line, where I shook hands with Nancy and Ronald Reagan. Reagan glowed with warmth. After introducing my date, I leaned forward and told him I had been a professor in California when he was governor.

"Oh, you must have hated me as governor," he chuckled.

"Oh, no, sir. I was one of your supporters."

He grabbed me by my shoulders, turned me toward the First Lady, and said, "Nancy, here's a professor who loved us in California, can you believe it?" She laughed and patted my hand.[10]

"Thank you," she said. It was a wonderful dinner, made special by the exchange with Reagan.

In less than a month, there was another falling-out between Reagan and Packwood. Lyn Nofziger sent a note over from the White House on October 6, saying that using the President's name in a fundraising letter that Packwood signed was inappropriate. Nofziger was particularly critical of Packwood making an issue out of the AWACS sale in the letter. The reference to the AWACS sale was removed, and I hoped that things could be smoothed over. I should have realized that both sides were looking for a fight.

One of the best things that Bob and Georgie Packwood did was to put on dinners for the sole purpose of engaging in stimulating conversation. I was invited to almost every one of these monthly salons. I met Mark Shields, the PBS political pundit, through one of these parties and we remained friends for years.

On November 6, 1981, I was summoned for a soiree at the Packwoods'. The *New Yorker*'s political columnist Elizabeth Drew was there with her husband David Welch, a British diplomat. Former Republican senator Edward Brooke of Massachusetts, an African American, was there with his beautiful wife. Daniel Boorstin and his wife talked to me about their son David, who served with me on the Ford speechwriting staff. Then Boorstin, a noted historian who was still serving as head of the Library of Congress, and I had an interesting discussion about history that captured the attention of everyone else in the room. To balance me at the dinner, Susan Alvarado was added to the mix. A former aide to Senator Ted Stevens, Susan was an avid tennis player who was now working on the White House legislative liaison staff. She and I would be doubles partners at various tennis events, one time playing against Senator Dan Quayle and his wife Marilyn.

After the guests left and Georgie retired, Packwood and I retreated to his basement lair. We commiserated on the evening. I thanked Packwood for letting me see how Washington worked up close and personal. He told me I was welcome, but he had something else on his mind. He wanted to turn his attention to civil liberties and particularly to First Amendment issues. "Why are you interested?" I asked.

"Frankly, I like the history of the issues going back to the Magna Carta. You know what an Anglophile I am. But there is another angle."

"What's that?"

He sipped his beer. "The news media loves their First Amendment rights. And if I can win them over, who knows what can come of it." So there it was. He was back to his presidential ambitions again. On November 13, he spoke to the Oregon Association of Broadcasters using information I had supplied. He wrote me on November 20, "On a scale of 10, it was a 12. . . . I love the way you have rewritten the Cotton Mather quote. It is much better than the way I say it." I rewrote the speech for him, and he committed it to memory for an address to the First Amendment Congress on December 22, 1981. Bob Packwood had embarked on a journey that would change my life and First Amendment law in America.

However, before that occurred, many events intervened. Back in California, I held Maureen Reagan's hand, trying to teach her the vicissitudes of campaigning for senator. She didn't get it. I told Pete Wilson's manager, George Gordon, that we were not allowed to endorse a candidate before the primary. Gordon threw me out of his office. I learned that there were many little secrets in Barry Goldwater Jr.'s past that would keep him from getting the senatorial nomination. I told Ted Bruinsma that being a college president was not enough to get elected to the U.S. Senate, even in a crowded field. Wilson went on to win the primary and eke out a win over Jerry

Brown in the general election. But by that time, I was no longer working for the Senatorial Campaign Committee, as we shall see. And we shall also see that Wilson would pop back into my life many years later.

After a short respite, I was off to North Dakota on another political assessment. I gave a guest lecture at the University of North Dakota in Grand Forks, which was great fun. Too often students find themselves listening to professors who have never been out in the "real world" and never tested their own theories. I provided a counterstatement to that anomaly, and it was not always welcomed by my hosts.

From there it was on to Seattle and a meeting with the Washington State Republican Committee. The new party leader, Jennifer Dunn, was articulate and attractive. I was helping her do in Washington State what Bill Harris had done in Alabama. She was so successful, she eventually got elected to the House of Representatives herself.

At the end of the fall of 1981, the NRSCC left our tiny digs atop a restaurant on Massachusetts Avenue and moved to our new offices on C Street. The open house went well. Each of us on the leadership team was given a nice potted chrysanthemum, with several others scattered about for effect. One day I came back from a trip and my mum had wilted. I complained to my secretary, who was supposed to be watering it. I put the mum in our bathroom shower, watered it, and left it to drain. A few hours later, I came back and the mum had completely revived. I happily put it back on my desk. The next morning I arrived to find the poor mum wilted again, so I put it in the shower. When I came back from lunch, it had revived. I put it on my desk and told my secretary I had a very odd mum that dried out very fast, and I couldn't figure out why. She smiled and said, "Well, maybe it's under a heat vent." Someone laughed in the background, but I believed it was the result of a nearby conversation, not ours. Sure enough, the next morning I came in and the mum was wilted, worse than ever. I dutifully took the plant into the shower again and returned to my desk. After lunch I retrieved the reborn mum, but as I was walking it to my desk, the staff was in hysterics. When I got to my desk, I saw why. There sat the shriveled mum. My staff had been rotating a healthy mum into the shower every time I put my shriveled one in. At night, they took back the healthy mum and replaced it on my desk with the shriveled one. It was the best practical joke anyone had ever played on me.

My staff was very loyal to me, and I was very loyal to them. However, I remained a closeted gay man who had to continue to be careful given the constituency of the National Republican Senatorial Campaign Committee. As deputy director, I realized a rule in political Washington: The higher your head, the easier it is to cut off. However, there were times when I let someone into my closet. For example, I received a phone call one day from Senator Alan Simpson's office. His chief of staff was trying to place one of his interns from Wyoming in a permanent job so he could go to law school at night at Georgetown. I told them to send him over. His name was Marty and he turned out to be cute as a button and sharp as a tack. We struck up a close friendship.

One night over dinner, he asked, "Can you keep a secret?"

"Sure, Marty. What is it?"

Marty toyed with his food. "It's risky. I'm not sure you'll want to know it."

I got a sense of what was coming. "Try me."

"Well,"—he took a deep breath—"I'm gay and I'm afraid if I come out, I'll lose my job. What do you think?"

"Marty, let me begin by trading secrets. I'm gay too." He dropped his fork. "You couldn't tell?"

"Not for a minute. I just liked you and respected you. You don't seem very gay to me."

"Well, I am, but I need you to keep it between us for obvious reasons."

"Of course, but what would you suggest in my case?"

"If you come out, you'll lose your job at the committee. If you lose your job at the committee, you'll have to drop out of night law school. Why don't you plan on coming out once you finish law school and get a job with a good firm?" And that is just what Marty did. By the time he finished law school, he had a partner, and he is a successful lawyer to this day, appreciated in a firm known for its diversity.

January 1982 began tragically. Someone came running into our offices and told us to turn on the television. In a snowstorm and during the evening rush hour, an Air Florida jet had crashed into the Fourteenth Street Bridge, the busiest one crossing the Potomac. Before rescue teams arrived, a man named Lenny Skutnik jumped into the icy river and began rescuing people. Soon word arrived that there had been a subway crash and the system was shut down. Like many others on Capitol Hill, I chose to sleep in my office since there was no convenient way home.

A few days later, Reagan was to give his first State of the Union Address. Presidents George Washington and John Adams delivered their State of the Union Addresses orally to a joint session of Congress. However, Thomas Jefferson, who was somewhat uncomfortable with public-speaking situations because of his stuttering, decided that he would write his Annual Message to Congress. The new tradition continued through the administration of the very large William Howard Taft, whose Inaugural read like a State of the Union Address, and whose State of the Union Addresses were epically detailed. President Woodrow Wilson, as part of his progressive agenda, decided that addressing the Congress as had Washington and Adams would be a major improvement in relations with Congress, which the Democrats had conquered in the 1912 election. And ever since, presidents have trudged up Capitol Hill to deliver their annual State of the Union Address.

During his Address, Ronald Reagan praised Skutnik's heroism. When Skutnik rose from his seat next to the First Lady to acknowledge the applause, the House was no longer divided and Americans could take pride in the virtue of one man who stood for us all. Ronald Reagan made that happen and a new tradition was established. It helped the Capitol recover from the tragedy.

We continued to monitor Senate races as we moved into the primary season for most of them. Unfortunately, there was also Tidewater v to plan. It would be the last. Not only had it outlived its usefulness, Packwood made a mistake that jeopardized his career and changed mine.

This misadventure started in late January 1982 when I received a call from a leading executive search firm. The headhunter said he would like to meet with me to discuss the possibility of becoming a speechwriter for a CEO of a major company, which he could not disclose. I was flattered and assumed he would fly me to New York City for the interview. On a lark, I accepted the invitation. Much to my disappointment, the interviewer came to Washington, D.C., to meet me over lunch. Without going into much detail about the company, he said it was in the top tier but was not located in New York City or Washington, D.C. I said, "With my luck, it's Chrysler." The interviewer dropped his glass of wine, which splashed over the table.

At this juncture, Chrysler had secured loan guarantees from the government—which Packwood opposed—and had avoided bankruptcy. I knew little about Detroit or about the auto industry, or any industry for that matter. The headhunter begged me to go to Detroit just to give them a chance to talk to me. So in February, I flew to Detroit to meet with Wendell Larsen, a vice president for public relations, to discuss the position. Basically, Lee Iacocca needed a writer who would work for him and no one else in the company. Other writers wrote for other executives—including Jerry Greenwalt, the president of the company, who was pretty much Iacocca's puppet. Iacocca had risen to the same position at Ford, but had refused to be Henry Ford's puppet. One day at recess on the campus of their Catholic School, Iacocca's daughters heard the news that their father had been fired. Ford had given the news to the media before he gave it to Iacocca. Lee never forgave Ford for doing that and never uttered Ford's name without preceding it with some form of the F-word. After being fired, Iacocca recovered a few days later by being named CEO of Chrysler. His ambition was to have Chrysler replace Ford as the country's number two automaker. But first he had to rescue Chrysler from the brink of bankruptcy, which he did by launching a massive lobbying campaign on Capitol Hill. Smartly, Iacocca pledged to keep the Chrysler headquarters in Highland Park, near downtown Detroit. And though he got his loan guarantees, the company never had to use them. Thanks to Iacocca, the company rebounded, though it was still struggling in the recession of 1981–82.

When I returned from Detroit, I politely turned Larsen's offer down and began to prepare for the Fifth Annual Tidewater Conference. But no sooner had I gotten to work than Packwood called me to say that he had made a huge mistake and needed my help. His voice was breaking up, something I'd never heard before. I rushed over to his office in the Russell Building.

On the previous Friday afternoon, Packwood sat drinking cheap box wine he kept in his small office refrigerator. He was being interviewed by a reporter from the Associated Press on the national debt. Near the end of the interview, Packwood admitted that previously he had been mistaken about some items on the Pentagon budget. "For example, I claimed that so-called big ticket items like the B-1 Bomber were the cause of the deficit when in fact they are just a fraction of the budget."

The reporter joked, "It's pretty dumb to make those assumptions."

Packwood replied, "If you think I'm dumb, you should have to go down to the White House and deal with Reagan." He then claimed, "Reagan told us, 'You know, a black man went into a grocery store and he had an orange in one hand and a bottle of vodka in the other, and he paid for the orange with food stamps and he took the change and paid for the vodka. That's what's wrong.' And we just shake our heads." On Saturday, the reporter filed the budget story without mentioning the anecdote about Reagan, but the story as released was damaging nonetheless. It claimed that Reagan's "idealized image" of America was driving women, blacks, and other minorities out of the party. I could hear the wine talking as I read Packwood's comments.

On Sunday, the Packwoods attended a state dinner at the White House, where Ronald and Nancy Reagan greeted them coldly in the reception line. On Monday morning, the AP reporter listened to his tape recording again, heard the anecdote about Reagan's view of food stamps, and wrote a story about Packwood portraying the President as a senile racist. The Reagans were furious. Packwood's colleagues were outraged that he had divulged something from what was to be a private, off-the-record meeting with the President. As we have seen, Packwood had previously criticized Reagan for revealing pieces of his private conversation with the President. Even worse, because the reporter had reissued the story on Monday, it appeared as if Packwood had embargoed it until after he had attended the White House function on Sunday. That was not true, and the reporter, to his credit, came to Packwood's defense on that charge.

When he read the reporter's rewritten story, Packwood saw his career flash before his eyes and called me in for help. I began by calling the Vice President, who agreed to intervene. Packwood was allowed to apologize by calling Air Force One, where the President was in flight. Reagan accepted the apology, but later told Howard Baker, the Senate leader, to "take care of the Packwood problem."[11] Nancy Reagan barred the Packwoods from all White House functions. Of all things you did not want to accuse Ronald Reagan of, it was being a racist. I sent Packwood a letter about my experience with Reagan when he was governor and advised him on how to ride out the crisis. He responded, "Your letter of March 6 [1982] to me gives advice ranking among the best I have ever received."[12]

The right wing of the Republican Party, which was already alienated from Packwood because of his position on abortion, was out for blood. Joe Coors, the conservative brewmaster, threatened to cut off all funds to the NRSCC unless Packwood was removed as its chair. Six conservative Republican senators asked Packwood to resign as head of the NRSCC. Resolutions were sent in for the Tidewater Conference that condemned Packwood. Ed Rollins stopped all of Reagan's fundraising letters on behalf of the NRSCC. The crisis jeopardized our ability to maintain a majority in the Senate in the 1982 elections. And we were about to go into the Tidewater Conference, which ended appropriately enough on the Ides of March!

As I walked into the Crystal and Blue Rooms of the Tidewater Inn for the first night's drinks and dinner, I knew this would be the last one. Despite some cancellations, the stars came out but our overall numbers were down. Congressman Jack Kemp of tax-cut fame held court in one corner of the room. Congressman Trent Lott, later senator and majority leader, circled here and there. Senators Pete Domenici (New Mexico), Slade Gorton (Washington), and Ted Stevens (Alaska) let people come to their tables while they swilled booze.[13]

We surprised everyone after they sat down for dinner when we played a personal videotape from Reagan; he greeted the guests and told them to have a great conference. Then he kidded Packwood: "I'm told that it's a tradition out there in Maryland to go crabbing. Of course, we all know it's been a tradition here [in Washington] too. But, again, I don't mean by anyone in *our* party."[14] The laughter was hearty. I looked over at Packwood and he winked at me. It's good to be friends with the vice president, I thought to myself. After dinner, clumps of celebrities gathered around the piano and sang songs, forgetting the nation's economic woes and Reagan's declining poll numbers.

The next morning the discussions began at various tables named for famous Republicans, such as Taft, Lincoln, and Teddy Roosevelt. The first resolution gently warned Reagan and the Congress that the huge deficits it was running up to end the recession were dangerous. "Voodoo economics" had become "supply side economics." David Stockman, the President's budget director, was on hand to fight and modify the resolution. He argued that spending was needed to stimulate the economy, and behind the scenes reminded those present that defense spending was aimed at crushing the Soviet economy. "We can spend them into the ground," he said, repeating Reagan's aphorism.[15]

The second resolution, initiated by Congressman Mickey Edwards of Oklahoma, begged Republicans to return to their civil rights roots to "fully integrate black Americans into the mainstream of the private economy." The resolution went right to the heart of the Reagan-Packwood feud. The third resolution, initiated by Congressman Newt Gingrich of Georgia, called for a thorough reform of the Defense Department to "streamline research, development, and procurement programs" and ensure "that every dollar will be spent wisely." The fourth resolution, initiated by Representative Claudine Schneider of Rhode Island, called for making America competitive in international markets by improving education at home. The fifth and final resolution, initiated by Congressman Jim Leach of Iowa, called for arms control. One of the "whereas" clauses said that while the United States had "a responsibility to take the lead in arms reduction negotiations," this house condemned the Soviet Union for its arms build-up, and its "invasion of Afghanistan."

I kept the house in order through all of the table discussions and debates while wining and dining the press in the evening. I often went "off the record" to say that the story Packwood told about Reagan was true, but it was not meant to imply that he was senile or a racist, only to point out that he was naive on budgetary matters. In the end, somehow Tidewater was again a success in terms of favorable press.

CHAPTER ELEVEN

Living Large with Lee Iacocca

Over Easter break I took a vacation in Maui, and then stopped in California on my way home, where Michael Douglas invited me to an Academy Awards party at Danny DeVito's house with the cast of the television comedy series *Taxi*. Michael had befriended Danny while they made the film *One Flew over the Cuckoo's Nest*. During the early evening, Michael toggled back and forth between the national champion basketball game and the awards show, clearly showing more enthusiasm for Georgetown's basketball team than Oscar nominees. I hate basketball, so I sat between Christopher Lloyd and Danny's wife Rhea watching the Oscars. When Diana Ross walked on stage, Danny looked over to me and said, "Barry Gordy needs to feed that woman."

CHRYSLER

When I came back to Washington, D.C., I received a call from Wendell Larsen at Chrysler. "Lee's going to be in D.C. and would like to take you to lunch on April 5. Please oblige him."

"Of course."

At our luncheon, Lido Anthony Iacocca cut an impressive figure. He was nattily dressed, well groomed, and tall. His face was full of expression, and, as I would learn, he would not take "no" for an answer. He told me he was willing to pay quite a lot for me to join his team. "Why me?" I asked. Lee explained that he had a vacation house near President Ford in Rancho Mirage, California. They were playing golf, and Lee told Ford that he needed a speechwriter who could move him to the next level. Ford recommended me.

"What are your goals?" I asked him while I played with my salad.

"I want to beat the crap out of Ford Motor Company, and I want my picture on the cover of *Time* magazine."

"Then you'll want to talk about national issues," I surmised.

"I already do. We need a national industrial policy. The damn Japanese are killing us with theirs. Reagan's deficit is keeping interest rates up so people can't get loans to buy cars. Chrysler operates a military tank company, so I can talk about national defense." At the conclusion of our conversation, in which Iacocca had no questions for me, he said that he would be sending a new offer within days. "Please consider it carefully. Your current boss is in some trouble." Iacocca had done his homework; I left the lunch impressed.

In Oregon over the Senate recess, Packwood was suddenly unrepentant. Perhaps he read Reagan's dipping poll numbers; the recession still held the economy down. In any case, in Portland before the Kiwanis Club on April 12, Packwood questioned the domestic program of the President. A few days later, in Astoria, he claimed that Reagan had "removed the glue that held everyone together in the Republican Party." He was not following my advice, and he was not making my job at the Senatorial Campaign Committee any easier. On the same day he was in Astoria, I called Senate press secretaries together to explain that Ed Rollins was cutting off the nose of the Republican Party to spite its face. He had every right to be mad at Packwood, but Rollins had no right to hinder our fundraising efforts on behalf of the Republican senators that were up for election. I told the press secretaries to get their bosses to call Rollins and get the decision reversed.

When I came to the office the next morning, there was a letter waiting for me from Chrysler. It provided $80,000 in compensation, a huge amount for anyone in the time of a recession, but particularly an executive speechwriter. I would be given a company car of my choosing. The cost of moving would be covered. I began calling my friends to discuss the situation. Packwood stood no chance of being reelected as head of the NRSCC, and since I had been so closely associated with him, I might be seen as a pariah in D.C. When I met with Vice President Bush, he recommended that "You get some business experience under your belt and get out of Dodge."

I replied, "Well, perhaps I'll get into one. Chrysler will let me have any car I want."

Chuckling, he recommended, "Get the New Yorker, it's their best car."

John Macksoud said it would be like "jumping off a cliff," but "you have done it before and survived. You tend to grow each time you take these chances, and that is a good thing." I called Ken Khachigian to get his opinion. Remarkably, Ken, who had started a PR firm in San Clemente after his stint at the Western White House with Nixon, was now Ronald Reagan's favorite writer, but he had promised his wife he would return to California after only a few months working for Reagan. She was not about to let him get ensnared in another Watergate. But after Reagan was shot, Ken had to stay longer than intended. He confirmed what many others told me: "Your connection to Packwood hurts you right now. Get out of town."

When I got home that evening, there was another omen. A letter said that my building would be converted from rentals to condominiums, and I would be paid to move out if I chose not to buy in. The sooner I moved, the more I got. Since Chrysler was paying for my move, I could pocket the move-out money from the condo conversion group.

If I had any doubts about leaving, they were eliminated four days later in a column by Rowland Evans and Robert Novak. The damaging part of the op-ed claimed that I had personally attacked Rollins in my meeting with press secretaries. Their paragraph read as follows:

> "You can thank Ed Rollins for this," a Packwood aide told distraught Senate Republicans. Both damage estimates and counter-offensive moves by Packwood escalated April 15 when Craig Smith, Packwood's top aide, told senatorial assistants that scrapping the Reagan [fundraising] letter would cost $30 million in campaign funds. . . . The game of political chicken between two giant "egos" could cost Republicans control of the Senate, said Smith, for which "the White House should be held accountable."

The column went on to claim that I was Packwood's "most conservative and Catholic advisor." I called Bob Novak, hoping he would print what I actually said. But Novak would not take my call. I had a note delivered to him putting my version of events in print. Still no retraction.

I met with Packwood, and he thanked me for what I told the Senate press aides. "I don't care if that fat ass Novak didn't quote you correctly, he did get the story out there. These people needed to know what that f—ker Rollins was doing to them."

I thanked him and told him I was going to accept the Chrysler offer effective May 10. He lowered his head, and said slowly and sadly, "I can't say as I blame you. It's quite an offer." On May first, I moved out of Arlington Towers and drove to our Pennsylvania house to visit with John Macksoud. We had a productive time together sorting my life out. Then it was on to a new life in a new city. When I arrived in Detroit, I rented a house on Windmill Point, a posh neighborhood on Lake St. Claire in Detroit. The house had a lovely screened porch looking out on a nice lawn maintained by the landlord. Spring was just arriving.

MY UN-LIFE IN DETROIT

The first thing I noticed in Detroit was the poverty. On the way to my office at Chrysler Headquarters in Highland Park, I saw people fighting in food-stamp lines. I had decided to give my Datsun 200SX to my sister, Avis, since I would be getting a Chrysler New Yorker from the company. Before she arrived, the Datsun's tires were slashed. There was no love for foreign cars in Detroit. After a nice visit with Avis, I replaced the tires and she drove away. A neighbor came over while I waved goodbye to my sister.

"I'm sorry about what happened to your car."

"My fault, I'm afraid; I couldn't get my sister out here any earlier to take it off my hands."

"Well, I understand why it happened, but in this neighborhood, crime is very, very rare."

"Why is that?" I asked.

"Oh, you don't know? This is where the head of a Mafia family lives. You'll see their guys patrolling the place all the time.[1] Very safe, very nice." And so it was.

The first major speech I wrote for Lee was for the Million Dollar Round-table in Atlanta, a gathering of overachieving insurance agents. The speech took four major drafts because much of the early advice I got was wrong. After filtering the speech through Larsen, I sat down with Lee, who didn't like it at all. I went down to the river and rewrote the speech completely from memory. Lee approved the new version, but thought it was too long. I revised it on the way down to Atlanta in Chrysler's private, rented jet. Lee was rather grumpy the whole way. He read the draft through, practicing it aloud once on the plane, and once again in his hotel room. Of all the clients I've had, none rehearsed more than Iacocca. It explains why, even though he was delivering a speech from manuscript, people in the audience thought he had it memorized. On this occasion, he pepped up as he walked on stage, drawing energy from the assembled multitude. Interrupted by applause, the speech received a standing ovation at its completion. Only then was Lee appreciative of my efforts. Proving yourself through another person's delivery is one of the most nerve-wracking parts of the speechwriter's job. But once it happens, a bond is created that is hard to break.

Wendell Larsen soon left to become a vice president at another company. So I had direct access to Lee whenever I needed it.[2] One of the nicest people at Chrysler during my time there was Bud Liebler, who took over public relations. One day as I was sitting bored in my office, Bud came in and invited me out to the test track in the Michigan hills. "It's about time you got the feel of the cars you are writing about." At the test track, I rode shotgun in an experimental Chrysler around an oval track with a steep angle of repose. When the car hit 90 miles an hour, the driver took his hands off the wheel.

"What are you doing?" I yelled.

"Don't worry, just watch." Sure enough, the tilt of the track held the car on course. "This is a great little baby. We are bringing Shelby in to help us with it." Carroll Shelby, the famous race-car driver, had developed the Mustang with Lee.

A few weeks later, Bud dropped by again. "Want to see how they make commercials?"

"Bud, I know how they make commercials. But yeah, anything to get out of the office."

On this particular day, Lee was filming with a production team from Kenyon and Eckhardt, the advertising firm led by Leo Kelmenson, who had helped Chrysler through the bad days.[3] The most famous moment with them, according to Lee, went this way: In 1980 in the midst of the Chrysler loan guarantee fight, Lee showed up to shoot a commercial. After makeup and blocking of positions, Lee was ready for the cameras to roll. But when he got into the script he stumbled, which was uncharacteristic. He apologized and walked to the back of the car. Then walked to the front and began again. He flubbed his lines again. On the next take, he came forward and deviated from the script by slapping the car with the palm of his hand, saying, "If you can find a better car, buy it." And the rest is history.

On this particular day in 1982, the shoot was outside, and everyone was in place as Bud and I arrived. We sat in some director's chairs that were available, but not the one with the words "Lee Iacocca" on the back. Lee's car arrived and he popped out the shotgun side. I went up to him and asked if it was all right for me to watch the shoot. "Why not?" he replied. "The more the merrier." The commercial went off without a hitch. But soon its effect was muted when a reporter wrote that "Mr. Buy American" was wearing a Burberry trench coat and Italian glasses and shoes in his commercials.

In the summer of 1982, as Iacocca's star continued to rise, the recession continued to erode Reagan's popularity. I traveled wherever Lee traveled, happy to leave Detroit behind. Like Iacocca, I loved visiting New York City,

Lee had many pals there. We flew over often from a private airport near Iacocca's Bloomfield Hills home. At the time, Lee's wife Mary was dying of diabetes. Her illness depressed Iacocca. In Manhattan, he could find solace among the friends and the glitter of what was always the Big Apple to a boy raised in Allentown, Pennsylvania.

There were several keys to Iacocca's successful rise to power. One was getting an engineering degree at Princeton, which gave him an eye for mechanical efficiency. The second was his ability to sell cars. He would go to the Division of Motor Vehicles and find out who had the oldest cars in town. He would arrive in their driveway in a new Ford and ask them to go for a spin. He quickly became the most successful Ford salesman in America.

Chrysler kept a suite at Waldorf Towers for Lee, and I had a regular hotel room next door. The Waldorf was *the* place to stay in those days. General MacArthur had an apartment there, as did Madame Chiang Kai-Shek. Iacocca was in constant competition with his pal Frank Sinatra, who lived a few floors up, to see who could have the most impressive suite. The rivalry led to more Forrest Gump moments in my life.

Because he didn't want to walk in alone or be left standing alone in the midst of various conversations, the rather shy Iacocca took to me to a party at Frank Sinatra's one night. I couldn't believe the view, nor how beautifully appointed the apartment was. Various political notables and notable stars were there. When we got back to Lee's that night, he called Chrysler head-quarters and said they needed to redo his apartment. Once it was finished in black and white with satin zebra-stripe wallpaper, Iacocca held an intimate party attended by Sinatra, Vic Damone, his wife Diahann Carroll, George Steinbrenner, and "Fuggy" Fugazie, the limousine mogul who purchased Chryslers for his fleet that serviced New York City. After Sinatra saw the redone Iacocca apartment, he ordered that his be redesigned. After Lee saw that new design a few months later, he asked that his apartment be redesigned again. "Keeping up with the Sinatras" became a little company joke.

One of the funniest moments I can remember at an Iacocca party was when one of New York's senators, Alphonse D'Amato, a Republican, and his wife dropped by early for a drink. As D'Amato came through the door, everyone, including Iacocca, turned to greet him. However, he ignored them when he spotted me and yelled, "Craig Smith, what are you doing here?" Before I could answer, D'Amato turned to the amazed Iacocca and said, "Do you know who this is? This guy ran the Republican Senatorial Campaign Committee; his research operation was the best, the best." I thanked D'Amato and shook his hand while Iacocca stood by dumbfounded.

New York City was much more fun than Detroit. At the Waldorf, I could wander down to Peacock Ally, where Bobby Short was playing the piano and singing beautiful jazzy songs. Or I could just go out and walk around seeing the sights and visiting good restaurants. I often dined with my former research assistant Johnny, who was now in Fordham Law School.

ELLIS ISLAND AND THE STATUE OF LIBERTY

By now Iacocca was being hailed nationally as a hero who had saved Chrysler in the midst of a national recession. Some in the media speculated that Iacocca was considering a run for president, since among other things, he had hired President Ford's speechwriter.[4] However, such speculation was laid to rest when President Reagan appointed Iacocca to head the Statue of Liberty–Ellis Island Commission. His job would be to raise funds to restore these national monuments. A PR firm was hired to write his speeches, but I was skeptical about their abilities; I remembered how bad the agency in Portland had been at the beginning of the Packwood campaign. Besides I would rather write about patriotic and historical matters than rubber polymers and miles-per-gallon statistics. So I bided my time.

Iacocca and I traveled to Ellis Island on a hot summer day to survey what we were up against. My maternal grandparents and Lee's parents had come through Ellis Island. When we set foot on the small island, we could see that it was in ruins; weeds grew everywhere. When our guide showed us through the cattle chutes, holding pens, and turnstiles our forebears endured, we both broke down and cried. Then it was on to the Statue of Liberty, which had also fallen on hard times. I showed Lee the entire poem that Emma Lazarus had written, not just the excerpt on the statue. When he reached the end, he cried again. "Let's use this. I can raise millions with this poem alone."

I wrote a speech on mandatory seatbelts for Lee to deliver to a joint session of the Michigan legislature. Packwood wrote me a note on July 14, 1982: "Just read Iacocca's (Smith's) speech on ideologues cloaked in the guise of testimony on seatbelts. Masterfully done!" We wanted Michigan to become the first state to require wearing seatbelts. The legislature passed the mandatory-seatbelt law. Soon other states followed, and many lives were saved. During our campaign for the laws, I wrote an editorial for Lee for the "My Turn" column in *Newsweek*,[5] and they told us it got the biggest response of any column to that date. Not all of these responses were positive; Ralph Nader wanted air bags, not seatbelts, and libertarians wanted no restraints at all.

One memorable evening of my tenure with Iacocca occurred on the night of the Italian American dinner in Washington, D.C., in September 1982 with Jack Valenti, a former speechwriter for President Johnson and now the head of the Motion Picture Association, as the MC. Besides Iacocca, the honorees for the evening were Bart Giametta, the president of Yale, and Sophia Loren, the Oscar-winning, statuesque actress. As the dignitaries gathered for the exclusive cocktail reception backstage, Iacocca asked me to get him a scotch. He preferred Dewars White Label and the bartender had it. Lee asked me, as he always did, whether I had his speech with me and what I thought of it. I told him it would be fine and showed him the ring binder under my arm. He asked if I was sure the speech would be no more than seven minutes long, the limit imposed on us by the head of the Italian American Association. "The remarks I prepared are six minutes long; you have one minute to ad lib. As always the first page is blank, so you can make notes."

"Good. Should be a short night," he mused as the crowd around him grew. I backed away and watched from a distance as more and more people came over to admire Iacocca and shake his hand. Just as I struck up a conversation with Valenti about speechwriting in the White House, Sophia Loren arrived in a stunning black gown. The Oscar-winning actress was much taller than I expected. The crowd, including Valenti, literally went dumb and then rushed over to meet her. Iacocca was left standing alone, scotch in hand. I rushed over to keep him company.

"Did you see that? She's really something." He licked his lips in lust. "Take me over to her. Introduce us."

"But I've never met her."

"Pretend, pretend. Who's to know?" he commanded. And so I steered Iacocca through the crowd and he got to meet one of his film favorites.

Once the banquet began, it became clear to me that Iacocca was wrong about the length of the evening. An hour went by before they got everyone into their seats. Another hour went by as we waded through the convocation and dinner. Finally, Jack Valenti rose and began to introduce notables in the audience. He went on and on; at almost every table, someone was asked to stand. When Iacocca finally secured the microphone, he got off the best line of the night by beginning, "If there is anyone in the audience who has not been introduced, I'd be glad to do it at this time." His speech on Ellis Island and his parentage moved the audience: "The fact is that one out of every eight persons who came through the gates of Ellis Island was an Italian. If they were like my parents, they came to this country with little more than the clothes on their backs. But they had something more important than material possessions; they had hope."

Sophia Loren spoke next, for about fifteen seconds. She simply thanked the association for honoring her and sat down. No such luck with Bart Giametta. To our horror, he gave a lecture on Renaissance Italy that lasted forty minutes. Wonderful as I thought the lecture was, this was not the place for it. I could see the steam coming out of Iacocca's ears and several people in the audience fidgeting like crazy. When Giametta concluded, there was a stampede for the restrooms.

Back in Detroit, I learned that the PR firm was paid $1 million for its first year to work on the Statue of Liberty–Ellis Island project and was a disaster. I couldn't believe how unprofessional they were. For example, they sent over a speech draft written in longhand! I took it in to Lee and told him to put me in charge of the writing operation. They could do the research, but I would write all the copy and his speeches. "You'll never have time for that," he countered.

"Lee, I'm a fast writer. I usually clear my desk here by noon."

"What in the hell do you do for the rest of the day?"

"I drive down to the river, read a book, come back to my office, and then check out." Chrysler required all employees, regardless of rank or how little they had to do, to come to work at 8:30 A.M. and leave no earlier than 5 P.M. I told Iacocca it was a stupid, inflexible rule.

He sighed. "I used to work to midnight all the time at Ford. They had to kick us out of the building. It isn't like that anymore."

No, I thought to myself, it is not—and thank God for that. So my speechwriting duties doubled and so did my travel. We were back in New York on September 16 to make another pitch for help with the Statue of Liberty–Ellis Island project. The media was all over the event. Lee and I had decided that as much as possible, we would let the Island and the Statue speak for themselves. Here are some excerpts from the standard speech I wrote for him:

> The Statue of Liberty was a gift given to America on July 4, 1884. . . . It has been a welcoming beacon of hope for all those who came to our shores through this harbor. It is a recognized symbol of hope and freedom throughout the world. Ellis Island was opened on January 1, 1892. For decades, millions of people—tired, destitute, but full of hope—passed through its gates. In November of 1954, it was closed after 62 years of service—62 years that saw the world give to America 16 million people yearning to be free. As we rebuild these symbols of our heritage, I hope all America will take part, and that the result will be a great renaissance of spirit across this great land. The restoration will also serve as a restoration of our heritage. It is a heritage that extends back through

the entry gates of Ellis Island—back across the Atlantic to England and Ireland, to France and Germany, to Spain and Italy, in fact, to all of the countries of Europe and beyond.

Lee was kind enough to make sure I was one of the people who got a Statue of Liberty medal for my work on the project. It rests on my mantel to this day.

Though the patriotic project was going well, there was still the business end of things with which to contend. In the same week in September of 1982 that Iacocca spoke about the Statue of Liberty, I attended the negotiations with the UAW, which increased my distaste for the leadership of unions. They demanded all kinds of perks that were exorbitant, particularly in the current economic environment. For example, Chrysler wanted a $50 deductible on plastic surgeries for spouses; the leaders said no. They were happy to sacrifice a decent contract for the workers in order for their wives to get free face-lifts! I begged Iacocca to go over the heads of the UAW leaders and make his case to the workers. But Douglas Fraser, the UAW head, sat on our board and Lee did not want to offend him. After weeks of wrangling, an agreement was reached, but it was not a sensible one.

Back on the speaking trail, one of my favorite moments came at the Tremont Hotel, where Lee addressed the prestigious Commercial Club of Chicago over a big monthly luncheon in October 1982. I loved the venue because both Lincoln and Douglas had spoken at the hotel during their campaign for Senate in 1858. Fifteen hundred people filled the floor and balcony at tables for the luncheon.

I incorporated some of that history into Lee's remarks. As usual he scribbled a few notes on the blank first page in his binder before rising to talk. At the time, Continental Illinois Bank had declared bankruptcy due to its issuing of bad loans. So Lee began by ad-libbing, "If I'd known how easy it was to get a loan from Continental Illinois, I would never have turned to the federal government." The audience laughed heartily, but what Lee didn't know was that the head of the now defunct bank was on the dais with him. After the luncheon, the bank president came after Lee to give him a piece of his mind. I stood guard by Lee.

He told the bank president, "If your skin is so thin that you can't take a joke, you'll never get your damn bank out of bankruptcy." The bank president turned on his heel and marched off.

A few days later, we were off to Manhattan again. Lee had been asked to march at the head of the Columbus Day Parade on Fifth Avenue, celebrated on Monday, October 13, which happened to be my birthday. So as a birthday present, he told me to march right behind him. It was a chilly day, so we were all buttoned up. The popular mayor of New York City, Ed Koch, was on one side of Iacocca, and the former city councilman from Queens and now lieutenant governor, Mario Cuomo, was on the other side. Koch had obtained loan guarantees for New York City before Lee had obtained them for Chrysler, and so there was some affinity between them. However, Lee also liked Cuomo, an Italian American whose star was rising. The truth was that Lee was marching in between two mortal enemies. In 1977, Koch had defeated the dark and brooding Cuomo in the mayoral Democratic primary, but instead of supporting Koch, Cuomo accepted the Liberal Party nomination. Infuriated, Koch beat him again in the general election. In the 1982 gubernatorial primary for governor, Cuomo got his revenge by defeating Koch. However, during a very dirty campaign, Cuomo refused to denounce signs held by his supporters that read, "Vote for Cuomo, not the homo."

The parade was great fun for me as I waved to the crowds on each side of Fifth Avenue who had no idea who I was. Poor Lee had to try to make conversation between Caesar and Brutus. When the parade was over, we had lunch in an Italian restaurant in the village with Cuomo, Koch, and other dignitaries. The room quickly divided into the Cuomo clique and the Koch clique. At one point Lee leaned over to me and said, "You know why Koch lost, don't you?"

"No, I don't. I figured with the New York base and Jewish vote he would win the primary."

"Koch is a queer."

"What?"

"Yeah, everybody knows it."

Koch was single and combative. And after I asked around, I found that there were a lot of rumors about his sexuality. Cuomo went on to become governor and then give one of the best keynote addresses ever in 1984 at the Democratic Convention. But he was indecisive about running for president and turned down a seat on the Supreme Court, in part because of the people with whom he was pictured at our little gathering on Columbus Day 1982, and at gathering after gathering.[6] You don't become city councilman from Queens without a little help from the Mob.[7]

The night of the Columbus Day Parade I had nothing planned. And I began to wonder how long I could continue with my itinerant life. While I had a place to live, I didn't have a home. I was so caught up in my duties that I had no personal life. I began to get depressed. So I went to the concierge in the Waldorf and asked him to recommend something on Broadway for me to see. He said that most of the plays and musicals were shut down because of Columbus Day; however, a play called *Torch Song Trilogy* was getting good reviews.

"What's it about?" I asked.

"Some homosexual's story. I don't know if that is your thing." By now the AIDS epidemic was on the nation's radar. I had checked with my high school buddy Tom Luhnow about the situation with him and his partner. "We were lucky," he said. "We became monogamous just when the plague started. We're clean, but losing friends all the time."

So I went to see Harvey Fierstein's *Torch Song Trilogy*. When I sat down, I was surprised at the number of celebrities I could recognize in the packed house. Phyllis Newman and her husband Adolph Green and his musical-comedy writing partner Betty Comden were sitting together. In the play, Estelle Getty, whom I loved from *Bonnie and Clyde*, was astounding as Harvey's mother. I wept heavily at the end of the play and had to hide my face in my handkerchief. The show brought all my feelings about being gay to the surface. I felt guilty about not coming out, about all the students for whom I could have been a role model, about all the wasted years without a relationship. So I drank myself to sleep in my hotel room.

In early November, I asked Lee to give me a break. I wanted to go to New York and work on election night at CBS again. Iacocca was impressed that I could land such a gig, but I could tell he wasn't too happy I would be away for a week. Little did he know that it was the beginning of the end of my full-time employment at Chrysler.

I was even more interested in covering the election than usual because the midterm election included many Senate contests for which my NRSCC division had provided the research. Dan Rather replaced Walter Cronkite as the anchorman. Rather had threatened to bolt the network if he didn't get Cronkite's chair when the old man retired. Roger Mudd was Rather's main competition and would have been a better choice. Mudd was stolid and a good news reader, but not much of an investigative reporter. Rather was terrific as an investigative reporter, as his stints on *60 Minutes* revealed. But he was wrong for the anchor post in my opinion; Marshall McLuhan would have seen him as too hot for television, a cool medium. Nonetheless, Rather would go on to become the longest-serving network anchor ever.

I reintroduced myself to Rather when I came onto the set for the first night of rehearsals. He remembered me from my previous work for CBS and as his daughter's boss in the Packwood campaign. She was one of our interns. Once we were on the air, I could see that Rather was taking the anchor position in a new direction. He spun out Texan aphorisms that sounded as phony as the emotion he tried to impart. He was terribly smarmy while trying to relate to his audience. Luckily for me, I was back to writing stories that interpreted the data for everyone, not just the anchor with the immense ego.

TOO MANY JOB OFFERS

It turned out that CBS was looking for a full-time person who could take the data generated by Warren Mitofsky's polling operation and write it into compelling stories for the reporters. The material would go through Marty Plissner, but it was clear that whoever got the job would be in line to replace him down the road. After two nights of rehearsals and dinner with Marty, I was told that he and Mitofsky supported me for the job. It would mean a pay cut to $65,000, and Manhattan's standard of living would make that salary even punier when compared to the one I had at Chrysler. Nonetheless, I was intrigued.

Over lunch on election day, Leslie Stahl commanded, "I want to know everything about the vote in the West." She had her usual spot to cover the results from the West. Hughes Rudd would cover the South, replacing Mudd, who left the network in a huff when he didn't get the anchor job.[8] Bob Shieffer would cover the Midwest, and Mike Wallace the East, all reporting to Rather as the anchorman. After our lunch, Leslie told her producer she wanted me in the producer's hole beside him during the broadcast. I got a big laugh every time I told someone that on election night I would be working in Leslie Stahl's hole. The results from the West are the last to come in, so we had lots of time to prepare. Election night went well, boosting my chances at the CBS job.

When I returned to Detroit, it was time to assess my life once again. Since arriving in Detroit, I had been careful about my health. I limited my drinking to one martini a night. I did exercises every day. I watched what I ate. But the ascetic life was boring. So I tried to refine my spiritual life at the same time. I often visited the Chapel of the Little Flower, which was the haunt of the infamous fascist Father Coughlin in the 1930s.[9] I returned to my studies of existentialism, Zen Buddhism, and Catholicism looking for a meaningful synthesis. It eventually included some observations for living a better life. For example, I found that if you did not turn the material or the personal toward the spiritual, they would let you down. In order to make that turn, it was important to assess your values and prioritize them. Is it more important to be loyal or honest? Is it more important to be artistic or truthful? In phone conversations, John Macksoud helped me through these reflective moments wherein I reformed my thinking and began to touch on a place where I could be happy while being alone. I got to know myself better and like myself more. Freud had said that we can't love others until we love ourselves. Maybe, I thought, that had been my problem.

On the professional side, I had learned a lot at Chrysler, but the business world was of no interest to me. The Statue of Liberty–Ellis Island project was meaningful, but by the end of 1982 consisted mainly of revising a standard fundraising speech. Worse, I wasn't happy in Detroit. It was a run-down, family-oriented town that had miserable winters. So I called CBS and told them to prepare a contract. I called Packwood to let him know I would be leaving Chrysler for CBS. He was surprised and told me he had a better idea for my future. He had perfected his idea about media First Amendment rights, and it would only work if I came back to Washington and headed the project. "But what will I tell CBS?" I asked.

"Don't worry about CBS. They are going to be a big contributor to our new foundation."

Packwood was putting together a consortium to support a foundation that would coordinate efforts to give broadcasters the same rights as newspaper publishers. Broadcasters were subject to such things as the equal-time and equal-access rules of the Federal Communications Commission. There was also a personal-attack rule, which required broadcasters to give response time to government officials or politicians they criticized. This rule was a corollary to the so-called "Fairness Doctrine," which required broadcasters to cover important issues and then provide on-air time for "contrasting views" on those issues from voices in the community. You may remember this from an earlier time when the local news often concluded its broadcast with the introduction of someone from the community. The introduction usually began, "And now for a contrasting view . . ."[10]

These rules had been upheld unanimously by the Supreme Court in 1969 in a horrible decision, *FCC v. Red Lion*. The decision caused the states to attempt to apply the rules against newspapers. Five years later, in a case brought by the *Miami Herald*, the Supreme Court unanimously ruled that the "free press clause" of the First Amendment prevented such regulation of newspapers. The ruling created a contradiction between treatment of the print and broadcast news. The Supreme Court eventually realized the rulings had created a problem, and sent a signal that it was ready to revisit the issue. Packwood told me, "You are the only one who can head this effort up. I need an academician who has political savvy."

"Have you raised the money for it?"

"I'm almost there. In my capacity as chairman of the Commerce Committee, which makes telecommunication law, I should have no trouble putting it together. AT&T alone has promised $250,000." Packwood had been one of the leaders of the deregulation movement, including phones, trucks, and airlines, under Carter. So it seemed natural that he would press again in other areas. Besides, deregulation was a hallmark of Republicanism, and he needed to get back into the good graces of the party after his contretemps with Reagan.

"OK," I told him. "Keep me posted and I'll think about it."

"Think about this, Craig. At CBS you'll be reporting the news. With me at a new foundation, you'll be making the news." Packwood knew he would not be reelected as head of the NRSCC, and in fact, would have no leadership position because of the bad blood with Reagan. He was striking out on his own. If he could not become majority leader, he was going to make a run at president, and the foundation was going to be his launch pad.

One of the last speeches I wrote for Iacocca was delivered in Boston to an elite group of 150 members of the Commercial Club on December 7, 1982. We flew into Boston at sunset and the city looked radiant. Our luxurious rooms in the Ritz-Carlton looked out over the Common. In our tuxedos, we headed over to the club; under its rules, no media were allowed. Iacocca would be off the record and free to ad-lib. Just before I nestled among the Cabots, the Lodges, and the Stoddards, I handed Iacocca's speech to him. Through dinner and various opening remarks by club members, Iacocca jotted notes on the blank first page.

Tonight, however, Lee decided not to be witty, but to vent. Using the anniversary of Pearl Harbor as a starting point, he lambasted the "Japs" for taking jobs away from his workers who had fought in World War II. "The damn Japs don't have to meet the OSHA and EPA standards that I do. They don't have to provide the health benefits that I do. They don't have to pay the taxes that we do." While these remarks offended me, they did not seem to offend the elderly white male audience. Once he got on script, things went well. At the end of the speech, he got a long standing ovation. The president of the Commercial Club moved to the microphone and said, "Lee, I have to tell you that in the 25 years I've been coming to this club, I've never before seen a standing ovation. In fact, I didn't know most of these guys could stand up!" When we returned to the hotel, Iacocca thanked me for the speech by giving me the plaque the Commercial Club had presented to him.

Months later, I was surprised to see Iacocca's picture on the cover of *Psychology Today* (February 1983) with a caption about his public speaking. I quickly bought a copy thinking that some psychiatrist had done an analysis of Iacocca based on my speeches. I found instead that the magazine had merely printed the Boston address without Lee's opening remarks. They were using his mug and my speech to sell copies of their magazine. A week after that, Iacocca was on the cover of *Business Week* (February 14, 1983), and a month after that, he finally made the cover of *Time* (March 21, 1983), his head jutting out of the grill of one of Chrysler's K-Cars. All through this period, he continued to use the speeches I had written for him. But I was no longer there.

By New Year's Day of 1983, Packwood had enough seed money from the media to operate the Freedom of Expression Foundation for a year. He promised to take care of me if the foundation ran out of money. I notified CBS that I would not be taking their offer after all, and explained to Marty that CBS Corporate supported the project I was going to head.[11] "Yeah," he said gloomily, "word came down from the top. And I mean the top." He meant Tom Wyman, the president of CBS, whom Packwood had called to get me off the hook.

WHO'S GLORIA SWANSON?

I decided to break the news to Iacocca during an auto show scheduled for January 12, 1983, at the Sheraton City Center in Manhattan, because he was leaving the next day for his annual two-week vacation in Boca Raton. The car display was situated in an incredibly glitzy event—lots of bars, stands of hors d'oeuvres, cooks making omelets and cutting huge slices of roast beef, and a massive dessert bar. Prominently displayed about the room were the vehicles that would restore the luster to the Chrysler name and make Iacocca even more famous: the first-ever minivan, called the "Caravan"; a new small car, the "Laser"; the redesigned trucks; and the stretch limousine.

I watched for a chance to corner Iacocca while the guests arrived. Suddenly, I saw that he had been left all alone near one of the cars. I rushed over and asked him how his drink was. "Empty, damn it."

"I thought so. Here's a fresh Dewar's," I offered.

He sipped the scotch. "I've been left here standing all alone. That just isn't supposed to happen. Tolley's not doing his job." Tolley was the new vice president for public relations. He seemed to me to be a superficial guy, but Iacocca had heard good things about him from a previous employer, American Motors, which Chrysler would eventually subsume.

I tried to console him. "Look, the press conferences went well today. People are dying over the cars. Tomorrow this will be written up as a big success."

"It better be. This little bash cost a f—kin' fortune. I just wish Sinatra and Steinbrenner would get here so I'd have someone to talk to."

Ignoring the slight, I took a sip for courage. "Well, it's just as well. There's something I wanted to talk to you about."

"Shoot," he said, panning the room looking for his friends.

"With the Ellis Island Commission on track and with this celebration of Chrysler's comeback, it looks like things are going pretty well for you."

"So?" he snorted, staring around the room and ignoring me.

"And since you'll be leaving for Boca Raton tomorrow, I thought I'd take this opportunity to tell you that I've decided to leave."

Misunderstanding me, he replied, "But the party is just beginning, you can't leave yet. Don't you want to see Sinatra?"

"That's not what I mean. I mean I want to leave Chrysler. Senator Packwood is setting up a foundation . . ."

"Oh, I get it. This is a shakedown. You want a raise. I'll talk to Tolley about it. We'll work something out."

"You don't understanding. I'll be taking a pay cut in my new job."

"You're joking. No one takes a pay cut."

"I'm serious. I'm going to be working for $30,000 less than I'm making here."

"Ah, at last, there's Steinbrenner." Turning to me, he said, "Look, Tolley will work something out. I need you to write for me. I'm going to do an autobiography and I've told Tolley to publish that speech I gave in Boston last month. So just name your price. It won't be a problem." And with that, he was off to greet the owner of the New York Yankees.

Relieved, I decided I could finally enjoy the party. I had invited Johnny to join me when he got done with his law class. He arrived a few minutes after Steinbrenner and we grabbed drinks. But the din in the room was incredible. We found ourselves shouting at one another. Since our dinner reservation wasn't for another hour, I led Johnny over to the big limousine and invited him in.

"Can we do this?" he asked, wide-eyed.

"Sure, I've got my Chrysler badge on." I pointed to the security tag and we jumped into the back seat of the huge limo. I slammed the door shut and the noise stopped. It was great.

After about ten minutes, the door next to me opened and this tiny old lady in a foxtail coat looked in. "Do you like this carriage, young man?"

The voice was unmistakable, and my knowledge of old movies came in handy. "Yes, ma'am. In fact, Miss Swanson, you'd love it."

"May I come sit in it?"

"Of course, of course." Gloria Swanson, the star of silent films and *Sunset Boulevard*, was also the former paramour of Joe Kennedy Sr. She crawled into the car and began to ask a dozen questions. How big was it? Was it available in other colors? I kept up with her as best I could, and then I saw something odd through the tinted windshield. Huge, bright lights were rolling toward us. Was I dreaming this? Had we all been reincarnated into *Sunset Boulevard*? Or was I just drunk?

Then it hit me: someone was making a commercial. I poked Johnny in the ribs and whispered, "We've got to get out of here." He promptly opened his door and slid out. I tried to exit after him, but Miss Swanson had more questions. She pulled me toward her, her bony hand on my wrist.

"You know," she said in her best diva voice, "Lee will give me one of these if I make a commercial about it right now. What do you think?"

"It's a great car for a great star."

"You rhymed," she laughed. Then she crooned, "I've always loved limousines."

Just then Iacocca came into view. He opened the door on her side of the car and looked in. Before Swanson could say a word, he looked at me and said, "What are you doing in here?"

Before I could answer, she saved me. "He's doing a wonderful job of selling me this car, Lee. How clever of you to have him sitting in here just when I arrived. Everyone says you are a genius and now I know why?"

I eased myself out of the limousine while Iacocca and Swanson made small talk. "Let's get out of here," I ordered Johnny. And we left. Once out the hotel door, I began to jabber on about meeting Gloria Swanson. Johnny made me feel very old when he asked, "Who is Gloria Swanson?"

Over dinner at the Edwardian Room in the Plaza Hotel, I explained to Johnny who Gloria Swanson was. He said, "I thought she was some bag lady who had her coat on inside out."

At the table next to us, I noticed that Hume Cronyn and Jessica Tandy were just finishing dinner. Johnny didn't know who they were either. So I explained that they had starred together in *The Gin Game* on Broadway, but tonight they were in a play about Appalachia, with music by Keith Carradine. I smiled at Ms. Tandy and gave her a little salute, and a charming smile came back.

The next day I learned that by resigning I had hurt Iacocca's Italian pride, and he started a rumor that he had fired me and that's why I was going to Washington, D.C., for a pay cut. My friends at Chrysler knew this claim to be untrue, but since it made sense out of the facts, it took a while for slander to die at the company. Lee went through three speech-writers in the next six months.[12] The rumor about my being fired wasn't finally killed off until 1986, when I was brought back to Chrysler as a consultant to write speeches that framed the launching of Chrysler products in Europe. This effort was headed by Bob Lutz, a brilliant man of Swiss descent who could speak several languages. He had my speeches translated into French and German, depending on the audience, and told me to make sure I used no metaphors that might confuse a foreign audience. Then in Paris, while answering a question about how Chrysler would know how many cars should be shipped to Europe, he said in French, "Well, I guess we will have to play that by ear." Suddenly, a sea of French economic and automobile reporters began touching their ears, not understanding Lutz's American metaphor. He eventually went to General Motors and became its leader after Lee refused to name him president of Chrysler because Lee was afraid Lutz would overshadow Lee's success.[13] Instead Iacocca chose the feckless Bob Eaton, who eventually sold Chrysler to Daimler Benz. By that time, Iacocca was in retirement but still a shareholder. He sued to have the deal canceled, but lost in court. In 2008, Daimler dropped Chrysler and it floundered, finally being bailed out by the federal government in 2009 and sold to Fiat, the Italian car maker.

CHAPTER TWELVE

President of a
National Foundation

ON SUPER BOWL WEEKEND IN 1983, I LEFT DETROIT, DROVE A
rented car to my Pennsylvania house, and had a heart-to-heart talk with
John Macksoud about my future. At age 38, my life could be described
as restless. I'd worked on three campuses, held several political positions,
moved to Detroit, and done some moonlighting with the networks and
George H. W. Bush. Sometimes I had to move on, as in the case of San
Diego State, the University of Virginia, and Ford's loss of the presidency.
But in other cases, such as leaving Birmingham, I had made the decision to
leave even though I had been offered a damn good position. Being closeted,
I continued to feel like a fish who couldn't find a suitable pond. That feeling
contributed to the need for change. However, the moving and resituating
further enhanced the feeling of being apart from others.

John provided some comfort by telling me he was happy I'd gotten the
business world and the political world out of my system, and thought I
could do some real good for freedom of expression in America. I would be
returning to a place that had been my home twice before, the Washington,
D.C. area, and I was happy to be running a nonpartisan think tank that
was closer to my academic roots than the business or political environment.
Maybe something permanent was finally coming together for me.

I drove through a tremendous snowstorm a day later, arriving in Arlington just in time to watch and celebrate with old friends the Redskins' victory
over the Dolphins in the Super Bowl. That Monday I moved into a twelfth-
floor apartment in Madison House; it had a great view down the Potomac
toward Mt. Vernon and was within walking distance of the Metro line and
quaint Old Town Alexandria.

I completed the legal work to set up the Freedom of Expression Foundation with the help of Paul Berger, Packwood's pal from law school. The advisory board included such luminaries as Katharine Graham, the publisher of the *Washington Post*; Arthur Ochs "Punch" Sulzberger, the publisher of the *New York Times*; Thornton Bradshaw, the head of RCA and hence its subsidiary, NBC; Jack Valenti, the head of the Motion Picture Association of America; Richard Munro, head of Time-Life Incorporated; Alan Neuharth, the head of *USA Today*; Eddie Fritts, the chubby president of the National Association of Broadcasters; Bob Erburu, the CEO of the Time-Mirror Corporation; Larry Jinks of the Knight-Ridder chain; Charlie Brown, head of AT&T; Tom Wyman, president of CBS; Drew Lewis, CEO of Warner/American Express; Robert Marbut, CEO of Harte-Hanks Communications; Thomas Wheeler, head of the National Television Cable Association; Thomas Krattenmaker of Georgetown Law School; and Leonard Goldenson, the founder and head of ABC. Hard to beat those creds.

As I dealt with the executive assistants of each of these media moguls, it became apparent that their companies were not going to contribute what they had pledged to Packwood in one lump sum. They were going to pay in yearly installments. So the $250,000 from AT&T became $25,000 a year. The $30,000 from the networks and large newspapers became $10,000 a year for three years with an option to renew. At first I was taken aback by this news, but in the end it worked to our advantage. No one contributor could dominate our operations. Furthermore, I was forced to find other contributors, which greatly broadened our coalition and our funding base. For example, the regional Bell operating companies each came on board for $10,000 a year.

The second thing the executive assistants told me was that we needed a two-tier system for board members. Katharine Graham was not going to sit on the same board with lobbyists like Fritts, Wheeler, and Valenti. So we put the association lobbyists on a "Policy Advisory Board," and the owners of famous entities, such as CBS and the *Washington Post*, on the "Research Advisory Board." The word "advisory" was crucial to my way of thinking because it prevented the boards from running the foundation; they could only "advise" it.[1] Both boards met together once a year. Senator Packwood ran the board meetings in his office at which I discussed strategy.

To attract board membership, Mrs. Graham agreed to host advisory-board dinners at her famous house on R Street in Georgetown after the work meetings in Packwood's office. As I entered Mrs. Graham's home for the first dinner, I saw on a side table a small, discrete black-and-white photo of her husband, Philip Graham. He had committed suicide in the house in the late '50s, and that's when she took over the company. Against all odds, she prevailed and improved the newspaper, which survived all of its rivals. It was the toast of the town in the Kennedy-Johnson era, but won two ears and a tail when it brought Nixon down over the Watergate cover-up.

The bright green back lawn sloped down toward the Potomac River; there, we sipped cocktails and watched the sun go down. In the large dining room, Mrs. Graham headed one table of guests and insisted that I sit next to her during our first dinner. Senator Packwood headed the other table, and then at dessert time we would play musical chairs and be reseated next to someone new. Over the years around the two intimate tables, I was privileged to hear Jack Valenti tell stories about Lyndon Johnson, Jackie Onassis, and John Kennedy. Drew Lewis revealed his ambition to be on Reagan's Cabinet. Leonard Goldenson talked about the founding of ABC. Tom Wyman was very interested in my experiences at CBS News.

Mrs. Graham's graciousness and candor enhanced her hosting abilities. One evening at the beginning of dinner, a hot pâté smeared onto a slice of pear arrived. It was supposed to be an appetizer. She took one bite and said to me, "I don't think this is very good. What do you think?"

"The combination doesn't work, I'm afraid." She quickly exited and then returned. The appetizers were replaced seconds later.

Making the Freedom of Expression Foundation into a credible force was hard work. The advisory boards gave us clout and opened a lot of doors; but the staffs of the trade associations were reluctant to give up power and follow my lead. I assembled a small, loyal staff. Joel Bolstein, from the Senator's Commerce Committee staff, would do the research while he attended law school at night. Johnny would intern over the summer of '83 while on break from Fordham Law School. Most important, I brought in my high school buddy Tom Luhnow from San Francisco, where he lived with his partner. He would do all the inside work: payroll, taxes, audits, and the like. Tom was a superb writer and I trusted him to edit all my prose from fundraising letters to books. It was also great to have someone to confide in. Tom and I often commiserated over the AIDS pandemic. The Christian Right took the crisis as a sign from God that homosexuals were going to hell. Heterosexuals got anxious when they learned the disease could spread to them. Scare tactics were pervasive and we all lived in fear. The mere possibility that you *might* be gay often sent people running. It was a dark time—almost a whole generation of gay people would be lost.

RUBBING ELBOWS

Thanks to our board members and Senator Packwood's clout, I was invited by ABC to the White House Correspondents' Dinner on April 23, 1983, in the Washington Hilton. The table included Congressman Edward Markey (D-MA) of the House Commerce Committee; he was handsome and articulate and very ambitious. He would soon become an arch enemy because he favored regulation of the content of the broadcast news media. Senator Packwood's former chief of staff Mimi Dawson, now from the Federal Communications Commission, was at the table and rather surprised that I was there. And sitting next to me was one of ABC's big stars, Barbara Walters, who looked much younger and even more attractive than she did on television. She and I got into a debate about the media declaring presidential elections before the polls had closed in all states. "I thought it was awful that the networks, including ours, would call Reagan the winner before West Coast polls had closed," she argued.

I replied, "The study we did at CBS News showed that equal numbers of Democrats and Republicans stayed away from the polls on the West Coast on election night in 1980. Calling Reagan the winner didn't make a difference in terms of party turnout."

"But that means there was a lower turnout in the West than the East."

"What is wrong with that?"

"Well, I just think the more people who vote the better."

In response, I revisited my anti-democratic side. "I don't want people voting who don't really care about the election. Most of the voters are pretty ignorant of the issues."

Mimi intervened and changed the subject, asking Walters what her key to success was. She answered, "Perseverance. I just never give up until I get the interview. That's how I got to Castro when no one else could." There is something to be said for that.[2]

Other perks became common. I was a guest of ABC whenever the Monday Night Football game was in Washington, D.C., which was great because I was a huge Redskins fan. George Allen was the coach of the L.A. Rams, my favorite team when I lived in California. When I moved to Virginia in 1973, Allen took over as head coach for the Redskins. He never had a losing season and won a couple of Super Bowls.[3] CBS had me in as a guest at the U.S. Open Tennis Tournament in Flushing every year, which was a thrill. NBC invited me to the taping of their *Christmas in Washington* show.

In the meantime, I ramped up the foundation's research agenda to enhance its credibility. The foundation's first research monograph was a book by John Armour called *Substance and Shadow*, which laid out the Founders' understanding of the First Amendment. I got a grant from the National Association of Broadcasters to go on a national lecture tour, and used my campus connections to get booked here and there. I lectured on the evils of the Fairness Doctrine at the University of Texas Law School one morning, and then on rhetorical theory for their School of Communication that afternoon. I returned to Penn State for a lecture to the Broadcast and Speech Departments, which allowed me a side trip to visit with John Macksoud at our little house on the hill in the woods. I was the guest speaker for South Dakota State's Journalism Day, and lectured at Rider College's Department of Journalism and then threw in a free lecture for the Philosophy Department on Heidegger for my old tennis buddy from Birmingham, Professor Bob Good.

Often campuses would invite speakers to debate me on whether the Fairness Doctrine should be repealed, and pay for the opponent's travel. The practice of paying people to come in and interrupt what was essentially my gig annoyed me, so I tended be merciless in these debates. One of them was carried statewide in Utah from the BYU campus in Provo.[4] I had great fun pointing out that if a broadcaster called for a law outlawing prostitution, he would have to provide under the terms of the Fairness Doctrine contrasting views from a representative of the prostitutes. Many a Mormon in Utah became an opponent to the Fairness Doctrine that day. We were eventually able to get enough money from the NAB to videotape my four major lectures, each with a different introducer. These included Dan Rather from CBS, Tom Jarriel from ABC, Tom Brokaw from NBC, and Daniel Schorr, then at NPR. Gannett, publisher of *USA Today*, gave us a grant to write up study guides for a course in First Amendment law to accompany the tapes we distributed to campuses. More contributors joined the foundation, including GTE, Newhouse Foundation, American Express, Getty Oil, Pulitzer Broadcasting, Cox Communications, Comsat, Hubbard Broadcasting, Playboy, Pulitzer, Scripps-Howard, Western Union, and yes, Chrysler.

In raising these funds, I learned several lessons. First, I had to make the pitch for the funds to the decision maker. No one else could explain the foundation's purpose, answer tough questions, and demonstrate how it worked to the contributor's advantage. When I went to J.C. Penny Company, I met with a vice president who assured me the foundation would be funded —after all, Sears had joined—but he would take the pitch "upstairs" for me. We never got a cent from J.C. Penny. For a long time I tried to get a meeting with John Kluge, the media mogul who ran Metromedia

Broadcasting. Finally, I was seated next to him at a luncheon and made my pitch. His response: "Why didn't you come to me sooner?"

"Because I couldn't get through your gatekeepers." Kluge not only became a donor, but treated me to the best seat in the house for *Cats* in New York City, a musical he had helped to produce.

Second, professional fundraisers are useless. Most of them won't work on commission because they know they can't raise you much money. They also rely on you to write their pitches for them, which they then take to the same people they have hit on time and again, or ones you supply to them. They rarely master enough information to answer difficult questions during their pitches.

Third, a famous board gives you enormous credibility. Few people in the media business had more credibility than Katharine Graham or Thornton Bradshaw. People wanted to meet them and would contribute to get that opportunity.

Fourth, have a patron with clout. While controversial, Senator Packwood was in an important position. The law says that people can pay for access to a member of Congress; they can't pay for influence. Talk about splitting hairs. In a classic case of how this worked, the executive director of the MacArthur Foundation, which funds the famous genius grants, wanted to meet with Senator Packwood to discussion a tax problem that his foundation faced. Senator Packwood, as a member of the Senate Finance Committee, could solve that problem. The executive director made a $25,000 grant to the foundation, and of course, *totally unrelated* to that, was given *access* to Senator Packwood.[5]

To raise money for the foundation, the Senator traveled to various locations. If the speeches went well, he would drink with me late into the evening. Like many other workaholic perfectionists, Senator Packwood's drinking was in direct proportion to his sense of accomplishment. On one occasion, after a speech at ABC headquarters in New York, Senator Packwood, two ABC lobbyists, and I sat down for drinks at a table in the bar of our plush hotel. After the first drink, the Senator told the lobbyists to "buzz off, because I need to talk to Craig about some strategic matters." As they left, I smiled to myself thinking how nice it was to be the Senator's close advisor. He burst that bubble when he said, "You see those two women at the bar?"

"Yeah."

"They are prostitutes. Let's take them up to our rooms."

I was stunned. So that's why he wanted the lobbyists to leave. More surprising, he must not have guessed that I was gay. I had been better at hiding my true identity than I thought. After I recovered, I responded, "I don't do that sort of thing." I looked over at the women, who were fashionably dressed in black, arms and shoulders bare, their spiked heels hooked into the bottom of the bar stools. When the Senator left the table, I finished my drink and went upstairs to my room, hoping to get some rest. I was finally beginning to fall asleep when I heard a key in my door. A drunk ABC executive who had been at the dinner flopped through the door holding onto a young man in a tuxedo. "Excuse me!" I yelled. The executive quickly apologized and vanished. Good lord, I thought, everyone's having fun tonight but me.

By this time, we were renting a townhouse a block south of the Capitol. The house had once been owned by Congresswoman Millicent Fenwick, made famous in Gary Trudeau's *Doonesbury* as Lacy Davenport. She had been a star at our Tidewater conferences before she resigned her seat in 1982 and made an unsuccessful run for the Senate. It was fun to explore the neighborhood of the House side of Capitol Hill. It had its pubs, like the Hawk and Dove (which only recently went out of business), quaint row houses, the National Republican Congressional Committee, and St. Peter's Roman Catholic Church, a gem into which I often retreated.

The House side of the Hill is different from the Senate side. Its bars are funkier and more down to earth. Clientele are younger because House aides tend to be younger than Senate aides. Remember, House members serve two-year terms; senators serve six-year terms. So there is more turnover on the House side and the salaries are lower. Having regularly to trek over to Packwood's office on the Senate side or to lunch with a lobbyist, I could see the difference on a daily basis at the upscale restaurants, such as La Brasserie, with an older crowd sitting along Massachusetts Avenue. The Senate side also had the advantage of being closer to Union Station for quick trips to New York on the Metroliner.

By the end of 1983, I was secure enough in my job and had enough money in the bank to buy a condo in my building on the Potomac. So I left my rented 12th floor view and moved down to a smaller 6th floor place. It faced north, so neither the light nor the view were as good. But it was mine, and it began to appreciate in value as the economy recovered and we moved into the Reagan boom years created by "voodoo"—that is, "supply side"—economics.

KILLING THE FAIRNESS DOCTRINE

Now that we had completed the research necessary to establish the foundation's and my credibility, Senator Packwood and I decided to hold three days of hearings (January 30, February 1 and 8, 1984) on legislation (S. 1917) to repeal the Fairness Doctrine and its corollaries.[6] Coordinating the three days of hearings was not easy, but when it was done, all sides were heard from, and Senator Packwood could revise his legislation and take it to the full committee for a vote. John Armour and I kicked off day one of the hearings, which was dedicated to scholars, historic research, and constitutional arguments. Armour and I covered the original intent of the colonial founders of the nation with regard to freedom of expression. When I finished my testimony, Senator Barry Goldwater joked that he didn't "go back to the colonial days" but nonetheless had some questions. At the end of the exchange, Goldwater agreed to cosponsor our legislation, eventually writing a preface to a study of mine on a completely different topic, the famous Compromise of 1850, which saved the nation from civil war for a decade.[7]

Later on the first day of hearings, such notable scholars as Thomas Krattenmaker of Georgetown Law School testified that the "Fairness Doctrine and its corollaries" were unconstitutional. A passel of deans of schools of journalism took the same position, as did the Society of Professional Journalists. The chief scientist for the FCC chimed in that the Supreme Court's argument from 1969 that the airwaves were scarce no longer applied. Technology had solved the problem of narrow bandwidth, and cable was now available to most Americans.

The next day, those who favored the Fairness Doctrine were sandwiched among more legal experts. We started with the Pentagon Papers lawyer Floyd Abrams, who gave a strong boost to our position.[8] Then came archconservative Elaine Donnelly, executive director of the Eagle Forum, who bragged that she used the Fairness Doctrine to defeat the Equal Rights Amendment for women. Senator Packwood questioned her extensively on how she had intimidated broadcasters into stopping their editorializing in favor of the ERA. She was so proud of what she had done that she failed to realize that she had just given us a terrific reason to do the Fairness Doctrine in.

From the left, Robert Gerz represented Ralph Nader, arguing that he couldn't get his argument in favor of airbags on the air without the Fairness Doctrine. I would later debate Ralph Nader at a forum in which he insisted that I speak first, that I give him a copy of my remarks a day ahead of time, and that there be no rebuttals. I conceded every point and the audience still thought I won the debate. Nader is a lousy speaker and an even worse debater. At one point, he compared me to Ronald Reagan, as if that would do me damage. The debate was printed in the *Free Speech Yearbook* after he was allowed to edit his transcripts.[9]

After the second day of testimony, we succeeded in conveying to a sympathetic press that our position was the responsible course that was opposed by extremists on the left and right. The third day of the hearings was the kicker. We brought in our high-powered broadcasting stars to attack the doctrine. James Batten, the head of Knight Ridder, testified—as did many others, including Bill Small on behalf of the Associated Press. But the hero of the day was Eugene Wilkins, a station manager in Spokane who got caught in the Catch-22 of the Fairness Doctrine. When the city voted to bring an international exposition to town, Wilkins's station supported the move, as did the local environmental group. But eight members of that group broke away and demanded that their opinion be put on the air as a "contrasting view." Wilkins refused, arguing that the splinter group was not a responsible minority that had standing under the Fairness Doctrine criteria. The splinter group filed a complaint with the FCC, which immediately began an investigation of Wilkins's station. The station was exonerated, but Wilkins was fired because of the legal bills the station incurred.

The hearings helped our efforts. However, the legislation was only one leg of a complex triangle. Reagan had appointed Mark Fowler, a former broadcaster, to head the FCC, and he was looking for a case to bring before it so that he could suspend the Fairness Doctrine. He found the case in Syracuse, New York, when a station (WTVH) owned by Meredith Broadcasting refused to provide response time to Nader, who opposed nuclear power. The FCC in upholding the station's position effectively suspended the doctrine. Nader appealed to the D.C. Court of Appeals and the battle was on. We might now win in court and not need to win in the Congress.

The third battle began with the development of a new technology called "teletexting." This allowed a television channel to scroll the news in hard print across its screen. Nader demanded that the FCC apply the Fairness Doctrine to the new technology. The FCC refused and that case was appealed to the D.C. Court of Appeals. It landed in the lap of a three-judge panel headed by Judge Robert Bork. He not only sided with the FCC, but wrote a very persuasive opinion undercutting many of the tenets of the 1969 *Red Lion* case. Nader appealed the ruling to the full fifteen-member Court of Appeals, which then sat *en banc* to hear oral arguments. They sided with Bork. At that juncture, the Fairness Doctrine had taken two hits and was sinking fast.

Early in 1984, Senator Packwood had become head of the power-ful Senate Finance Committee, the chief tax-writing body in the Senate. That helped us raise money for the foundation; however, the Senator did much less for us than he could have. There were two reasons: First, though it was perfectly legal to pay his expenses when he spoke on behalf of the foundation, he refused to accept any funding, fearing it could be seen as unethical.[10] Second, Senator Packwood's top priority was raising money for his reelection campaign in 1986.

He continued to offer me as a substitute for him when he received invita-tions he could not fulfill due to work in Washington. On one such occasion, I flew to Medford, Oregon, by commercial jet, and then was flown in a single-engine plane from Medford to Gold Beach on the coast. In front of the Oregon Logging Association, I was to speak about presidential cam-paigns.[11] I could see that the group was disappointed that the Senator had not come. Nervous, I spoke on the beach in front of a bonfire at nightfall. The crowd warmed to me slightly during the host's introduction when they learned I had been a presidential speechwriter for President Ford. I began by saying, "You have no idea how hard it is to write speeches for a man with an 80-word vocabulary." That broke the ice, and the anecdotes about presi-dential campaigns that followed cheered them even more. They invited me back in the following year.[12]

I also kept my iron in the scholarly fire. I continued to publish articles on how language can help people connect with spirit, and how interrela-tional existentialism can grow out of joint artistic projects or partnerships. The latter article, completed with Paul Arntson at Northwestern University, explored how couples inspired one another to transcendent spirit. These included George Sand and Frederick Chopin, Vincent Van Gogh and Paul Gaugin, and William Wordsworth and his sister.[13]

THE 1984 PRESIDENTIAL CAMPAIGN

In the summer of 1984, it was time for the political conventions. Meet-ing in San Francisco, the Democrats nominated Walter Mondale, Carter's vice president and the former senator from Minnesota. He surprised the country by picking Congresswoman Geraldine Ferraro of New York as his running mate.

Given my work for the GOP, I was precluded from covering the Demo-cratic Convention for CBS. However, I was called in to work at the Republican

Convention, which took place in sweltering Dallas starting on August 20. Just as the convention began, a young man named Gregory Johnson burned an American flag on the steps of the convention hall. He was arrested for violating a Texas law against desecration of the flag. His case eventually went to the Supreme Court, where in a narrow 5–4 ruling, his right to engage in "symbolic speech" was said to be protected by the First Amendment. That I was there and witnessed the burning gave my lectures on First Amendment law a new sense of reality for my audience.

This convention was Dan Rather's first Republican Convention in the anchor booth. In a rare moment of humility, he claimed that he needed my knowledge of conventions in general and Republicans in particular. As I've shown, his approach was different than Cronkite's, in part because by 1984, there was not much news being made on the floor of the highly scripted conventions. Much more time would be spent on interviews in the anchor booth featuring Rather. I found this approach frustrating because instead of watching the convention, we were watching the Dan Rather Show. I had my own little booth below Rather's from which I could spot people on the floor of the convention for our reporters, and also provide research and tips to Rather over a headset.

On the Sunday leading into the convention, Rather let me sit in on the *Evening News* set. CBS president Tom Wyman was there and we talked about the foundation. On Monday, Rather had a sit-down with all the reporters, and I sensed that Leslie Stahl felt very threatened by the new kid on the block, Diane Sawyer. Rather interviewed Ford in the anchor booth during our live coverage, and I was able to give him a brief hello on his way out. On Tuesday, I started the day by beating Warren Mitofsky at tennis in the insufferable heat. I spoke to the students visiting from the Washington Center, and then listened to the Ferraro news conference focusing on her husband's tax problems. I briefed Rather on Vice President Bush for his interview that evening; this interview would be much friendlier than the confrontation the nation was to witness four years later.

The last two days of the convention were fairly boring until Rather made a crack about me. Not knowing that I could hear the conversation, Rather told the executive producer that a story I gave him was probably inaccurate because "Craig is kind of a right-wing nut, isn't he?" Having failed to get an appointment in the Reagan administration because I was a moderate and too close to Senator Packwood, I exploded at the remark. Rather and I settled our differences later over coffee. But we argued again when he asked me how the convention was going, and I complained that we had missed several important stories while he interviewed people in the anchor booth.

The stories included gold medal winners from the Olympics endorsing Reagan, and Rosey Grier, the man in whose arms Robert Kennedy died, coming forward to explain why he had converted to Republicanism! Worse, though they had showed the film introducing Mondale at the DNC, CBS refused to show the film introducing Ronald Reagan, and we later learned that millions of viewers turned to the other networks so they could see the film. Rather was advancing an ideological agenda and it was not Republican.

We did get one scoop. As Reagan gave his acceptance speech, I noticed that something was wrong and told Rather to pay particular attention. "What do you mean?" he asked.

"He's off his rhythm. It's not like him." Near the end of the speech, Reagan lost his place and went off script. We had advance copies of the speech in front of us. Since it was part of my MA thesis, I realized where he was going. He started talking about there being no real Left or Right, there was only an up or down. And America must always stay on the upward path. I told Rather to report that Reagan had lost his place and fallen back on the speech he had given on behalf of Barry Goldwater twenty years earlier during the 1964 presidential campaign. We scooped everybody on the story. But when Ray Charles was led to the stage by the Reagans to sing "God Bless America," CBS again cut away. This move was particularly prejudicial in light of the fact that CBS had covered Jennifer Holiday closing the Democratic Convention. Knowing she was a Republican, I took Diane Sawyer aside and complained about the situation. She was as mad about it as I was, but didn't yet have the clout to do anything.

Back in Washington in the fall, I sent advice to George Bush about his impending debate with Geraldine Ferraro. The press was saying he couldn't win. If he was aggressive, he would appear to be bullying Ferraro. If he was nice to her, all those stories about him being a wimpy Ivy Leaguer would come back to haunt him. When Reagan performed badly in the first debate with Mondale,[14] the pressure on Bush was enormous. I advised him to stick to the issues, to ignore Ferraro at all costs, and to look straight into the camera after acknowledging the question from a reporter. "Kennedy ignored Nixon in the first debate of 1960 and played to the audience."[15] If you watch a videotape of the Bush-Ferraro debate, you'll see that Bush followed my advice until about three-quarters of the way into the debate.

For her part, I learned that Ferraro had changed clothes many times right before the debate, unable to decide what to wear.[16] She settled on a fluffy suit with large houndstooth squares that made her look like a grandmother. Throughout the debate, she continually looked down into her lectern, obviously bothered by the television lights, which led people to believe she was reading prompting notes. And then Ferraro made a naive comment about foreign policy. Bush couldn't resist. He turned toward her and said, "Let me help you with that, Geraldine." I put my head in my hands while he gave her a lesson in foreign policy.

She looked straight at him in her reply. "Don't you patronize me, Mr. Bush. I don't have to know war to love peace." It was her best and his worst moment. That night and the next day, Bush was declared the winner of the debate, but that one moment was played over and over again in news reports. As usual, the news media was looking for zingers that would arouse their audiences; reporting on the substance of the debate was more difficult and less interesting.[17]

After his failure in the first debate, Nancy told Reagan's advisors to "Let Ronnie be Ronnie." And in the second debate, the old Reagan was back. He demolished Mondale, who for some reason wore tons of makeup and it showed. Reagan and Bush soared in the polls, but more among men than women.

For election night 1984 at CBS in New York, Diane Sawyer requested that I work with her. It was a natural move for me because she was taking over John Hart's role at the Trend Desk, and I had worked with him on previous election nights. It would be her first election night for CBS and she wanted to do well. She had worked for Nixon and followed him into his exile to San Clemente. She was there when David Frost finally broke through to Nixon's guilt during their famous interviews. She and I became a solid team. At the time, she was dating Richard Holbrook, who was making a name for himself in the Reagan State Department. I was surprised because, to put it kindly, Holbrook was not the prettiest peach on the tree. So I wondered what Sawyer saw in him. "Oh, Craig," she responded, "he's sooooo bright." He was also her secret source for lots of stories. When she later married Mike Nichols, I understood why. He too is very, very bright.

On election night, our job was to develop stories from material gleaned from the exit polls: how were Catholics, or blue-collar workers, or African Americans voting. Diane was a team player and kept morale high among herself, me, and Andy Haywood, her producer. She seemed like a young coed as she worked with us. We giggled and laughed. She even gave me a shoulder rub at one point. Then when she went on the air, astonishingly she became Grace Kelly, the epitome of cool sophistication. Her seriously furrowed brow is visible to this day on the *ABC Evening News*.

Our most effective story of the evening was on how self-identified "computer nerds" were voting. About 80 percent of them voted for Reagan, and

Diane speculated that it was because many computer enthusiasts were libertarian and individualist.[18] On election night 1986, I would return and work with her again.

REAGAN'S SECOND TERM

On January 20, 1985, the CBS trailers were parked on the West Lawn of the Capitol grounds in preparation for one of the coldest inaugurals ever. The temperature was minus 5 degrees, with a wind chill of minus 25. The pipes in the foundation's townhouse were frozen. It was as cold as anything I'd seen in Chicago during my frigid stay there in 1979. This was not supposed to happen in Washington, D.C. It was decided that Reagan and Bush would be sworn in at the White House on Sunday, and then Reagan would give his Inaugural in the Capitol Rotunda on Monday the 21st.

CBS brought me on board to work with Dan Rather for this inauguration. I was in the booth with Rather early on inauguration day, having prepared a briefing book on the history of inaugurals and interesting inaugural moments. For example, William Henry Harrison ("Old Tippecanoe") ignored the advice of Daniel Webster to cut his speech in half and delivered a 75-minute inaugural address in the cold rain. He died of pneumonia a month later. Thus, he gave the longest inaugural address ever and had the shortest presidency ever. Another interesting moment was when First Lady Lucy Hayes refused to serve liquor at the inaugural ball of 1877, and was quickly dubbed "Lemonade Lucy."

I reported to Rather, who then reported to the nation, that this was the first indoor inaugural since that of William Howard Taft, who gave his address in the House Chamber. That night I attended the inaugural ball at the Kennedy Center, where I bumped into actors Michael York and Jill Clayburgh, and some friends from Birmingham and the media community. But for many reasons, the magic had gone out of the inaugural balls. There were too many of them. They were being used to raise money for the party. Since the Packwoods decided not to attend, I wasn't the guest of someone with a private box.

In early February, I took a lecture swing on the West Coast visiting San Jose State, UC Davis, Stanford, CSU Fullerton, Pepperdine, and the University of San Diego. While most of my host professors were kind and courteous, and their students were attentive, there were some professors who wanted to protect the Fairness Doctrine at all costs. This led to some uneasy situations in which I did not want to embarrass my host, but also did not want to give the impression that I agreed with her or his position. On the plus side, the trip allowed me to visit many of my friends. My former UVA student Bill Post actually served me dinner atop his apartment building on Larkin Street in San Francisco as we watched the sun go down and the fog come in.

Campus lectures later in the year at the University of Wisconsin, Northwestern, and many more were very satisfying. I visited Anheuser-Busch in St. Louis, gave a lecture in the preserved courtroom where Dred Scott had been sentenced to return to slavery, took a dinner boat ride on the Lake of the Ozarks with August Busch IV, and then I traveled on down to Springfield to lecture at Southwest Missouri State, where my MA thesis advisor taught in semi-retirement. One of the benefits of a teaching career is that you develop a network of friends and associates across the country.

In 1985, I hit on two new First Amendment issues.[19] The first was freedom to advertise. I developed the legal position that banning the advertising of legal, non-harmful products violated the First Amendment rights of advertisers and the companies that made the products. When legislation was introduced in Congress to ban beer and wine advertising on television and radio, I asked to speak at the hearing, which was chaired by Florida Senator Paula Hawkins, a Mormon and a Republican. In my testimony, I made the counterintuitive point that there was no correlation between advertising and increased consumption of beer and wine. In fact, despite huge increases in the money spent on such advertising, even allowing for inflation, "beer sales were flat." After the laughter died down, I continued: "The fact is that advertising moves those who drink from one product to another; it does not add people who do not drink to the mix." More laughter. "Furthermore," I continued, "without advertising, lite beers would never have created a market niche, and therefore, a healthy product would have been denied to millions of users." I also pointed out that unlike cigarettes, studies had shown that having two drinks a day is actually healthy. My claim was based on a study of 30,000 people conducted by the health insurance industry. "So," I told the committee members, "you can have four drinks a day and break even." Hawkins's legislation went nowhere. I was able to add contributors to the foundation, like Philip Morris, which stayed with us a very long time. When I was criticized for accepting money from the tobacco industry, I rationalized that I would take money from the devil in order to defend the First Amendment. Better I take the money and use it for a just cause than the industry keep it and use it to advertise a poisonous product, I also published a book on *First Amendment Rights of Advertisers*, which the Freedom to Read Committee of the Association of American Publishers endorsed.

The second issue was the cross-ownership rule. In the wake of Watergate, the Nixon-appointed head of the FCC, Richard Wiley, imposed a rule that said newspapers could not own television stations in their own cities. The rule was aimed at the *Washington Post*, which quickly complied by swapping its station in D.C. for one in Detroit with a newspaper there that was caught in the same bind. However, other newspapers fought the rule, and the Supreme Court ultimately ruled in the late 1970s that newspapers that owned broadcast stations in their own cities before the rule went into effect were grandfathered in. Thus, the *Chicago Tribune* could retain its television station in Chicago, WGN, but the *Chicago Sun-Times*, which did not own one, could not buy one if it wanted to. This created an uneven playing field in which the *Tribune* could use profits from its television station to prop up its newspaper. To its credit, the *Tribune*, which was a member of my foundation, joined us in fighting the rule.

By 1985, it was apparent that the cross-ownership rule not only created an unfair competitive environment, but was hampering the ability of independent newspapers to survive. With so many channels available to viewers on cable, it made no sense to prevent newspapers from owning a station in their own towns. They would not have a monopoly on opinion, and the cash flow from a television station might keep the non-chain papers alive. Our coalition swung into action and the FCC agreed to hear our plea. I was invited to speak at the prestigious D.C. Bar Association to present our position on this issue. Many favorable editorials followed.

In June I invited my nephew Danny to come to D.C. and intern with us. I was helping Danny get a degree at San Diego State and thought a visit to the nation's capital would do him good. To celebrate the official start of summer, we sailed across the Chesapeake Bay, docked in St. Michael's, and enjoyed blue crabs and beer. We slept on the boat and then sailed back to Annapolis the next day. On the Fourth of July, Danny was completely taken with the fireworks display over the Potomac and was able to retreat with his friends to our office on South Capitol to spend the night and not fight the mobs to get back to my condominium. Later in the summer, we were the guests of Legg-Mason, who handled the foundation's accounts, at their professional tennis tournament in Rock Creek Park. We had wonderful seats and could see all the big-time players of the time, including Connors, Vilas, Lendl, and McEnroe.[20] Lendl was my favorite—always a perfect gentleman and self-made, not a natural talent. I could identify with that.

The Fairness Doctrine fight continued in earnest when the FCC held a hearing on it in preparation for their ruling in the *Meredith* case. We put together a great lineup for the event. CBS's Eric Sevareid came out of retirement to oppose the doctrine, as did Bill Monroe of NBC News.[21] My testimony reviewed the standard arguments against the Fairness Doctrine: it chilled speech and was unconstitutional; it was not justified by the scarcity-of-spectrum argument because cable had solved that problem and now spectrum space for channels went begging for buyers; it contradicted the Supreme Court's ruling in the *Miami Herald* case, which said that newspapers could not be required to present contrasting views. Now, all we had to do was wait for the FCC ruling.

AT THE MONASTERY

Balancing my policy work were the visits with John Macksoud. He had become something of a monk, relying on the philosophy of Søren Kierkegaard, who argued that the only way to God was down a singular and lonely path that ended with a leap of faith. By this point in his life, John had contact only with his girlfriend Judy, who lived near him, and me. He had stopped drinking alcohol and consuming meat. His psychological analysis of people was based entirely on Freud, and was always fascinating and sometimes scary.

My visits were a retreat into a monastery, which cleared my mind and made me a better writer and thinker. I was expected to perform certain tasks, such as pruning the trees and clearing brambles, cleaning out the cellar, and painting here and there. I had to check my ego at the door. However, I began to realize that John was trying to re-create me in his own image. John's method, one used by many a professor in the mode of Socrates, was to question your every premise until it was destroyed. It is so much easier to tear down ideas and beliefs than to build them up. His hope, I suppose, was that when nothing was left, I would embrace his way of thinking.

However, in my case, I never got to that point. My search for a transcendent sense of spirit saved me. I had concluded that I had a soul and that it would allow me to associate with or glimpse spirit beyond the material world and personal disappointments, and certainly beyond logic. Because spirit was perfect, nothing could be added or subtracted from it. Hence, while we could expand our souls and bring spirituality to our lives and our creations, we could not become one with spirit. At best, once our bodies gave out, our souls could enter an eternal stream of superconsciousness that associated with spirit.

When John realized he could not possess my soul, he decided that it would be better for us to continue our conversations by phone only. I was no longer welcome at the Pennsylvania retreat, which I owned. I had bought John's interest out to supplement his income. "Bodies get in the way," he claimed. "Better for only our minds to connect." I reluctantly complied with his wishes. He promised to take care of the house for me. While we talked on the phone weekly, it would be years before I saw his face again.

REWRITING THE TAX CODE

After almost two years as head of the Finance Committee, Senator Packwood failed to achieve the tax reform he had sought, despite working closely with Senator Bill Bradley, Democrat of New Jersey, a terribly bright and decent man who had once been the star of the New York Knicks basketball team. The senators' efforts to put together a legislative package were frustrated by infighting, deal-making, and Packwood's own missteps. Initially, he saw loopholes in the tax law as incentives to channel investments to needed areas. The tax-incentive method was more effective, he rightly noted in a press conference, than legislative mandates or allocation of government funds. For example, tax incentives for people to put money into IRAS (Individual Retirement Accounts) encouraged savings, which in turn allowed banks to loan out more money at lower rates, which in turn encouraged building, which in turn led to more money being available for houses and businesses and thus higher levels of employment. Tax shelters for those investing in senior housing provided employment and places for poorer seniors to stay.

These benefits were what Packwood had in mind when, during a news conference, he said that he "kind of liked the tax system the way it was." That line and the Senator's own protection of Oregon's special interests sent a signal in early 1986 that the new tax bill would not differ much from the old system. Senators on the Finance Committee began to roll out their own plans for projects in their states. It began raining earmarks, which in those days we called "pork barrel spending."

Taking his aide Bill Diefendorfer to the Irish Times bar on the House side of Capitol Hill, Packwood admitted defeat. Diefendorfer suggested a whole different approach, using Senator Bill Bradley's flat tax as a foundation. On a napkin, Packwood and Diefendorfer wrote a new legislative package. Packwood and Bradley then pushed the new, simplified version in the corridors of the Senate. The investment tax credit, which cost the government $25 billion a year, would be repealed; a minimum corporate income tax would be imposed so that over all, corporate income taxes could be lowered from 46 percent to 33 percent, and provide $100 billion over the next five years to lower individual income taxes. The bill ended tax shelters and streamlined itemized deductions in return for dropping the income tax rates to 15 to 27 percent, instead of the 50 percent top rate at the time. The standard deduction was raised to $2,000 per individual. Months later, after midnight on May 8, 1986, the roll call of the Finance Committee began. When it was completed, the vote was unanimous for the Packwood-Bradley proposal. The committee rose and gave Packwood an ovation. In tears, he thanked them.

That was only the beginning of the battle. The bill had to go to the House for approval, but the House came up with its own version of the tax reform. A conference committee tried to reconcile the bills. In late August, the 83-page compromise hit another bump when some members of Congress asked that they be allowed to take the bill to their constituents over the Labor Day break. However, Packwood knew that would kill the bill. Voters would find some part of the compromise they did not like and tear the bill to pieces. He and Bradley held their colleagues' feet to the fire and kept them in session. Congressman Dan Rostenkowski did the same in the House. At 9:35 P.M. on August 16, the compromise bill that had been approved in the House was approved in the Senate and sent to the President. Reagan happily signed it and claimed it as one of the great achievements of his presidency. However, it was in reality the crowning achievement of Bob Packwood's career.[22]

CHAPTER THIRTEEN

Protecting Broadcasters' First Amendment Rights

ONE DAY IN EARLY AUGUST OF 1986, MY REALTOR CALLED TO SAY that an elderly woman who lived on the 12th floor of my building, in a condo with a south- and west-facing wraparound balcony, wanted to sell her place without listing it. She wanted a quick sale, providing enough money to get her into a retirement home in Williamsburg. I had 24 hours to make a bid before it went public. It took me five minutes to OK the deal. I moved up to the top floor of Madison House and once again looked down the Potomac and into the sunset.

During the summer of 1986, I would move up in another way. After the New York Times Company gave me a grant to write a book on the history of First Amendment challenges in America, I received a call from News America Corporation inviting me to New York for a private lunch with the Australian turned U.S. citizen Rupert Murdoch. Up to this time, I had been unsuccessful in getting Murdoch to join the foundation. Here was my chance. A limousine picked me up at LaGuardia Airport at 11 A.M. and whisked me off to Murdoch's office in the building that housed his company and the *New York Post*, his salacious tabloid. The context for my visit was clear: In 1981, Murdoch had purchased the *Boston Herald* from the Hearst Corporation; his company, Fox Broadcasting, also owned a Boston television station. He had been given a waiver by the FCC under the cross-ownership rule because the *Herald* would have gone under if it couldn't transfer revenue from the television station. Murdoch was not at all unhappy that the newspaper he bought regularly attacked Senator Ted Kennedy, often referring to him as "fat boy." Kennedy was furious and decided to introduce legislation ending Murdoch's waiver under the cross-ownership rules.

I was ushered into Murdoch's "Citizen Kane" office, where we made a little small talk and then adjourned to a private dining room overlooking the East River. We were joined by the editor of the *Post*, who barely said a word during our lunch. I noted that Murdoch served a Sanford chardonnay with our salmon; Sanford is a wonderful Santa Barbara winery. Was it a coincidence? Or had Murdoch read my resumé and learned that I graduated from UC Santa Barbara? He asked what I planned to say in my filing at the FCC regarding how the agency would carry out the Kennedy mandate. (His legislation was passed because it was attached to a spending bill that Reagan couldn't veto without bringing the government to a halt.) I repeated the arguments against the cross-ownership rule from memory. A week later, a check for $10,000 arrived to support the work of the foundation, the same amount we received from our other newspaper supporters.

When he had introduced his bill in late 1987 to end Murdoch's cross-ownership waiver, Kennedy said, among other things, that the Freedom of Expression Foundation was "a front" for Murdoch. I was furious and happy at the same time. Furious, because Kennedy had slandered the foundation, which had many more supporters than Murdoch, including Kennedy's friends at the *New York Times* and the *Washington Post*, and we had attacked the cross-ownership rules long before Murdoch came into the picture. Happy, because I could use the attack by Kennedy to raise funds for the foundation from conservatives. I held a press conference in which I listed all of our contributors and our board members, including Katharine Graham. I then pointed out to the press that Kennedy could not be sued for anything he said on the floor of the Senate, but if he was not on the floor of the Senate or in one of its committees, his speech was not protected.[1] Therefore, I challenged him to come off the floor of the Senate and repeat his charges about the foundation. "If he does," I declared dramatically, "I will sue him for slander." Needless to say, Kennedy never took up the challenge, and the coffers of the foundation were filled anew.

In the meantime, the press, including Graham's liberal *Washington Post*, went after Kennedy and his sneaky tactics. On January 5, 1988, the *Post* wrote, "It is disgusting that these all-inclusive spending bills . . . become vehicles for special, personal and even petty interests pursued by legislators when they think no one is looking." Six days later, I was quoted in the *New York Times* on the issue. On January 6, 1988, the *Wall Street Journal* weighed in: "Senator Ted Kennedy now admits he plotted to kill a newspaper he doesn't like; indeed he boasted about it."

Murdoch was forced to sue the FCC, which was commissioned to carry out Kennedy's legislative mandate. When the case of *News America*

Corporation v. FCC was finally resolved, we were vindicated. The Kennedy legislation was condemned as a "bill of attainder," that is, aimed not at a group or category of businesses, but at one man, Murdoch, and therefore it was unconstitutional. In footnote 11, the U.S. Court of Appeals for the District of Columbia wrote:

> Senator Kennedy appeared to believe that the Freedom of Expression Foundation was little more than a Murdoch front organization working in concert with News America. . . . That perception is not borne out by the record in this case. Freedom of Expression Foundation is a nonprofit organization supported by numerous daily newspaper publishers, broadcast licensees, newspaper and broadcast trade associations, and other corporations. For instance, the *Washington Post* and the *Times Mirror* organizations are major contributors; News America is a relatively minor one.[2]

The foundation was an even bigger player on the First Amendment stage. The decision reestablished the FCC's right to issue waivers for the cross-ownership rule. We filed papers asking the FCC to abolish cross-ownership rules altogether. In response, they voted to reform them in a way that allowed for more waivers and expanded cross-ownership opportunities.

MAKING A RUN AT THE FCC

For his 1986 Senate race, Packwood had amassed a huge $4 million campaign war chest. His opposition in the Republican primary was a fundamentalist minister who attacked Packwood on the abortion issue and for his disloyalty to Reagan. Against my advice, Packwood decided to hammer the minister with negative radio ads. The strategy backfired when voters decided Packwood was using his money unfairly. He won the primary, but it was closer than it should have been. Learning his lesson, Packwood went on to an overwhelming general election victory as I sat on the set at CBS doing another stint with Diane Sawyer. We were saddened by the fact that the Republicans lost their majority in the Senate despite Packwood's win.

Packwood found himself without the prestige of being a committee chairman, and with his wife Georgie beginning to protest his drinking. She demanded that Packwood and their children enter counseling. The children must have squirmed through these sessions, especially when Packwood admitted that his career was more important to him than his family.

I learned this sad story on one of the many days that he and I sipped wine in his underground chamber in the Capitol building late in the afternoon. (Senior senators get these special rooms in the bowels of the Capitol for their private use.)

Nineteen eighty-seven began with a bang when Mark Fowler resigned from the FCC and I became a candidate for the Republican opening on the commission. I was supported by Packwood, which wasn't much of an endorsement with Reagan, who would make the appointment. Vice President Bush told me he would support me after his personal candidate, an African American aide, was eliminated. However, Eddie Fritts of the NAB and other members of the foundation's boards badly wanted me on the FCC and let the White House know. I called in chits from all the senators I had helped over the years. When letters came in from Senators Alan Simpson, Strom Thurmond, Pete Domenici, Mitch McConnell, and Barry Goldwater, it was clear I was the Senate's candidate for the job and I would have no trouble getting confirmed if nominated.

But getting the President to nominate me was another matter. The evangelicals wanted one of their broadcasters on the FCC, and the White House tried to appease them, given their support for Reagan. However, it was eventually discovered that the evangelicals' potential nominee was a closet atheist! Another candidate moved forward from another quarter, only to be found guilty of tax evasion. Bush's candidate languished on the list.

As lead candidates bubbled up, they could be seen at various functions on the arm of the former chair of the FCC, Dick Wiley, whose claim to fame was imposing the cross-ownership rule in 1975 to punish the *Washington Post* for its role in the Watergate crisis. He now opposed the cross-ownership rule, realizing that it was broadcasters who buttered his bread. After stepping down from the chairmanship of the FCC, he had formed his own law firm and by 1987 was the preeminent communications lawyer in the nation. He would volunteer to show potential FCC nominees around, wine and dine them, and then assure them that he could coach them through the confirmation process.[3] Wiley, with whom I had played some doubles tennis at NAB events, paid no attention to me until May. That's because on May 5, Tom Griscom, assistant to the President for communications and planning, wrote, "I have looked into the situation regarding the seat to be vacated by Mark Fowler and am happy to advise you that you are very definitely a candidate for the position. . . . You are very much in the running. I'm hoping it won't be long before I have something nice to tell you!" Since Griscom had worked for and was close to Minority Leader Howard Baker, his words meant a lot. Sure enough, I was finally called to the White House for an interview with Patrick Dennis, the head of White House Personnel; my name then appeared all over the trade publications, which claimed I was sure to get the nomination. Dick Wiley took me by the arm at the first party at which he spotted me and began acting as if he had been my mentor for years. Then nothing happened for weeks. Finally it was announced that Patrick Dennis would be the new nominee. Tom Griscom called me from the White House and personally apologized: "I thought you had it; I really did. But the Reagan people weren't going to let a Packwood guy onto the FCC. So they picked one of their own from the inside."

The failure to get the FCC nomination upset me more than any of the other jobs I failed to get. It also led to another moment in my life when an existential assessment was in order. I had continued to mentor friends and help them with their lives. One was having trouble with depression despite a successful career in law. "I'm happy when I'm around Ann, but struggle everywhere else," he confessed.

"So marry Ann," I told him. He took my advice, and they are still married over twenty-five years later. However, in their jobs and marriages, often building families with children, my mentees had much less time to spend with me.[4] Others were having trouble as adults. Two were going through divorces, which led them to question their judgment. When they did have time to get together, they were less interested in philosophical issues and less available for one-to-one dinners. Furthermore, my personal life was empty. I began to think it might be time to move on or get onto a campus where your social life and vocation are intertwined. My vacations in California had their problems. I was transient in California, as visitors often are. I sometimes had nothing to do during the day while I waited for people to get off work and be ready for dinner. What if I had my own home and life there again? An excuse to move soon presented itself.

THE COMPLEX DEATH OF THE FAIRNESS DOCTRINE

Let me begin by summarizing our progress up to 1987 on getting the Fairness Doctrine repealed. After our hearings of 1984, Chairman Mark Fowler of the FCC had instituted its investigation of the doctrine. We filed the results of the Senate hearings, and I testified before the FCC along with others seeking repeal of the doctrine. The FCC concluded that it was "constitutionally suspect," but that they were obligated to impose it because it had been codified in 1959. The FCC then found Meredith Broadcasting in violation of the doctrine because its station in Syracuse did not give the Syracuse Peace Council, yet another Nader subsidiary, the right to present a contrasting point of view regarding the use of nuclear energy. On September 30, 1986, the case came before Judge Laurence Silberman, the husband of Packwood's former press secretary; he was highly critical of the FCC during oral arguments. Earlier in the month, Justice Bork of the D.C. Court of Appeals, with Judge Antonin Scalia concurring, ruled on the teletext case, saying that the Fairness Doctrine had not been codified in 1959; that 1959 amendment to the Communication Act of 1934 only said that the FCC had the right to impose the doctrine, not that the doctrine had been codified.[5] If they could impose the doctrine, they could suspend it. Relying on this ruling, Silberman issued his decision in January 1987, which remanded the *Meredith* case back to the FCC for rehearing. The FCC suspended the Fairness Doctrine on August 4, 1987. The Supreme Court then upheld the FCC's action by denying Nader's appeal. It was a great victory for our coalition.

We still had a battle to fight on another front. When the Bork decision came down, several members of the House and Senate vowed to codify the Fairness Doctrine, arguing that had been the intent of Congress in 1959.[6] Senator Fritz Hollings (D-SC), who replaced Packwood as chair of the Commerce Committee, initiated the effort. I was allowed to testify at the hearing in March of 1987 and embarrassed some of the Democrats who constituted the majority on the committee by pointing out that the right-wing Eagle Forum, among others, supported the doctrine and had used it to kill the Equal Rights Amendment. I also relied on Bork's decision to stress that the argument about airwaves being scarce was invalid. I cited the case of Frederick Berg, a man who filed a fairness complaint against NBC alleging that the World War II Holocaust never happened, and demanding that his contrasting point of view be put on the air. Instead of dismissing the complaint out of hand, the FCC had the obligation under the law to pursue it, costing NBC a fortune in legal fees. I was backed up over the next week with editorials I requested from *USA Today*, the *Washington Post*, the *Wall Street Journal*, and many more. The campaign of persuasion was in full swing.

When Hollings's bill came to the floor of the Senate, Packwood gave a magnificent speech attacking the bill as an assault on the First Amendment. Near the end of the address, Packwood pulled a letter from his pocket from the Justice Department. It had recommended to President Reagan that he veto this bill if it came to his desk. The bill passed, as expected, but it did not carry by enough votes to override a veto. The House also passed the bill because most politicians hate the press, because it has at some time reported something inaccurately and/or uncovered their scandals—financial, sexual—and their unethical conduct. So any attempt to deregulate the media always meets with massive resistance on Capitol Hill.

Luckily for our side, Ronald Reagan had once been a broadcaster and was open to their arguments. He vetoed the legislation and announced the fact in his radio address to the nation on Saturday, June 20, 1987. The bill was dead in the Congress, and so was the Fairness Doctrine, or so we thought. Hollings was not finished. In December, he used Kennedy's tactic of attaching an amendment to the continuing resolution for the funding of the government. The amendment would have reinstated the Fairness Doctrine. The House included the amendment in its version of the continuing resolution, and the resolution then went into a conference committee to have the differences worked out. President Reagan made clear that there were only two pieces of the resolution that would cause him to veto it and bring the government to a halt. One was the limitation on aid to Nicaraguan rebels, the Contras, and the other was the codification of the Fairness Doctrine. The Senate conferees sided with the President by a vote of 14 to 13, and the House reluctantly went along. The Fairness Doctrine was finally dead.[7] And our fight had made national headlines. The foundation was more credible than ever.

At that juncture, it would have been easy for the advisory boards to have declared victory and dissolved the foundation. But to a person, they said they valued the research I provided and wanted the foundation to continue. I told them I would think about it. It hit me that the foundation might serve as an entree to a campus as a kind of First Amendment research center.

THE BORK FIGHT

However, before I could run that idea past the Senator, he got into another battle with the White House. It afforded me an inside look at the Supreme Court nomination process. When President Reagan nominated Robert Bork to the Supreme Court, many conservatives were delighted. He was a distinguished scholar as well as a strict constructionist judge. And from my perspective, he had been very helpful during the Fairness Doctrine fight. However, adding another conservative to the Supreme Court set off alarm bells in the liberal community, particularly among women's groups that feared repeal of *Roe v. Wade*, which gave women the right to choose to have an abortion.

Liberal groups knew that Bork had lots of baggage. As a Yale professor, he had defended strict construction and close reading of the Constitution, and attacked judicial activism. As a member of the D.C. Circuit Court of Appeals, he had put his philosophy into his rulings. More troubling was the fact that as acting attorney general, Bork had fired Watergate prosecutor Archibald Cox when no one else would do it. The ABA divided on the Bork nomination, with the majority declaring him "well qualified," and the minority claiming he was "not qualified." In contrast, in the earlier cases of William Rehnquist and Antonin Scalia, the "well qualified" designation had been unanimous. The ABA majority report claimed that Bork's rulings had been "fair" and "balanced."[8] Bork's essays and books revealed that he did not believe the Constitution should be interpreted liberally. He drew the most attention for his 1963 article in the *New Republic* and his lectures that were published in the *Indiana Law Journal*. In the former, he implied that the 1964 Civil Rights Act violated the rights of white property owners; in the latter, he made clear that only explicit language in the Constitution gives Congress power to act. Furthermore, his literal readings of laws often ignored legislative intent, which worked against the interpretations put in place by the Warren Court in general, and *Roe v. Wade* in particular.

Since Bork was not tainted by any financial or other kinds of scandals, he would have to be attacked on ideological grounds if his nomination was to be stopped. That tactic had not been used before; only conflicts of interest, financial scandals, or past racism had stopped previous nominees.[9] In an appearance on *Face the Nation*, Senator Joseph Biden, who was considering a run for president in 1988 and was the chair of the Judiciary Committee, had warned that if the President nominated Bork, the Senate would resist because Bork had an unacceptable "predisposition" on all major issues. The day after Bork's nomination, Ted Kennedy hyperbolically proclaimed that "Robert Bork's America is a land in which women would be forced into back alley abortions, blacks would sit at segregated lunch counters, rogue police could break down citizens' doors in midnight raids, school children could not be taught about evolution." A week later, Biden pleaded with the public to become more active because the administration was moving the Supreme Court back in time. When Biden continued to assure groups that he would oppose the Bork nomination, even the *Washington Post* faulted him: "While claiming that Judge Bork will have a full and fair hearing, Sen. Joseph Biden this week pledged to civil rights groups that he will lead the opposition to the confirmation. As the Queen of Hearts said to Alice, 'sentence first—verdict afterwards.'"

However, Bork became his own worst enemy. I watched as he humorlessly engaged Senator Arlen Specter (R-PA) in a long philosophical debate on the Constitution. He claimed to have changed his mind about *Hess v. Indiana*, another free-speech case. Stunningly, he said that he would not overturn *Roe v. Wade*, and that commercial and broadcast speech probably deserved more First Amendment protection than he had previously believed. Bork was dismissive toward the Ninth Amendment, which reads, "The enumeration in the Constitution, of certain rights, shall not be construed to deny or disparage others retained by the people." Senator Leahy (D-VT) claimed that Bork was undergoing a "confirmation conversion." Bork's craven, lackluster performance gave Packwood his rationale for opposing the nomination.

However, the White House gained an advantage when press reports of plagiarism eliminated Senator Biden from the ongoing Democratic presidential nomination process. Biden borrowed liberally from a speech by Neil Kinnock, the Labour candidate for prime minister of Great Britain. Reporters soon found paragraphs from Robert Kennedy's speeches unacknowledged in Biden's campaign talks. Then a reporter discovered that Biden had been suspended from law school because of plagiarism. Three strikes and Biden was out.

President Reagan went on the offensive; eventually, he would make more than thirty public statements in support of Bork—some on national television to the viewing public. This campaign of persuasion was another major turning point in the nomination process because from here on out, presidents would make public statements supporting their nominees, a practice that was quite rare prior to Reagan. Nomination debates moved from the Senate to the public sphere.

Packwood attacked Bork in a speech on the floor of the Senate after the public and media pressure forced the full Senate to take up the nomination. George Will then attacked Packwood in the *Washington Post*.[10] After three days of dramatic debate, six moderate Republicans, including Packwood, voted against Bork. The nomination was defeated 58 to 42 on October 23, 1987. The White House public-relations machine and congressional liaison office could not overcome Bork's rhetorical inadequacies, change of positions on important cases, record on political issues, and the major media opinion leaders turning against him.

FINDING A HOME

During the Bork fiasco, Vice President Bush began to campaign in earnest for the Republican nomination. I had begun working with Jim Pinkerton, Bush's "issues guy," in April of 1987. One of the first documents I worked on was a position on "Trade Policy."[11] Along with it I suggested that Bush's speeches needed to project the persona of a man who was "a straight shooter, a guy who plays by the rules, and an intelligent guy who is not afraid to be tough. Let's kill this wimp stuff now." Because of his Ivy League background and Gentleman Jim approach to life, Bush was seen as something of a softy by some reporters and columnists.

When Bush made his formal announcement, I provided language to deal with the fact that no sitting vice president had been elected to the presidency since Martin Van Buren in 1836. Addressing this issue, Bush would state that "records were made to be broken." He wrote a note thanking me for "putting old Martin Van Buren to rest." I then helped Bush get ready for the Republican primary debates, in which he performed rather well. My favorite moment came when former governor of Delaware Pete Dupont asked Bush to "give peace a chance." Bush responded, "Let me tell you something, Pierre," which was his real name, "America must always operate from strength." That prick burst Dupont's bubble and he vanished as a viable candidate.

THE JOB HUNT

I continued to seek an avenue back into academia. One opportunity occurred in November 1987 when I was invited to speak at the National Communication Association's annual meeting in Boston. The NCA had rented Faneuil Hall, where Daniel Webster had given a number of his famous speeches. I was invited to present a paper on Webster since I had published research about the remarkable Massachusetts senator and two-time secretary of state. It was wonderful to give the lecture in the old hall where Webster had given a eulogy to Thomas Jefferson and John Adams, who happened to die on the same day, July 4th, fifty years after they had signed the Declaration of Independence. Behind me was a mural that portrayed Webster's famous 1830 Senate debate with Senator Robert Hayne. My appearance ended a busy year that included lectures at Drake University in Iowa, DePauw University in Indiana, Clemson University in South Carolina, and, much to my delight, the University of Virginia.

To keep the board of the foundation happy, if I were to move to a campus, I would have to be near a media center, and I knew there were only a few places I wanted to live. The choices were further narrowed by the available openings for full professors with tenure. Eventually, I was asked to interviews at the University of Maryland and George Mason University, both near Washington. On the other side of the country were interviews at the University of California, Berkeley and California State University, Long Beach.

I set up preliminary meetings at Berkeley and Long Beach during my Christmas break in California. I liked the fact that the Berkeley department had the courage to call itself "Rhetoric" where so many others shied away from the term and went with the new catchall "Communication Studies." The University of California was a "research one" university, meaning the emphasis was on publication of research, not the teaching of students. I had published numerous scholarly articles and headed a prestigious foundation. However, as I have mentioned, the University of California usually required that a professor publish a university press book before tenure could be obtained. I had published two textbooks and a study of the ratification debates surrounding the Constitution, but none was a university press publication. The department chair at Berkeley tried to ease my anxiety on the matter. He said that they could give me all the credit I needed to be eligible for tenure within a year of my being hired. While I had a scholarly book in the works, I did not have a university press contract. So I was leery of the Berkeley arrangement, particularly having watched professors of mine perish when I was an undergraduate.

On January 5, I drove to Long Beach State to meet with Richard Porter, the chair of their Speech Communication Department. The interview got off on the wrong foot because traffic delayed my arrival, so a meeting with the dean of the college, which Porter had arranged, was canceled. Porter, a former Navy man, told me that the department had gotten the job line for which I was applying because the department had a very good record in terms of hiring minorities and women. "It's kind of ironic that a white, male Republican would be our hire using a position we received as a reward for our affirmative action record!" Well, I thought to myself, if you only knew the diversity I would be bringing to the place.

BUSH BOXES WITH RATHER

Back in Washington, the 1988 presidential campaign was in full swing. I was regularly sending issue-position papers to the Bush camp, and memos on how he should conduct himself in debates. Then came one of the strangest nights in American political history.

On the evening of Ronald Reagan's last State of the Union Address, Dan Rather was to interview Bush on the *CBS Evening News*. Around the city, people gathered over cocktails and dinner to watch the Bush interview and then the State of the Union Address. I knew that Bush was concerned about being tied to the Iran-Contra scandal in which the United States had shipped arms into Iran, who then sent other arms to our allies in Nicaragua to fight Daniel Ortega's Communist government there. Roger Ailes, who was advising Bush at the time, told me that Rather's producer assured Bush that after a question or two on Iran-Contra, the interview would move on to other issues. Bush insisted that the interview be live so that it could not be re-edited by CBS. Ailes was in Bush's vice-presidential office during the interview, and I watched from a dinner party, martini in hand, as millions of Americans tuned in at 6:30 P.M. Eastern Standard Time that cold January evening.

After the headlines, Rather turned to interview Bush, who appeared on a screen in front of Rather. Of the three anchors of the evening news shows, Rather was by this time the most sensational. For example, he had caused a stir when CBS refused to interrupt a football game for the *CBS Evening News*, and Rather had stormed off the set. As expected, Rather began the interview by peppering Bush with questions about Iran-Contra, and Bush defended himself, saying he was "out of the loop" on the deal. Rather didn't buy it. He quoted former secretary of state George Shultz and Bush's aide Donald Gregg to the effect that Bush was informed about what was going on. Bush told Rather that he had answered the questions on Iran-Contra and wanted to move on to other issues. Rather refused and continued to question Bush about Iran-Contra. Bush said that Rather's producer had promised that other issues would be covered. Rather ignored him. Angered, Bush finally said we all make mistakes. "How would you like it if I judged your career by those seven minutes you walked off the set? I have respect for you, but I don't have respect for what you are doing tonight."

Rather looked stunned but pushed on. "Mr. Vice President, I think you'll agree your qualifications for president. . . . are much more important than what you just referred to." He then asked Bush to participate in a full press conference on the issue. Bush responded that he had done 86 news conferences since March of 1987. Rather put words in Bush's mouth: "I gather the answer is no. Thank you very much for being with us." Turning away from the monitor on which Bush's face could be seen, Rather said, "We'll be back in a moment."

The shock of Rather cutting the Vice President of the United States off stimulated a chatter across the nation as we all waited in anticipation for Reagan's last State of the Union Address. Two and half hours later, the President arrived in the House chamber to more than the usual huzzahs and cheers at 9 P.M. Eastern Standard Time. Even though the House and Senate were now in the hands of the Democrats, civility demanded that Reagan be given his last hurrah. As he moved up to the dais, Reagan handed a copy of his speech to the Speaker of the House, Tip O'Neal, and another to Bush, both of whom sat behind a high desk that was behind Reagan.

Reagan began by acknowledging the record of his presidency, but said, "Let's leave that to history: we're not finished yet. My message to you tonight is, put on your work shoes—we're still on the job." The audience cheered. He humorously reasserted his philosophy: "Chinese philosopher, Lao-tzu, said, 'Govern a great nation as you would cook a small fish; do not overdo it.'" This principle was used to support a spirit of bipartisanship, which Reagan hoped would pervade the Congress.

After this introduction, Reagan announced that his speech would be organized around "four basic objectives." The first focused on strengthening the economy. The second on social programs, particularly schools. The third on global strategies for economic development and the spread of democracy. The fourth objective was to enhance national security. This was an important and effective move since it consolidated his speech in understandable blocks instead of covering 51 issues in 51 minutes, which is too often the case with State of the Union Addresses.

He then turned to economic growth as the Vice President and the Speaker could be seen turning pages and following along. Reagan's underrated use of statistics could be seen in this section as he wove evidence into the speech: "We have had a balanced budget only 8 times in the last 57 years. For the first time in 14 years, the federal government has spent less in real terms last year than the year before. We took $73 billion off last year's deficit. . . . The deficit itself has moved from 6.3 per cent of the Gross National Product to only 3.4 per cent." As he often did, Reagan concluded his litany of statistics with a punch line: "I can assure you, the bipartisan leadership of Congress, of my help in fighting off any attempt to bust our budget agreement. And this includes the swift and certain use of the veto . . ."

Two paragraphs later, Reagan launched another litany that was prologue to one of the most unconventional moments of any State of the Union

Address. Reagan pointed out that only 10 of 91 appropriation bills had made it to his desk on time: "Last year, of the 13 appropriations bills due by October 1st, none of them made it. Instead, we had four continuing resolutions lasting 41 days, then 36 days, and two days, and three days. And then along came these behemoths." Suddenly, everyone's attention, including the television cameras, was drawn to tall stacks of paper sitting near the President. He moved over and lifted one up and brought it back to his lectern: "This is the conference report—a 1,053 page report weighing 14 pounds." He plopped the stack down to much laughter. He stepped over and picked up another one. "Then this—a reconciliation bill six months late . . . 1,186 pages long, weighing 15 pounds." He plopped it down and picked up another stack, again to continuing laughter and cheers. "The long-term continuing resolution—1,057 pages long, weighing 14 pounds." He dropped it on the table and then continued to much laughter, "That was a total of 43 pounds of paper and ink. You had three hours—yes, three hours—to consider each, and it took 300 people at my Office of Management and Budget just to read the bill so the government wouldn't shut down. Congress should not send another one of these. . . . And if you do, I will not sign it." The House Chamber erupted with applause and cheers. This passage was signature Reagan taken to new heights. The use of a litany of statistics, visually illustrated by heavy props, and concluded with an effective punch line.

Reagan then called for education and welfare reforms. On welfare, Reagan uttered this line contributed by Peggy Noonan: "There are a thousand sparks of genius in 50 states . . ."[12] On the issue of drugs, again Reagan was unconventional. The moment went this way: "The war against drugs is a war of individual battles, a crusade of many heroes—including . . . someone very special to me. . . . Nancy, much credit belongs to you, and I want to express to you your husband's pride and your country's thanks." The audience cheered as the First Lady took a bow from the gallery. With a wink, Reagan added, "Surprised you, didn't I?"

Near the end of the speech, Reagan argued that progress was being made in terms of returning Latin America to democracy. His proof played right into the Iran-Contra scandal, which had been the subject of Rather's fight with Bush hours earlier. Having won over the audience, Reagan could now help his vice president out. "The Sandinista regime knows the tide is turning and the cause of Nicaraguan freedom is riding at its crest. Because of the freedom fighters . . . the Sandinistas have been forced to extend some democratic rights, negotiate with Church authorities, and release a few political prisoners." Reagan called on Congress to "sustain the freedom fighters," clearly indicating that the Iran-Contra crisis was behind him. In fact, Reagan claimed that we could be for Nicaragua what foreigners like "Lafayette, Pulaski, and Von Steuben" were to the American Revolution.

Reagan closed by taking his audience outside of the House Chamber and down to the Potomac, where they could see the lights of Washington, D.C., reflected in the river. It had become his "shining city on a hill."

The fallout from the earlier Bush-Rather dustup had begun immediately. The CBS switchboard lit up like the Eiffel Tower on Bastille Day. During his lead-in to ABC's coverage of the State of the Union Address, Sam Donaldson took a shot at Rather by saying he went "too far," and accused him of "arrogance." The next night Rather tried to rationalize what he had done: "Now, a personal word if I may about last night's interview with Vice President Bush. First, no, CBS did not mislead the Vice President about the subject matter. . . . Secondly, I of course respect the office of the vice presidency. . . . Trying to ask honest questions and trying to be persistent about answers is part of a reporter's job. . . . The fact that more attention is given to the heat than the light is regrettable, but it goes with the territory."

Neither man was helped by the exchange. Despite his disclaimer, Rather had violated the rules of the interview and been rude to the Vice President. Bush had hit Rather with a cheap shot, a tactic that tarnished Bush's image. On the Republican side in the Iowa caucuses, the winner was Bob Dole, even though Bush had the better ground team. Bush faced the challenge of having to win in New Hampshire, or being out of the race. Luckily, Bush ran ahead of the pack there, and then consolidated his victory on Super Tuesday across the South. At that juncture, he asked me to rewrite his standard campaign speech and make it sound "presidential"—no more petty stuff, because he believed he had won the nomination fight and wanted to run as a national leader, not as a politician seeking the nomination. At last he had seen the light.

A CALIFORNIA CONNECTION

My job interview process continued when I flew back to Long Beach for a full day of conversations and a lecture to the students on the campus. The dean and the provost were excited about bringing in my foundation. At the end of my lecture, the students peppered me with questions. My interview with the faculty went well until a senior member of the department asked,

"These job lines are hard to get. What guarantee have we that you will stay? After all, you've jumped all over the place in your career."

Before I could answer what seemed like a fair question, another faculty member jumped in. "Don't answer that. You don't have to answer that. It is none of our business. Our job is just to hire the most qualified person for the job."

Before a fight could break out, I interjected that I did not mind answering the question, and proceeded to say, while there were no guarantees, I believed I was "at a point in my life where I'm ready to settle down. And as a native Southern Californian, Long Beach makes a lot of sense to me. My parents are only 100 miles down the road." At the end of the day, Richard Porter told me I would receive an offer of a full professorship with one class off each semester to run the foundation on the campus. I told him I looked forward to working out a contract, not knowing how difficult that would eventually prove to be.

In late March, I received word that the president of George Mason University had confiscated the job line in communication and turned it over to the Economics Department so they could hire a Nobel Prize–winning economist. However, the job at Maryland was still open and I was invited to spend April 6th on the campus, interviewing and giving a guest lecture on political campaigns. My problem with the Maryland position was that the administration did not seem to have full faith in the department. Having been through the debacle at Virginia, I did not want to take the risk of joining a department that might be done in.[13]

A few weeks later, the job offer had not yet arrived from the dean at Long Beach, so I called to inquire about the delay. He said there were a couple of problems that needed to be worked out. First, the Chancellor's Office was leery about having the foundation move to the campus and use the university's charitable status with the IRS. I told the dean that we had our own 501(c)(3) status with the IRS, and that I would make all of our books available to the Chancellor's office. "Well, what about this?" he suggested. "Why don't you keep the foundation off the campus, and start a new center on the campus that the foundation would fund?"

"That's fine with me," I replied. "In fact, it works to my advantage. I just can't imagine why they want to do it that way."

"There is no explaining how lawyers' minds work."

"What's the second problem?"

"Well, that's a bit more difficult. It turns out that we have never brought anyone to this campus with tenure. So we would like to give you credit toward tenure, and bring you up for tenure after your first year. How does that sound?"

"I'm afraid that's unacceptable. I had tenure at the University of Alabama in Birmingham."

"Yes, I know, but we've never done this before."

"My board will not allow me to move the foundation and its staff to California without a tenure guarantee. I can go to Berkeley for the same terms you've offered me."

That seemed to surprise the dean, who concluded our conversation by saying, "Let me see what I can do." I was beginning to think I'd have to spend another year in Washington and start to search for an acceptable job all over again. In the interim, I was a guest speaker at the Bill of Rights celebration at the University of Virginia and then, with other presenters, treated to a candlelit dinner in the famous Rotunda at one end of the lawn in the center of the campus. A week later I gave the first Carroll Arnold Lecture at Penn State. In my opening remarks, I was very happy to be given the opportunity to acknowledge everything Carroll had done for me while I was his student. Silver-haired, he beamed from the front row of the auditorium.

By May things began to fall into place. Bush had sewn up the nomination as the Soviets withdrew from Afghanistan, giving the administration a boost. He prepared for the Republican Convention scheduled for New Orleans in August. He had me appointed to the Convention Special Proceedings Staff where I would help speakers with their speeches and contribute lines for his. I couldn't help wondering if there might be a place for me in the Bush administration if he won the election. My subsequent meetings with Roger Bolton, Bush's chief of staff, did nothing to lower my expectations. In Atlanta, the Democrats nominated Michael Dukakis, the governor of Massachusetts, who selected Senator Lloyd Bentsen of Texas as his running mate. It was the first conjunction of a Massachusetts-Texas ticket since JFK and LBJ. And the Democratic ticket moved into the lead in the polls.

The dean at Long Beach called to say that the decision on tenure would be left to the department. If they voted for it, he would grant it. I was relieved because I believed I could carry that vote. A week later, word arrived that the department had indeed voted to grant me tenure. I began to make preparations to move myself and the foundation to California. I met with Packwood in the Senate Caucus Room. When I described the job to him, he congratulated me on my return to academia but expressed sadness at my leaving Washington.

I put my condo overlooking the Potomac on the market, and it sold for a nice profit a few weeks later. I could now afford a place to live in Long Beach. I resolved that I was not going to be a California commuter; I wanted to live close to the campus, which luckily was only a few miles from the beach. So I could live near the beach, avoiding the smog and blight of the larger Los Angeles metropolitan area, and still get to work quickly. My new home was a short walk to the beach. It sat on a peninsula that jutted into a bay.

My going-away dinner back in Virginia took place at the apartment of Phil Bane, one of my former students. All of my friends who were former Virginia students showed up and we had a grand time. Each one had a story to tell about me—some funny, some moving, some life-changing. I promised to visit often and told them to come to California when they got the chance.

After the movers pulled out, I began my drive across the country on July 25, 1988, heading down to Bristol, Virginia, my first night on the hot and humid road. I drove across the length of Tennessee the next day from the mountains to the Mississippi River flats. I had dinner with a former student in Memphis, Mason Granger, who was the station director of the NBC affiliate there. I spent the 27th and 28th in Arlington, Texas, with my former student from San Diego State, Jack Williams, who had fathered my godson. He had moved up at American Airlines and with his wife Judy created a wonderful family.

On July 29, I drove to Amarillo to stay with one of the quirkiest contributors to the Freedom of Expression Foundation. Stanley Marsh ran the ABC-TV affiliate there, and through his wife, the couple inherited a small fortune, since her grandfather had invented barbed wire. They used their money in innovative ways. First, they adopted many children. Then they built their home, Toad Ranch, where I stayed; it contained a small menagerie of various animals. There were camels, llamas, peacocks—who woke me in the morning with their shrieks—pigs, horses, sheep, and even an island for black swans.

A DIGRESSION: ME, PAUL, AND MICHAEL

The 30th was marked by an easy drive to Albuquerque, where I stayed with my college chum Paul Bardacke and his wife in their house on the bank of the Rio Grande River. I came to catch up on things and play some tennis. The next day was blistering hot. Luckily our tennis match was interrupted by a rare summer rain. However, just as the rain started, Paul screamed, "Run for the house!" It was as if he was allergic to raindrops. When we got into his house, I said, "What in the hell was the rush? The rain was nice."

"Look at your socks."

Suddenly, I saw blood coming through the top of my socks in several places. "Oh, my God. What did that?"

"Mosquitoes. They are the most vicious I've encountered anywhere in my life." Calamine lotion was applied to the bites and I had learned about the famous killer mosquitoes of Albuquerque.

It was good to relax with Paul. We had met as rival debaters in high school and then wound up on the same debate squad in college. As I mentioned earlier, it was Paul who introduced me to Michael Douglas. At that time, Paul was very liberal, and his older brother, who attended Berkeley, was an avowed socialist who played a part in the Free Speech demonstrations there in the '60s. Paul's parents were socialist English professors. He was one of my many buddies who thought someday he might become president of the United States.

After graduation, Paul went on to law school, became a very successful lawyer in Albuquerque, and began to talk about making a difference in the world. I encouraged him. Then I received a letter in which he wrote, "I would like to be Attorney General [of New Mexico]. But I am nervous about politics—about running for office—about possibly losing—about reorganizing my life. I guess I called you just because I wanted you to say 'do it, have fun, learn from it.' I think you said that."[14] And I had.

In 1982, when Paul ran for attorney general of New Mexico, Michael and I came to help out when I could get free of my duties at Chrysler. Because of his celebrity status, Michael was very helpful in raising money. His wife at the time was Diandra, a shy but beautiful daughter of the Spanish ambassador to America. Michael and Diandra had met at Jimmy Carter's inaugural. He literally fell in love with her across a crowded room. At the fundraisers we did for Paul, Diandra felt uncomfortable in the crowds seeking to get close to Michael. So my job was to keep her company, which also served to keep me away from the Democrats at these events who might object to Paul having a Republican advisor. Diandra and I became good friends.

I wrote Paul's main campaign speech, rehearsed him for events, and worked on his campaign commercials, which Michael then filmed. Michael and I became much closer. One night in Santa Fe, Michael, Diandra, and their infant son Cameron were put up in one cabin and I was in another behind Forrest Fenn's art gallery, where we held a fundraiser for Paul. After the gallery emptied, Michael and I stayed up and drank before the fire in my cabin reminiscing about old times. That night, we also talked about gun control. Michael lived only blocks from where John Lennon had been shot in 1980.

Working with his friend Jann Wenner, the editor in chief of *Rolling Stone*, Michael had helped to create Cease Fire, an organization that fought for gun-control legislation. I was able to get Senator Packwood to help us out behind the scenes on one important piece of legislation, and then I wrote speeches for Michael on the topic. For me, it was the beginning of both a renewed relationship with Michael and a new cause. Eventually, he was named an "Ambassador of Peace" by the United Nations and expanded his area of concern to land mines, small arms, and children used as soldiers. I continued to write speeches for him to give around the world. He also helped my campus center by raising funds for it; in fact, while making the film *Wonder Boys* in Pittsburgh in 1999, he sent a letter to his friends begging them to send funds to the center.[15]

During his election campaign in 1982, Paul had fire in his belly and easily won. He served for four years with distinction; in fact, the Justice Department Building in Santa Fe is named for him. Paul was a leader of all the states' attorneys general in their suits against the tobacco companies. He ended a lot of corruption in New Mexico and strengthened its criminal code.

However, term limits prohibited Paul from running for statewide office for four years. So it wasn't until 1990 that Paul could seek the governorship.[16] Former governor Bruce King entered the Democratic primary against Paul. We did what we could, but King won with 52 percent of the vote, and Paul was heartbroken. That did not stop him over the ensuing years from being a very successful lawyer; he even appeared before the Supreme Court.

After leaving Albuquerque, I traveled on to Flagstaff and finally to see my aunt in Laguna Niguel, who acted as my realtor. I visited my parents and then moved into my condo on August 4th. It felt wonderful to be home in California again. Soon I was visiting my parents regularly, renewing old friendships, and starting new ones. And importantly, learning the virtues of living in Los Angeles.

But first, it was off to another political convention.

CHAPTER FOURTEEN

The Rise and Fall of George Bush

THE TRIP TO NEW ORLEANS FOR THE REPUBLICAN CONVENTION interrupted my course preparations, the first I had done in over a decade. By the oddest of coincidences, when I changed planes in Dallas, I was seated next to Senator Dan Quayle of Indiana for the short flight to New Orleans. He seemed happy that I remembered who he was, a second-term senator who had won his seat from the redoubtable Birch Bayh by beating him in a statewide televised debate in 1980. Quayle had easily won reelection in 1986, in the same cycle with Senator Packwood. We had a pleasant chat all the way to New Orleans, part of which was spent speculating on who George Bush might select for a running mate. "I hope it's not Bob Dole," I told him.

"Why not? He's been a good leader in the party," replied Quayle.

"Yeah, but he was a bad running mate for Ford in 1976. He's great in the Senate but not so great on the hustings."

"People usually don't vote for the vice-presidential candidate. So he only matters in a very close election or where the presidential candidate is very old."

"You're probably right," I told the senator. "I'm looking forward to Bush's acceptance speech. That's what the convention comes down to."

"Are you working on it?" he asked.

"You never know what's retained in the final draft until it is delivered. But since I was a little boy, I've always loved acceptance speeches."

"I'll watch from my home in D.C. I'm not interested in staying for the coronation." Quayle was doing some work on the Republican platform and would leave Monday night, at the end of the first day of the convention.

Once I got settled into my hotel room, I walked over to the convention center in the Superdome and was briefed on my assignments on the Official Proceedings Staff. I would write talking points and background papers for Bush spokespersons who would visit state delegations and inform them of where we wanted to go on the issues. I would also write, edit, and/or rehearse assigned speakers for the convention. My former student Tommy Scully was there working on the legal staff and provided good company. Each day of the convention would be instantiated with a theme, and we were to write speeches for convention speakers that reenforced that "theme of the day." Governor Dukakis was still ahead in the polls, so we had a lot of work to do.

All went well the first two days of the convention; I worked on speeches for Governor Jim Thompson of Illinois, Senator Alan Simpson of Wyoming, and Secretary of Treasury Jim Baker. However, on Wednesday of convention week, the wheels almost came off the Bush bandwagon over the selection of a vice-presidential nominee. Bush first approached Senator Simpson, who demurred because he was in favor of a woman's right to choose an abortion, and he had offended the AARP by criticizing their lobbying tactics. Simpson said his pro-choice stance would be a deal breaker with the Christian Right, and that was not what Bush needed at this point in the campaign. Bush then sent his campaign manager, Lee Atwater, over to talk to Dole about coming on the ticket. Dole told Atwater he would be glad to, but he would not report to the Bush campaign. He would run his own operation. That was unacceptable to Bush.

With Dole out of the picture, Bob Teeter, Bush's pollster, and Roger Ailes, Bush's media advisor, came forward with a choice of their own. I was rehearsing former President Ford for his speech to the convention, when the news of the choice for vice president came to us. A Ford aide came into our rehearsal room and announced, "Bush is picking some senator from Indiana to be his running mate."

"Dick Lugar," Ford retorted.

"No, the other one. The young one."

"Dan Quayle?" Ford said incredulously. "You've got to be kidding."

But Quayle it was. He flew back to New Orleans. On Wednesday at a riverside rally, with a big paddle-wheeler in the background, Bush endorsed Quayle, who acted like a little kid at Disneyland.

By that evening, the press had trotted out every story they could find to ding Quayle. The most damaging was the claim that he had ducked service in Vietnam by hiding in the National Guard. At one point, I caught up with Mark Shields on an escalator, who turned to me and said, "This is bad, Craig. They've got to retract this Quayle thing fast."

If Bush was seen to have bungled his first major appointment, he would be badly damaged; the McGovern debacle of 1972 was still fresh in reporters' minds. Teeter and Ailes assured Bush that they could deal with the negative stories in the same way that they had in Quayle's past Senate campaigns. Bush decided to stick with Quayle; however, the "theme of the day" that had been slipped under the hotel door of every delegate had been blown away.

On the last night of the convention, our job was to get everybody back on the same page. This was all about George H. W. Bush. So speaker after speaker praised him. Quayle gave a credible acceptance speech, attacking Dukakis and praising Bush in masculine terms to reduce the pesky wimp factor. Nonetheless, Bush needed to give the speech of a lifetime.

Bush had hired Peggy Noonan and Vic Gold to be the main writers of the speech, but accepted ideas, paragraphs, and slogans from others. For example, Ford's (my) line about the Democrats "promise, and we perform" was incorporated into Bush's remarks. Bush rehearsed the speech several times until he felt comfortable with it. As he began to speak, I could see that he was confident and the cheering, adoring delegates made him feel at home. The famous lines hit their mark. Volunteers would "spread like stars, like a thousand points of light in a broad and peaceful sky." For once Bush was not reluctant about talking about himself: "I'm a man who sees life in terms of missions—missions defined and missions completed." He invoked his plea for a "kinder, gentler nation," a part of Bush's authentic persona that I had tried to bring out during the 1980 run. To deal with the wimp factor, drop-dead language was incorporated, such as the frontier metaphor about not changing the party of the president when things are going well: "But when you have to change horses in midstream, doesn't it make sense to switch to one going the same way?" In the same vein, Bush said that if Congress kept pushing him to raise taxes he would tell them, "Read my lips, no new taxes." The line brought the house down, and it would eventually bring down George Bush.

The most important passages in the speech came when Bush used the strategy of redefinition that I had proposed.[1] Like Jimmy Carter in his 1976 acceptance speech, Dukakis had to be vague in 1988 in order to hold the Democratic Party together. If he got specific, various special interest groups would begin to fall away, despite Jesse Jackson's appeal for them to pull together like the patches in a quilt. Dukakis's vagueness left him open to redefinition, as did his reliance on being competent, another trick Carter had used. In a veiled reference to Italian dictator Benito Mussolini, Bush took care of the competence ploy by arguing that "Competence makes the trains run on time, but doesn't know where they're going. Competence is the creed of the technocrat who makes sure the gears mesh, but doesn't for a second understand the magic of the machine." Bush further redefined Dukakis by contrasting stands with him:

> Should public school teachers be required to lead our children in the pledge of allegiance? My opponent says no—but I say yes. Should society be allowed to impose the death penalty on those who commit crimes of extraordinary cruelty and violence? My opponent says no—but I say yes. Should our children have the right to say a voluntary prayer, or even observe a moment of silence in the schools? My opponent says no—but I say yes. Should free men and women have the right to own a gun to protect their home? My opponent says no— but I say yes. Is it right to believe in the sanctity of life and protect the lives of innocent children? My opponent says no—but I say yes. We must change from abortion—to adoption. I have an adopted granddaughter. The day of her christening we wept with joy. I thank God her parents chose life. I'm the one who believes it is a scandal to give a weekend furlough to a hardened first degree killer who hasn't even served enough time to be eligible for parole.[2]

Going into the Republican Convention, Bush was 17 points behind Dukakis. Coming out of the convention, he was 7 to 10 points ahead, depending on which poll you read. That's the biggest bounce coming out of a convention that I can remember. Now all Bush had to do was get through the debates with Dukakis, and survive the small matter of Dan Quayle debating Senator Bentsen.

After the last speech of the last night of the convention, a bunch of us, including Tommy Scully, went out to celebrate. We wound up at Café du Monde on the Mississippi River and drank coffee diablos, a mix of coffee and liquors. After two of them, I playfully tossed a beignet at Tommy, covering his dark suit with confectionary sugar. He fired one right back at me and the fight was on, using beignets as snowballs and hiding behind overturned tables. Once we finished, we left lots of money to a horrified proprietor.

As the sun rose on the way back to the Hyatt, we saw that Jane Pauley and Bryant Gumbel were setting up for NBC's *Today Show* in Jackson Park. Tommy wanted to harass them, and I agreed because both of them seemed incredibly pompous. So we began to yell things at them until we heard a siren. Fearing a headline such as "Sugar-Coated Bush Aides Arrested for Harassing Pauley and Gumbel," we ran all the way back to our hotel.

In the ensuing campaign, Bush performed well in the debates. He not only held his own against the cool, technocratic Dukakis, he bested him on many points. However, the tipping point came in an unexpected moment.

Bernard Shaw of CNN asked Dukakis if he would still oppose the death penalty for someone who raped and killed his wife. The audience gasped at the question, but Dukakis had been asked the question before and should have been able to field it. Instead, he gave a very unemotional, legal response to the question. Bush's response was devastating: "Now I know why they call him the ice man." The moment was replayed for the next 24-hour news cycle and Dukakis fell further behind in the polls. Then, trying portray himself as strong on national defense, Dukakis appeared in a commercial riding in a tank, helmet and bulging earphones in place, his head sticking out of the hatch. As the tank rumbled around, Dukakis's head bobbled from side to side as he sported a forced grin. Even Democrats were appalled at how silly the governor looked.

The Democrats' only hope was the debate between Quayle and Bentsen. Quayle rehearsed in three mock debates with Senator Packwood—a fine debater, but more importantly, Bentsen's colleague on the Finance Committee. Packwood could imitate Bentsen's positions. Quayle did very well in each practice round, even on the question of what he would do in the case of the unfortunate situation wherein the president was assassinated. However, when the mock reporters questioned Quayle about his experience, his wife Marilyn suggested that Quayle claim he was more experienced than John Kennedy had been when he was elected president. While the claim was true, it was irrelevant, as Lee Atwater quickly pointed out. Kennedy was a martyred saint and the comparison would be ridiculed. The senator agreed and Lee thought that was the end of the matter.

Bentsen practiced with the young and charismatic Ohio Congressman Dennis Eckart. During one of their practice rounds, Eckersly playing Quayle said, "I don't know if you realize this, but I'm more qualified now than John Kennedy was when he ran for president." Bentsen laughed and said, "Quayle would never be so silly as to say anything like that."[3]

As I watched Quayle come on stage on the night of the actual debate, I recognized the look on his face. It was the look of a novice debater who had made it into the finals of a tournament. Everything went out of the debater's head, and he just stared at the audience. Meg Greenfield described Quayle as a deer looking into oncoming headlights.

Somehow Quayle hung in there through the first half of the debate. Using Ailes's advice, if he was unsure about a question, he would rephrase it into something he could answer. By this point, he had twice been asked, "What would be the first thing you would do if the president were incapacitated?" Note, the reporter did not say "killed" or "assassinated," in which case Quayle would take the oath of office; he said "incapacitated," which invokes the provisions of the Twenty-fifth Amendment, a much more complicated scenario. So Quayle dodged by saying in effect, "What you are really asking is if I'm qualified to be president?" And then he listed his qualifications.

Tom Brokaw asked the question again, and again Quayle tried to deflect. Smelling blood, Brokaw would not let him off the hook. So Quayle took refuge in Marilyn's line. On the videotape, you can see Bentsen smiling and literally licking his lips as Quayle said he was more qualified now than John Kennedy was when he ran for president. Bentsen's response has become legendary: "I knew Jack Kennedy. Jack Kennedy was a friend of mine. And Senator, you are no Jack Kennedy." The crowd went wild, and when they finally calmed down, Quayle said, "Senator, that was uncalled for." A mild cheer came from the Republican side. However, that night and over the next few days, all that was played on the air was Quayle's claim and Bentsen's response. Atwater was furious and feared what the next poll would show. Stunningly, there was no change in the standings. Quayle had been right during our plane ride when he said, "People don't usually vote for the vice-presidential running mate."

TEACHING AGAIN

Through the autumn, it felt wonderful to be in the classroom. The students inspired me. Some whom I befriended in my first year, like Paul Prince, and others like Nina Reich, Angela Aguayo, and Glenn Evans, are still very close friends. Too many to name have become excellent professors in their own right, and more than a few in my own department after going off to get their PhDs and returning to us. My favorite moments came when I learned something from the students as we were working a problem out on the blackboard. My best class was on the history of rhetorical theory, a kind of Great Ideas class wherein I deduced theories of persuasion—when they didn't spell it out themselves—from the great thinkers in Western Civilization. Eventually, I converted these thoughts into the textbook *Rhetoric and Human Consciousness*, which is now in its fourth edition; my students refer to it as a "smart pill."

In the Los Angeles and Orange Country areas, I talked about the election and my past experiences to Republican Women's, Lions, Rotary, and Kiwanis Clubs. I commented on the debates for various local media. On election night, I held a party for my students. It is so much easier watching returns on the West Coast than the East. The time delay means that the

Eastern returns are coming in while you eat dinner, instead of when you are ready for bed. The night went well for Bush, and I knew I would be involved in helping with the transition. But I wasn't sure if there would be a place for me in the new administration, or if I even wanted one. I didn't want to be on the speechwriting staff, and as in 1980, probably wanted a position that was so far up the food chain it would go to someone with more direct involvement in the campaign, or someone who donated a lot of money to it. Soon after his inaugural, Bush made the mistake of isolating the writing staff from him, hiring young and relatively inexperienced people, and farming his big speeches out to writers like Noonan and Ray Price.

I traveled to Washington from Long Beach to work on the transition team, particularly on formulating issues related to communication policy. I was happy my positions were adopted. That fact gave me the courage to tell the Bush team that I couldn't accept anything less than the rank of assistant secretary, perhaps assistant secretary for higher education, or an appointment to the FCC. Good news of a sort soon arrived. David Bates, Bush's deputy chief of staff; Janet Mullins (who had worked for Packwood), from Bush's congressional liaison team; and James Pinkerton, director of policy development for Bush, all wrote me that I was under consideration by the President-elect for a position in his administration. My name was again bandied about for a seat on the FCC. When I flew into D.C. for Bush's inaugural, I also had time to spend the evening before the event with Packwood, who threw one of his charade parties for the staff.[4] He also assured me that Bush would find a place for me in the administration. But I had become too removed from Bush's inner circle to get anything I wanted. The offers that came did not attract me. I had held some high-flying jobs at the Senate Republican Conference and at the National Republican Senatorial Campaign Committee. I wasn't going to become a bureaucrat in some office somewhere off the Mall. Furthermore, my status was about to change at the university.

RUNNING A DEPARTMENT

Dick Porter was promoted to associate dean at CSU Long Beach, leaving the chairmanship of the department open. Having been around only a few months, I did not think the faculty would turn to me. However, one by one, faculty came to me and asked me to take over the department. And so I did, starting in the spring semester of 1989.

I also picked up some consulting money writing speeches for executives. Ed Orley at Michigan Health Care needed lots of help when he moved up to CEO from being the chief financial officer; bean counters are not usually rhetorically adept. John Bryant, the head of a large food conglomerate, needed a homecoming speech in Mississippi. The mayor of Long Beach needed a speech now and then. A councilman in Redondo Beach wanted to run for Assembly and needed an advisor. I thought of this income as play money, which really helps when your only steady income is that of a professor.

Of course the work of the off-campus foundation and the on-campus center needed to continue, and the bicentennial of the signing of the Constitution provided an excellent opportunity. There were three highlights of the many engagements I accepted. One was to speak at the Freedom Foundation in Valley Forge, the place where President Ford had delivered one of the speeches I wrote for the Bicentennial of the Declaration of Independence thirteen years earlier. Another was a speech at the University of Virginia, and finally, I was a participant in ABC Radio's programs on the event. We also brought visitors to the campus such as Tommy Griscom, who had served as President Reagan's communications director and had tried to get me on the FCC.

In 1990, I wrote more studies recommended by Freedom to Read Committee of the Association of American Publishers; these included *The Road to the Bill of Rights: The Constitutional Ratification Debates of 1787–88*, and *The Ratification of the Bill of Rights, 1789–91.*[5] The University of South Carolina Press published *Freedom of Expression and Partisan Politics.*[6] The most important review came from Jeffrey St. John, winner of the National Press Foundation's Benjamin Franklin Award; he called it "an Emancipation Proclamation for the electronic media. . . . A rare, remarkable work with uncommon clarity." I was flattered and I had published the first of several university press books.

FIGHTING THE RIGHT WING

In the summer of 1990, I presented a paper at a conference in Amsterdam and heard a wonderful keynote address by the philosopher Stephen Toulmin. I was glad to have associates and friends to meet up with in the city that had haunted my 1971 trip. I visited the incredible Van Gogh paintings again and walked the canals. Then I flew to Dublin to present another paper at another conference.

Even in late June, Dublin was dank, with only splashes of sunshine. I remember walking through a park one cloudy day and cursing the incessant rain. An old man walking by happened to hear me and said, "Don't curse the rain, lad, that's what makes the whiskey taste so good." Yeah, I thought, and that's what makes you a nation of alcoholics.

After the conference in Dublin concluded, I made my way to London for a few days. It was much warmer than Dublin; the late June sun didn't set until quite late. Since Wimbledon was underway, it was not uncommon to see a tennis star along the street or in one of the restaurants. In front of Harrods department store, I said hello to Evonne Goolagong. At one dinner, I sat a table away from the very handsome Stefan Edberg, one of my favorites, and his beautiful wife. After I paid my bill, I gave him a salute from the door, which he sheepishly acknowledged.

Back in America, I was greeted by a call from one of the contributors to my Center for First Amendment Studies. Had I read about the controversy over a photographic display in Cincinnati? No, I had been out of the country, but I would check it out.

For the reader to understand this controversy a bit better, I want to remind you of the case law surrounding obscenity. First, what most people don't know is that it is legal to own obscene material, but your state or local government can prevent the sale of such material. Second, in order for such laws to stand up to constitutional scrutiny, they must define what is obscene in very detailed and graphic ways. Furthermore, the burden of proof on the state is heavy. The law must specifically define obscene matter, whether written, filmed, drawn, or photographed. It must show that the material in question panders to prurient (sexual) interests; that taken as a whole, the work has no socially redeeming values (literary merit); and that it offends community values.[7]

Robert Mapplethorpe's homoerotic photographs from 1979–80 were being shown in Cincinnati along with the controversial photos by Robert Serrano. The National Endowment for the Arts had funded a traveling retrospective of Mapplethorpe's called *A Perfect Moment*. His photographic perspective focused on the male body, with a particular appreciation of African Americans.[8] He had died of AIDS in 1989, leaving funds to a foundation to care for those with the illness. At the same time, the NEA funded a showing of Robert Serrano's photos, including one of a crucifix immersed in urine, called *Piss Christ*. In response, Congress cut the NEA's budget by $45,000, the amount given for the Mapplethorpe and Serrano displays.

The Congress then required that the NEA *not* fund obscene material. The NEA, therefore, implemented a requirement that all grantees certify in writing that they would not utilize federal funding for projects inconsistent with the criteria in the amendment to the 1990 appropriations bill. The amendment empowered the NEA to declare certain materials obscene and, therefore, not eligible for funding. These included "depictions of sadomasochism, homoeroticism, the sexual exploitation of children, or individuals engaged in sex acts." However, that certification requirement was subsequently invalidated as unconstitutionally vague by a federal district court using the standards I reviewed above.[9] When the NEA did not appeal the decision, John Frohnmayer, the liberal Republican head of the NEA, came under attack. Eventually, he was fired by the Bush administration to appease the radical Right, who were attacking Bush using Patrick Buchanan as their leader. It would not be the last time that Bush caved to Buchanan while I protested from the sidelines.

Nonetheless, by the summer of 1990, *A Perfect Moment* had made its way into the Contemporary Art Center in Cincinnati, where its director was promptly arrested for displaying and selling obscene material. I booked a flight to Cincinnati, toured *A Perfect Moment*, and met with the editorial boards of both major papers there. (They were part of the Scripps Howard and Pulitzer chains that supported my Freedom of Expression Foundation.) They were reluctant to take on this fight because Cincinnati was a Republican stronghold and right-wing staging ground, all the way back to the Ku Klux Klan. However, I warned them that if they did not fight the Right at this juncture, it would further empower the radicals, and newspaper content would be on their list for censorship.

Some of us had hoped that the religious Right would die down after their agenda was not advanced by Ronald Reagan. He was good at giving them lip service; he attended the annual conference of evangelical ministers every year of his administration. He may even have ignored the AIDS crisis to cater to them. However, the major items on their agenda were not approved, and some of the ministers, Cal Thomas being the most prominent, suggested that their flocks return to their churches and pray, rather than trying to change things through politics.

That respite did not last long. Senator Jesse Helms (R-NC), Donald Wildmon of the American Family Association, and art critic Hilton Kramer took out ads in the *New York Times* attacking homosexual lifestyles. I immediately called Punch Sulzberger, the publisher of the *Times* and a former board member of my foundation, and complained about the tone of the ads and why he should be ashamed that his paper printed them. He did not have much of a response. The Mapplethorpe and Serrano exhibits gave new life to the right-wing movement. Jerry Falwell of the Moral Majority, who had claimed AIDS was God's punishment for homosexuals, joined in with another screed of his own. At the time, more than a million Americans were infected with HIV; by 1992, 150,000 people would be dead from AIDS.

The exhibit in Cincinnati was in a separate room of the museum, and the entrance clearly warned visitors about what they were going to see. Hence, the photographs were protected speech under the First Amendment; this showing was in effect a private viewing. However, local prosecutors argued that by selling tickets to the display, Dennis Barrie, the director of the Contemporary Art Center, was pandering to the public and selling obscene material—a violation of the law. Since the newspapers wouldn't run pictures of the photos, the public's imagination ran wild about what was actually in the exhibition room.

Soon the *Post* and the *Enquirer* ran editorials in favor of tolerance that repeated my arguments about First Amendment protection. Barrie was eventually acquitted. But the controversy did not end there. The Congress amended the NEA and NEH charters, requiring that their chairpersons ensure that "artistic excellence and artistic merit are the criteria by which [grant] applications are judged, taking into consideration *general standards of decency* and respect for the diverse beliefs and values of the American public." The assessing panels should reflect "diverse artistic and cultural points of view" and include "wide geographic, ethnic, and minority representation," as well as "lay individuals who are knowledgeable about the arts" [§ 959(c)(1)-(2)].

Using the new standards, applications that had been approved by the advisory panels were subsequently vetoed by the National Council for the Arts, which reviews the advisory panel recommendations. Eventually, the NEA bowed to congressional pressure and stopped funding individual artists altogether.

In the meantime, the applicants who had been approved and then disapproved took their case all the way to the Supreme Court. They became known as the NEA Four and included Tim Miller, who was a teaching adjunct at California State University, Los Angeles at the time. My friend David Olsen, who teaches at California State University, Los Angeles, began working on a book on the crisis, and I asked him if he could send me a study we could post on my Center for First Amendment Studies' website. He obliged, and it is still there, outlining the tactics of the radical Right.[10]

At the hearing, the government sought to protect the National Endowment for the Arts' right to set criteria for its competition for grants, even if those guidelines were suggested by Congress in appropriation legislation. Let's be honest; nowhere are the criteria for assessment more subjective than in the arts. Van Gogh sold one painting in his lifetime, and that for 15 francs. In the 1990s, one of his paintings sold for $147 million, another for $110 million. Jackson Pollock, whose paintings Mark Rothko despised, made lots of money in his own time by dribbling paint on canvases, as did Rothko by creating large, simple, primitive dialectics of color; these works are nowhere near as inspirational as Van Gogh's. So the government argued that even though the criteria of the NEA might seem vague, they had a right to impose them as they saw fit.

Furthermore, the government claimed that the NEA provided proper assessment by ensuring that its panels of judges were diverse and reflected national standards of decency and artistic merit. The NEA had considered "decency" and "respect" for diverse beliefs and values as additional, not the only criteria for its award. And the government argued that such a procedure did not "disallow any particular viewpoints." In other words, the language of the controversial amendment from Congress was advisory, not mandatory. It provided additional criteria, but did not preclude other criteria. Justice Sandra Day O'Connor, writing for the Court's majority, agreed: "Thus, we do not perceive a realistic danger that § 954(d)(1) will compromise First Amendment values. As respondents' own arguments demonstrate, the considerations that the provision introduces, by their nature, do not engender the kind of directed viewpoint discrimination that would prompt this Court to invalidate a statute on its face." The new criteria to be "considered" are in fact, according to the majority, in line with the vision and mission of the NEA.

Justice Scalia saw through the government's tactics. He argued that the criteria in the amendment were meant to be mandatory and should have been upheld that way. Scalia began his opinion with the comment that "'The operation was a success, but the patient died.' What such a procedure is to medicine, the Court's opinion in this case is to the law. It sustains the constitutionality of [the congressional amendment] 20 U.S.C. 954(d)(1) by gutting it." In other words, he opposed the compromise of the majority, which reduced the congressional language to hortatory suggestions instead of mandatory standards. No one was happy with the resolution of this issue. And questions about indecency standards plague the Supreme Court and hence the rest of us to this day.

WATCHING PACKWOOD FROM A DISTANCE

With the children off to college, Bob and Georgie Packwood divorced; he was involved with Elaine Franklin, the volunteer coordinator in his 1980 campaign and his campaign manager in 1986. By the spring of 1991, Senator Packwood was preparing for his 1992 reelection campaign and the stars were aligning for him, though a few black holes lingered on the electoral horizon. While Bush had run the most efficient war in the history of the nation, his administration was in trouble because the economy was faltering and he had broken his promise about raising taxes. If he ran behind in the 1992 election, he might pull some GOP senators down with him, including Packwood, who was beginning to look a little gray around the gills. Worse yet, the popular, articulate, and somewhat good-looking congressman from the Portland area, Les AuCoin, was the favorite for the Democratic nomination to run against Packwood. AuCoin was itching for this fight. He had wanted to run in 1986, but feared Packwood's fundraising ability; he had been told by women's and Jewish groups not to run against Packwood, and to keep his powder dry for some other race. Yet in the six intervening years, nothing had come his way. So in 1992, AuCoin decided to challenge Packwood.

In the meantime, President Bush nominated Clarence Thomas to the Supreme Court to replace Thurgood Marshall. Packwood, who had opposed the nomination of Robert Bork to the Supreme Court, announced that he would do the same in Thomas's case. Women's groups praised Packwood for his stand. Republicans condemned him.

Born in the segregated South, and raised in Pin Point, Georgia,[11] Thomas was an attractive nominee—a product of poverty, Catholic boarding schools, and hard work. He eventually entered and left two seminaries, the victim of racism. After graduating from Holy Cross College with honors, he attended Yale Law School. From there he went to work for moderate Republican senator John Danforth and changed his voter registration to Republican. Thomas's early life provided a potent narrative that President Bush and his advisors used to influence the nomination process by taking the story to the public.[12] On July 8, Bush claimed that Thomas offered a "stirring testament to what people can do."[13] On August 6, the President said he was "deeply moved" by Thomas's life story.[14] The President continued his unprecedented pre-hearings campaign of persuasion in mid-August by claiming that "his personal story cannot help but move people."[15] The same strategy was used in a teleconference with the National Governors Association on August 18; in a speech to the National Association of Towns and Townships and a speech to the nation, both on September 6; and at a fund-raising dinner in Philadelphia on September 12, 1991. No president prior to Bush had made so many statements in support of a nominee to the Supreme Court before his or her hearings than Bush did for Thomas. Bush clearly sought to replace questions about ideology, which had sunk Bork, with the narrative of Thomas's life, which was much more accessible to the public than theoretical considerations. The press was quick to take up the same theme.[16]

Thomas had other virtues. In 1981 and 1982, he served as assistant secretary for civil rights in the Department of Education. Reagan then chose Thomas to head the Equal Employment Opportunity Commission (EEOC), which supported most affirmative-action programs. While the Civil Rights Commission was critical of the Reagan administration in many areas, it singled Thomas out for praise. In fact, Thomas's EEOC was critical of the Reagan Justice Department, deciding not to file amicus briefs opposing it only after major pressure from the White House. The EEOC in 1983 resolved over 74,000 complaints, compared with less than 58,000 in 1980 under Carter. Only after 1984 did Thomas openly begin to question the hiring regulations of the EEOC in particular, and the use of quotas for reparations for past abuses.[17] Thomas's sixteen months of noncontroversial service on the D.C. Circuit Court of Appeals, his conversion on the issue of affirmative action, and his support of "natural rights" made him attractive to the Bush administration, particularly to White House counsel C. Boyden Gray, who helped usher the nominee through the confirmation process.

Just as the Senate was about to vote on Thomas, National Public Radio broke a story: Anita Hill, an African American former employee of Thomas at the Department of Education and a professor of law at the University of Oklahoma, had claimed in testimony to the FBI that he had sexually harassed her.[18] Thus, a second round of hearings began on October 11, 1991, in which Thomas angrily denied the charges. With ABC, NBC, and CBS providing live coverage, Hill repeated her testimony to the FBI about intimate sexual innuendos.[19] That evening, Thomas's testimony in reply drew huge television ratings.[20] An electric moment came when Thomas accused the panel of conducting a "high-tech lynching of an uppity black man."[21] Thomas's indignation and passionate delivery stood in marked contrast to his previous testimony.

Over the next 48 hours, Hill returned and new witnesses were called on the specific charge of sexual harassment. Republican senators accused Hill of lying, or of being part of a conspiracy to stop the nomination.[22] Why had she followed Thomas from one post to another if she was being harassed?

Thomas returned one more time to protest how he was being treated, and refused to withdraw his name.[23] Throughout the two sets of hearings over eleven days, the committee heard from representatives of fifty different interest groups, most of which opposed the nomination. After more media coverage and debate in the Senate, Thomas was confirmed on a vote of 52 to 48, the closest confirmation vote in the twentieth century. Thomas's nomination battle was won not only because of the rhetorical strategies of Bush and his Justice Department, but also because of Thomas's own ability to manipulate the media at a live hearing that was being watched by the public.[24]

THE '92 PACKWOOD CAMPAIGN

In the following spring, Packwood easily won the Republican primary. However, the Democratic primary was hotly contested. During it, Packwood again ignored my advice and ran negative ads in the other guy's primary. The ads claimed that Congressman AuCoin had bounced checks in the bank of the House of Representatives. As I predicted, the press and the public were outraged that Packwood would interfere in the other party's primary. Packwood's worst fear was realized when AuCoin won a very close recount, many people voting for AuCoin simply to spite Packwood.

At this juncture, Packwood had a discussion with Senator Phil Gramm (R-TX), the new head of the National Republican Senatorial Campaign Committee. While the committee could only give Packwood's campaign $17,500 under the law, it could also provide funds to the Oregon Republican Party for "party building purposes," using a loophole in the campaign contribution laws. Gramm and Packwood agreed to a scheme wherein $96,500 would be given to the Oregon party, most of it earmarked for Packwood's reelection campaign. On March 6, 1992, Packwood told his tape-recorded diary, "What was said in that room would be enough to convict us all."[25]

At the same time, Elaine Franklin, now Packwood's chief of staff, negotiated with the National Independent Automobile Dealers Association to get them to spend money on behalf of Packwood, which is legal as long as there was no "coordination" with Packwood's campaign. Franklin's "negotiating" was a violation of Federal Election Campaign rules, which Packwood acknowledged in his diary on March 20, 1992. In the fall campaign, the political action committee of the association spent $65,539 for phone banks on Packwood's behalf.

For this general election, Packwood abandoned his usual grassroots, lawn-sign approach and decided to spend almost all of his funds on media advertising. In a letter dated July 11, 1992, he wrote to me, "There are no full-time campaign employees. We have a bunch of part-timers. I must admit trepidation about this strategy. It's the first time we haven't had thousands of volunteers." He closed by joking that I would be welcome to speak for him in Baker, Oregon, as I did in 1980. At that juncture in the campaign, Packwood had raised over $3,000,000 to AuCoin's $200,000. He led in the polls by a margin of 46 to 33 percent.

That summer Bush again called me to be on the Official Proceedings Staff of the Republican Convention, this time meeting in his hometown of Houston. Bush was in trouble for all sorts of reasons. One of the main ones was that he was not featured in his best venue: press conferences. These should have been put on in prime time. At press conferences, Bush was witty, totally in command of information, and knew the names of every member of the White House press corps. But Bush said he did not want to be seen as imitating Reagan. We told him that the nighttime press conference had not been invented by Reagan, but by Kennedy, and Nixon had used them to great success. By the time he finally agreed to do a press conference at night, the networks refused to cover it, arguing that the nation was too far into the electoral process and it would be unfair to cover the President and not his opponents.

Houston was hot and muggy, but I enjoyed working at the convention. On the weekend preceding the convention, we set up shop, and I learned that there was a plot afoot to substitute Colin Powell, the former head of the Joint Chiefs of Staff, for Quayle as the vice-presidential nominee. Quayle was a liability; Powell could shake the election up. Like Thomas, Powell was African American, and Bush enjoyed a good rapport with that ethnic group dating back to his days as a Houston congressman. And if a Republican can run well among African Americans, he cuts into a normally Democratic ethnic stronghold.

The plan was for Quayle to come forward on Wednesday night of the convention and announce that for the good of the party, he was not seeking renomination. He would then give a speech nominating Powell. That all sounded wonderful to me. President Ford, who had dumped his vice president, Nelson Rockefeller, in 1976, supported the plan. But President Bush wouldn't hear of it. People had tried to dump him from the Reagan ticket in 1984 and Reagan had remained loyal. Bush would remain loyal to his vice president too.

Once the convention got underway, I was given some prime writing assignments. Surrounded by Missouri state troopers, Governor John

Ashcroft came in with a speech that was four times as long as his allotted time. When I told him I would work with his staff to cut it, he walked out in a huff and went over my head to Rich Bond, who was running the convention. Bond told Ashcroft to cut the speech to eight minutes or he would not be allowed to speak at all. The humbled governor returned, and we cut the speech and the governor's ego down to size.

The high point of the convention for me was working with Condoleezza Rice on her speech celebrating the fall of the Berlin Wall and the collapse of the Soviet Union. "America triumphed in the Cold War because we were committed to a strong defense, because we believed in free markets, and because our diplomatic skill was second to none. . . . Sometimes the American spirit finds its clearest reflection in the eyes of those still seeking democracy's promise—a Polish worker, a Russian peasant, a black South African child." I found Rice to be a very bright woman, and she certainly knew how to deliver a speech. That was important, because she would precede Patrick Buchanan, who would then be followed by former President Reagan.

Buchanan had attacked President Bush in several primaries before dropping out of the race.[26] I argued that he should be confined to a ten-minute speech in the middle of the afternoon. But Rich Bond knew that the election would be close and believed that Buchanan's endorsement would help Bush rally social conservatives. So an agreement was reached. If he would endorse Bush, Buchanan would speak in prime time, sandwiched between two more moderate speakers, Rice and Reagan.

Condi Rice's speech went very well, and then Buchanan was introduced. He went on so long that Reagan did not speak in prime time in most time zones. Worse yet, Buchanan's speech was a right-wing screed that claimed America was involved in a "culture war." He tied the Republican Convention to his agenda and only endorsed Bush at the end. It was disaster for a party seeking its way back to the middle ground; Bill Clinton's people would exploit the moment and win the middle ground for themselves in the campaign.

For the last night of the convention, I rewrote a speech Bob Dole's staff had given him and then rehearsed him through it. He was cranky during the process but wound up giving a fairly good speech of introduction for Bush. On the same night, I worked with Bob Hartmann, my boss in 1976 in the White House, on a speech for President Ford. Prior to our convention, the Democrats had nominated Bill Clinton, and throughout their convention had taunted Bush with the refrain "Where was George?" Ford answered the query, providing a fine review of Bush's record, repeating the line "George was there." And then Bush came forward and gave a good acceptance speech, but not good enough to regain the lead over Clinton. When Ross Perot reentered the race for president a few weeks later as a third-party candidate, Bush's hopes for reelection were dashed.

Packwood's general election campaign was nasty and negative except for the debates, which were spirited and excellent. The final debate from Portland was televised statewide, and Packwood won it with several devastating revelations about AuCoin's voting record and ambition, and a chilling conclusion which charged that electing AuCoin was a "suicide pact for Oregon."

Just when it looked like Packwood might move into the lead for good in the polls, he was called by Florence Graves, a freelance reporter, about claims that he had pressured employees for sex. Packwood's chief accuser was a staff member from 1969, Julie Williamson (see chapter 8), who had gone to work for AuCoin. She had encouraged Graves to find other women who would corroborate her claims that Packwood was coming on to employees. The *Washington Post* considered buying Graves's story, but before it did, it gave Packwood a chance to respond. He denied the story, and his staff began to systematically attack the credibility of the women who had talked to Graves. When interviewing Packwood to determine whether to endorse him or AuCoin, the leading paper in the state, the *Oregonian*, asked point-blank whether the Senator was being investigated for sexual harassment. Sitting in on the meeting, Elaine Franklin interrupted the interview and denied the story. The *Oregonian* then endorsed Packwood. At the same time, the *Post* decided not to run with the story because the election was so close, because they did not originate the story, because only four of the accusers would allow their names to be used, and because the testimony of some of the women had not been corroborated or was highly suspect.

Election night 1992 was a cliffhanger for Packwood. While the networks projected him as the winner, he discovered that large numbers of Democratic precincts in Portland had not reported their votes. He quickly calculated that despite media projections, he could easily lose the election. It turned out that the outstanding Democratic votes were in suburbs loyal to Packwood. He won the election 52 to 48 percent but wasn't sure of victory until 2 A.M. He would not be allowed to savor it for long.

CHAPTER FIFTEEN

The Fall of Bob Packwood

I HAD WITNESSED THE FALL OF RICHARD NIXON FROM A DISTANCE. The revelations hurt me personally—how could I have been so wrong about the man? The resignation speech touched me emotionally because I identified with Nixon's California roots, experience in debate, and rise from the lower class. In the case of Bob Packwood, I was on the inside and an advisor through the crisis, albeit from California. And even though I had warned Packwood about some of the tactics he was using, his fall would prove gut-wrenching.

It began two weeks after the election on November 22, 1992, when I was awakened by a call from a friend, who read me a front-page story from the *Washington Post* accusing Packwood of ten instances of sexual misbehavior: PACKWOOD ACCUSED OF SEXUAL ADVANCES; ALLEGED BEHAVIOR PATTERN COUNTERS IMAGE. One of the accusers was Gena Hutton, who claimed in the newspaper account that she had told me about her incident—an attempted French kiss in a parking lot—during the 1980 campaign. This eventually led to calls to me from the *Post* and the Senate Ethics Committee. I told them that while I knew Gena to be an honest person, I did not remember her telling me about the incident. Furthermore, according to the dates she gave, the incident she was talking about occurred before I became campaign manager. Perhaps she told the first campaign manager who preceded me. I called Gena, and after some discussion, we realized that she told me about the incident not in 1980, but when we met for a dinner in Las Vegas in 1984. Gena had also signed on to the 1986 Packwood campaign. So she could not have been all that offended by what happened in 1980. In any case, the Senate Ethics Committee decided not to call me as a witness after I clarified things with their staff in several phone interviews.

Georgie Packwood told the *Post* that these allegations had floated around for some time, but she had no knowledge of them. She regretted the fact that her children would now read about them. Mimi Dawson said the charges were "rubbish," and pointed out that many women on Packwood's staff had been promoted and gone on to wonderful careers without ever having been harassed by him. Others in the Packwood camp continued attacking the credibility of the women who had come forward. The *Wall Street Journal* opined that many of these charges were insignificant (an attempted French kiss) or the result of publicity seekers.

However, the controversy was revived when women's groups in Oregon vented their outrage at Packwood as some of their members corroborated the *Post's* story. Chief among these was Mary Heffernan of NARAL (National Abortion Rights Action League), who claimed that Packwood had put his arms around her and kissed her in his office in 1980. I knew Mary because she had worked in the 1980 campaign. We were on opposite sides of most issues, but realized that we had to work together if Packwood was to be elected. In the *Post* story, she claimed she did not report Packwood's sexual advances because she was afraid she would hurt the NARAL movement. Jean McMahon claimed that while she was attempting to write a speech for Packwood, he chased her around a motel room. The staff claimed that no one had ever heard of her being given such an assignment. And I knew that Packwood never used a speechwriter.

Paige Wagers, a mail clerk, claimed she was called into Packwood's office one day, only to find the door locked behind her and him running his fingers through her hair. She pushed him away and moved on to another job. Five years later she found herself walking with Packwood through a dark corridor of the Capitol. He allegedly forced her into his hideaway office and attempted to make love to her. She resisted and left. In her testimony to the *Post*, she said she made "clear in the nicest way possible that I wasn't interested." In his defense, many supporters pointed out that in every case when the woman told Packwood to stop, he stopped and never bothered the woman again. Many remained on his staff for years after such incidents, feeling perfectly safe.

But the crisis continued to blossom like a bad blister. The *Oregonian*, claiming it had been a victim of Franklin's deception, asked Packwood to resign. He went into seclusion and then into a Minnesota clinic for alcohol dependency. He was assigned to an Alcoholics Anonymous group in Washington, D.C. I spoke to Packwood after he returned to Washington. He said he did not like Alcoholics Anonymous's methods, particularly their calling on a higher power. He held a news conference on December 10, 1992, to rationalize his wrongdoing. He claimed to have an alcohol problem, told about how he was raised in a man's world, and concluded, "I didn't get it then; I do get it now. . . . If any of my comments or actions have indeed been unwelcome or if I have conducted myself in any way that has caused any individual discomfort or embarrassment, for that I am sincerely sorry. . . . My actions were just plain wrong. . . . I pledge to restructure, drastically and totally, my attitude and my professional relationships."

The statement was hard to watch, given that Packwood had supported the feminist movement and surely understood how the world had changed since his upbringing. Under severe questioning, Packwood refused to say anything about specific charges or the women who made them. Instead, Packwood requested that the Senate Ethics Committee investigate the matter, knowing full well they probably would have investigated it anyway. I called Packwood and told him to be honest, open, and cooperative with the committee. On December 14, 1992, I received a short letter from the Senator that reads in part: "Thanks for the advice. Needless to say, it's not a happy time. My shoulders are broad, however, and I have no intention of resigning."

Nonetheless, Packwood ignored my advice and followed his lawyer's recommendations on two crucial strategy decisions, both of which would prove disastrous. First, Packwood would not grant interviews; he would retreat into the bunker of his office. His lawyer did not trust his client with the news media. Second, Packwood would pass sections of diaries to his legal team, who would screen them and pass relevant pages on to the Ethics Committee. Packwood hoped that the move would demonstrate a cooperative attitude while at the same time showing that some of the women making the charges had their facts wrong.

The bunker strategy failed for a number of reasons. Packwood is combative and usually quite good with the press, as he would later prove in interviews with Barbara Walters and Larry King. To tie his tongue was a mistake. Furthermore, the strategy appeared to be an admission of guilt, especially when Packwood would respond to a question with, "My lawyers have advised me not to respond." A poll in the *Oregonian* showed that 78 percent of the respondents believed Packwood was guilty of the charges; 61 percent thought he should resign. Only a month before, he had been reelected to the Senate!

Packwood hired Jake Stein to replace his first legal team, and went on the offensive. He began to score well with audiences and the press; he never drank again; his own morale improved immensely. In fact, he felt empowered enough to help the Republicans defeat the Clinton healthcare package being pushed by the First Lady. The Republicans stood united against the bill, and the Democrats were unable to break the filibuster; they had 56 votes, four shy of the necessary 60. Packwood cracked, "We've killed health-care reform. Now we've got to make sure our fingerprints are not on it."

Then came another blunder caused by the lawyers. Even though the diaries were screened by Packwood's law firm, they allowed his bragging about manipulating the divorce court to slip through. A staffer on the Ethics Committee discovered the passage, and the committee widened its investigation into the impropriety of contacting former employees who were lobbyists in order to gain an advantage over his wife in a divorce settlement. The diaries revealed that Packwood called Sean (yes, the same one who recruited me in 1979), a lobbyist, and asked him to put Georgie on retainer. According to the diaries, Sean replied, "How much?" Packwood asked for "$7,500 a year." (Should his wife have outside income, Packwood would pay less in alimony.) Sean repeated the figure. Packwood said, "Yeah." Sean replied, "Consider it done." Within a week, Senator Packwood took a position favorable to Sean's company before the Senate Finance Committee. When he learned that the Ethics Committee had expanded its investigation to new charges, he cut off access to his diaries. Clearly, the ghost of Richard Nixon was haunting Packwood.

The committee had gotten passages of the diaries up to 1989; the complete typed diaries ran over 8,000 pages. On October 20, 1993, sensing that Packwood was playing games, the three Republicans and three Democrats on the committee unanimously agreed to issue a subpoena for the 1989 through 1992 diaries to examine the context of his last race for Senate and the new charges about soliciting help from lobbyists. Packwood, supported by the ACLU, took his case to the floor of the Senate, where he argued that the committee had violated its agreement by going into new areas of investigation beyond sexual misconduct. Ignoring the Watergate precedent, Packwood claimed that his diaries, even though composed in his Capitol office on government equipment and transcribed by a government employee, were "protected by a constitutional right to privacy." The most offensive moment of this speech came when he threatened his colleagues that the diaries would reveal sexual affairs between other senators and staff members. Senators in the room were infuriated and horrified. Packwood concluded by saying that taking his diaries violated the prohibition against self-incrimination in the Fifth Amendment. The day after Halloween, he took the Senate floor and again repeated his threats about what might be revealed if the diaries were released to a court of law. Echoing Nixon, he stunningly proclaimed, "I want you to understand the fear that any one of us has about leaks."

Neither the committee nor the Senate at large was buying Packwood's case. By surrendering some of his diaries, he had lost the right to conceal any of them. The legal doctrine of "in for a penny, in for a pound" prevailed. So behind the scenes, he tried to cut a deal wherein the diaries would be turned over to the former solicitor general of the Bush administration, Judge Kenneth Starr, who would examine them only with regard to the specific charges of sexual misconduct and the manipulation of the divorce proceedings. Senator John Kerry (D-MA) surmised, "We are being tested here. Let's tell the American people we are not going to cover up and we're not going to have a double standard." In response, Packwood pleaded, "The Senate Ethics Committee is behaving like prosecutor, jury, and judge." The venerable Senator Robert Byrd (D-WV) then rose to defend the decorum of the Senate and proclaimed, "It is time for you to go." On November 2, 1993, almost a year after his reelection, Packwood lost the Senate vote 94 to 5 and took his case to federal court.

In the meantime, the Senate Ethics Committee interrogated the secretary who transcribed the diaries from 1969 on. Under questioning, she admitted that since the Senate subpoena was issued, Packwood had taken the tapes of the diaries and revised them. Tearfully she confessed that the difference in volume and background noise clearly indicated that Packwood had tampered with the original taping sessions. The disclosure opened Packwood to charges of obstructing justice. Nixon's ghost was now chasing Packwood down the corridors of power. And not so oddly, Packwood came to rely on some of Nixon's staunchest supporters. William Safire, one of Nixon's favorite speechwriters, was now an editorialist for the *New York Times* and a longtime Packwood crony. He penned an editorial in support of Packwood's right to keep the diaries private.

It was to no avail. U.S. District Judge Thomas Penfield Jackson ordered the diaries turned over to the court for safekeeping, and then on January 24, 1994, ruled in favor of the Ethics Committee: "Senator Packwood enjoys no Fifth Amendment privilege to avoid surrendering his personal diaries to the Ethics Committee, the act itself presenting no risk of incrimination beyond that he has already reduced to written or recorded form." Knowing it was over, Packwood worked with Senator Dole on a resignation scenario. However, negotiations were interrupted when the Justice Department announced it would investigate possible felony charges against Packwood for influence peddling and obstruction of justice. Packwood told Dole he must stay in the Senate to retain his bargaining chip of resignation.

Senator Packwood appealed Judge Jackson's ruling to the Supreme Court, where Chief Justice William Rehnquist, a personal and philosophical ally of nominees to the Court that Packwood opposed, relished denying Packwood's appeal in a lengthy decision. On March 2, 1994, Rehnquist ruled that Packwood had undermined his case by altering the very diaries he had agreed to give to the committee: "Evidence of tampering very likely renders all of the requested diary entries relevant to the investigation." The diaries were turned over to Judge Starr, who decided what was relevant to the ethics probe and what was not.

Packwood responded that "a precedent has been set that will not protect the private thoughts and property of American citizens from government snooping." In an interview on ABC's *20/20* with Barbara Walters, he described himself as a coke-bottle-glasses nerd in high school who was always afraid of being rejected by girls. He confessed to binge drinking and making "boorish passes" once he became a senator. But he also defended what he had done: "If you try to kiss a woman in the hopes . . . that she might want to be kissed and she doesn't, is that sexual misconduct? Or is it just misperceived? You perceive one thing and she perceived another. . . . Some people talk to their psychiatrist . . . I talk to my diaries." It was Packwood's best public defense. The campaign on his behalf continued as former female employees tried to discredit some of the twenty-six women who had by this time made charges against him.

The Justice Department announced that it did not have enough evidence to pursue charges of obstruction of justice and influence-peddling against Packwood. That was the good news. The bad news was that the Justice Department decision freed the Senate Ethics Committee to act. On May 16, 1995, it released the lurid details of seventeen corroborated incidents of sexual misconduct. Despite the report, Senator Alfonse D'Amato (R-NY) said, "Packwood is entitled to all the presumptions of innocence that any citizen is, and until this is over, he should continue his work." Senator Barbara Boxer (D-CA) took a different tack: "It would be better for Senator Packwood, for the women, and for the Senate if he were to resign."

On June 27, 1995, Packwood appeared before the Ethics Committee in closed session for three hours to give his side of the story. Afterward, in a heated debate, the committee split 3–3 on whether to have open hearings. Thus, the motion failed, and the committee continued in private. However, Senator Boxer brought the issue to the floor of the Senate, where Republicans and Democrats fought over the issue of open hearings. Senator Simpson (R-WY) defended Packwood's right to a closed-door hearing, arguing that open hearings would do immeasurable harm to the reputations of some of the women, and that the committee had a right to proceed as it saw fit. The Republicans closed ranks and Packwood won a 52–48 vote for closed hearings. Boxer was livid.

Matters took a turn for the worse for Senator Packwood when two new allegations came to the committee in August. The most egregious case was made by a woman who claimed that when she was seventeen, Packwood came to her home, knowing her parents weren't there, and forced himself on her. Boxer renewed her call for an open hearing. To defend himself, Packwood appeared on *Dateline* with Jane Pauley and read a letter from the seventeen-year-old thanking him at that time for all he had done for her. Packwood argued that no one who had been abused would have written such a letter. Taking some journalistic license, Pauley responded that she might have written just such a letter under the circumstances if it meant advancing her career. Packwood appeared flabbergasted by her assertion.

On August 31, 1995, in an about-face, Packwood called for public hearings, which riled his Republican supporters in the Senate. Packwood was running back and forth like a rat trapped in a small cage. Nonetheless, Senator Dole worked feverishly to get a compromise in which Packwood would give up his chairmanship of the Finance Committee, but stay in the Senate. But Dole's efforts were undercut when Senator Mitch McConnell (R-KY), whom Packwood had recruited to run for Senate, announced that the Ethics Committee had voted unanimously to expel Packwood from the Senate. On the morning of September 7, 1995, McConnell claimed, "The evidence is compelling. The appropriate response is to resign."

Packwood held a press conference at which he attempted to refute the charges, attacked the jurisdiction of the Ethics Committee, and reasserted that he would not resign. But during the day, senators besieged him in his hideaway in the basement of the Capitol, where he was joined by his chief defenders, Senators Simpson and McCain. They told him the crisis had to end. After a few minutes, Senator Dole joined them. Looking directly at Packwood, he said, "Bob, you're killing the party and you're killing the Congress."

An hour later, Packwood took the floor of the Senate, and in a meandering speech reminiscent of Nixon's farewell to his staff, he tearfully resigned in the name of "duty, honor, and country. It is my duty to resign. It is the honorable thing to do for this country, for this Senate. I leave this institution not with malice but with love." He had held on for almost three years after the initial charges had been made.

A number of things struck me as I listened to Packwood's resignation speech. The most astounding is the parallel with Nixon. Both men kept taped evidence, which they tried to alter. Both men prided themselves on their Machiavellian tactics. Both men admired Benjamin Disraeli, the nineteenth-century British prime minister known for his political and foreign-policy skills. Both men took delight in pulling off tricks that short-circuited the political system. Both had fathers that they did not admire.[1] Both Nixon and Packwood had saintly mothers who inculcated a sense of guilt in their sons. Like Nixon, I suspect more of Packwood's ambition came from his efforts to live up to his mother's standards than from trying to win his father's attention. His mother was a stern teacher who was a perfectionist. She was a tough, no-nonsense woman, who regularly criticized her son and his campaign operation. That was also true of Packwood's wife Georgie.

The criticism from their mothers developed a sense of unworthiness in both Packwood and Nixon. So when they had spectacular successes—Nixon's 49-state sweep in 1972, Packwood successful reelection in 1992—they found ways, perhaps unconsciously, to punish themselves. And so for both Nixon and Packwood, what began as an offense—or in Packwood's case, boorish behavior—exploded into a full-blown crime because of an effort to cover up the original offense. Each of them sullied their reputations with the words they uttered into tape recorders. Instead of being reprimanded for bad behavior, Packwood would be expelled from the Senate, having chosen to ignore the lessons of history taught by the example of Nixon, the very man who was elected president on the same night that Packwood was first elected to the U.S. Senate. In the end, Packwood chose to be Nixon rather than to learn from Nixon's mistakes.

Recently I found a striking passage in a book by Ray Price, Nixon's best speechwriter. He wrote, "One part of Richard Nixon is exceptionally considerate, exceptionally caring, sentimental, generous of spirit, kind. Another part is coldly calculating, devious, craftily manipulative. A third part is angry, vindictive, ill-tempered, mean-spirited."[2] This was true of Bob Packwood as well, and it helped shape his political tragedy. Cultivating his mind, he rose from obscurity to become one of the most impressive members of the United States Senate. However, like many other politicians, the longer he stayed, the more immune to criticism he became. The burning desire to do well for his constituents had balanced his ambition in the beginning. But cynicism and the desire to affirm a damaged ego eventually eroded the moral fiber that kept his dark side in check. The better angels of his nature were driven into exile as Packwood willingly entered a realm without spiritual guidance.

Packwood married Elaine Franklin, and she maintained their home in Portland while she worked as a campaign consultant in the Northwest. Packwood became a lobbyist for several companies whom he had helped when he was chair of the Finance Committee. He lived six months of the year in Washington, and six in Portland. One night, during one of my visits to D.C., the two of us retreated to a dinner in Georgetown. He told me that he would have resigned from the Senate much earlier if he knew how much money he could make as a lobbyist. "As long as the Republicans control the

Senate, I can make lots of money." He claimed that his bicoastal marriage was much better than "having to live with the same person night and day year round."

When the check came, the waitress said, "Here you go, Senator."

He looked at me and asked, "Did she just call me 'Senator'?"

"That she did, Bob."

"Wow. They still remember." I felt sorry for him, having to rely on such moments for the grains of recognition that would sustain his psyche.[3]

A REPUBLICAN PROFESSOR

Through the three years that marked the decline and fall of Bob Packwood, I adapted to academic life. I raised enough money to maintain the Center for First Amendment Studies on the campus, fund graduate fellowships, and publish research on the First Amendment.[4] I continued to explore the relationship between rhetoric and spirituality. I had noted that all the way back to the Greek Sophists, there were theorists who had pursued rhetorical theory as a way of creating sublime speeches that called people to spirit. However, it was nigh unto impossible to get anything published on the subject. I complained about this treatment in an article[5] that built on the work I had done in linking Heidegger's theory to a spiritual pathway to God.[6]

I also continued to lecture around the country on various topics. Again hosted by my mentor Carroll Arnold at Penn State, I lectured on the innovations in media coverage resulting from reporters being embedded with combat troops during the Gulf War. At William and Mary, I talked about the challenges the First Amendment had faced in our history. At Northwestern, where my co-author Michael Hyde had relocated, I talked to his seminar about rhetoric and transcendence. I regularly presented several research papers a year at the annual meeting of the National Communication Association, and most of these were competitively selected, after which I converted them into scholarly articles or book chapters.

In 1993, I was surprised to receive the Distinguished Scholarly Research Award from the university. I rewarded myself with a trip to Italy to attend an academic conference in Turin and then travel on to Milan, Florence, and Venice. While in Venice, I wandered a little way off of St. Mark's Square and found the Church of St. Zulian. I went inside and, overwhelmed with a sense of spirituality, I prayed to the Virgin Mary to prevent me from ever getting depressed again. The black dog of depression is always lurking, and so depressives not only live with depression but with the threat of depression, and hence in fear. When I finished my rosary, I heard the words "write, write." And ever since I have tried to write every day, and lo and behold the depression has never returned.

Throughout this period, particularly when I visited other campuses to lecture on the First Amendment, colleagues would ask, "How can you be a Republican?" I had to admit that by 1994, it was getting tougher and tougher. The Republican Party had been good to me, and I had long admired its conscientious conservatives who protected the Constitution. To this day I fear that liberal justices on the Supreme Court have such a plastic view of the Constitution that it can be molded into anything they want. And sure enough, with the activist conservatives on the Supreme Court, they too have molded it to their philosophies instead of interpreting in terms of genuine hermeneutics or even original intent. But on balance, I believe there is less danger to the Constitution from conservative justices than there is from liberal ones.

I also admired the Eisenhower, Nixon, Kissinger, Bush Sr. realpolitik in foreign policy, and still reeled from the failures of Truman and Kennedy on that score. Obviously, I evolved into what became known as a moderate Republican, who could trace their agendas back to Lincoln, Teddy Roosevelt, Claire Booth Luce, Margaret Chase Smith, and Eisenhower. But by 1994, even die-hard conservatives like President Ford were being tossed into the moderate camp. The reason was that social conservatives guided by the religious Right were taking over the party and moving it further to the right. It was uncomfortable, and getting more so with every passing election. The Pat Buchanan episode at the 1992 Republican Convention had been traumatic. Even Mr. Conservative, Senator Barry Goldwater, complained in 1994 about what was happening, and to my delight also defended gays in the Republican Party at the same time. In a column in the *Washington Post*, he started by saying that he believed in keeping the government "out of our pockets, off our backs and out of our bedrooms. . . . Gays and lesbians are part of every American family. They should not be shortchanged in their efforts to better their lives and serve their communities. Some will paint this as a liberal or religious issue. I am a conservative, but I believe in democracy and the separation of church and state." Goldwater rightly recognized that authentic conservatism is neither populist nor exclusively Christian. Like him, I stayed in the Republican Party to continue that fight from within.

In 1995, I was eligible for a sabbatical, but in the California State University, they are for one semester at full pay instead of a whole year, as at major universities. On top of that, you have to submit a proposal for research or creative activity. When I accepted the sabbatical, I had to give up the department chairmanship. After six years in that post, I gladly did so. I would not miss the student and faculty complaints, the scheduling difficulties, and constant budget fights. Furthermore, I had appointed Professor Sharon Downey as my vice-chair to get her ready for my departure. She easily outshone me and served for a record fifteen years.

I took my sabbatical in the spring of 1995 to write *The Quest for Charisma*, which began by correcting the definition of charisma.[7] The news media used the term to refer to someone who was good-looking and rhetorically adept. However, the true meaning of charisma is to be imbued with spirit or grace. I was upset by the fact that many leaders were called charismatic—in 1995 it was President Clinton—when in fact they were merely talented speakers. After straightening things out, the book laid out pathways to spirituality that would allow a person to become genuinely charismatic. In late April of 1995, I flew to Grand Cayman Island to stay in the empty condo of a friend and put the finishing touches on the book. The condo was located on the eastern side of the island on a beautiful aquamarine bay. I would write all morning long, then go out to see sights. On the way back to the condo, I would snorkel in a new spot each day. When I got home, I would write some more and then follow Dennis Connor on television as he won the America's Cup sailing regatta. In the evening, I had a martini and fixed myself dinner.

Before my arrival, I wondered if I could survive a week of living alone. However, the writing went well, the snorkeling gave me exercise, and the regatta held my attention. I returned home with a completed manuscript that was eventually published by Praeger Press. I had a chance to publicize the book at a conference in Scotland the next summer. It would be the first time that I faced a crisis at an academic event.

I traveled to London and then on to Edinburgh, where I was to present a paper on St. Augustine and talk to colleagues about my new book. As I watched one of the academic panels to get a feel for this international conference on the history of rhetoric, I saw that the participants were very well prepared and ready to pounce on any mistake anyone made. That evening when I got back to my room, I read my paper and was heartsick. It simply would not do given the quality of presentations I had witnessed. I tried rewriting it, but there was not enough time. I had a terrible, sleepless night.

The next morning I arrived at my panel and the room was packed. I assumed this was because the noted scholar Brian Vickers was on the panel with me. Since he would go first, I assumed many people would leave after he gave his talk. When he finished, I looked around the room; no one left.

In fact, more people came through the door. What in the world was I to do to avoid embarrassment?

I shoved my written presentation aside and began to talk about the influences on St. Augustine's writing, especially book 4 of *De Doctrina Christiana*, which includes his recommendations with regard to preaching. I quickly ran through the influence of Plato since this audience was well aware of it. I then talked about the influence of Cicero on St. Augustine, but again breezed through the subject matter because I knew that the audience was very familiar with Cicero's influence on Augustine. At that juncture, I had nothing left to say, and so I opened my mouth to conclude when this thought came out:

> While many of you are no doubt familiar with the influence of Plato and Cicero on St. Augustine, I have found very little in our literature about the influence of Jesus on St. Augustine. I find this odd since Augustine wrote several commentaries on the Gospels and would have been very familiar with Jesus as a rhetorician. [I heard a gasp in the room but continued.] Jesus had an uncanny knack for adjusting His rhetoric to His audience. And He had at least four. He did not preach to children because He claimed they were innocent and pure, and therefore, not in need of his words. He did preach to the masses and used parables so they could understand his thoughts. The Sadducees, Pharisees, scribes and high priests comprised His third audience, with whom He engaged in argumentative disputation. Finally, came those who had faith, such as his apostles, who believed and were in no need of persuasion. Let me now argue that each of these audiences shows up in the work of St. Augustine and he provides a different rhetorical style for addressing each one.

I then provided a detailed analysis of St. Augustine on style and its relationship to audience. And concluded that Augustine was the father of both scholasticism and humanism. Scholastics who believed one could reason one's way to God could find much in St. Augustine to support their view, especially his reduction of rhetoric to a presentational skill as opposed to an epistemic one. However, the humanistic desire to retrieve the classics was also rooted in St. Augustine's reliance on Plato and Cicero. When I finished, the audience applauded, and several members came up to me after the panel and thanked me for sharing the paper. To this day, I believe that my spiritualism saved me that morning in Edinburgh. I rewarded myself by touring the city, winding up on Arthur's Seat, a high hill that overlooks the city and its castles.

A POLITICAL FLING

Since a presidential election year was getting closer, I expected to sit back and watch the jockeying for position going on in the spring and summer of 1995. But it was not to be. I received a call from Ken Khachigian asking me if I'd be interested in writing for California Governor Pete Wilson's campaign for president. Over the next 24 hours, I thought about the consulting position. An ex-Marine, Wilson had been a superb mayor of San Diego. His career in the Senate was less effective. But to his credit, he realized he was better at administration than legislation. So he left the Senate to run for governor and won. In 1994, he won again, along with the Republicans taking control of the U.S. House of Representatives for the first time since 1954. As governor, Wilson had made effective reforms that put the state back on a stable financial footing. I also had been impressed by his fairness to the faculty on our campuses. After I studied Wilson's record, I concluded that I could be enthusiastic about his candidacy. The projected starting date for me would be June 1, 1995.

On my first visit to Sacramento, I learned that Pete Wilson had worked with Republican pollster and strategist Don Sipple to create a coherent value system we could use as a backdrop for his rhetoric. This strategy was reminiscent of Reagan's run for governor in 1966. In the Wilson campaign, my job was to develop a matching issue-position system and then build speeches from the value and issue systems. Wilson had wanted to start his campaign in April, but decided to have throat surgery to remove a polyp on his vocal chords. Unfortunately, his recovery took much longer than his doctors predicted; his brilliant wife Gayle had to deliver some of the speeches I wrote for Pete. He was back to normal at the end of June, by which time he had opened a campaign office for the Iowa caucuses and told Larry King he would be a candidate for president.

While Wilson met with his strategy team to come up with something that would move him ahead in the pack,[8] my mother called and told me to come to National City immediately. My father had fallen and cracked his pelvis. When I arrived at the hospital, Dad believed he was going to die and told me to start processing all the paperwork for a funeral. He did not die, but his idea about the paperwork was a good one. I soon knew where all his files were. We brought him home a few days later. Since he was bedridden, Mother and I nursed him along as best we could. And I also hired a nurse to help Mom. Thank God this happened during the summer when I was off from teaching. It is amazing to me what you can do when you have to do it.

Changing my father's diapers was no fun, but I managed. After all, at one point, he had changed mine.

So my summer of 1995 became very busy. I made the two-hour run down to National City whenever possible, and then flew to Sacramento to write speeches for Pete Wilson whenever they were needed. By mid-August, my father was up on a walker and I was exhausted. However, I could get no rest. As a lead-up to the formal presidential announcement, Governor Wilson had scheduled a number of major speeches in late August. In Boston on August 25, Wilson spoke in Faneuil Hall. After creating a sense of place, Wilson said, "The federal government is taxing the pursuit of happiness to death. It has proven Webster's famous maxim that 'The unlimited power to tax involves, necessarily, a power to destroy.' If he were alive today, I'll bet he'd help us throw another 'Tea Party' in Boston harbor." We were ahead of our time. The speech then took up the issue of crime prevention and there were the usual horrific statistics. But each point was supported with a personal story about someone with whom Wilson had a connection. The press ate it up.

In Philadelphia, Wilson reinforced the crime theme by appearing at the Fraternal Order of Police Lodge Number 5. After a bow to Ben Franklin, Wilson went on the attack: "I'm sick and tired of the cult of victimage that makes every murderer into a celebrity and forgets about the family of the victims. I'm sick and tired of clueless movie stars and naive novelists gaining publicity for cop killers on death row while the victim's family watches in grief and anguish." Wilson then "set the record straight" regarding the crimes and trial of Mumi Abu-Jamal, "A.K.A. Wesley Cook, who put a bullet between the eyes of Danny Faulkner, a 26 year old police officer Jamal had already shot in the back." It was tough stuff that played well in Philadelphia.

Then came the big one. Wilson would make it official and announce his candidacy in New York Harbor, with the Statue of Liberty as a backdrop, on August 28, 1995. The speech, "Lady Liberty's Promise," was delivered on a sunny, hot day with lots of media coverage. It took up most of page 6 of the *New York Times* and got the front-page treatment back in California. Wilson argued that "American optimism is being undermined by a federal government that is out of step, out of touch, and out of control." Some of my students called to say they had instantly recognized my periodic style in Wilson's phrasing. He argued that citizens needed to take responsibility for their decisions, and the government needed to do the same by balancing the budget, overhauling welfare, halting illegal immigration, and doing away with affirmative action. He continued:

Look with me into this harbor. To understand America is to see it through this lady's eyes. She promises freedom—not a free ride. She promises fairness—not favoritism. She promises unlimited hope—not a guaranteed result. The answer, my friends, isn't someone who blows in the wind. America wants a leader with the courage of his convictions—right now!

When the event was over, Wilson flew to New Hampshire to begin his campaign there at a tax opponents' picnic. Talk about walking into the lion's den. In this speech, he used his experience as governor of California to show that he was fiscally responsible:

> The story begins when I first came into office as Governor in 1991. I inherited the largest budget deficit any state generated in American history—a $14 billion, "B" as in billion, budget shortfall. At the same time, the economy was going into the dumper and California's defense industry was being killed by cuts in the defense budget. . . . Like Ronald Reagan when he became governor in 1967, I realized that some tax increases would be required to close the yawning gap. . . . My story has a happy ending. By the end of my third year as governor, we had a $1.1 billion surplus.

Then it was time to praise his audience: "You are the one group in America that can't be fooled with false claims and dummied-up numbers. You have a wonderful reputation for holding candidates accountable for the claims they make." The *Los Angeles Times* wrote, "Wilson and his wordsmith have sprinkled the new stump speech with Reaganesque language. There is a touch of hope and optimism to smooth the negative edges."[9]

It was a valiant effort, but Wilson faced too many obstacles to succeed. First, there were the other declared candidates, among them Bob Dole, Patrick Buchanan, and Phil Gramm. Second, he had not done enough over the years in support of the party and its candidates. He was supported by only one in ten Republicans and had placed eighth in the Iowa straw poll earlier in the year. Third, his fundraising efforts were hampered by the fact that Colin Powell was a possible nominee, and until Powell officially removed himself from contention, some Republican moderates would sit on their wallets. Wilson called Powell and begged him to make a decision. Powell waited. Wilson called the fat cats and begged them to support him. They said they would if Powell withdrew. Fourth, fights began to break out between Wilson's California team and the new national advisors. While his gubernatorial speechwriters deferred to my judgment, his California political advisors would not bow to the GOP presidential consultants.

There were some ups. Governor William Weld of Massachusetts endorsed Wilson and tried to help him raise funds. We put Wilson on teleprompter to prevent him from wandering off his text. Said the *Los Angeles Times*, "The result has been a more focused, forceful delivery. His voice is nearly back to normal after a long recovery from throat surgery."[10]

But his candidacy didn't catch fire. Even in California, he ran behind Dole by 12 points in polls taken at the end of September. His teleprompter failed at an important Iowa event, and he had to improvise his speech to finish. The poll numbers did not move in New Hampshire, where negative columns informed anti-tax New Hampshire Republicans that Wilson had raised taxes in California. Wilson's pro-choice stand was used against him in Iowa, and the campaign ran out of money.[11] There was also some talk about Wilson being a potential vice-presidential nominee if he were to opt out of the process quickly and gracefully. Thus, on September 29, 1995, Wilson withdrew from the presidential contest, perhaps the shortest campaign for president ever. It was only a month since he had delivered the "Lady Liberty" speech.

AN APPOINTMENT

It wasn't long into the fall semester when Governor Wilson called, asking if I wanted to fill an opening on the California Commission on Teacher Credentialing. I accepted and was unanimously approved by the California Senate to begin a two-year term in January of 1996. The commission met once a month to set policy regarding what was required to get a teaching credential in California, along with a number of other issues. We monitored charter schools to make sure they were up to standards. We reviewed colleges of education to make sure they did the proper fieldwork with teacher trainees and met the criteria we set. We approved emergency credentials for people who did not meet the state's standards but were needed because of teacher shortages. (At the time, nearly 10 percent of California teachers were on emergency credentials.) From people who had lost their credentials due to various infractions, we heard requests for reinstatement.

The problem was that the commission was staff-driven. The staff was making and carrying out policy and expecting the commission to rubber-stamp it. I was one of several commissioners who stopped that practice. Then we demanded that the staff set up a program whereby teachers on emergency credentials could earn credits to convert to regular credentials.

Third, we gave credit for life experiences to older people who wanted to teach. Fourth, we made it easier for credentialed teachers in other states to transfer into California.

COMING OUT

One day I arrived home from Sacramento to find many messages on my phone. They were from relatives telling me to call my mother immediately. I had no idea was what wrong and hurriedly dialed her number. My cousin Adrienne was at Mom's house and told me that my mother had found my father dead beside his bed that morning. After repacking my bag, I left for National City, where I would spend the next few days arranging for the funeral of my father and taking care of my mother, who was grief stricken and afraid. While I was doing that and arranging for relatives to fly in, I had some time to think about where I was in my life. I decided I would come out at the first opportunity, now that the news couldn't hurt my father.

After the service at St. Mary's Church, I gave the graveside eulogy; Navy sailors followed with a gun salute and bugled taps, then handed me the flag that had draped my father's coffin. The next day I talked with Mom about what she wanted to do. She told me she wanted to stay in "her house." I had already triangulated my parents with caring neighbors and relatives whom I could call if I needed to check on my parents or make sure they got the groceries they needed when I couldn't come down to do the shopping. That arrangement would now continue with my mom. I would also come down to see her every weekend to make sure she had what she needed and to take her to visit her older sister, who lived nearby.

During the funeral and all the next day, I had kept my feelings under control. But as I drove back to Long Beach, I fell apart and had to pull my car off Interstate 5. I wept for my father and for the fact that he never really knew who I was.

A week later I was teaching a mass lecture class on protest rhetoric in America. I was reviewing the great speakers who had led various movements. I commented that the "Freedom Now" movement had Martin Luther King Jr. as its spokesperson. The Native American movement had Russell Means. The women's movement had Gloria Steinem and Betty Friedan, among others. The farm workers movement had Cesar Chavez. I then began to talk about gay leaders, starting with Harvey Milk. A hand shot up in the front row, and I recognized the student. She asked, "Are you gay?"

So there it was. How do you answer that question? If I denied it, it would be a lie. If I avoided it as "inappropriate," it would be perceived as a "yes." Here's my chance, I thought. So I answered honestly. And then continued on about Milk. But there was a lot of buzzing going on, so I thought it best to close things off. "That's enough excitement for one day. I'll see you next class."

Tim Murphy was my teaching assistant for the class and chased me down outside. "That was brave," he said.

"No, not so brave. I should have done it a long time ago."

"Then why didn't you?"

I thought for a moment. "Because of my career choices, I got used to hiding that part of me in a closet. Coming out would have hurt my father; I had hid from him too. But I was wrong on that score. I've probably done more damage by not being the role model I could have been for gay kids in my classes all these years."

When I got back to my office, I sent a hasty message to the faculty telling them what had happened in my classroom. I didn't want them blindsided by student questions. Over the next week, I received supportive messages from every member of the faculty except one. Ironically, he was in the closet.

That night I had a good deal of time to think about the closet I was leaving. It had protected me in my youth and during my professional life. It had given me agency to do remarkable things I could not have done in my generation had I been out. It had become more and more comfortable over the years, especially when it was populated by some straight and gay friends. Having been born at the end of World War II, I was thrown into a homophobic environment that was readily apparent to me. People were not shy about saying how they felt about homosexuality, particularly my father's Navy friends and my mother's relatives who lived nearby. They reinforced one another's opinion that to be homosexual was to be depraved, mentally ill, and disgusting.

For some reason, I never believed that. I was, as I have written, often depressed, but I did not believe the depression flowed from my homosexuality or the suppression of it. I did not believe it flowed from not being myself. Even though I often felt like a fish out of water, for some reason I liked that fish and decided to protect it. So I learned to cope. I would work harder in school than anyone else. I lost myself in television shows and films, coming out of my closet and going into the silver screen. I would fight for recognition, admiration, and success. When I discovered high school debate—or better, when it discovered me—I hit on the one thing that could bring me what I needed most: acknowledgment.

Being in the closet, hiding my true identity became just one more challenge that I was going to have to meet. It didn't take long for the habits of survival to form: role-playing, wit, being knowledgeable, being needed. College proved to be an even more closeted space than high school. On a campus that was known as a "party surfer school," physical appearance mattered and so did masculinity. Though threatened by this world, I navigated through it and actually came to enjoy it. There was good company to be had. And there were very pleasant young men to look at, even if I could never touch them.

By the time I came on the job market, I was sought after. But when I took the job in San Diego as a professor, I found myself in an all-male homophobic department. Of course, I'd seen some prejudice in graduate school, but it was often condemned. At Queens College, my master's thesis advisor was out. At Penn State there seemed to be an openness to all sorts of lifestyles. So it was disappointing to hear anti-gay remarks in academia, particularly in a department in which I had some prior experience running their summer debate institute. By this time, however, I finally had some gay friends—some in the closet, some out—who provided badly needed conversations about our mutual experiences.

When I moved to the University of Virginia, I found a much more accepting environment. Though married and with children, a department head told me he was gay and took his "pleasures down the road in Richmond." One of the major departments was filled with closeted professors who threw wonderful parties. At UVA at that time, the policy of don't ask, don't tell felt like a step in the right direction. However, any temptation to step out of the closet was quashed when my tenure battle began. Knowing I might have to look for a new job killed any chance of my coming out, as did the miracle of becoming a speechwriter for the president of the United States.

My political career was off and running. I was being rewarded for what I had learned and how I performed, and for being in the closet. There was no turning back. It would be twenty years before I came out. And in that time, I was not a "closet queen," nor did I find any acceptable outlet for my sexual desire. I remained a devout Catholic living the life of a penitent. Let me be clear, I certainly condemn the Church's priests for their heinous crimes and the Church for covering them up. My Catholicism was theology, and modified, as I've stated, with a healthy dose of existentialism. I also let people know that in Catholic canon law, you have the right to disagree with the Church as long as you submit your disagreement to an agent of the Church (a priest will do) and allow that agent to attempt to change your mind. I had learned this when working on the abortion issue in Oregon. If the priest fails to change your mind, and you continue to sincerely hold to your belief, it is not a sin and you cannot be expelled from the Catholic Church. One hopes the Church will not only continue to clean up its act, but move forward on many issues of personhood that would make the world a better place. The Bible evolved from being an advocate of multiple wives to presenting a loving Jesus who never mentioned homosexuality but had an apostle known as "the one Jesus loved" or the "beloved apostle, John."

Nonetheless, before I came out of my hope-, fantasy-, and friend-filled closet, I chose to lock in a portion of my persona that is an *existentielle*, a deep part of my being. I not only withheld it from public view, I buried it so deep that I've been celibate for most of my life. So while the closet helped me professionally, it hindered me personally. For a long time, the professional substituted for the personal. That explains sixteen books and over sixty scholarly articles and book chapters; it explains the promotions, the fundraising, the department chairmanships, the boards, and the travels. Eventually, I learned to live with lost emotional opportunities by investing in spiritual connections. I have the love that the Catholic philosopher Karl Jaspers talks about in his theory of interrelational existentialism. It is transcendent and pure.

That being said, the night after I came out, I reflected on the fact that I had not done enough to help the gay world, but did try to do some good when the opportunity presented itself. Once I was free of Washington and involved in the fight for freedom of expression, I could do more. All through my closeted days, I mentored employees and students, gay and straight, male and female, who did me proud. And many of them remain close friends to this day. There was some immediate good news after I came out. When the story leaked across the campus, it prompted two department chairs and several professors to follow suit. We celebrated over lunch one day in the faculty dining room.

My reverie over lifting a terrible weight off my shoulders was interrupted by a call from the National City police department that my mother was complaining to them regularly about the neighbors trying to break into her house. None of her complaints had any merit. Mom had always been a little eccentric, but we believed it to be her way of being funny. It was now clear that Dad's death had pushed her over some brink. So I took her to a psychiatrist for analysis. The bad news was that Mother had paranoid dementia; the good news was that a new drug had just come out to treat it. It was called Risperdal. For some patients, it not only checked the paranoia, but reversed it.

I asked the psychiatrist if I could move my mom to Long Beach. He strongly advised against it. "She needs all the security she can get," he told me. "Just continue to have the neighbors watch her, and come down when you can. When she's ready to move, she'll let you know. My guess is that it will be about a year after your father's death."

A few weeks after Mom started taking the Risperdal, I found her in her bedroom crying. Taking her hand, I asked, "Mom, what's wrong?"

She looked up at me and smiled. "I didn't know people could be this happy. I've never felt this way in my entire life." Mark one up for science.

The year following my father's death went by quickly. Friends, even those who had not figured out I was gay, were very supportive. I helped the son of one of those friends come out to his father, and both of them were very grateful to me.

Since I was out of politics, I could watch the presidential election in the fall of 1996 with some objectivity, and work my class in campaign persuasion through the process. When Pat Buchanan won the Louisiana primary, party leaders panicked and rushed to support Bob Dole, who got the nomination from an unenthusiastic convention. The Dole on stage during the presidential debates was laconic, stiff, and dark. It was the same Dole who had damaged the ticket in 1976; it was the same stubborn Dole who had caused Bush to put Quayle on the ticket in 1988. So it came as no surprise that Dole lost badly to Bill Clinton. The miracle was that the Republicans retained majorities in the House and Senate.

I continued my monthly trips to Sacramento for the Commission on Teacher Credentialing, my weekly trips to take care of Mom, and my daily trips to my classes. A week after the anniversary of my father's death, my mother told me that she was ready to move if I could find a duplex that would provide her with her own space and me with mine. I was relieved that I wouldn't have to continue the back and forth to National City, and happy she wanted her own space. Now all I had to do was find a place for us, sell her house, sell my condo, and the move would be complete.

CHAPTER SIXTEEN

There's More Politics
in Education Than
Education in Politics

BEFORE I EVEN STARTED LOOKING FOR A PLACE FOR US, THE FORMER
chair who had hired me, Dick Porter, and his wife Rosemary invited me
to their home for dinner. Their Spanish-style duplex was built in 1923,
one block off a bay with a swimming beach and two blocks off the ocean
with a very wide and long beach. The ocean, calmed by a breakwater, was
often filled with dolphins, seals, and once a misguided baby whale. The air
was full butterflies, seagulls, pelicans, hummingbirds, and a pair of green
parrots. Both units of the duplex were two bedrooms, one bath; each had
a small kitchen and a decent dining room. Dick told me that he and Rosemary were going to move to northern California. "What are you going to
do with your house?" I asked.

"We'll sell it."

"Have you put it on the market yet?"

"Not yet."

"Have I got a plan for you," I explained. We could save on real estate
commissions and do our own escrow if I bought the house for a fair price.
The deal was struck and we closed on the house at the end of April 1997. In
May, I moved into the upstairs unit and Mom moved into the lower one. I
put my condo and Mom's house on the market.

At school, just before graduation day, I was doubly surprised and enor-
mously grateful: I received the Outstanding Teaching Award from the
university and then got word that I was selected for the Outstanding Professor Award from the National Speakers Association, a group of professional
speakers that included lawyers and business leaders.[1] It had been a tough but

ultimately rewarding spring. In the summer things got even better when my condo sold, albeit at a loss, and I sold Mom's home on July 4th to a family who wandered by while I was watering the front lawn.

With Mom settled in and an end to political involvement, one would think I would finally give a little time to the personal side of my life. However, anyone reading the next chapters of this book will realize that the professional workaholic lifestyle is difficult to abandon. As one close friend told me, "If you spent as much time working on your personal life as you do on your professional life, you'd have sixteen lovers instead of sixteen books." Just as when I was coaching college debate, I was too immersed in what I was doing to realize that I was actually shutting out the personal side of things in a whirl of activity.

For example, in late July, I received a call from the dean of the College of Liberal Arts asking me to consider becoming interim chair of the Journalism Department. It had lost its accreditation. Always up for a challenge, I accepted the assignment. Soon I was putting the school paper back on a sound financial footing by hiring an advertising manager. I got the department to cut its number of major options from five (there were only five full-time professors in the department) to three, concentrating on their strengths and eliminating their weaknesses. I recruited new, young faculty who knew what was going on in the field. I even opened an exchange program with China, which brought their journalists to our department in the summer for training. The Chinese were always amazed at how freedom of expression was guaranteed by our First Amendment.

Around this time, I was shocked with the news of the tragic killing of Matthew Shepard, a gay student at the University of Wyoming who was beaten to death by homophobic thugs in October of 1998. When in the world was it going to end? A few years later, Matthew's mother, Judy, spoke at the luncheon of the Western States Communication Association's annual convention. There wasn't a dry eye in the house.

GUN CONTROL

One day I had a brainstorm regarding gun control. I believed the FBI could digitalize the "riflings" each gun made on a bullet head, encrypt them, and keep them on file, just like they did with fingerprints. When a crime was committed with a gun, police would have a much better chance of catching the criminal if they could match bullets taken from bodies with the digitalized national FBI file. I spoke with police officers about the plan and, to a person, they said it would work. The *Miami Herald* printed my plan under my byline in July, and then I went to Sacramento to encourage California to become the leader on the issue. Here are excerpts from my testimony before the state Senate Judiciary Committee:

> Currently, Congress and the NRA are dancing around the issue of gun control in an effort to retain loopholes for gun buyers. They have presented California with an opportunity to show national leadership on this issue by implementing all of the constitutional measures available. To that end, I am proposing a constitutional way to strengthen current statutes. The need for such legislation is overwhelming: On an average day in America, ten children and 48 adults are killed by handguns; 33 women are raped by someone holding a gun to their head; 570 robberies are committed using a handgun; and over 1,000 assaults occur where a handgun is involved. Multiply that by 365 days, and you begin to see the enormity of the problem. Gun violence costs $20 billion a year. In California alone in 1998 there were 1,315 handgun homicides. That is about four a day. These 1,315 handgun homicides constituted over 60% of all homicides in the state, up from 53% in 1989. The citizens of California have had enough. Polls show that 78% would ban assault weapons; 89% would extend federal background checks to gun shows; 80% would require trigger locks; and 70% would ban the sale of guns on the internet. Surely, they support this proposal which is far less constitutionally suspect than others and far more effective in terms of preventing crime. . . . One of the most dangerous practices in this country is the use of a "straw purchaser" to obtain a gun for a criminal or someone who is under age. This proposal ties the gun to the "straw purchaser"; should that person turn the gun over to someone else, they do so with great risk. For if that gun is used in a crime, it would be traced directly back to the purchaser unless that person recorded an interim bill of sale. One way to curb the violence is to "fingerprint" every handgun sold in America. Every gun barrel makes *unique* markings on any bullet fired through it. Every gun bears a serial number. And every handgun sale is registered with local police authorities. Since every gun is test-fired by the manufacturer before it is put on the market, there is a bullet available that holds the unique barrel markings of that particular gun. If manufacturers were required to make one bullet marking from each gun they produced available to the Federal Bureau of Investigation, the Bureau could digitalize the unique barrel markings of each gun and keep them on file along with the serial number of the gun and the name and address of the owner when the gun is purchased. Handguns that have already been sold can be brought in to a local test-firing facility, test-fired, and their riflings would also

be registered with the Federal Bureau of Investigation, a procedure to which no law abiding citizen should object. Since handguns are now registered at time of sale anyway, it is a small step to call them in and make sure their barrel markings are registered also. Then the Federal Bureau of Investigation (and of course all local law enforcement agencies to which the information would be made available on request) would have a new and extremely efficient way of putting the bullet from the crime-scene together with the gun that was used for the crime, and the name and address of its owner, since the markings on the spent bullets could be compared with the digitalized files housed at the Federal Bureau of Investigation, much in the same way as California now compares fingerprints for teachers who enter our classrooms. Moreover, handguns traded between private individuals would inevitably be reported. You can bet that under such a system a person who sold or gave a gun to someone else would surely want the state to know about the transfer of ownership since the gun would be so easy to trace.

I got a lot of support for my proposal from chiefs of police, and through intermediaries got to President Clinton's domestic council. I was stunned when he endorsed my proposal in his State of the Union Address in 1999. I'll never forget his words:

> To strengthen the hand of the prosecutors, we will invest more in the ATF's National Gun Tracing Center and supply local law enforcement agencies with the tools they need to utilize that center from computers to training. We want to make it possible and we can make it possible to trace the origin of every single gun used in every single crime in the United States. . . . We will create a groundbreaking national ballistics network that eventually will enable us to trace almost any bullet left at a crime scene anywhere in America to the gun of the criminal who fired it.

We then created S. 2324 with support from a coalition that was led by Senators Herb Kohl (D-WI) and Dianne Feinstein (D-CA) to "require ballistics testing of all firearms manufactured and all firearms in custody of Federal agencies, and to add ballistic testing to existing firearms enforcement strategies."[2] The bill was introduced in the House as H.R. 4150 by Congressman Xavier Becerra (D-Los Angeles). After reviewing the information we provided, David Bejarano, the chief of police of San Diego, wrote to me to say, "Your proposed solution is bold and potentially very effective. Please keep me informed as you pursue the passage of the Gun Ballistics Safety Act." He was not alone. Every law enforcement person I talked with supported our proposal. Nonetheless, we lost that round. In February 2001, Congressman Andrews reintroduced the "Gun Ballistics Safety Act of 2001" (H.R. 408) before the House Judiciary Committee. In the meantime, because of our efforts, the White House picked Long Beach to participate in a special program to track handguns used in crime. The federal program aimed at reducing crime by identifying illegal gun traffickers. According to the ATF and FBI, the new Crime Gun Trace Report provided instant information on nearly 64,000 guns.

However, the thrill of this success soon dissipated over the next few years. We never overcame opposition led by the NRA. California, New York, and Maryland adopted proposals like mine, but they did not sweep the country. And in order for the plan to be effective, every state would need to adopt it.

While the issue of gun control bubbled through the courts, Michael Douglas, Jann Wenner (publisher of *Rolling Stone*), and I believed we had a chance at securing a state's right to control guns in light of a correct reading of the Second Amendment. Again, I editorialized in various papers on the topic because of contrary appellate decisions. Eventually, the Supreme Court intervened. In its brief to the Supreme Court on the D.C. case, even the Bush administration admitted that the states have the right to control guns. U.S. Solicitor General Paul D. Clement said guns are subject to "reasonable regulation" by the government and that all federal restrictions on guns should be upheld. The NRA was furious with the administration.

I argued that the Court should take another ruling into account. Placing the amendment in context, the Ninth Circuit Court of Appeals had ruled that the Second Amendment does *not* prohibit states or the federal government from restricting the possession of guns. This ruling was consistent with the last Supreme Court decision on the issue, which came in 1939 in *U.S. v. Miller*. Most important, in writing this decision, Judge Reinhardt used the conservative standards of "original intent" and "strict construction of the Constitution" to reach his court's unanimous conclusion. Commenting on the Second Amendment—"A well-regulated militia being necessary to the security of a free state, the right of the people to keep and bear arms shall not be infringed"—Reinhardt concluded that "'well-regulated' confirms that 'militia' can only reasonably be construed as referring to a military force established and controlled by a government entity." Reinhardt traced the amendment back through James Madison and the need for some states to protect themselves from disturbances within their borders. At that time, Shays' Rebellion in Western Massachusetts had frightened many states—hence, the right to protect themselves by creating militias. Both the Pennsylvania frame and the Massachusetts constitution argued that the people have the right to keep and bear arms, but only for "the common defense." Thus, using the criteria established by conservatives for reading the Constitution into the context of the intent of the framers, the Ninth Circuit concluded that the Second Amendment allows states, not individuals, to form militias and thereby confer on individuals of the state the right to bear arms.[3]

However, when the Supreme Court finally weighed in, the conservatives violated their own standards by ignoring the original intent of the Founders, and took the Second Amendment out of its context to find for individual gun owners in cases coming from D.C. (2008) and Chicago (2010). Because of this tortured interpretation of the amendment, we were forced to shift our emphasis. Now that all citizens are allowed to carry guns, it became even more imperative to fingerprint guns nationally. The problem has not been solved as I write, and more and more tragedies seem to occur with more deadly force, from Aurora, Colorado, to Newtown, Connecticut.

As all this was going on, I continued my regular routine, having repaired the Journalism Department and ended my term on the Commission for Teacher Credentialing.[4] My Center for First Amendment Studies web page had gained an international reputation; its publications got solid reviewers and were adopted in college classes around the country. All of this made my continued service in the Academic Senate seem paltry. Out of frustration about the way faculty were being treated by its union and by the chancellor, I wrote an editorial in the *Los Angeles Times* condemning both. Our pay lagged behind comparable institutions, yet our teaching loads were higher, not to mention our cost of living. The union wasted its time on strange agendas, while the chancellor ignored suggestions to improve the system. A few days after the editorial appeared, I was scheduled to speak at the home of the president of the university at a meeting of the faculty supper club. My topic was the First Amendment and academic freedom. When I arrived, President Bob Maxson took me aside and said that Chancellor Charles Reed was coming to the dinner. "Why?" I asked. "I've never even met the man."

"Because he wants to see who you are. Your editorial really pissed him off."

"Fine," I retorted. "I'd be glad to repeat it to his face."

"Don't you dare. Let me handle things. You'll find he's gruff but reasonable."

While the faculty was eating, Maxson, Reed, and I met in a small study and, as they say in diplomatic circles, we had a healthy exchange of views. The chancellor told me he wanted to provide more money for faculty salaries, but couldn't because the union was interested in other matters such as protecting lecturers and kicking graduate teaching assistants out of the bargaining unit. I agreed that the union was a problem and had said so in my editorial, but argued he could do more for us in Sacramento with the legislature than he was doing. In the end, we shook hands, and I went out and delivered my lecture. I had no idea at the time that our paths would cross again, and I would in effect become his boss.

AN UNUSUAL COAUTHOR

Near the end of the spring, news arrived of the tragic death of John Macksoud's daughter Meredith, whom I had regularly visited in Santa Barbara over the years. I had known Meredith since she was born. I gave her eulogy on a bright June day with her mother, Jackie, looking on; we placed Meredith's ashes beneath a bench with a plaque to her on it. The bench sat under a tree that looked out to the ocean from a retreat house in Montecito. A few months later, I brought my mother up to visit with Jackie, and on the way back, we stopped at the bench in Montecito and looked out over the ocean. Mother took my hand and we both cried.

Meredith was working on a book at the time of her death, and Jackie asked me if I would finish it. I had no idea what I was getting myself into, but agreed because I believed the project would give Jackie closure. The book was a filmic biography of the character actor Arthur Kennedy. He had been a lead actor in a number of famous Arthur Miller plays on Broadway, including *The Crucible* and *All My Sons*. He also starred in the initial production of *Becket*, but was not used in the film version. However, his film career was stellar and brought him several Academy Award nominations, including for his roles in *Lawrence of Arabia* and *Elmer Gantry*, where he played cynical reporters. He had many supporting roles in Westerns.

Meredith had completed some descriptions of his film roles and had lots of notes about his life, including some letters from his daughter who had agreed to support the project. Pulling all of this together into a coherent book was a challenge, but *Arthur Kennedy, Man of Characters* came out in 2003 with a foreword by Laurie Kennedy. We gave Meredith first author, "with Craig Smith and Jackie Lohrke" trailing after. I thought her mom deserved a credit too.

MOM MOVES OUT

It was at this time that I realized that Mom needed more care and attention than I could give her. She was now using a wheelchair most of the time. We had gone from driving up to see my sister to flying to Sacramento and driving from there. However, such trips were getting too taxing for Mom. Loading her into a wheelchair was unpleasant and embarrassing for her, particularly for the airline flights. It was time that she made the permanent trip to my sister's place. She needed Mom's pension to help make ends meet; but more important, my sister was a retired nurse. Soon Mom had her own suite in Renée's house, so her privacy, when she wanted it, was assured. I also promised to visit often. And there was the bonus of being able to go fishing with my brother-in-law in the pristine rivers and lakes around Mount Shasta. However, saying goodbye to Mom at the end of each of those visits was tearful and difficult.

For the 1999–2000 school year, I was asked by the Department of Comparative Literature and Classics to consider becoming its interim chair. I accepted. Here was another chance to do some tangible good, and at the same time I could model being a gay chair. And this department was a kindred department to mine. After all, I had published research in the classics, particularly on Aristotle and Cicero. My textbook *Rhetoric and Human Consciousness: A History* had just come out. So I accepted the post effective for July of 1999, and began to familiarize myself with the department.

I won't bore you with the details of the problems of the department except to say I tried to solve them. By this time, I had prioritized the concerns of a department chair. First and foremost, protect your faculty; most of them are going to be around indefinitely. Students will eventually move on. My second concern was for graduate students because they were self- and departmentally selected standouts. Often they would become professors and researchers in their own right. Third came undergraduate majors. A department's major count is always an indication of strength. Fourth came the staff, particularly the department secretary, who was usually the face of the department. Fifth came representing the department to the campus and local community. Sixth came fundraising, though this item sometimes moves up in times of budget crises. Matters of curriculum, office space, classroom allocation, course scheduling, budget, hiring, retention, promotion, and tenure should be assessed and prioritized within this framework. A good chair will create a climate of consensus that rewards good citizens and isolates bad ones. A good chair will keep the faculty fully informed and know how to run an efficient faculty meeting.

Once the Department of Comparative Literature and Classics brought me in, we revised the curriculum, changed the department name, and recruited majors. I'm most proud of converting two overworked part-time lecturers to full-time status, and ending their abusive treatment in terms of running up the number of students they had to take into their classes without providing the proper assistance for them.

BUSH V. GORE

As the fall semester of 2000 began, with Mom gone and me no longer being chair of a department, I had much more free time and could focus on the presidential campaign. Luckily, I was teaching my usual election year class in campaign persuasion. I filled the class in on the vicissitudes of politics. For example, the nomination of Governor George W. Bush for president had not been the game plan intended by my former client, his father George H. W. Bush; he wanted his son Jeb to be the nominee. However, Jeb had lost the 1998 race for governor of Florida to Lawton Chiles, while George Jr. upset Ann Richards for governor of Texas. After he won the nomination, Bush put Dick Cheney in charge of selecting the running mate. Cheney emerged as a father figure to George, and so George put him on the ticket.

I often took the thoughts I shared with my students to other venues. I told the Rotary Club of Long Beach that while Gore would carry the popular vote, he would not carry his home state. I claimed that it was very likely that the electoral vote would go to Bush, or that the election would be thrown into the House of Representatives. At USC's Annenberg School close to election day, I pointed out that while Bush was not the best debater in the world, he had a consistent persona. Gore projected a different persona in each debate, being artificially annoyed in debate one, much too obsequious in debate two, and a silly bully in debate three. In the vice-presidential debate, Cheney chewed up Senator Joe Lieberman (D-CT), who sounds like Elmer Fudd.

Election night hadn't started well for my set of predictions. In fact by about 9 P.M. Pacific Time, my guests, mostly liberal colleagues, began to head for home when most networks called Florida for Gore. I told everyone to sit tight because there were more absentee ballots than ever in that state and they tended to be from Republicans, the elderly, and people in the military, which boded well for Bush. Several of my guests exited anyway, happily claiming, "The networks wouldn't make a mistake like that." In the meantime, Gore lost his home state of Tennessee. And then Florida changed from blue, to red, and finally to neutral as we all looked on with open mouths. Coincidentally, the night the Supreme Court finally resolved the election was the night of the final for my campaign persuasion class, December 13, 2000.

The whole debacle prompted me to write an article that criticized the liberals and the conservatives on the Supreme Court for their hypocrisy in the *Bush v. Gore* ruling. The conservatives had abandoned states' rights and overturned Florida's courts, clearly violating their own calls for judicial restraint and protection of states' rights.[5] The liberals had abandoned federal intervention through the Fourteenth Amendment and become defenders of states' rights. In the old days, when the Court was going to overturn precedent, the chief justice attempted to put together a large if not unanimous majority. For example, the decision in *Brown v. Board of Education*, which ended segregation, was unanimous. However, in *Bush v. Gore*, it was Justice Anthony Kennedy who coalesced a majority around his Fourteen Amendment argument; Chief Justice Rehnquist wrote a concurring opinion on different grounds, with only Justices Scalia and Thomas in support. The divided Court reflected a divided nation.

And then came 9/11.

The impact was monumental. As the Twin Towers crumbled, so did American confidence. The crisis changed George W. Bush from a pretender to the throne to a president when he gave a very effective speech to a joint session of Congress on September 20, 2011. I was disgusted when Jerry Falwell and his buddy Pat Robertson claimed that the attack on New York City was a punishment for America for harboring pagans, abortionists, gays, and lesbians. How could the Republicans dance with these devils? In any case, we went to war in Afghanistan against Al-Qaeda and their sponsors, the Taliban Party, which we had armed to fight the Soviet Union during the Carter and Reagan administrations.

Once things calmed down a bit, I flew to Washington, D.C., to stay with my old friend, freshman debate partner, and junior-year roommate, David Hunsaker, and start work on a book we had talked about for a long time. I had written my first textbook, *The Bases of Argument*, with David, and Bobbs-Merrill had published it. Given his expertise in communication law and my work on freedom of expression, it was a no-brainer to do a book together, which we entitled *The Four Freedoms of the First Amendment*. I enjoyed visiting David because he had become a consummate cook and retained his wonderful sense of humor. We put together a detailed outline of the book project and then divided the first drafting of chapters between us.

By the fall of 2002, my life was in a nice groove. I taught classes I loved to diverse students, who were hungry to improve their lives. I had dinner with good friends. I was heavily involved in academic leadership; in fact, I had been elected to the California State University Statewide Academic Senate, composed of representatives from its twenty-three campuses. I was writing almost every day, when I wasn't traveling to conferences or universities to give lectures. I published another editorial on gun control called "Ballistic Identification of Handguns" in the *Los Angeles Times*. The First Amendment Center at Vanderbilt University asked me to author their reference page on "Violence and the Media."

ANOTHER DYSFUNCTIONAL DEPARTMENT

In April 2003, Don Para, the dean of the College of the Arts, asked me if I would be interested in chairing the Department of Film and Electronic Arts (FEA). The idea struck me as a good one for several reasons. It would activate my creative side. By immersing myself in administrative work during the day, I developed a hunger for creative work at other times. I had written on film theory and criticism: one book chapter on ideology in *Casablanca*, one article on *Bonnie and Clyde*, and the book with Meredith on the actor Arthur Kennedy.

Nonetheless, I told Dean Para that I would not take the job unless the department voted to bring me in. I did not want to be "imposed" on them. After an interview with them individually and together, they unanimously invited me to be their chair. By the end of April, I had moved into my new office and saw why they needed an "outside, interim chair." The department proved to be the most dysfunctional I had ever witnessed, and that was saying something. The outgoing chair had resigned in a dispute with the dean. Her predecessor had resigned in a dispute with the previous dean. One of my first tasks was to withdraw the proposal for the joint MFA with the English Department from the agenda of the Academic Senate, because the English Department chair notified me that her department was pulling out of the project because "we just can't take it on right now." She was being polite. The truth was that the English faculty assigned to the project did not get along with the Film faculty assigned to the project.

Despite all the craziness, we were able to rebuild the MFA by partnering with the Theatre Arts Department. To get support for the MFA, I wrote a grant proposal to Steven Spielberg, who had come back to the university and finished his degree in 2002 under an assumed name. The grant wasn't advancing in Spielberg's shop until the gods intervened. One dark and stormy night, the satellite dish of our building was ripped out, leaving a gaping hole in the roof. Our equipment room was flooded. I wrote an urgent letter to George Lucas, Spielberg's mentor, begging for funds to replace or fix the damaged equipment. I received a form letter rejecting my request. Unhappy, and in one of my "what have we got to lose" modes, I called Lucas's office. His secretary answered and I explained the situation. She said, "Well, he's right here. Do you want to talk to him?"

George Lucas pledged to send $100,000 immediately and to speak with Spielberg about making a proper grant. That did the trick. Spielberg eventually provided $1.4 million over three years (2005–2008). The money allowed me to kick the department up a notch. I created a faculty exchange with a Swiss film school. I cultivated alums[6] and brought in resident artists.[7] I hired Donna Thomas as the new department secretary. She had twenty years of experience on the campus, but looked much younger than her age. She was a very attractive African American woman who treated students with respect and care. She was the best hire I ever made in my whole career and became my compatriot in what was about to become a major civil war in the department.

In the fall of 2003, I decided that I didn't want the experience in the Film and Electronic Arts Department to be like those in Journalism and Comparative Literature. After I left those departments, after a year, some of my reforms were undone. I wanted a full term of three years in my new department. The faculty unanimously granted, and the dean approved, my request. I rewrote the mission statement of the department and came up with a new mantra, which they approved: "We teach our students that theory informs practice and that practice refines theory." The slogan synthesized the course content of theory classes with practicum.

The new synthesis required a curricular revision. When I came in, the major was 63 units, more than half of the units needed to graduate. Many students were taking six to seven years to finish while waiting for the right courses to be offered to meet all their requirements. Every professor had inserted some class or other into the required list. After several contentious faculty meetings, a new major was approved that dropped the required units to 51. Our graduation rate increased significantly over the remainder of my term, and our students would still win more awards in various competitions than the other schools in the csu, and would have a higher placement rate for jobs than students graduating from usc or ucla.

Eventually, I wrote a proposal to the Hollywood Foreign Press Association. We not only got the funding, but I got to attend their annual luncheon where stars handed out the campus grant money flowing from the Golden Globes Award show. Jack Nicholson, Annette Bening, James Franco, Diane Lane, Felicity Huffman, Dustin Hoffman, Edward James Olmos, and many other stars attended the event and sat at tables surrounding ours. They talked directly to us before, during, and after the luncheon, which was a thrill for the students we brought to the event. I couldn't resist having a private word with James Franco, but given his looks, it was impossible to focus on the conversation. Things continued to go well when one of the alums allowed us to share in the profits from the world premiere of his film *The Chronicles of Riddick*, starring Vin Diesel. It was the first Hollywood premiere I ever attended. (My advice is to arrive late, and stay for the party after. It is likely to be better than the film.)

However, the department was far from a bed of roses. I received several complaints from students that one of their professors was berating them in class and on their film shoots. I called the professor in and asked him to respond to the allegations. He said that students needed to toughen up if they were going to work in Hollywood. I warned him that what might pass for normal language on a Hollywood set would not pass muster on campus, where civility is prized. He said he would change his ways. But only a few days later, as I arrived on the second floor of our classroom building, a student came tearing out of the same professor's classroom. Two seconds later the professor came out running after the student, spewing a string of expletives. When he saw me, he froze. I told him to be in my office the minute his class ended. There we had one of those "We can do this the easy way or we can do this the hard way" conversations. He resigned effective the end of the year. Little did I know this was only the first of several forced departures.

PUBLICATIONS

Since I had no romance in my life, I continued to channel my energy into writing. I finished my magnum opus on Daniel Webster, the culmination of much previous work on the subject. The new book from the University of Missouri Press was an "oratorical biography" that followed a tradition in our field of looking at a major historical figure from the perspective of their public addresses.[8] Webster had been the ultimate triple threat. He was probably the best deliberative orator in the Senate's history, particularly in his famous second reply to Senator Hayne. He was twice secretary of state. He had argued cases before the Supreme Court that are precedents to this day. Chief Justice John Marshall often plagiarized from Webster's legal briefs for his majority rulings. Webster was the master of the ceremonial address, overwhelming the audience in his prime at the Bunker Hill Monument, or at the laying of the cornerstone of the addition to the Capitol in the year of his death.[9]

I also finished *The Four Freedoms of the First Amendment* with David Hunsaker and packed it off to the publisher.[10] But just as I mailed it, David's wife called to tell me that he had died of a heart attack. I was devastated. And cried again when the book came out.

The fall was dominated by the 2004 presidential campaign. I was a regular on news radio shows around the country right after the presidential debate on September 30. President Bush looked awful against Senator John Kerry, but I noticed a tone of condescension in the senator's voice. The debate between Senator John Edwards and Vice President Cheney was closer; talk about contrasting personalities: youth versus age, beauty versus toughness, talkative versus laconic, Southern versus Western. In the next presidential debate, Kerry began to make the mistake most senators who run for president do: his answers to questions were too long and complicated. The line about being "for" the war in Iraq on one vote and "against" it on another became what Karl Rove called the "gift that just keeps giving."

Speaking of Rove, his strategy was to produce a huge turnout of the Christian Right vote for Bush. Knowing what was up, I predicted in interviews that Bush would carry the popular vote. Many commentators questioned my judgment. But I was confident for a number of reasons besides the turnout strategy. First, Kerry's wife spoke with a heavy accent developed in her youth in Namibia. It reinforced the perception of the couple as arrogant and aristocratic. Second, Bush had not run to the center as most candidates do in presidential elections. Bush maintained his conservative stance and cowboy persona. He was the guy you'd want to have a beer with, particularly if you were a blue-collar worker. America had yet to tire of its wars in Afghanistan and Iraq. And so it was that Bush, Cheney, and the Republican Congress were returned to power.

Commenting on and teaching about the election led me to consider a campaign myself, though on a much, much smaller scale. In the Statewide Academic Senate, I was approached by a few senators who asked me to consider being nominated for the position of faculty trustee on the CSU Board of Trustees. I began lobbying for the position in January 2005 at the first meeting of the New Year. I was quickly reminded that no Republican had represented the Academic Senate on the board since the first faculty trustee in the early 1970s. That man was Bob Kully, a debate coach at CSU Los Angeles when I was debating at UCSB; he had become a close friend and advised me on this campaign. However, my campaign was interrupted by the death of my most important mentor.

JOHN MACKSOUD GOES AWAY

One evening in February, I received a call informing me that John Macksoud had been found dead in our house and his partner, Judy, had committed suicide. I notified Jackie as gently as I could and then made plans to travel to Pennsylvania to meet with our lawyer and work out the details prescribed in John's will. In a confused and dazed state, I set out on what would become one of the strangest journeys of my life.

I flew to Harrisburg on February 8, landing at 4 P.M. local time in the miserable cold of central Pennsylvania. I rented a car and drove in the dark 90 miles northwest of Harrisburg to State College, where I decided to stay throughout the ordeal. The town had been my home for two years, and it gave me some comfort to be able to go to my old haunts for dinner and breakfast.

Luckily, our lawyer, John Carfly, was well connected. He had a realtor lined up to put the house on the market. He knew the president of the bank, across the street from his office, where John had an account. I arrived at his office in Philipsburg after the 35-mile drive from State College. Ironically, it was Ash Wednesday and Carfly had a dark cross on his forehead. "I wish I knew where I could get some ashes," I told him.

"You a Catholic too?"

"Yes."

"Well, we may not have time to get you ashes. Was John a Catholic?"

"In his youth, but not in his adult life. He had his own religion," I informed him.

"What did he want done with his body?"

"He wants it cremated."

"Will you want the ashes?"

"No, he wanted them disposed of, not kept or scattered or whatever. He believed that when the soul left the body, the body was an empty shell."

"All right. I'll take care of it."

"Thank you."

We went out to the house; it was a mess. I was devastated because John had promised to "take care of" the house for me when I bought his share of it. Now all I saw was that everything was in shambles. But in a locked file for which I had the key, we found a manila envelope John had left for me with gold coins I had also purchased from him to keep him afloat financially after the house money ran out. When we turned in John's guns to the state troopers, they gave us traveler's checks worth $5,000 that they had found on his body. We then located a bank account with about $4,000 in it. While I was filling out the paperwork for the account, the clerk asked if I wanted to open his safety deposit box. Surprised that he had one, I found more funds and a key to another safety deposit box at another bank 30 miles away. That box was filled with more gold coins and a passbook for a Swiss bank account. I was eventually able to collect the $10,000 in Swiss francs in the account. What began with tragedy and disappointment ended up being a mystery, with compensation making up for the loss of the house. I suspect that all along John knew he was creating a trail of money that would reinforce my opinion of him as a complex creature who would always haunt my life. Eventually, Purdue University Press at my behest would publish John Macksoud's formerly self-published book on rhetorical theory, with my introduction and commentary, and an appendix by another of his former students, Gregory Desilet, comparing John's theories with those of the famous deconstructionist Jacques Derrida. We demonstrate that while Derrida was developing his theory in France, John was developing a very similar theory at the same time in America. That publication gave me further closure of the loss of my most important mentor.

AGAINST THE ODDS

My trip to Pennsylvania cost me campaign time for the trusteeship because the Academic Senate happened to have their February meeting on the days I was away. Nonetheless, I filed my application a week after my return. In my application I stressed my knowledge of First Amendment issues, such as academic freedom, hoping that would overcome prejudice against my Republican background.

On March 10, in the afternoon, the rules were explained to the Statewide Academic Senate. The four certified nominees would give their speeches and answer questions. The next morning the senate would vote. Under the rules, the senate was required to send at least two names forward to the governor; however, it took a two-thirds vote to be nominated. My heart sank. I had assumed incorrectly that all that was needed was a simple majority. I did not believe I could possibly get two-thirds of this very liberal group to vote to put my name on the governor's desk.

Before I could recover I was herded into a small office off the floor of the Statewide Academic Senate chamber along with the three other nominees. One was the incumbent appointed by the previous governor, Kathy Kaiser—a good friend, a liberal Democrat and union advocate. If she were nominated, I did not believe the governor, Republican Arnold Schwarzenegger, would select her if he had a viable alternative. The other nominees were professors from other csu campuses, whom I had never met. We were not allowed to hear each others' presentations, so I had no idea what my competition was saying.

As the third to speak, I explained my commitment to shared governance of the csu system, relying on my record as a department chair. I argued that I could be persuasive with the board of trustees since I came "from where some of them dwell," a not so subtle acknowledgment that my Republicanism might actually work to the advantage of the faculty. I reviewed my academic record and argued it would provide the board with firsthand knowledge of what professors do. I reminded the senate that my entire teaching career had been spent at public institutions, three of them in urban settings with diverse student bodies. And at the end of my speech, I thanked the assembled group for their tolerance, a not-so-subtle reference to my homosexuality.

The balloting took place the next morning. On the first ballot, the incumbent received the necessary two-thirds vote. Then began the second ballot. It seemed to take the senators forever to mark their vote on a small piece of paper. These were collected and taken out of the room, where the clerk counted them under the watchful eye of the chair of the Academic Senate. He returned to announce that "on the second ballot, Senator Smith has received two-thirds of the votes and therefore his name shall be forwarded to the governor as one of your approved nominees." I was shocked and thrilled.

Then came a motion that the nominations be closed. If this motion passed, I would be the next faculty trustee, because Schwarzenegger would pick me over a union Democrat. The motion passed. Sure enough, after an interview in May to make sure I did not have horns, the governor's office announced my appointment.

My first official meeting as the faculty trustee for the board of trustees was July 19, 2005, the annual budget meeting. Since the board selects and evaluates the chancellor, I was treated like royalty by Chancellor Reed, who recalled our first contentious meeting years earlier. The other members of the board came from various walks of life. Roberta Achtenberg, the chair of the board, was a San Francisco activist, lesbian, and feminist who served in the Clinton administration. She and I hit it off immediately.

Bill Hauck, a former chair of the board, was head of the Business Roundtable and a conservative Democrat. Jeff Bleich was a leading lawyer from San Francisco and would eventually be named an ambassador during the Obama administration. Carol Chandler was in agribusiness and a Republican who became a close ally on many issues. Herb Carter, a former campus president, was an eloquent African American with a sensible perspective on what needed to be done. Then there was the labor leader who hardly ever came to meetings; he had been appointed by Governor Gray Davis, Schwarzenegger's predecessor, as had been Debra Farrar, the wife of a Democratic mega-fundraiser. Bob Foster was the head of Southern California Edison and eventually mayor of Long Beach. Business people rounded out the group along with a student and an alumni trustee.

I had vowed that in my capacity as faculty trustee, I would visit every campus in the system by the end of my first year on the job. And I succeeded in that goal, the only trustee ever to do so. These visits created a working relationship for me with local campus academic senates, student bodies, staff unions, and presidents. Sometimes when I visited these campuses, I would lecture to communication classes or give campus-wide lectures on First Amendment issues.

The unique role of the faculty trustee is to make sure that CSU Board policies are being properly implemented. I often found that campus presidents or provosts were reinterpreting board policy to advance their own agenda. This tactic made the board look bad, often getting blamed for dictatorial procedures that began as suggestions when the board approved them. My job also included taking input about unique campus problems, and discovering best practices with regard to such issues as curriculum development, student advising, faculty workload, student graduation rates, shared governance, and the like. The faculty trustee also voted on the appointment and assessment of each campus president. Because the board mainly consists of citizens who volunteer their time and come from many walks of life, the faculty trustee sits on board committees and attends its general meetings to apprise the other trustees of academic matters and to answer any questions they may have regarding the 22,000 teachers in the system. The faculty trustee votes on such important matters as tuition increases for students, campus building projects, and compensation for faculty, staff, and administrators. Needless to say, the position is a full-time job, so to keep me on as chair of the Film Department, I was paid overtime at 120 percent of salary on a year-round basis and released from all teaching assignments.

While all this was going on, I still had to maintain my Center for First Amendment Studies, which I did gratis. For example, in October 2005,

I published an editorial in the *San Francisco Examiner* on violence in the media and its effect on society. An assemblyman in California was trying to equate violence with obscenity so that video games could be regulated by the legislature. Refuting his position, I pointed out that the social-scientific data on which he relied was methodologically unsound, and then concluded, "The courts have found that violent programming should not be equated with obscenity and cannot be regulated because no harm has been proved." It was not the most popular position, but it was one that was consistent with the First Amendment. The legislation eventually passed and was signed by the governor. But my position was vindicated when the U.S. Supreme Court struck the law down.[11]

At the beginning of 2006, I was asked to join the board of the Rancho Los Cerritos. Why, you might ask, would I take on more responsibilities? The answer is twofold. That particular board contains many of the leaders of Long Beach, and being associated with them would help me raise funds for my Center. Second, the Rancho is a pretty neat place. It is a product of the Spanish land-grant system. The Rancho's grant had once run from the Los Angeles River to the San Gabriel River, basically including what is now Long Beach. After the California revolt during the Mexican-American War, the land grant was broken into smaller pieces, the largest going to the shepherding and cattle-ranching Hathaway family into which the Bixbys married. The Hathaways had raised the money for their share of the land by selling equipment to gold miners in 1849 and '50. With the Bixby alliance, sheep and cattle grown on the land were sold to the Union during the Civil War, bringing in even more money. The Rancho then became the founding site for the city of Long Beach, and soon after, oil was found on the Bixby property. This goose just kept laying golden eggs.

While the board members could contribute large amounts of money for the refurbishing of the Rancho, I could not. I had my relatives and my Center to take care of and made little money by the board's standards. However, I could help with fundraising by giving lectures on historic figures and tying them to events at the Rancho. I tried to personalize these lectures as much as possible for the community. For example, in the lecture on President James Madison, I told the audience the story about how he had been jilted by his first love when she broke off their engagement by sending him a note in a loaf of rye bread. I speculated that "she might have had another loaf in the oven . . . or a wry sense of humor." In the lecture on President Zachary Taylor, a hero of the Mexican-American War, I told the audience how he had been killed by a cocktail.[12] These lectures attracted large audiences, who often became "friends of the Rancho."

MY DINNER WITH ANDRE

As the spring semester of 2007 began, I received a call from Jack Williams, now retired from the presidency of the Royal Caribbean Cruise Line.[13] Jack met Andre Agassi, of tennis fame, when they raised money for cystic fibrosis research; they became such good friends that Andre stayed at Jack's house in Coconut Grove when he came to play tennis at the then Lipton Open on Key Biscayne. When Andre formed a foundation to fund a K–12 college prep school in a poor neighborhood in Las Vegas, he invited Jack onto the board. The school admitted mainly at-risk kids. Jack served as an auctioneer at the Agassi Foundation's annual "Grand Slam" fundraiser. After a few years, Jack realized that like many boards, its members knew how to raise money, but didn't have a clue about education. Jack suspected that some of the school officials were snowing the board with data that wasn't valid. So he suggested that I be added to the board, given my experience on the California Commission on Teacher Credentialing and my current status as a member of the board of trustees for the California State University system.

I soon found myself attending semiannual board meetings in Las Vegas, where we were put up at swanky hotels and, after a hard day's work, treated to dinner at an upscale restaurant. Happily I was told not to worry about fundraising but to focus on the school. I reported what I found and reforms were made. Every member of the first class to graduate from Agassi Prep was accepted into college. And every time I see Andre, he gives me a bear hug. Over dinner he'll pick my brain about all sorts of things. He's just the kind of student I love in my classes, open to all kinds of learning.

Obviously, I was wearing a lot of hats. I was able to manage because I simply didn't have an intimate personal life. The busier I became, the less I felt the personal void.[14] I also found the array of jobs and board memberships energizing. For example, as the faculty trustee, when I met with legislators, I often found that they were concerned about admissions policies and graduation rates, but not much about the four or five years in between, which is what education is all about. So I would try to fill them in.

Worse, they were cutting back on what they provided, which meant we would have to raise tuition to meet the shortfall. The state provided $12,000 per student when I joined the board; by the time I left, the state was providing only $8,000 per student, so tuition went up considerably.[15] We did mandate that one-third of all the tuition collected be redistributed to lower-income students to cover their tuition. The good news is that by the time I left the board, 110,000 students out of the 440,000 in the system were receiving state grants and not paying any tuition.[16] The bad news is that as I write, the system is horribly underfunded, and the State of California is only providing stop-gap Band-Aids to solve the problem.

Under these circumstances it is impossible to lower faculty workloads from their four courses a semester, plus service, plus research. Thus, faculty often leave for places with lower teaching loads, not to mention much lower costs of living and higher salaries. Out of Communication Studies alone, we have lost promising, publishing young professors to Lewis & Clark University, the University of Oklahoma, the University of Ohio, the University of Arizona, Northern Colorado University, and the National Institutes of Health in Atlanta. The CSU has become a farm club for other universities.

At the end of the spring semester as the faculty trustee, I made my usual round of commencements, starting with my favorite at the Maritime Academy and including our own lavender graduation, where I was the keynote speaker for the lesbian, gay, bisexual, and transgendered students about to graduate. I did not talk about my life; I talked about theirs and the challenges they would face. I hoped we had provided them with the equipment to cope with a sometimes hostile but also rewarding world.

By this time, to many people I had become a liberal Republican. My work on freedom of expression and gun control moved me to the left while my party moved to the right. That split was reinforced during the fall semester with the visit of Valerie Plame to the campus. She had become a sensation when members of the Bush administration outed her as a covert CIA agent in retaliation for her husband's attack on the President's war in Iraq. As the MC for her lecture, I met with her backstage at the campus's Carpenter Center and discovered that she went to Penn State and remained a loyal Republican despite what Richard Armitage, Karl Rove, and Bob Novak had done to her. Onstage, she gave a magnificent lecture and then sat down with me for an interview in front of a packed house. She talked about her experiences, and in answer to one question made clear that the sins of the administration should not be attributed to the entire Republican Party.

RESUMÉ FRAUD?

At the same time, the Film Department continued to devolve toward chaos. One day I found myself in a sleazy law office filled with ambulance chasers, where I was required to give a deposition in a lawsuit brought by the former chair of the department against the university, claiming she had been defamed in their finding regarding her workplace harassment.[17] Anything having to do with the courts terrifies me. I've been lucky enough never to have been picked for jury duty, though as I sat waiting to be called into the jury box, my palms would sweat until I was passed over. So now I sat in a room at a table with a university lawyer by my side and the former chair and her lawyer on the other side. As the clock approached noon, her lawyer directed yet another line of questioning at me: "Did you invite Professor Xavier to your house for drinks or dinner?"[18]

"Yes."

"Did you invite Professor Yatz to your house for drinks or dinner?"

"Yes."

"Did you invite Professor Zed to your home for drinks or dinner?"

"Yes."

"Did you have any of them over more than once?"

"Yes." I responded.

"Well, don't you think that might give the impression that you were running a white male heterosexual operation?"

"Well," I smiled, "since I'm gay, and since I had several female faculty members whom I hired to my home for dinner, I don't think we fit that picture." The lawyer asked that we take our lunch break. At lunch the lawyer and I were called and told that the deposition was over. Apparently, the former chair had failed to inform her lawyer that I was gay. She eventually settled her lawsuit with the university, which was kept confidential.

Things got worse. Professor Zed as a member of the Retention, Tenure, and Promotion Committee had worked with me to advise Professor Yatz on what he needed to do to get tenure. When he came up for tenure, Professor Yatz claimed he had done what we instructed in terms of publications and creative work. However, on his own Professor Zed decided to investigate these claims. It turned out some were not true, and therefore, we could not recommend Professor Yatz for tenure. However, his friend, Professor Xavier, protested not only to me, but to his students that Yatz had been unfairly treated. This unprofessional conduct was annoying to me, and it sent Professor Zed into orbit because tenure proceedings are confidential and we could not correct the allegations of Professor Xavier without violating confidentiality. So Professor Zed made an independent investigation of Professor Xavier's resumé and found that it, too, contained false claims. For example, he claimed to have received an MA from an Ivy League school, but they had no record of it. When the administration dragged its feet on the matter, in his estimation, Professor Zed gave the story to the *Chronicle of*

Higher Education. It was a terrible blow to the department, which imploded as various professors and students took different sides in the dispute.

I called a meeting of all the film majors to try to quiet things down. An associate vice president was sent to monitor my remarks. I explained to about two hundred film majors how the tenure system worked, making clear that there was more to promotion, tenure, and retention than being a popular teacher. That might be fine for high school or a junior college, where teaching loads were heavy, but at a university, where teaching loads were lighter, creative and/or scholarly activity and service were required. Every faculty member receiving tenure had to sustain a record of creative and/or scholarly work that was reviewed favorably somewhere. Then I told the students that it would be very unfair to them if we did not hold the faculty to the same standards we imposed on our students in terms of credits for their films and what they put in their portfolios to sell themselves in Hollywood. I concluded by telling them that since the situation was under review in both cases, I could not comment on them specifically. But the students filled in the missing information and got the picture.

I took student questions for another thirty minutes before another class arrived at the hall in which we were meeting. I told the students, "Let's go outside. I'm perfectly willing to continue to take your questions and comments in the quad until I have exhausted them"—which I did for another hour. Many of the students were concerned about getting jobs after they graduated from a department that had been beset by scandal. Over the next weeks, it was clear that the students had seen the light. They calmed down, and when faculty brought the issue up in class, they chastised the faculty members and told them to get on with what the class was really about. I was very proud of them.

In the end, the administration bought Professor Xavier out of the remainder of his contract and terminated Yatz with a paid leave for a year. Both were forbidden to come to the campus ever again. The untenured faculty were naturally anxiety-ridden, but I assured them that I would protect them as best I could as long as they were honest with me and worked hard. The students, much to their credit, continued to produce high-quality short films that won many awards.

A few years after I left the department, Professor Zed went after another faculty member because she had listed an MA as an MFA on her resumé when she was hired. The union did not defend her and she was forced to leave, given what had gone on before. A few years after that, Professor Zed was sent a letter of dismissal alleging that he had taken kickbacks from student scholarships and wrongly collected course fees from his students. He appealed the dismissal and worked out an agreement with the university that basically paid him to leave and forbade him from teaching at any CSU campus. Steven Spielberg never gave the department another cent, though I did talk him into making a free sneak peek at *Lincoln* available exclusively to students on the campus.

CHAPTER SEVENTEEN

Last Lessons out of the Whirl of Events

WHILE MANAGING THE MESS IN THE FILM DEPARTMENT, I CONTIN-ued to maintain my academic publishing. In a law-review article entitled "Violence as Indecency: *Pacifica*'s Open Door Policy,"[1] I attacked a bad, but still standing Supreme Court decision from 1978. It upheld the right of the Federal Communications Commission to reprimand a radio station for broadcasting a monologue by comedian George Carlin. The FCC then expanded its power to censor implied indecency based on context instead of specific words. Rulings based on context had become fairly arbitrary, which by most lights meant they were unconstitutional. For example, the FCC fined the radio network that carried Howard Stern, even though he did not say the condemned words; but similar implications about erections and even masturbation on CBS's *Will and Grace* and *Two and Half Men* were not penalized.

Robert O'Neill, the leading scholar on the First Amendment came out of my field and then went on to law school, eventually becoming dean of the University of Cincinnati Law School, president of the University of Wisconsin system, and president of the University of Virginia. Now he was director of the Thomas Jefferson Center. Bob told me he had a grant to set up a summit on the First Amendment at the National Archives Building in Washington, D.C., and he wanted me to participate.

In the fall, some graduate students, faculty, and I published an e-book on my Center's site, *The First Amendment and Religious Freedom*, and presented it at the National Communication Association's annual meeting in November 2008, and at the President's Forum for Human Rights on campus in March 2009. In November 2009 we presented "A First Amendment Profile of the Sitting Justices of the Supreme Court" to the NCA convention, and it was eventually published as a book by John Cabot University Press in 2011. I was very pleased that these outlets for the work of graduate students and faculty helped the graduate students get into PhD programs, and helped the faculty get tenured and promoted.[2]

THE 2008 PRESIDENTIAL CAMPAIGN

The primary season was underway for a successor to George W. Bush, whose administration had fallen on hard times. It bungled the crisis caused by Hurricane Katrina's flooding New Orleans; the wars in Iraq and Afghanistan were indecisive and prolonged. The speculation going into 2008 was that Hillary Clinton had a lock on the Democratic nomination and Rudy Giuliani, the hero mayor of New York City during 9/11, had a lock on the Republican nomination. In December of 2007, I had warned on several talk shows that the early presumptive nominees rarely won their party's nomination. Being in front of the pack means being a target for the other candidates and the media, who want to make a race out of it. Michigan Governor George Romney, the father of Mitt, had stumbled in 1968 when he said in an interview that he had been "brainwashed" by generals in Vietnam. Standing on a flatbed truck trying to address a crowd of supporters, Senator Edmund Muskie was reduced to tears during the New Hampshire primary of 1972 when the *Manchester Union Leader* revealed the foulmouthed utterances of his wife. In 1975, no one thought an ex-governor of Georgia who was a peanut farmer could win his party's nomination; but in 1976, he not only got the nomination, he won the presidency. In 1979, the pundits thought Ronald Reagan was too old to win his party's nomination; in November of 1980, he was president-elect. As late as January of 1992, the press was writing former governor Bill Clinton off because of sex scandals, but he became "the comeback kid." And the rise of George W. Bush is almost beyond comprehension.

By February 2008, Barack Obama was giving Hillary Clinton a run for the nomination. So she put all of her resources in the Super Tuesday primaries of February 5, attempting to score a knockout. It didn't work. Obama won a number of small states and scored heavily with his eloquent victory speeches. However, as I pointed out in my media interviews, he failed to ever match his poll-projected numbers in his victories, running roughly 3 to 6 percent behind them in each case depending on whose poll you read. I also pointed out that he did not debate well; on points, Hillary beat him in most of their debates. However, she was an unlikable schoolmarm in most of these exchanges. The press helped Obama along by lobbing easy questions at him until a skit on *Saturday Night Live* shamed them into equal treatment of the candidates.

As I made clear in guest lectures, no one shone on the Republican side. Giuliani avoided the New Hampshire primary and bet a win in the Florida primary would catapult him into the lead. However, his campaign was so disorganized that it could generate neither funds nor enthusiasm. He was out of the race, and the field eventually narrowed to Senator John McCain and former governor Mitt Romney. McCain won that battle.

At the political conventions, Obama gave his acceptance speech in Denver, which was something of a letdown. His advisors had decided he should give a workmanlike address with pragmatic approaches to problems instead of relying on his usual high-flown campaign rhetoric. His address was delivered outdoors—almost always a bad idea, because nature sucks the energy out of the venue. (Kennedy's acceptance of the nomination outdoors at the Los Angeles Coliseum was weak enough to induce Nixon to accept the offer of debates.) The Republican Convention seemed ready to take advantage of the situation. If McCain could define Obama in an unfavorable way while heightening his own credibility—the same strategy Bush Sr. used on Dukakis in 1988—the Republicans could win the election.

McCain surprised everyone by selecting Governor Sarah Palin as his running mate. She had very little experience, being a small-time mayor who became governor when her opponents self-destructed. On the last night of the convention, Palin gave a speech that received solid marks, and McCain followed with a speech that was muddled until his peroration, where he finally hit his stride and brought the crowd to its feet. I was not surprised over the next few days when the polls showed that McCain-Palin got a bump out of the GOP convention. They would lead in the polls through mid-September, when the mortgage crisis brought the economy and McCain's campaign to a halt. It didn't help that Palin was revealed to be a lightweight. Tina Fey did a spot-on imitation of Palin that was so good that to this day, people swear that Palin said, "I can see Russia from my front porch." She actually said, "You can see Russia from Alaska." It didn't matter, since that fact hardly qualifies as foreign-policy experience. Though she held her own in the vice-presidential debate with Senator Joe Biden,[3] gaffes continued to haunt her on the campaign trail. She was out of her depth, and given McCain's age, many people could not stomach the thought of her being a heartbeat away from the presidency. Had he won, McCain would have been the oldest man elected to the presidency. I watched how the game was played and commented on it. But I was content not to be directly involved.

So I did commentaries on the election on KFWB locally and other news outlets around the nation, such as the Rocky Mountain Radio Network. I watched as McCain gamely tried to defend Bush's wars, while Obama promised to end them posthaste. During the debates, it was shocking to me that McCain could not close the deal when it came to making an argument. He seemed to believe that the audience would fill in the missing pieces and infer the proper conclusion. In the town hall debate, he wandered around the stage as if looking for a lost cat. In all of the debates, he looked old and tired. Because of prisoner-of-war injuries, his gestures were stiff and limited. When in the last debate he sighed when he heard something from Obama he did not like, McCain reminded the audience of Gore in his first, eye-rolling debate with Bush in 2000. Television is a cool medium; overacting is detected immediately. And so a great patriot became a failed campaigner in part because of his rhetorical inadequacies.

Though Obama again ran behind the poll projections, which averaged an 11 percent advantage, he still won the election by a margin of 54 to 46 percent. His campaign had created an e-mail list of ten million supporters who were ready to phone others, walk precincts, and monitor polling places. Almost 62 percent of eligible voters turned out, the highest percentage since 1968. Republicans suffered many losses in the House and Senate; in the latter, the Democrats could now stop Republican filibusters. The only good news for Republicans was that the Democrats would have no excuses if they could not produce on the promises they made during the campaign. That would lead to the Republican comeback of 2010 and the decline of Obama's popularity. But in November of 2008, things looked pretty bleak for the Republicans.

TEACHING IN ROME

As the fall semester grew to a close, I was excited about a whole new adventure. I would be going to Rome with my friend Karl Squitier for three weeks to teach a class abroad for our students. We planned to take them on various excursions that illustrated what we were teaching, whether it be the Senate House in the Forum or Villa d'Este in the hills.

On January 2, I arrived at our apartment on the Tiber: two bedrooms, two baths, and in the fashionable Prati neighborhood, an easy walking distance to the Campo di Fiori and other famous sites. Karl and I quickly learned how to choreograph the preparation of meals in our tiny kitchen. Each night we traded the roles of master chef and sous-chef. We found the best local butcher, the best grocery story, the best liquor store, and were set for our three-week stay. Karl also found a lovely local bar/restaurant. The woman who ran the place was energetic and clearly in love with her gorgeous and brooding son, who was the brains of the operation. Almost every night we stopped in for an after-dinner *digestivo* (Campari, soda, lime) and were welcomed like visiting princes. We caught up on gossip and gave advice to the family, who took us under their wing. After we got in each night, Karl would call his partner back in California to report on the day's events. And I would sit alone, reading.

One high point of the trip came at Hadrian's huge villa, replete with ponds, a swimming pool, statues, and ruins. I told the students about Hadrian's gay relationship with Antinous, a young man he discovered in Bithynia. When Antinous sacrificed himself to the Nile to end a drought, Hadrian created more statues of him than existed for anyone else in antiquity. He also struck a coin in his honor.

One night we cooked for Mary Merva, the dean at John Cabot University in Rome, a wonderful liberal arts American university on the Tiber.[4] She brought her delightful husband, Stefano, whom she had met when she came to teach in Rome the first time. A few days later, Mary called to invite me to give a lecture on famous inaugural addresses as a lead-in to Barack Obama's inaugural. I must say it was a great thrill to see him sworn in. The inaugural has a whole different feel when you watch it from a foreign country. My pre-lecture was carried on Italian television, followed by the President's inaugural address live at 6 P.M. Italian time. After it was over, the president of John Cabot University asked me to teach a course there in the summer, and I've been going back ever since.

Early in the spring semester of 2009, I went up to see Mom. My sister warned me that "Mom seems out of it." It never failed, however, that when I walked into her room, Mom immediately brightened up. What had been slurred speech was suddenly clear and fluent. I spent the rest of my arrival day with her. The next day I spent the morning with her, then went off and caught my limit of fish at Little Medicine Lake with my brother-in-law. When we returned, Mom loved it when I brought the stringer of trout into her room for examination.

Also in the spring, I decided that six years was long enough to have been chair of the Film Department, and that two terms was long enough to be on the CSU Board. California's budget was in the dumper along with the economy. Being chair of a dysfunctional department was bad enough. I didn't need the added headache of no replacements for the departing faculty and no equipment money once the Spielberg funds ran out. As for the board of trustees, being forced to raise students' tuition was galling. So on May 7, I gave a farewell address to the Statewide Academic Senate, urging them to become more proactive and not to be overshadowed by the self-defeating faculty union. I received a resolution commending my service. A week later, I said my farewell to the board and was named "Trustee Emeritus." The most moving moment came when the chair called me "the conscience of the board."

The semester wound down, our graduation was completed, and I was finished as chair of the Film Department. I settled back into writing, exploration of spiritual ties, cooking for friends (most of whom were former students), playing tennis, and walking on the beach. The new, simpler rhythm of my life was interrupted by a call from my sister. Mom had suddenly fallen into a coma and was going fast. "Should I come up?" I asked.

"She's not talking to anyone, and I'm not sure you can get here in time." As I was packing, I received another call. My mother had passed away. At the end, with only her granddaughter in the room, my mother had lifted her arms toward heaven and given out a sigh, and died. Now, I needed to arrange for her to be buried next to Dad in National City.

When the hearse arrived at St. Mary's Church, I nearly lost my composure. Surrounded by relatives, we wheeled the casket into the church where I had been baptized and received my First Holy Communion. At the gravesite, I gave a eulogy in which I tried to relieve my sister's grief. I told those assembled that Mom was proud of what my sister Avis and I had accomplished in life, but it did not compare to what my sister Renée had given her: grandchildren. They were the lights of my mother's life. I concluded: "It is a long way from the woods of Pennsylvania to the clouds of heaven, but Mother has now completed that journey." My sister fell apart when the casket was lowered into the ground. Then we all commiserated for a while and headed for home. It wasn't until a week later, when everyone had finally departed, that I got some rest and was able to let go of my feelings. Mom had lived to be ninety-three. She was at peace and it was her time.

On the Fourth of July, 2009, I landed in Rome, where the temperatures were tolerable but I could feel that they were going to get much hotter and combine with the humidity coming off the Tiber, one block away. However, every evening a soft breeze came down the river and cooled things off. To celebrate the summer, Romans lined the Tiber with open-air bars, restaurants, and other amusements. One night I taught a bartender how to make a decent martini.

I decided to take a day trip to Orvieto and was delighted to find that when I exited the funicular at the top of the plateau, it was much cooler than below in the train station. However, while in the cathedral with a beautiful variegated front, I was suddenly struck with anxiety. I would be going home to teach as a regular faculty member for the first time in six years; no board of trustees, no chair of a department. The year would be my lead-in to the semiretirement program (half-time teaching, full retirement salary, plus half of my regular salary). What would I do with myself? My anxiety increased on the train back to Rome.

My class at John Cabot was composed of a dozen students from Cal State Long Beach and three students from Europe. They all earned A's or B's, doing very well on the final exams. Their five weeks in Rome and around Europe on the weekends changed their lives, as did their newfound knowledge of the power of rhetoric. And I had some great teaching experiences. One student had returned from soldiering in Iraq and was just beginning his college education. He thought of himself as a slow learner. I worked closely with him, allowing him, as I do with most students, to rewrite his papers in light of what I hoped was constructive criticism. The first time he rewrote a paper, a light went on. He came to me with tears in his eyes when he saw that he got an A.

I needn't have worried about adjusting to my fall schedule. I realized that throughout my life, I had gotten a wonderful education that continued to blossom in new publications and new ways of teaching. My love for history gave me a sense of prudence and opened the door to writing about historic events and important speakers. My immersion in films and the study of English literature, particularly Shakespeare and Hemingway, gave me a feel for language and the difference between the spoken and the written word. These experiences continually expanded my vocabulary, which is important if you are trying to say something in just the right way. It is as simple as this: the more words you know, the more precisely you can say things. Hemingway taught other lessons. First, watch for unneeded adverbs and adjectives. Second, if you get writer's block, try to think of one important, true sentence. Use it as a conclusion and inductively work your way back to it. If you read a good Hemingway story or book chapter, you'll find that it often ends with one important, true sentence to which you are led by all that has gone on before it.[5]

Being immersed in rhetorical theory had made me adaptable to new job situations and had given me the ability to write for a variety of occasions, from the Bicentennial of the nation to a speech on the new product line at Chrysler. My years in competitive debate and public speaking, both as a participant and a coach, gave me an appreciation of research for sound evidence to produce solid arguments. These skills led to my advancement at CBS, the White House, the National Republican Senatorial Campaign Committee, and Chrysler, and contributed to my academic publication record over the years. I continue to pass these skills on to my students as best as I can.

My relaxed schedule gave me more time to explore Los Angeles and its environs, which I have come to appreciate. The diversity of neighborhoods and cultures cannot be found anywhere else in the world. Our symphony orchestra is superb given the lineage from Zubin Mehta to Esa Pekka Salonen to Gustavo Dudamel. The opera is run by Placido Domingo, who brought us the innovative and over-the-top Ring Cycle of Wagner done with puppets, masks, and lots of neon. The combination of the Music Center, the Mark Taper Forum, and Disney Hall gives Los Angeles some wonderful venues. Then there are the museums: the Los Angeles County Museum is world-renowned; the Getty, sitting on its hill overlooking all of L.A. is beautifully designed; the Getty Villa on the ocean in Malibu is filled with ancient treasures. The Norton Simon Museum in Pasadena, and the Huntington with its gardens and Gainsboroughs in San Marino are perfect for a day's visit. The beaches are all different, some facing south, some west. They are accessible all year long, refreshed by a soft, cool ocean breeze. It serves to keep our climate moderate; in fact, I don't believe there is a better place to live year-round than along the coast in Southern California.

HISTORY REPEATS ITSELF

The spring semester of 2010 led into campaigning for the midterm elections and therefore, calls from local cable shows and national radio programs. I dwell on this moment in history because as I write, it mirrors in some ways where Republicans find themselves in 2013: lacking a national majority. If they could bring the party back in 2010, they may be able to do it again in 2014. So let's see what happened in 2010.

In my media interviews, I argued that 2010 paralleled 1966. In 1964, the Republicans had suffered a devastating defeat at the hands of Lyndon Johnson. At the top of the ticket, Senator Barry Goldwater had been painted as an extremist. (If only we could have his kind of "extremism" now.) He received only 40 percent of the vote and took many a senator and congressman down with him. Newspaper editorials predicted the demise of the Republican Party. But in the midterm elections of 1966, the Republicans came roaring back. Two years after that, Richard Nixon captured the White House and the Republican Party was back in the saddle.

I predicted a 1966-like comeback for the Republicans in November of 2010. I based this prediction on a number of factors. First, many Democrats who won new House seats in 2006 and 2008 won by very close margins and could be picked off if the Republicans played their cards right. Second, the 2008 presidential loss was less devastating than the media portrayed it. The fact is, Barack Obama, as he always did, ran behind his poll numbers. Remember too that Obama's endorsements of candidates had proven toxic as early as 2009 in Virginia and New Jersey for governor, and, heaven help him, in Massachusetts for senator, where the Republicans had picked up Teddy Kennedy's seat, ending the Democrats' filibuster-proof hold on the Senate.[6] Third, the country was not recovering from the Great Recession despite all the stimulus Obama and his House and Senate majorities provided. Unemployment remained very high. On January 20, 2010, the second anniversary of Obama's inaugural, the chair of the congressional panel appointed to oversee the bank bailout reported that 20 percent, that's one-fifth, of all Americans were either jobless, underemployed, or had given up on finding a job. People were hurting as they lost their jobs and/or their homes.

Fourth, the President lost his leftist and youth bases because he did not deliver on his promise to end the wars in Iraq and Afghanistan quickly. He also defaulted on the "don't ask, don't tell" policy on homosexuality in the military. There were more "Defense Department contractors" in Iraq than when the President took office. He continued the rendition program of the CIA and turned those apprehended over to other countries for torture. He expanded the terrorist prisons at Guantanamo Bay, Cuba. His approval of the use of drones often resulted in civilian casualties.

Fifth, Obamacare was unpopular across the country. Sixth, while a great campaign speaker, Obama was lackluster from his inaugural address through the 2010 election. Somehow, he had become a boring president. Reading from teleprompters at press conferences is a turn-off, as is not scheduling them in the evening when the public has time to watch, or not scheduling them at all because you don't want to answer tough questions.

Even the dumbest Republicans could see that 2010 presented them with an opportunity. Understanding the numbers, the Republicans, under the leadership of Senate Minority Leader Mitch McConnell and House Minority Leader John, "the dour but well-tanned," Boehner, decided not only to say "no" to Obama's policies but to say "hell no!" They launched a passive-aggressive strategy that proved effective. The passive part was to just sit back and circle their wagons in partisan unity while the Democrats whooped and yelled and ran up the deficit. The aggressive part was to be negative and positive. Republicans opposed the stimulus package, and when it failed to produce results, they said, "I told you so." They opposed the healthcare reform, particularly on the hustings in town hall meetings, and eventually got the majority of Americans to oppose the program too. They charged that Obama could campaign, but could not govern. Smartly, and better late than never, the Republicans aggressively recruited Hispanic candidates for public office, from Abel Maldonado for lieutenant governor of California to the charismatic Marco Rubio for senator in Florida. When all the votes were counted, Susanna Martinez became the Republican governor of New Mexico; Brian Sandoval became the Republican governor of Nevada. Many house races featured Latino and Latina Republicans.

The rhetoric of Republican resistance emboldened two other groups that proved important in the election. In January 2010, that is, just as we were heading into the midterm elections, the Supreme Court narrowly ruled in the *Citizens United* case that corporations and unions could spend independently and to their heart's content in federal elections. The FEC reports that the U.S. Chamber of Commerce poured $75 million into the midterm election. American Crossroads, which was founded by Karl Rove, spent $52 million; free-market backer Americans for Prosperity spent $45 million; and the conservative Club for Growth spent $24 million. Many more joined in. This money was particularly effective in down-ticket races for the state legislatures.

Just as important, out of the discontent of 2009, the Tea Party movement emerged to energize the election and the conservative wing of the GOP. Flogged on by Sarah Palin and the sophistic Glenn Beck, Tea Party members helped turn out disaffected voters, and that, combined with the unenthusiasm of Democrats, particularly the young, gave momentum to the Grand Old Party.

Other important variables in the elections of 2010 included early absentee voting during a time when the President and his party were particularly unpopular, and a toxic political environment in which compromise was nearly impossible and negative advertising reigned supreme. This environment was reenforced by commentators such as the rational Rachel Maddow and William Kristol, to the semi-rational Bill O'Reilly and Chris Matthews, and the irrational Keith Olbermann, Ann Coulter, and Rush Limbaugh. Almost anything you wanted to believe could be reinforced somewhere on a cable channel by some talking head. You can fool some of the people all of the time, as Lincoln suggested in one of his debates with Douglas. Americans were becoming more and more segregated and dogmatic. They believed they knew it all because even their dumbest positions, such as "There is no global warming," were being reinforced on some cable channel by some nut somewhere. The situation was also ridiculed by comedy news shows, including Jon Stewart's telling quotation-for-quotation matchup between George W. Bush and Barack Obama on the wars and the deficit. It didn't seem to matter who the president was; the same policies were being embraced by the Democrat that had been endorsed by the Republican.

In a stunning Gallup Poll, Americans claimed to have confidence in only three of the sixteen standard institutions that make up the country: the military, small businesses, and police. Others in which there was less than a 25 percent confidence rating included the media, banks, health insurers, and Congress. The Supreme Court and organized religion did better, but failed to achieve a 50 percent rating.

A typical example of the rhetoric of Republican resistance came on Friday the 13th (hello) in August. The President gave a speech at a Ramadan dinner (hello) in which he addressed the question of the right of Muslims to build a mosque near the tragic site of the attack on the World Trade Center. The President was correct, in my opinion, when he said, "[Muslims] have the same right to practice their religion as everyone else in this country. That includes the right to build a place of worship and a community center on private property in Lower Manhattan, in accordance with local laws." However, Representative Peter King (R-NY) immediately responded that "It is insensitive and uncaring for the Muslim community to build a mosque in the shadow of ground zero. While the Muslim community has the right to build the mosque, they are abusing the right by needlessly offending so many people who have suffered so much. . . . Unfortunately the President caved into political correctness." Would Representative King have resisted the President's defense of the First Amendment had he not seen a CNN/Opinion Research Poll earlier in August which showed that 68 percent of the public opposed plans to build the mosque?

By Labor Day, the Gallup Poll found that voters preferred Republicans over Democrats for Congress by a margin of 51 percent to 41 percent, the largest gap Gallup had ever found in favor of Republicans in the history of its polling. Furthermore, the poll revealed that Republicans were far more enthusiastic about voting than were Democrats. The Pew Research Center Poll showed that since the 2008 election, Obama had lost 14 percent of the support he had from single women, moderates, and white men; he had lost 13 percent of the support he had received in the election from Latinos, suburbanites, older voters, and younger voters. He had lost 9 percent of the support he had from liberals.

As I had predicted as early as November 2009 at the National Communication Association's annual meeting in Chicago, the result was a massive defeat for Democrats in the House, governor's races, and statehouse seats. Republicans also made a moderate gain in the Senate. They picked up 63 House seats, the largest gain by a party since 1948. But what is often overlooked is the depth of the Republican victory in statehouses. The Republicans won control of the legislatures *and* governorships of twenty states, including Wisconsin, Michigan, Ohio, Florida, and Pennsylvania. In only six states did the Democrats control all three branches of governance.

Thus, Republicans controlled most of the redistricting across the country, which would have important consequences in the 2012 election. They quickly passed laws requiring voter identification and went after public employee and other labor unions.[7]

The problem was that leading into the presidential campaign of 2012, the system had produced gridlock, the Republicans did not expand their appeal to minorities, and the Republican field of candidates was very weak. Each side had become more entrenched. And the Republican Party continued to slide to the right, away from sensible positions on gay rights, gun control, and freedom of expression. In the Republican presidential primary debates, it was horribly disheartening to listen to the likes of Congresswoman Michele Bachmann and former senator Rick Santorum spew their venom. It was even more upsetting to see the former sensible governor of Massachusetts, Mitt Romney, cave in to the Republican Right to get the nomination. That more than anything else put him at a severe disadvantage in the general election. Romney's elitist core was revealed when he claimed at a fundraising dinner that he would never get the support of the 47 percent of voters who paid no taxes and relied on government support.

The general election, though closer than expected because of Romney's performance in the first presidential debate, accomplished little. The most remarkable statistic from the election indicates voters' dissatisfaction with the system. This was no mandate, and had the Republicans run a candidate less prone to errors and revelations about his true values, they might have won.

Let's look at the numbers. President Obama was returned to office by a margin of 51.3 percent to 48.7 percent. However, a closer reading of the election statistics should send tremors through both parties. In the final count, Romney ran about 300,000 votes behind McCain's total vote of

2008.[8] And Obama ran 6 million votes behind his vote total from 2008.[9] In other words, the voters basically said, a plague on both your houses. It is almost unfathomable that a sitting president would run 6 million votes behind his first-term election numbers and be returned to office. Even when Franklin Roosevelt broke tradition and ran for a third term, he maintained his total vote following from the previous elections.

But don't let these statistics paper over deeper cleavages in the electorate.[10] White voters, particularly males, voted overwhelmingly for Romney, while women and minorities gave their support to Obama. Even among women there was a huge divide; married women supported Romney by a margin of 53 to 46 percent, while single women supported Obama by a margin of 67 to 31 percent. Suburban and rural voters went Republican; city dwellers went Democratic.

Often neglected among the exit-poll statistics was the fact that Obama ran even better among Asian Americans than among Hispanics. He received over 70 percent of the vote of each group, but the turnaround among Asian Americans was the most spectacular. Libertarian Republicans could take some pleasure in the fact that four states approved same-sex marriage and two legalized recreational pot smoking. However, because the House remained in Republican hands, it will be extremely difficult for this system of checks and balances to reduce unemployment and the deficit, monitor wars abroad, deal with climate change and international trade policy, to name just a few of the challenges we face. Social issues continue to be shunted off to ballot propositions or the Supreme Court, where one hopes they will continue to come down on the side of civil rights for all citizens.

The Democrats added a few seats to their majority in the Senate because Senate races are less influenced by super PAC money, and, let's face it, the Democrats had better candidates, and some Republican Senate candidates said such outrageous things that their remarks disrupted the presidential campaign by bringing to the fore issues that Romney wanted to ignore. However, even with these wins, the Democrats cannot prevent filibusters, one of the most anti-democratic parliamentary procedures ever adopted in this republic.[11]

It should now be clear that the Republican Party needs to revise its manifesto. The party's flirtation with the radical, religious Right produced some wins over the years and will probably keep Republicans in power in the more rural states and congressional districts, but such pandering will no longer produce a national consensus in favor of a Republican presidential candidate. If the Republicans want to remain a minority party, stay the course. However, if Republicans want to return to a time when they controlled the

House, the Senate, and the presidency, they need to take several important steps, as they did in 1966 and in 2010.

First, the party should show some pride in its past. The Republican Party under the leadership of Lincoln freed the slaves and passed the Thirteenth Amendment. In his martyred name, it passed the Fourteenth and Fifteenth Amendments to the Constitution. Those amendments gave African American men the vote, while extending equal protection under the law and due process of it to the states. Over the objections of the Democrats, Republicans got suffrage for women; the first female members of the House and Senate were Republicans, as was the first woman to sit on the Supreme Court. Teddy Roosevelt was a superb diplomat, winning the Nobel Peace Prize for negotiating the end of a war between Japan and Russia. He was a conservationist who created our national parks system. Dwight Eisenhower gave us peace and prosperity while negotiating the difficulties of the nuclear age and fixing the nation's infrastructure. Nixon and Ford continued that tradition with fiscal responsibility and environmental concern. And it wouldn't hurt to remind people that the SALT I limits were signed and the voting age was lowered to eighteen under Nixon. Ronald Reagan continued the battle for disarmament and taught Republicans not to speak ill of one another, to be optimistic rather than divisive, to transcend party lines when possible (remember those Reagan Democrats), and to communicate their message effectively.

Second, Republicans should have learned from him that when you favor an unpopular position, such as prohibiting abortion, do so in a rational and compassionate way. When you support a strict reading of the Constitution in its historical context, include the Bill of Rights, which means freedom of expression and religion, separation of church and state, and a right to privacy and fair trial. You can't invoke the Constitution on such issues as gun control without embracing the rest of the document. In other words, if you are going to be conservative, be sensible about it. True conservatism, the conservatism of Edmund Burke and William F. Buckley, is very attractive to most voters. They know that we need a strong defense; that we shouldn't entangle America in unwinnable foreign wars that are not in the national interest; that civil rights should protect individual freedom; that creativity should be nurtured and rewarded; that the states can function as laboratories for better policies (Massachusetts's healthcare plan developed under Romney became the model for Obama's national program); that unless it is vital to the national interest, education should be left to the states and localities; that religion is essential to the national spirit, but must be a private matter.

Third, it doesn't take a rocket scientist to tell you that nominating troglodytes and witches for senator at the expense of seasoned veterans will cost you elections. These nuts will get airtime and pop up into the national election with their ridiculously uninformed and/or offensive remarks. Whether for House, Senate, or president, picking a strong candidate is the most important element in producing a victory on election day. Given the huge numbers of voters who now call themselves independents, people are voting more and more for the person rather than for the party.

Fourth, Republicans must adjust to their audiences. In states like New York, California, and Maine, moderate Republicans need to be nominated for office. In most of the South, Republicans can rely on a traditional conservative framework to carry the day as long as extreme positions don't puncture that framework of the national election. But even in such states as Texas and Arizona, as they did in 2010, Republicans need to nominate well-qualified Latinos/as for office because that population is growing. The successes of Hispanic Republicans in Florida, New Mexico, and Nevada, among others, should have found the Republicans nominating many more Hispanic candidates in 2012. Of course they need to appeal to women, who make up over half of the electorate. They did this by electing Susan Collins and Olympia Snow as the U.S. senators from Maine, and Susana Martinez and Nikki Haley as governors of New Mexico and South Carolina respectively.[12] They must also find Asian American candidates, as they did a decade ago in California.

Fifth, and for now, Republicans can function as the loyal opposition and score points with the public on many issues. They should monitor foreign policy and make sure the administration is engaged in realpolitik instead of romanticism. They should call the President out when he violates the War Powers Act (as he did in the Libyan intervention), and they should consider questioning the moral and legal implications of using torture and drones as weapons against terrorism. They should point out that when you add income taxes, property taxes, state taxes, Social Security taxes, Medicare taxes, city taxes, and sales taxes, you'll find that many Americans are paying half their income to their governments. If they are getting the services they want for those fees, fine; if they are not, we've gone down the wrong road. It is also fair to point out that the federal government continues to grow and take on more and more responsibilities that were once the province of the states while running a national debt that is going to come due with a vengeance someday soon. They should continue to protest that the states have lost many powers to the federal government while being burdened with unfunded mandates and regulations tied to federal aid. They should reveal the bloat and fraud in the welfare system, as well as in defense spending.

Sixth, be smart. Read the poll data to figure out what the voters want to hear about and what their positions are on the issues. With the help of super PACs, the Republican Party should nurture young, promising candidates from city-council and assembly seats all the way to the White House. Recruit at the lower levels of the electoral system and support a career that is promising.

If the Republicans don't make these changes, the party will not only continue to lose people like me, it will wind up nationally where it now sits in California, where the Democrats have super-majorities in both houses of the legislature and hold the governorship. The Republican Party of Earl Warren, Richard Nixon, Ronald Reagan, and Pete Wilson is now irrelevant to governance in this state. I give this advice because America needs a two-party system; it is out of the dialectic between them that sensible policies used to emerge.

THE LAST ACT?

Between the midterm elections of 2010 and the presidential election of 2012, I continued to teach and run my Center. I participated in a grant the campus received from the Doris Duke Foundation by giving ten lectures in downtown Long Beach to the community. Five lectures concerned the terrible times of blacklisting in Hollywood, and five lectures concerned censorship of violence and indecency. Each lecture was followed by a feature film that was either written or directed by a blacklisted artist, or illustrated the point of the lecture. That such artists could be censored in an America that had just won a world war in the name of protecting freedom and democracy should give us pause.

The Center runs forums in Rome with John Cabot University each summer on freedom of expression, often comparing American freedoms to those of European nations. We have completed six episodes of a cable series on *The First Amendment and You*,[13] which tries to bring an understanding of all the clauses of the amendment to the public. It also points them to our website, where they can find objective studies of issues surrounding freedom of religion and expression. Under a grant, we have expanded our program of fellowships to graduate and law students around the country.

In 2010, I was humbled to receive a letter informing me that I would be given the Douglas Ehninger Award from the National Communication Association for "distinguished scholarship in rhetorical studies." At the convention, as the MC read my accomplishments, I looked out over the sea of academics and reflected on the arc of my life. There were a lot of successes. But I learned more from the failures. After the event, some of my friends speculated that semi-retirement would be difficult for me. Because of my publication record in the midst of a busy life outside of academia, they often see me as a Type A. However, I had made some major adjustments after I returned from Rome. I am happy to sleep in every morning, make my breakfast, and spend an hour quietly reading the *Los Angeles Times*. If the morning is open, I write. At school, I'm happy to pour my abilities into just one class a semester, and to mentor as many students outside of class as is feasible. Being out of the closet, I can make up for lost time helping LGBT students. I'm happy to go on long walks beholding birds on the beach, to watch the evening news at the end of the day, to cook for my friends, including students, several times a week. I'm happy to share my sense of spirituality with them and see it surface in their work, hoping they can pass it along to others. Though a step or two slower than I used to be, I play tennis whenever I can get a game up. I'm happy to putter in my garden and read good books.

As a genuine conservative in Edmund Burke's definition of the term, I hate changes. Yet, as this narrative makes clear, I've had to endure many. My training in rhetoric, more than anything else, has helped me cope with and adapt to these changes. If there is anything I'm sure of, it is that you can't have it all. With no romantic relationships, not to mention a partner, I've had plenty of time to do the work I do. I have found contentment by reducing desire and enhancing spirituality. And I have been blessed with many spiritual relationships that have stood the test of time. Yes, it is difficult to balance spiritualism with reality and to keep dreaming in a world that lets you down. However, if you develop an association with spirit, refine it, and use it, your talent can take you to places you've never dreamed of. From there, you can reach back and bring others along. You can expand the sense of spirit in the world, diminishing the pain of living in a troubled environment, and thereby make this world a better place, one that nurtures and inspires.

Notes

CHAPTER ONE. MEETING RICHARD
NIXON AND ROBERT KENNEDY

1. These perceptions were simplistic. In fact, Lou Harris became famous as a pollster because of his work in the 1960 campaign for John Kennedy. Harris divided the public into 280 subcategories, and Kennedy adjusted his message to those subcategories most likely to be in his specific audience. Learning from this targeting, Nixon would put together, as we shall see, a very sophisticated polling operation for his 1968 run for the presidency.

CHAPTER TWO. GEOGRAPHY LESSONS

1. During World War II, during the Nazi occupation, many of these Jews and their children were sent to death camps. Today Sanok is part of Poland but very near the Ukrainian border.
2. The census form in my father's papers has his father's name as Erwin, which is incorrect.
3. They lived at 4511 40th Street in Long Island City until January of 1941.
4. She became a member of the International Association of Machinists, Lodge # 755, paying dues starting in June 1943.
5. I always believed it quite ironic that I was conceived in a town that called itself "no f–k."
6. The front lawn was edged with banana trees and Eugenia berry bushes. Unhappy with the soil in our backyard, my father dug huge holes, filled them with topsoil, and then planted apricot, peach, and plum trees. Later a grape arbor was added.
7. Hiss was eventually convicted of treason. FBI files show that his wife's typewriter was used to type up 65 confidential State Department documents that were then conveyed to Soviet agents.

8. The 1948 presidential election had the lowest turnout of eligible voters in history. Many Republicans were so confident of winning that they did not vote. George Gallup was so confident of his prediction that Dewey would win that he suspended polling three weeks before the election. He would never make that mistake again.

9. The movie *The Manchurian Candidate*, starring Frank Sinatra and Lawrence Harvey, was based on these events.

10. I was able to retrieve my father's service records from the Navy, a marvelous treasure trove. My comments on his activities in the Navy are based on these records.

11. In 1945 and again in 1947, he had been cited for being overweight, and it would occur again in 1956.

12. As I was writing this memoir, I wondered what the real reason was for my father being let go. Could it have been the drinking? After much beer, he actually peed beside the road on the way back from a Navy picnic as other officers drove by honking. Could it have been the temper tantrums on the golf course? That could have been construed as behavior unbecoming to an officer. My father's Navy records included his regular "fitness reports." The fact is, they are consistently superior. The first is from the shakedown cruise of the USS *Cushing*; my father received 3.9's and 3.8's on a 4.0 scale in June of 1944. In September 1945, he is ranked among the top 20 percent of the men evaluated. His superior writes, "This officer is a mature, well trained officer with an excellent knowledge of fire-control and electrical engineering. He has a good sense of humor and is a good shipmate." A few months later, the next report claims that "He is well liked by his fellow officers." By June 1946, he is ranked in the top 10 percent of his peers and is described as "mature and well-grounded." In early 1947 the report reads, "Smith has, by virtue of the rapid demobilization, been thrust into a position normally filled by an officer of greater seniority. But despite initial unfamiliarity with many details of the Executive Officer's duties, he has acquitted himself well in his task which is not an easy one. Smith's loyalty to the service is above reproach." The reports continue in this vein well into 1949, where he is described as an "exceptionally loyal officer." Still in the top 10 percent in 1950, he is described as "extremely conscientious; his outlook and attitude are excellent." By 1951 he has become "an excellent instructor." When he enters the Korean War in 1951, his superior writes, "His actions against the enemy have been highly commendable." In 1953 he is commended for "mature judgment and understanding [making] him a particularly effective summary court and special court martial president." Once in Dahlgren, Virginia, as a lieutenant commander, the same praise continues along with the high marks. In Norfolk at Sewells Point, he

receives all "outstandings" on his report and is complimented for "his pleasant personality and cooperative spirit." All of these reports recommend him for promotion. His last report in part bemoans the fact that he has been retired; it reads, "A fine officer and a loss to this command on his retirement."

13. The other novice team from our school made the finals. Joe wouldn't let us debate one another and we had no desire to do so. So we shared first- and second-place trophies.

CHAPTER THREE. FROM STUDENT BODY PRESIDENT TO CBS NEWS

1. One of the seniors on the squad was Mike Leff, who went on to become the leading authority on Cicero in our field. We became close friends at Santa Barbara and remained so the rest of his life, which ended too early due to cancer.

2. We now know that this protocol was so sensitive that even Vice President Johnson did not know about it. We also know that apologists for the Kennedy administration varied widely from the truth. See Sheldon M. Stern, *The Cuban Missile Crisis in American Memory* (Palo Alto, CA: Stanford University Press, 2012). Stern studied the Ex-Com (Executive Committee of the National Security Council) documents of the period. He was the historian at the John F. Kennedy Library for 23 years.

3. Eddy was a direct descendent of Mary Baker Eddy, the founder of Christian Science.

4. Rockefeller's wife "Happy" had given birth just days before the primary, reminding voters that she was Rockefeller's second wife, and that he had divorced his first. Many believe the timing of the birth caused Rockefeller's defeat in the primary.

5. I took first place in impromptu speaking, second place in original oratory with a speech condemning the Soviet Union for oppressing Eastern Europe, and Mike Talley and I made the semifinals of debate.

6. I returned to the Western Tournament with an oration on the evils of the tenure system and took first place.

7. Hagen would be denied tenure and eventually end up teaching for 30 years at the University of Utah, where he continued to rile his students and colleagues with his unconventional teaching.

8. Burke began his writing career as a music critic in Greenwich Village. Once when John visited Burke in his New Jersey home, John played some classical

music. John had been a child prodigy. When John finished the piece, Burke looked at him and said, "That's quite an investment you've got there." Burke was an ecologist before his time. His house had no electricity or indoor bathrooms until the late 1950s.

9. Reagan's reconstruction of baseball box scores being telegraphed to him is legendary. He was aided by a sound man who imitated the sound of a ball hitting a bat and played a recording that imitated the cheers of the baseball fans. Bill Boyarsky, *The Rise of Ronald Reagan* (New York: Random House, 1968), 56–57.

10. Ronald Reagan and Richard Hubler, *Where's the Rest of Me?* (New York: Duell, Sloan and Pearce, 1965), 116.

11. Reagan and Hubler, *Where's the Rest of Me?*, 257.

12. General Electric began the process of ending the program when John Kennedy won the White House. When Reagan's contract came up for renewal, GE decided against it.

13. Lou Cannon, *Governor Reagan: His Rise to Power* (PublicAffairs, 2003), 109. Throughout this period, Reagan was also a guest on other television programs, from the *Ford Television Theatre* (1954–53) to the *Kraft Suspense Theater* (1964).

14. Ironically, Spencer and Roberts had run Rockefeller's unsuccessful California primary campaign against Goldwater in 1964.

15. Boyarsky, *The Rise of Ronald Reagan*, 108.

16. Boyarsky, *The Rise of Ronald Reagan*, 139.

17. The only writers who got this story right were British. Lewis Chester, Geoffrey Hodgson, and Brian Page included it in their insightful book *An American Melodrama: The Presidential Campaign of 1968* (New York: Viking Press, 1969).

18. Gavin's memoirs are available from Michigan State University Press.

19. *Rights in Conflict: Convention Week in Chicago, August 25–29, 1968.* A Report submitted by Daniel Walker, Director of the Chicago Study Team, to the National Commission on the Causes and Prevention of Violence, introduction by Max Frankel (New York: E.P. Dutton, 1968), 303, 372–77.

20. Little did I know that events across the country in Oregon regarding the issue of political debates would have an impact on my life. A young political whiz named Bob Packwood would be elected to the U.S. Senate against all odds.

CHAPTER FOUR. FIRST JOB SYNDROME

1. She married a few months after her graduation.
2. John could not know that in France, Jacques Derrida was developing some of the same theories and would incorporate them a few years later into his postmodern theory of deconstruction, which he would propagate in America from Yale. (In the last chapter of this book, I return to John's work and what eventually happened to it.)
3. Don Coleman, "SDSC Council to Continue Voting: Professor Cites Intimidation by Ethnic Groups," *San Diego Evening Tribune*, April 25, 1970, A2.
4. This was typical of Reagan on civil rights issues. During his run for governor, his primary opponent, George Christopher, implied in a joint meeting that Reagan was a racist. Reagan rose to "a point of personal privilege," and said: "I resent the implication that there is any bigotry in my nature. Don't anyone ever imply I lacked integrity. I will not stand silent and let any imply that—in this group or any other." He then slammed his fist into his hand and walked out of the meeting. Boyarsky, *The Rise of Ronald Reagan*, 149.
5. It was Greenwood to whom Richard Nixon was mainly referring in 1962 when in his infamous "last press conference," Nixon said, "You won't have Nixon to kick around anymore."
6. Noel Greenwood and William Tromley, "Ouster of UC's Heyns Topic of Secret Reagan Parley," *Los Angeles Times*, June 13, 1970, A1, 19.
7. Noel Greenwood, "UC Faculty Dossiers Urged; Reagan Calls It 'Witch Hunt,'" *Los Angeles Times*, June 16, 1970, A1, 22.
8. In 2009, the faculty in the California State University system voted to take a 10 percent one-year-only pay cut to save the jobs of their colleagues. This after not having received a raise in two years!
9. He must have felt as if he were back in Venezuela in 1959. He had been stoned and spit on there and become something of a hero back in the United States when he returned from the trip.
10. Garland was an icon of the gay movement for a number of reasons. She was gay-friendly; her father was gay; but most important, her songs could easily be sung as gay torch songs. Remember "The Man that Got Away."
11. If the fountains were left on all the time, the farmers in Louis's day would be drained of all water. But the Sun King wanted to tell people they were on all the time. So a simple scheme was set in place. Just before he was about to go outside, he would give a signal. The fountains would be turned on, and he could pretend that they were always running while he was king. When he went back inside, the fountains were turned off.
12. This story was later verified by Philip Hilts in "Eye on the White House," *Potomac Magazine* (*Washington Post*), April 21, 1974, 26–30.

CHAPTER FIVE. WORKING AT MR. JEFFERSON'S UNIVERSITY

1. Years later, when one of my nemeses was promoted to full professor and elected chair by the department at San Diego State, Golding denied the appointment and the promotion. The professor resigned in a huff. It was the beginning of a reform that would eventually result in the department becoming one of the best MA-granting communication studies departments in the country. Today, one of my former students there is now a full professor and teaches the courses I taught him.

2. His room was preserved and could be viewed through a wrought-iron grate where the door had been. One day I read in the student paper that a thin young man and his girlfriend decided to have sex on Poe's bed. In the middle of the night, they slipped through the grate, had sex, and then found themselves trapped. Evidently, sex causes the body to expand. Once they were freed, they were brought before some sort of tribunal, but since no cheating, stealing, or lying was involved, they were left to go free, and no doubt, practice safer sex.

3. While I certainly saw Hartmann with a drink in his hand at receptions and the like, I never saw a time when he was unable to function.

4. Cheney got the job by writing a five-page letter to Rumsfeld telling what he would do if Cheney were chief of staff.

5. Jules Witcover, *Marathon: The Pursuit of the Presidency, 1972–1976* (New York: Signet, 1977), 49.

6. Dick Cheney, *In My Time* (New York: Threshold Editions, 2011), 94.

7. I've written extensively elsewhere about speechwriting. See, for example, Craig R. Smith, "Contemporary Political Speech Writing," *Southern Speech Communication Journal* 42 (1976): 52–67. But for verification of many of the claims I make in this chapter, see Robert Schlesinger, *White House Ghosts: Presidents and their Speechwriters* (New York: Simon and Schuster, 2008), 258–66.

CHAPTER SIX. WRITING FOR PRESIDENT FORD

1. I will always be grateful to Charlie and Grace Skelly, the parents of one of my best students and still friend Paul Skelly, for putting me up for a few days in their home in Alexandria while I looked for a place to live. Paul went on to become a prominent lawyer at the largest law firm in the world.

2. In his memoirs, Dick Cheney claims that Hartmann circumvented the staffing of speeches. But my experience does not support Cheney's claim. Cheney, *In My Time*, 94.

3. Gerald R. Ford, "Remarks on Taking the Oath of Office, August 9, 1974," *Public Papers of the Presidents of the United States: Gerald R. Ford, 1974*, book 1 (Washington, DC: Government Printing Office, 1975), 1–2.

4. Witcover, *Marathon*, 50.

5. For a thorough look at the development of rhetorical theory, see my *Rhetoric and Human Consciousness: A History*, 4th ed. (Long Grove, IL: Waveland Press, 2013).

6. I find it annoying that to this day, press reports claim that Reagan made up this story. Our research found that while he may have exaggerated the story, it was basically true. Google it, and you'll find coverage in the *New York Times*.

7. For this reason, good speechwriters need to study psychology. However, Aristotle's book on that subject, *De Anima (On the Soul)*, is much less sophisticated on psychology than what he writes in his *Rhetoric*.

8. Michael McGee, "The 'Ideograph': A Link between Rhetoric and Ideology," *Quarterly Journal of Speech* 66 (1980): 1–16. For a revision of this position see McGee's "Text, Context, and the Fragmentation of Contemporary Culture," *Western Journal of Speech Communication* 54 (1990): 274–89. See also McGee, "In Search of 'The People': A Rhetorical Alternative," *Quarterly Journal of Speech* 61 (1975): 245–47; "A Materialist's Conception of Rhetoric," in *Explorations in Rhetoric: Studies in Honor of Douglas Ehninger*, ed. R. E. McKerrow (Glenview, IL: Scott Foresman, 1982), 23–48; and McGee and Martha Martin, "Public Knowledge and Ideological Argumentation," *Communication Monographs* 50 (1983): 47–65.

9. President James K. Polk borrowed this phrase from a New York newspaper to justify his imperialist war policy.

10. This phrase was coined by President Franklin D. Roosevelt and repeated by Ronald Reagan, starting with his speech in support of the candidacy of Senator Barry Goldwater in 1964.

11. Just to be clear, this kind of writing takes a lot of training. Thomas Gibbons cataloged 288 tropes and figures in 1767 in *Rhetoric; or, a View of Its Principal Tropes and Figures, in Their Origin and Powers*. He is not to be confused with Edward Gibbon, who wrote *The History of the Decline and Fall of the Roman Empire*.

12. The article was written by William Willoughby, "Righteous Ford Talks Like Carter, Wows Baptists," *Washington Star*, June 16, 1976, A1, 15. He reports that Ford was interrupted 16 times by applause. The text can be found in Gerald R. Ford, "Remarks at the Southern Baptist Convention, Norfolk, Virginia, June 15, 1976," *Public Papers of the Presidents of the United States: Ford, 1976–77*, book 2, 1877–80. The speech can be accessed online at *www.presidency.ucsb.edu/ws/index.php?pid=6127*.

13. My office number was OEOB 120; ironically, that was next door to 122, which had been Ken Khachigian's office in the Nixon administration.

14. I believe my ability to write speeches quickly can be traced to my high school and college training as an impromptu and extemporaneous competitive speaker. In the former case, you are handed a topic and have two minutes to prepare a five-minute speech about it. In the latter you were given a contemporary news headline, and then given 45 minutes to prepare a seven-minute speech about it.

15. Stalin, being only 5' 5," had used the same trick at Yalta and Potsdam with Churchill and FDR.

16. The Bicentennial speeches, which were published in a book by the Government Printing Office, can be found in chronological order in *Public Papers of the Presidents of the United States: Gerald R. Ford, 1976–77*, book 2 (Washington, DC: Government Printing Office, 1978), 1941–43, 1961–62, 1963–65, 1966–71, and 1973–77.

17. "Not unexpectedly the museum address drew derisive comments from some White House aides who have been critical of the Ford's speech writers." "President Kicks Off Bicentennial at Air and Space Museum," *Washington Star*, July 2, 1976, 10.

18. In his memoirs, Hartmann said the speeches of the summer of 1976 were the best that Ford had delivered in his lifetime. Robert Hartmann, *Palace Politics: An Inside Account of the Ford Years* (New York: McGraw Hill, 1980), 386. In a footnote on the next page, he wrote of my work: "Craig Smith, a bearded University of Virginia speech professor who filled in during the summer trying to disprove that 'those who can't, teach.'"

19. I knew about Spencer from my thesis research; as we have seen, he had helped Reagan win the governorship of California in 1966.

20. Cheney, *In My Time*, 100.

21. My version of these events aligns with Yanek Mieczkowski, "Gerald Ford's Near Miracle in 1976," *American History*, November 30, 2007 (online journal).

22. The next day Dole and Ford flew to nearby Russell, Kansas. Dole wept during the speech he made there, somewhat humanizing him.

CHAPTER SEVEN. WRITING FOR PRESIDENT GEORGE H. W. BUSH

1. Michael J. Hyde and Craig R. Smith, "Hermeneutics and Rhetoric" (lead article), *Quarterly Journal of Speech* 65 (1979): 347–63. See Craig R. Smith, "Heidegger's Theory of Authentic Discourse," *Analecta Husserliana*, vol. 15, ed. Calvin Schrag (Boston: World Institute for Advanced Phenomenological Research; D. Reidel Publishing Co., 1983), 209–17. Craig R. Smith, "Martin Heidegger and the Dialogue with Being," *Central States Speech Journal* 36 (1985): 256–69; Michael J. Hyde and Craig R. Smith, "Rethinking the Public: The Role of Emotion in Being-with-Others," *Quarterly Journal of Speech* 77 (1991): 446–66.
2. Guy Hunt went down to massive defeat in 1978. But in 1986, he did succeed, becoming the first Republican governor of the state since Reconstruction. He was reelected for a second term.
3. I liked Jennifer, and we remained friends for many years. I was saddened when in the 1992 campaign an illicit romance between her and the President was alleged. Nothing could be further from the truth. Mrs. Bush knew her well, and while Bush was vice president, Jennifer served as his Senate liaison officer, hardly a post you would give to your lover. This was one of those cases where men and women are not allowed to work together without the media or others assuming a relationship between them.
4. Dick Cheney tells a similar story about a meeting he had with George W. Bush in 1999. I guess this kind of hospitality runs in the family. See Cheney, *In My Time*, 252.
5. Adam Clymer, "Bush Hot Property on GOP Dinner Circuit," *New York Times*, February 19, 1978, A26.
6. "George Bush: Campaign 80's Early Bird," *Newsweek*, December 11, 1978, 37.
7. Letter of March 10, 1977.

CHAPTER EIGHT. WORKING FOR THE UNITED STATES SENATE

1. Letter from Bush of January 8, 1979.
2. I could also reconnect with some of my students who were now friends and moving into major law firms in Washington, D.C. One of my favorite dinners was with Phil Bane and his parents. After Phil and his mom would slip

off to bed, I would stay up late with his father, Howard, who was a legend at the CIA. He regaled me with stories of Tibetan freedom fighters and his efforts to undo Communist plots in Africa. After 9/11 Howard was called back into service as head of the anti-terrorism unit of the CIA.

3. See Keith Hinson, "Wallace Talks Shop in CA Class," *Kaleidoscope* (Birmingham: University of Alabama), June 25, 1979, A1.

4. When Wallace was termed out as governor years earlier, he had run his wife Lurleen for the post and she won. She later died of cancer. He then married Cornelia, the former Miss Alabama.

5. Letter of November 8, 1979. Hayakawa, a noted semanticist, had been embarrassed that staff composing letters under his name had made syntactical and grammatical errors.

6. After my infamous performance at the staff retreat, Packwood sent me an autographed picture of himself, which was dedicated, "To a genius of the fast bark." His handwriting, however, is so bad that I've always told people it reads, "To a genius of the first rank." No one has ever doubted my translation.

7. Coward had gone from songwriter to performer. One of his most famous stunts was to sing "Mad Dogs and Englishmen" at a very rapid clip. He could also do the number by the general from *The Pirates of Penzance* in the same way.

8. It was later converted to the River Place condominiums and the huge USA TODAY building was erected right next to it.

9. Packwood had met her during his first run for the legislature. She had been married before and then quietly divorced. Four years into her marriage with Packwood, Georgie had a stillborn child, a trauma from which she never fully recovered. However, the couple adopted a little boy, Bill, and a little girl, Shyla.

10. In 1992, when she told this story, Williamson was working for Packwood's opponent. See chapter 14.

11. From this campaign on, Packwood would implore his pollsters to find another issue that would prove as successful as saving the whales. It had ranked 10th on the 1974 poll. No one on his staff except his pollster argued for addressing it. The pollster's argument, however, caught Packwood's attention. By coming out in favor of saving the whales, you offend no one in Oregon and you pick up the conservationist vote, another unnatural constituency for Republicans.

12. He sent our strategy committee a memo on April 19, 1982, comparing our social activities with those of Benjamin Disraeli, the famous British parliamentarian. He too loved charades.

13. Tragically, Heinz was killed in a plane crash and never realized his potential.

14. Memo of January 7, 1980.
15. This last bit of advice eventually led to the most famous line in Bush's 1988 acceptance speech: "I see a kinder, gentler nation." That was the real Bush speaking.
16. Letter of April 3, 1980, the P.S.
17. He continued to send personal letters of thanks. For example, letter of January 7, 1980.

CHAPTER NINE. RUNNING A SENATE CAMPAIGN

1. Conversations in these memoirs are created from notes made soon after they took place.
2. Bush was given the nickname "Poppy" by his teammates on the Yale baseball team, which won the national championship. He was called "Poppy" because he hit an inordinate number of pop-up flies. When his kids came along, they took to calling him "Poppy" as an extension of "pop."
3. I continued to mentor him for many years.
4. The lone dissenter, Melissa Maxey, was from Georgia.

CHAPTER TEN. THE NATIONAL REPUBLICAN SENATORIAL CAMPAIGN COMMITTEE

1. I received a note from Elaine a few days later (dated November 21, 1980). She told me she was going to have a talk with her husband when he returned from China, and I shouldn't be surprised if her duties as a housewife were reduced. I took this to be a women's liberation moment, but it turned out to be a signal that Elaine was pursuing Packwood. Later in her note she wrote, "One thing will remain clear in my own mind; without your played down leadership, your humour, your sensitivity and your diplomacy, my place in the campaign would have been less tolerable." She then complained about Mimi. "My intelligence was insulted. So was yours and you handled it much better than I did." She then invited me to dance with her at the inaugural ball.
2. John informed me that the novelist John Gardner, who also taught at SUNY Binghamton, had written a novel that used for its plot a professor who runs off with a graduate student and lives as a hermit in the Pennsylvania woods.

Since John had struck up a friendship with Gardner, it is possible the plot was based on John's resignation from the campus and his romance with Judy. The novel is called *Nickel Mountain* and the professor, Soames, does bear a resemblance to Professor Macksoud.

3. The Center for Disease Control discovered at least three cases in 1980; the most noted was a flight attendant, Gayton Dugas, who may have spread the disease in New York City bathhouses. AIDS soon became associated with the gay lifestyle. The first known death from the disease occurred in January 1981 in New York City. On May 18, Lawrence Mass became the first journalist to write about the potential epidemic. His story, carried in a gay periodical, migrated to mainline media a few months later. By the end of the year, the disease had spread from New York to California, and at least 121 people had died of it.

4. In March 1981, Packwood sent me a handwritten note: "Once more, thanks. You are a whale of a guy. What you are doing is essential to what I hope is the direction we both want our party to go."

5. June 28, 1981, as carried by the *Oregonian*.

6. Paul Newman replaced Forbes Hill. Paul was brilliant but never finished his PhD at Iowa and so was not retained at UCSB. However, he and I would work together 15 years later.

7. There is a medieval art of letter writing called *dictamin* that I write about in my book *Rhetoric and Human Consciousness*, 176–78.

8. At one point, Packwood believed he had 55 senate votes against the AWACS sale and brought the issue to a vote. To his horror, only 47 senators stuck with him, and the sale was approved.

9. That reference came on March 8, 1983, in Reagan's speech to the National Association of Evangelical Ministers. He addressed the group every year he was president.

10. A picture of the event hangs in my office.

11. I had become of a friend of Tommy Griscom, the White House communications director, when he was the press aide to Senator Howard Baker.

12. Letter from Packwood dated March 10, 1982.

13. Domenici was a moderate and an ally of Packwood's on fiscal issues. Gorton was beholden because he had been elected from Washington State during the 1980 Reagan landslide. During Gorton's campaign, Packwood had provided advice. Stevens, second-in-command in the Senate, was a friend of Packwood's.

14. See Elizabeth Drew, "A Reporter in Washington: The Republicans," *New Yorker* (April 5, 1982): 132–50 for complete coverage of the conference.

15. I know of no credible Washington, D.C., insider that believed the Strategic Defense Initiative would work. They did believe it could force the hand of

Premier Gorbachev at the bargaining table. I even wrote a speech for Senator John Chafee, Republican of Rhode Island, which he delivered to the Oxford Union, in which he publicly decried the Initiative as full of holes, a threat to peace, a violation of the ABM Treaty, and too expensive. But the Soviets did believe it would work. Their paranoia got the best of them. Eventually, Gorbachev agreed to nuclear-arms reductions, and of course eventually his government fell, in part due to economic hardships in the Soviet Union caused by its military spending.

CHAPTER ELEVEN. LIVING LARGE WITH LEE IACOCCA

1. In 1997, John Cusack would star in a movie about all this called *Grosse Pointe Blank*.
2. Years later, I found it amazing that Iacocca gave no credit in his autobiography to the people who had written speeches for him over the years. I was followed by several writers who eventually left because of the workload. Iacocca claimed to have learned all he needed to know about speechmaking in a Dale Carnegie course. What Iacocca learned in that course was how to deliver a speech, not how to write one.
3. Ron De Luca was in charge of the Chrysler account.
4. See, for example, Amanda Bennett, "President Iacocca? No, but in Detroit It Sounds Plausible," *Wall Street Journal*, June 28, 1982, 1. The more Iacocca denied the rumors, the more they intensified.
5. Lee Iacocca, "How to Cut Interest Rates," *Newsweek*, August 16, 1982, 6.
6. Because of his indecisiveness, Cuomo became known as "Hamlet of the Hudson." He lost his bid for a fourth term in 1994 to Republican George Pataki.
7. My uncle, who lived in Bayonne, had worked *for* an organized crime syndicate. He was not part *of* the syndicate because he was not Italian. When my uncle's sister-in-law became first lady of the State of New Jersey in 1963, he was given a nice patronage job, and later so was his son, my cousin. Ironically, that governor went on to become chief justice of the New Jersey Supreme Court.
8. When CBS made the mistake of picking Rather over Roger Mudd for anchor, Mudd went to NBC.
9. Along with Gerald L. K. Smith and Senator Huey Long, Coughlin gave President Roosevelt fits. Coughlin's radio rants were often more popular than the President's fireside chats.
10. Gilda Radner became a sensation on *Saturday Night Live* when she played Emily Latella, a busybody who presented contrasting views on the evening

news, but got things mixed up. My favorite began, "What is all this talk about violins on television?" She had misheard the word "violence." When corrected, she would conclude with two words, "Never mind."

11. Dotty West, a Democratic political consultant, got the job I was offered and held it for more than 25 years.

12. I had started work on Iacocca's autobiography, *Iacocca*, before I left. Bill Novak was brought in to finish it. He was paid $50,000. When the book became a big hit, Novak asked Iacocca for a bonus. Lee turned him down flat.

13. In 2012, I saw Lutz on *Real Time with Bill Maher* on HBO and was stunned when he claimed there was no such thing as global warming.

CHAPTER TWELVE. PRESIDENT OF A NATIONAL FOUNDATION

1. The board of directors included me, Jack Faust, Cathy Cormack Wagner, and Dave Barrows, a longtime Packwood crony.

2. Barbara Walters continues to persevere in order to get her interview. In 2011 she landed an interview with Syrian President Bashar Al-Assad. She is the only Western journalist who has been allowed to interview him since the rebellion in Syria broke out.

3. Ironically, when I came to CSU Long Beach, they also hired George Allen out of retirement to coach the failing football team. Allen was 5 and 5 going into his last game of the season. He had never had a losing season, so winning this last one was crucial. It was close, but he won it. The team then dumped a bucket of Gatorade on Allen in celebration. When he caught pneumonia and died, so did the football program.

4. The debate occurred on March 19 against Bob Gerz, a Nader minion. The day before, I had lectured in three classes and that night discovered that Provo was a totally dry town. When I arrived in Salt Lake City the evening of the 19th, I was greeted by Professor Dennis Alexander, my pal at the University of Utah, who immediately rushed me to a "club" where you could get a good martini. I was very grateful. He said, "I knew you'd need a transfusion once you spent some time in Provo."

5. The meeting took place on May 17, 1983. This may explain why I never got a genius grant (wink).

6. We had taken the equal time and equal access rules off the table since most members of Congress supported them.

7. Eventually, I would become enough of an expert on the First Amendment to contribute regularly to the scholarly *Free Speech Yearbook*, to write for

law journals and publish several university press books, and to turn out a textbook.

8. Abrams had defended the right of the *New York Times* to publish Daniel Ellsberg's release of classified Vietnam War documents.

9. My other high-profile debate was on commercial speech against Congressman Joe Kennedy of Massachusetts. He was a bit of a bully, but I held my own and got my point across.

10. Senator Bob Dole regularly had his foundation pay for his travel. On December 24, 1984, on page 8, the *New York Times* wrote a story on this issue entitled "Lesson on How to Build Power on Power," which focused on Packwood's Freedom of Expression Foundation and Dole's foundation for people with disabilities. Andrew Schwartzman, head of Nader's pro–Fairness Doctrine lobby, criticized people who contributed to our foundation as a way of getting access to the Senator. The article quotes my response: "I would say he writes a couple of hundred letters a year to such groups as the Business Roundtable and senior broadcast executives. . . . Given our status with the Internal Revenue Service, anyone who gives money to the foundation knows it can't flow back to the Senator. . . . If they want to make a political contribution, they would give to Mr. Packwood's political organization." The *Times* praised my scholarly output and the transparency of our operation. They were less kind about Dole's foundation.

11. August 10, 1984.

12. In November 1984, I substituted for Packwood at the Jaycees dinner meeting in D.C. Their master of ceremonies wrote to me afterward: "As I mentioned on the phone this afternoon, the response to your talk has been extremely positive indeed. Both Steve Smith, our chapter president, and I have received numerous phone calls from other members who were calling to say they found your talk very interesting. I should also thank you for making me look good. After you had left, Mike Cash, who was sitting to your immediate right, announced to the group that I was the one who arranged to have you speak and I received a round of applause, further indicating how well received your remarks were." Letter from Richard Reid of November 29, 1984.

13. "Identification in Interpersonal Relationships: One Foundation of Creativity," *Southern Communication Journal* 57 (1991): 61–72.

14. This is the moment that Ron Reagan Jr. claims revealed to him that his father had Alzheimer's disease.

15. See copy of memo to Bush and his letter of thanks of July 27, 1984. I kidded Bush, "Ask why she never served in the armed forces."

16. After the election, staffers from both sides of the vice-presidential contest met for lunch and to compare notes. Ann Wexler was at the lunch and told me this story.

17. I had noticed this tendency in the primaries. In one Democratic debate, Walter Mondale had attacked front-runner Senator Gary Hart by asking of his policies, "Where's the beef?" which was at the time a line from a funny hamburger commercial. Mondale's remark was played over and over on the media. However, the line was a cheap shot. Of all the candidates, Hart had put out the most substantial description of his plans for each important issue. The media ignored the facts, went with the one-liner, and no doubt increased their ratings while debasing the democratic process.

18. Just after New Year's 1985, I received a handwritten note from Diane Sawyer concerning election night. It read in part, "Your steady hand, strong mind, and quick sense of what should be *communicated* made the event a great time."

19. See letter from Packwood dated March 21, 1985.

20. Connors had the foulest mouth of any sportsperson I have ever witnessed. He turned his head in just such a way that umpires and television microphones could not pick it up, but kids in the stands could hear him. It was disgusting. McEnroe used a different technique. Instead of profanity, he relied on sarcasm to unnerve his opponents and ridicule the umpires.

21. From 1964 to 1977, Sevareid had given his famous two-minute editorials, at the end of "The CBS Evening News with Walter Cronkite." I found them superficial and formulaic.

22. Packwood received an invitation from President Ford on June 27, 1984, to come to Colorado State University and celebrate "Broadcast Day" with a speech there. Packwood turned the offer down and recommended that they take me instead. They preferred a name politician.

CHAPTER THIRTEEN. PROTECTING BROADCASTERS' FIRST AMENDMENT RIGHTS

1. Senator William Proxmire (D-WI) had learned this the hard way. He presented one of his Golden Fleece Awards to a scientist who Proxmire claimed had fleeced the government. He presented the mock award off of Capitol Hill and was promptly sued for slander by the scientist, who won an award for damages.

2. The Court also pointed out that in floor debate Senator Hollings (D-SC) stated the legislation only applied to Murdoch; see 134 Congressional Record S 63 (January 26, 1988).

3. I had known him since the time in 1981 when he helped Packwood's chief of staff Mimi Dawson get appointed to the FCC.

4. Some of the best lawyers in Washington, D.C., today are former students of mine and remain close friends. Tom Farrell is the head of Virginia Electric and Power Company. He was often kidded that he majored in Craig Smith since fifteen of his units were in my courses.

5. *Telecommunications Research and Action Center v. FCC* reads, "We do not believe that language adopted in 1959 made the fairness doctrine a binding statutory obligation."

6. In my opinion, they were right. Any reading of the 1959 debate over the amendment makes clear that its intent was to codify the "Fairness Doctrine" so that the FCC couldn't repeal it. We consistently held to that position because we wanted the Supreme Court to declare the law unconstitutional and end the doctrine and its corollaries once and for all. That way, it could not be resurrected by Congress. But the Supreme Court sided with Bork on the matter and returned jurisdiction to the FCC. That meant Congress could intervene and reestablish the doctrine.

7. Hollings reintroduced his codification bill in 1988 and 1989, but it went nowhere. On February 10, 1989, the U.S. Court of Appeals unanimously upheld the FCC's suspension of the doctrine.

8. I wonder to this day if this is where Fox News got its slogan.

9. For example, when President Johnson tried to move his close friend Justice Abe Fortas up to chief justice, it was discovered that Fortas was receiving a large yearly consulting fee from a private foundation. The nomination was withdrawn. Nixon's nomination of Clement Haynsworth was undone when it was discovered he held a small amount of stock in a company he ruled in favor of. Nixon's nomination of G. Harold Carswell failed when it was discovered that he had made racist remarks in 1948.

10. George Will, "Packwood Revving Up Mob Instincts against Bork," *Washington Post*, October 1, 1987, A21.

11. Memo of April 28, 1987, to Pinkerton.

12. Later she would rephrase the line for Vice President Bush's acceptance speech in New Orleans at the Republican Convention. There, on the issue of volunteerism, he would call for "a thousand points of light."

13. The Maryland department survived a crisis and now thrives.

14. Letter of July 25, 1981.

15. By that time, Michael had gone through a divorce and lost half of his fortune to Diandra, including the eight-million-dollar house in Montecito, near Santa Barbara. However, Michael was able to retain the family compound on

Bermuda and share the house on Majorca, off the coast of Spain, for alternate six-month periods. Having won his first Oscar as the producer of *One Flew over the Cuckoo's Nest* in the mid '70s, he won another one for best actor in *Wall Street*, while making a new fortune in films. Then he met and wedded the very bright Catherine Zeta-Jones, by whom he had more children.

16. We began planning in the summer of 1989. I visited with Paul and his committee on July 28–30.

CHAPTER FOURTEEN. THE RISE AND FALL OF GEORGE BUSH

1. As any rhetorical theorist can tell you, I borrowed it from the great critic Kenneth Burke.
2. This line would lead to an independent group putting a commercial together that attacked Dukakis for releasing Willie Horton from jail. Once out, Horton committed more atrocious crimes.
3. As four years earlier, those of us involved in the debate preparations got together to swap war stories after the election.
4. In a letter dated January 30, 1989, he wrote, "You are a perpetual delight and comrade. Your wit and continued good natured help means more to Georgie and me than you'll ever realize."
5. The flagship journal of the National Communication Association, the *Quarterly Journal of Speech*, wrote of the former book: "Each of the three purposes is satisfied. . . . It gives the reader an excellent feel for the nature of the debates."
6. *The Book Reader* called the study "refreshingly non-partisan . . . thoughtful, amusing, extraordinarily erudite." A review in *American Journalism* claimed that "Professor Smith brings considerable expertise to his study of political expression. . . . Smith has contributed to a scholarly, conservative treatment of his topic. . . . Smith's expertise in rhetorical theory and experience as a television network news consultant enable him to integrate in a useful way his discussion of rhetorical strategies with the realities of modern journalistic organizations. Readers with journalism backgrounds will appreciate his firsthand knowledge of television news."
7. There are a number of important Supreme Court cases that have set up these criteria. The most important are *Stanley v. Georgia* (394 U.S. 557, 1969), *Miller v. California* (413 U.S. 15, 1973), and *Roth v. United States* (354 U.S. 476, 1957). These and other First Amendment cases are explored in my book with David Hunsaker, *The Four Freedoms of the First Amendment* (Long Grove, IL: Waveland Press, 2004).

8. Mapplethorpe also took beautiful photographs of flowers, some of which adorn the walls of Elton John's house.

9. *Bella Lewitzky Dance Foundation v. Frohnmayer*, 754 F. Supp. 774 (CD Cal. 1991).

10. Go to *www.firstamendmentstudies.org*. In October 2012, Tim Miller came to our campus, and I participated with him in a review of the NEA Four ruling.

11. Pin Point could be seen across a large lake by the rich folks living on the other side. One of the rich kids that came to Pin Point to play with the black kids was Johnny Mercer, who eventually became one of America's premier songwriters, employing the rhythms he heard in Pin Point.

12. Jane Mayer and Jill Abramson point out that the Justice Department sought to "bury ideology and sell biography" using the "Pin Point story." *Strange Justice: The Selling of Clarence Thomas* (Boston: Houghton Mifflin, 1994), 30.

13. "Remarks Announcing the New American Schools Development Corporation Board, July 8, 1991," *Public Papers of the Presidents of the United States: George Bush, 1991*, book 2 (Washington, DC: Government Printing Office, 1992), 830.

14. "Remarks at the Annual Convention of the National Fraternal Order of Police in Pittsburgh, Pennsylvania, August 14, 1991," *Public Papers of the Presidents of the United States: George Bush, 1991*, book 2 (Washington, DC: Government Printing Office, 1992), 1041.

15. "Remarks at a Kickoff Ceremony for the Eighth Annual National Night Out Against Crime in Arlington, Virginia, August 6, 1991," *Public Papers of the Presidents of the United States: George Bush, 1991*, book 2 (Washington, DC: Government Printing Office, 1992), 1119.

16. Trevor Parry-Giles, "Celebritized Justice, Civil Rights, and the Clarence Thomas Nomination," in *The White House and Civil Rights Policy*, ed. James Aune (College Station, TX: Texas A&M University Press, 2004).

17. Trevor Parry-Giles, "Celebritized Justice."

18. Due to a staff error, committee chair Senator Joe Biden had failed to provide the information to the other committee members.

19. Her argument was that references to pornographic videos, pubic hair, and the like were tantamount to sexual harassment.

20. John Anthony Maltese, *The Selling of Supreme Court Nominees* (Baltimore: Johns Hopkins University Press, 1995), 93.

21. Senate Committee on the Judiciary, *Nomination of Judge Clarence Thomas to Be Associate Justice of the Supreme Court of the United States*, 102nd Cong., 1st Session, October 13, 1991, p. 157–58. Like Hugo Black's radio address of 1937 when he was in trouble for his past association with the KKK, Thomas's outburst broke through the mediating screen of news reporters and commentators.

Earlier, Thomas had previewed this strategy when he said, "I have been able . . . to defy poverty, avoid prison, overcome segregation, bigotry, racism, and obtain one of the finest educations available in this country. But I have not been able to overcome this process. . . . I will not provide the rope for my own lynching." Senate Committee on the Judiciary, *Nomination of Judge Clarence Thomas to Be Associate Justice of the Supreme Court of the United States*, 102nd Cong., 1st Session, October 13, 1991, 8–10. ABC's *Nightline* ran three programs on the hearings.

22. Vanessa Bowles Beasley, "The Logic of Power in the Hill-Thomas Hearings: A Rhetorical Analysis," *Political Communication* 11 (1994): 287–97.

23. For a full analysis, see William L. Benoit and Dawn M. Nill, "A Critical Analysis of Judge Clarence Thomas' Statement before the Senate Judiciary Committee," *Communication Studies* 49 (1998): 179–95; Michael J. Gerhardt, "Divided Justice: A Commentary on the Nomination and Confirmation of Justice Thomas," *George Washington Law Review* 60 (1992): 969–96.

24. See Joseph Faria and David Markey, "Supreme Court Appointments after the Thomas Nomination: Reforming the Confirmation Process," *Journal of Legal Commentary* 7 (1991): 389–416; John Massaro, "President Bush's Management of the Thomas Nomination," *Presidential Studies Quarterly* 26 (1996): 816–27.

25. As we shall see, in a Nixonian twist, Packwood was forced to turn his diaries over to the investigators. The diaries were transcribed from his dictated tapes by his loyal secretary Cathy Wagner Cormack.

26. Buchanan aired an obnoxious anti-Bush ad in the Georgia primary that showed gays cavorting in a Gay Pride parade and implied that Bush was in favor of their lifestyle. While Bush was certainly more sympathetic to the plight of HIV/AIDS victims, he was a conservative on gay issues.

CHAPTER FIFTEEN. THE FALL OF BOB PACKWOOD

1. In Packwood's case, it was a father who drank heavily and was not a very successful lobbyist. A victim of polio, Fred Packwood was mean to himself, his wife, and his son, whom he raised to be studious and ambitious. He also discouraged him from making friends with his peers and encouraged him to spend time with his aunts, uncles, and father's clients.

2. The quotation is from Raymond Price's *With Nixon* (New York: Viking House Press, 1977) as quoted in Walter R. Newell, *Soul of a Leader* (New York: Harper Collins, 2009), 73.

3. In 2010, Packwood was called to serve on the commission headed by Senator Simpson and Erskine Bowles examining ways by which the national debt could be curtailed.

4. Eventually, I would receive the Robert M. O'Neil Award twice for articles published in the *Free Speech Yearbook*. That meant a lot to me because I had enormous respect for the career and writing of Bob O'Neil.

5. "The Problem with Writing on Rhetorical Charisma, Power, and Spirituality" appeared as the lead article in the *Journal of Communication and Religion* in 1993.

6. See "Finding the Spiritual Dimension in Rhetoric," *Western Journal of Communication* 57 (1993): 266–71; "Heidegger and Aristotle on Emotion: Questions of Time and Space" (with Hyde), in *The Critical Turn: Rhetoric and Philosophy in Postmodern Discourse*, ed. Ian Angus and Lenore Langsdorf (Carbondale: Southern Illinois University Press, 1992): 68–99; "Existential Responsibility and Roman Decorum: A New Praxis," *Western Journal of Communication* 56 (1992): 68–89.

7. It is available as an e-book now but was originally published by Praeger Press.

8. The issue would be illegal immigration. Though the issue would work well in Republican primaries, it would be the beginning of the end of Hispanics voting for Republicans in respectable numbers in national elections.

9. August 31, 1995.

10. August 31, 1995.

11. I never received my last paycheck.

CHAPTER SIXTEEN. THERE'S MORE POLITICS IN EDUCATION THAN EDUCATION IN POLITICS

1. These humbling honors would continue to accumulate. In the spring semester of 2000, I was named the Outstanding Professor on the campus. At the beginning of the spring semester of 2001, I was inducted into Phi Beta Kappa. Even nicer was that since I had helped so many Associated Student officers with leadership training, the Associated Students gave me a lifetime pass to all events on campus. In 2006, I was presented with the Nicholas Perkins Hardeman Award for Academic Leadership. I couldn't help but reflect that I had come a long way from the days of trial and tribulation at San Diego State and the University of Virginia. I began to worry a little that I was becoming too much a part of the establishment. However, my weekly calls from John Macksoud kept that in check.

2. The short title for the act was the Ballistics, Law Assistance, and Safety Technology Act (BLAST). The act went on to "establish a computer system" for identification of the bullet head markings.

3. I have expressed this opinion and the ones above in many editorials over the years. Invariably, they lead to death threats. I've not taken them seriously; however, one of our allies in Seattle was shot to death because of his work on gun-control measures there.

4. The new governor, Gray Davis, was a Democrat who promptly politicized the board, doing the bidding of the teachers union.

5. Clarke Rountree was kind enough to cite my article in his book *Judging the Supreme Court: Constructions of Motives in* Bush v. Gore (East Lansing: Michigan State University Press, 2007).

6. David Twohy had written *Pitch Black* for Vin Diesel, and when he wrote and directed *The Chronicles of Riddick* for Vin, David allowed us to take the profits from the premiere at Universal Studios.

7. The most famous and kindest to the students was Reidar Jönsson, who wrote the Swedish novel *My Life as a Dog*, which was turned into an award-winning film.

8. These studies in American public address tended to be chapters in books about many orators, or scholarly articles in journals about single speeches. My book was one of the first full-blown books on a single orator.

9. The book met with generally good reviews. I was very moved when Karlyn Campbell, a notable in public-address criticism, took the time to send me a personal letter praising the book, particularly its analysis of how Webster braided forms of public address to generate his powerful rhetoric. A review in the *Historian* stated, "Although Webster has many biographers, Craig R. Smith . . . makes a significant contribution in this volume with what amounts to an interdisciplinary history of the statesman's speeches. Smith's method is to place rhetorical analyses of Webster's major orations within a narrative of his political career"; vol. 69, no. 1.

10. While the book did not sell very well, I took some comfort from the fact that the book eventually came out to very good reviews. For example, the reviewer in the *Free Speech Yearbook*, Professor McKay, wrote, "This is a book I intend to use the next time I teach my course. . . . It offers a well written narrative providing both a historical perspective and a contemporary view of freedom in America as guaranteed by the constitutional interpretations and judgments of our federal court system. . . . The authors review the genesis of the First Amendment from the period of colonial America to our 21st Century in an intelligent and uncomplicated fashion. . . . I am pleased that their observations are thoughtful and challenging, underscoring the importance of citizens knowing about their rights."

11. See *Brown v. Entertainment Merchants Assn.*, 564 U.S. No. 08-1448 (2011).

12. On the very hot afternoon of July 4, 1850, Taylor, in dress blues, began drinking his favorite drink, a Cajun Cherry. It consisted of a tumbler half full of pitted cherries that were covered with cream and bourbon. The drink may have been tainted, because it caused his stomach to rupture and he died shortly after.

13. Jack had been a student of mine at San Diego State. In 2000, he hired me as a consultant to Royal Caribbean to help with educational programs for the ships' crews. That consultantship ended with 9/11 since cruise-ship bookings declined steeply.

14. I even accepted an invitation from one of my former students, David Kennedy, to be an overnight guest on the USS *Ronald Reagan*, a nuclear-powered aircraft carrier. David had been one of the student body chairs at UVA that I had advised. He eventually became a captain in the Navy, and then retired into advising it. I participated in a tailhook landing on the ship off the coast of California, toured the ship, talked with pilots all night long since it was too noisy to sleep, met with the admiral in charge of the Pacific Fleet, and participated in a catapult takeoff back to Coronado Island the following day. It was a blast.

15. The crisis has continued. Tuition is now around $6,000 per student and the state is only paying a little more than $5,000 for each student.

16. This does not count those receiving Pell grants from the government or other scholarships. The fee of about $3,500 a year was still one of the lowest in the United States. But as we have seen, the fee rose to around $6,000 a year by 2012.

17. The finding was composed by a Hispanic woman who ran the Office of Equity and Diversity.

18. These X, Y, Z names are invented.

CHAPTER SEVENTEEN. LAST LESSONS
OUT OF THE WHIRL OF EVENTS

1. The article was published in the *Law Journal of Florida International University*.

2. The second edition of my *Silencing the Opposition: How the U.S. Government Suppresses Freedom of Expression during Major Crises* (Albany, NY: SUNY Press, 2011) includes chapters by five colleagues.

3. One of the great facts of American politics is that if you hang around long enough, you eventually get nominated for president or vice president. As we

saw earlier in this book, Biden made his first run at the presidential nomination in 1987, twenty-one years before he finally got nominated as the vice-presidential candidate of the Democratic Party.

4. Mary had gotten her BA in economics at Cal State Long Beach, so the connection was a natural one.

5. See, for example, the end of the first chapter in his posthumously published *The Garden of Eden.*

6. This did not change in the following year. Just after Labor Day in 2010, Lou Harris released a poll that showed that an endorsement from Obama was more likely to hurt a candidate than help a candidate.

7. The voter ID laws were generally suspended pending further review. The attempt to recall the governor of Wisconsin for signing the anti-union law was repulsed, but courts in some states overturned some of the anti-union legislation. However, Republicans were successful against the unions in Ohio and Michigan.

8. The fact is that Romney received a lower percentage of even the Mormon vote than did McCain.

9. McCain received about 59,950,000 in 2008; Romney received 59,650,000 in 2012. Obama received about 69,500,000 in 2008 and only about 63,500,000 in 2012.

10. One of the most interesting items about the 2012 election was the accuracy of the polls. Republican pundits such as Peggy Noonan, Michael Barone, George Will, and Karl Rove looked pretty bad relying on crowd size and anecdotal evidence to predict a Romney win. It always surprises me when conservatives have no sense of history. In 1960, Nixon drew his largest crowds in Georgia, but failed to carry the state; Kennedy drew his largest crowds in Ohio, but failed to carry the state. The statisticians, led by Nate Silver, who got all 50 states right in the electoral college, won the day. That had not happened before, particularly on the state level, where polls tended to be way off.

11. An attempt to mildly reform the filibuster was being floated by Senate Majority Leader Harry Reid but went nowhere.

12. I might add that Governor Nikki Haley wisely picked a black man to replace Jim DeMint in the Senate. Tim Scott is the first African American senator from South Carolina, which has a large African American population.

13. Also available on YouTube.

Bibliography

Aristotle. *On Rhetoric: A Theory of Civic Discourse.* Trans. George Kennedy. 2nd ed. New York: Oxford University Press, 2007.

Arntson, Paul, and Craig R. Smith. "Identification in Interpersonal Relationships: One Foundation of Creativity." *Southern Communication Journal* 57 (1991): 61–72.

Beasley, Vanessa Bowles. "The Logic of Power in the Hill-Thomas Hearings: A Rhetorical Analysis." *Political Communication* 11 (1994): 287–97.

Bella Lewitzky Dance Foundation v. Frohnmayer, 754 F. Supp. 774 (CD Cal. 1991).

Bennett, Amanda. "President Iacocca? No, but in Detroit It Sounds Plausible." *Wall Street Journal*, June 28, 1982, 1.

Benoit, William L., and Dawn M. Nill. "A Critical Analysis of Judge Clarence Thomas' Statement before the Senate Judiciary Committee." *Communication Studies* 49 (1998): 179–95.

Boyarsky, Bill. *The Rise of Ronald Reagan.* New York: Random House, 1968.

Brown v. Entertainment Merchants Assn., 564 U.S. No. 08-1448 (2011).

Bush, George H. W. "Remarks Announcing the New American Schools Development Corporation Board, July 8, 1991." *Public Papers of the Presidents of the United States: George Bush, 1991*, book 2, p. 830. Washington, DC: Government Printing Office, 1992.

———. "Remarks at the Annual Convention of the National Fraternal Order of Police in Pittsburgh, Pennsylvania, August 14, 1991." *Public Papers of the Presidents of the United States: George Bush, 1991*, book 2, p. 1041. Washington, DC: Government Printing Office, 1992.

———. "Remarks at a Kickoff Ceremony for the Eighth Annual National Night Out Against Crime in Arlington, Virginia, August 6, 1991." *Public Papers of the Presidents of the United States: George Bush, 1991*, book 2, p. 1119. Washington, DC: Government Printing Office, 1992.

Cheney, Dick. *In My Time.* New York: Threshold Editions, 2011.

Chester, Lewis, Geoffrey Hodgson, and Brian Page. *An American Melodrama: The Presidential Campaign of 1968.* New York: Viking Press, 1969.

Clymer, Adam. "Bush Hot Property on GOP Dinner Circuit." *New York Times*, February 19, 1978, A26.

Coleman, Don. "SDSC Council to Continue Voting: Professor Cites Intimidation by Ethnic Groups." *San Diego Evening Tribune*, April 25, 1970, A2.

Drew, Elizabeth. "A Reporter in Washington: The Republicans," *New Yorker* (April 5, 1982): 132–50.

Faria, Joseph, and David Markey. "Supreme Court Appointments after the Thomas Nomination: Reforming the Confirmation Process." *Journal of Legal Commentary* 7 (1991): 389–416.

Ford, Gerald R. "Remarks at the Southern Baptist Convention, Norfolk, Virginia, June 15, 1976." *Public Papers of the Presidents of the United States: Gerald R. Ford, 1976–77*, book 2, pp. 1877–80. Washington, DC: Government Printing Office, 1978.

———. "Remarks on Taking the Oath of Office, August 9, 1974." *Public Papers of the Presidents of the United States: Gerald R. Ford, 1974*, book 1, pp. 1–2. Washington, DC: Government Printing Office, 1975,

Gardner, John. *Nickel Mountain.* New York: New Directions Publishing Co., 1973.

Gavin, William F. *Speechwright: An Insider's Take on Political Rhetoric.* East Lansing: Michigan State University Press, 2010.

"George Bush: Campaign 80's Early Bird." *Newsweek*, December 11, 1978, 37–39.

Gerhardt, Michael J. "Divided Justice: A Commentary on the Nomination and Confirmation of Justice Thomas." *George Washington Law Review* 60 (1992): 969–96.

Greenwood, Noel. "UC Faculty Dossiers Urged; Reagan Calls It 'Witch Hunt.'" *Los Angeles Times*, June 16, 1970, A1, 22.

Greenwood, Noel, and William Tromley. "Ouster of UC's Heyns Topic of Secret Reagan Parley." *Los Angeles Times*, June 13, 1970, A1, 19.

Hartmann, Robert. *Palace Politics: An Inside Account of the Ford Years.* New York: McGraw Hill, 1980.

Hilts, Philip. "Eye on the White House." *Potomac Magazine (Washington Post)*, April 21, 1974, 26–30.

Hinson, Keith. "Wallace Talks Shop in CA Class." *Kaleidoscope* (Birmingham: University of Alabama), June 25, 1979, A1.

Hunsaker, David, and Craig Smith. *The Four Freedoms of the First Amendment.* Long Grove, IL: Waveland Press, 2004.

Hyde, Michael, and Craig Smith. "Heidegger and Aristotle on Emotion: Questions of Time and Space." In *The Critical Turn: Rhetoric and Philosophy in Postmodern Discourse*, ed. Ian Angus and Lenore Langsdorf, 68–99. Carbondale: Southern Illinois University Press, 1992.

Iacocca, Lee. "How to Cut Interest Rates." *Newsweek*, August 16, 1982, 6.

Maltese, John Anthony. *The Selling of Supreme Court Nominees.* Baltimore: Johns Hopkins University Press, 1995.

Massaro, John. "President Bush's Management of the Thomas Nomination." *Presidential Studies Quarterly* 26 (1996): 816–27.

Mayer, Jane, and Jill Abramson. *Strange Justice: The Selling of Clarence Thomas.* Boston: Houghton Mifflin, 1994.

McGee, Michael. "The 'Ideograph': A Link between Rhetoric and Ideology." *Quarterly Journal of Speech* 66 (1980): 1–16.

———. "In Search of 'The People': A Rhetorical Alternative." *Quarterly Journal of Speech* 61 (1975): 245–47.

———. "A Materialist's Conception of Rhetoric." In *Explorations in Rhetoric: Studies in Honor of Douglas Ehninger*, ed. R. E. McKerrow, 23–48. Glenview, IL: Scott Foresman, 1982.

———. "Text, Context, and the Fragmentation of Contemporary Culture." *Western Journal of Speech Communication* 54 (1990): 274–89.

McGee, Michael, and Martha Martin. "Public Knowledge and Ideological Argumentation." *Communication Monographs* 50 (1983): 47–65.

Mieczkowski, Yanek. "Gerald Ford's Near Miracle in 1976." *American History*, November 30, 2007 (online journal).

Miller v. California, 413 U.S. 15 (1973).

Newell, Walter R. *Soul of a Leader.* New York: Harper Collins, 2009.

Parry-Giles, Trevor. "Celebritized Justice, Civil Rights, and the Clarence Thomas Nomination." In *The White House and Civil Rights Policy*, ed. James Aune. College Station, TX: Texas A&M University Press, 2004.

"President Kicks Off Bicentennial at Air and Space Museum." *Washington Star*, July 2, 1976, 10.

Price, Raymond. *With Nixon.* New York: Viking House Press, 1977.

Reagan, Ronald, and Richard G. Hubler. *Where's the Rest of Me?* New York: Duell, Sloan and Pearce, 1965.

Roth v. United States, 354 U.S. 476 (1957).

Rountree, Clarke. *Judging the Supreme Court: Constructions of Motives in* Bush v. Gore. East Lansing: Michigan State University Press, 2007.

Schlesinger, Robert. *White House Ghosts: Presidents and Their Speechwriters.* New York: Simon and Schuster, 2008.

Senate Committee on the Judiciary. *Nomination of Judge Clarence Thomas to Be Associate Justice of the Supreme Court of the United States.* 102nd Cong., 1st Session, October 13, 1991.

Smith, Craig R. "Contemporary Political Speech Writing." *Southern Speech Communication Journal* 42 (1976): 52–67.

———. "Existential Responsibility and Roman Decorum: A New Praxis." *Western Journal of Communication* 56 (1992): 68–89.

———. "Finding the Spiritual Dimension in Rhetoric." *Western Journal of Communication* 57 (1993): 266–71.

———. "Heidegger's Theory of Authentic Discourse." In *Analecta Husserliana*, vol. 15, ed. Calvin Schrag, 209–17. World Institute for Advanced Phenomenological Research; D. Reidel Publishing Co., 1983.

———. "Martin Heidegger and the Dialogue with Being." *Central States Speech Journal* 36 (1985): 256–69.

———. *Rhetoric and Human Consciousness: A History.* 4th ed. Long Grove, IL: Waveland Press, 2013.

———. *Silencing the Opposition: How the U.S. Government Suppresses Freedom of Expression during Major Crises.* 2nd ed. Albany: SUNY Press, 2011.

Smith, Craig R., and Michael Hyde. "Hermeneutics and Rhetoric." *Quarterly Journal of Speech* 65 (1979): 347–63.

———. "Rethinking the Public: The Role of Emotion in Being-with-Others." *Quarterly Journal of Speech* 77 (1991): 446–66.

Stanley v. Georgia, 394 U.S. 557 (1969).

Stern, Sheldon M. *The Cuban Missile Crisis in American Memory.* Palo Alto, CA: Stanford University Press, 2012.

Telecommunications Research and Action Center v. FCC, 750 F 2d, 70 (1984).

Walker, Daniel. *Rights in Conflict: Convention Week in Chicago, August 25–29, 1968.* A Report submitted by Daniel Walker, Director of the Chicago Study Team, to the National Commission on the Causes and Prevention of Violence. Introduction by Max Frankel. New York: E.P. Dutton, 1968.

Will, George. "Packwood Revving Up Mob Instincts against Bork." *Washington Post*, October 1, 1987, A21.

Willoughby, William. "Righteous Ford Talks Like Carter, Wows Baptists." *Washington Star*, June 16, 1976, A1, 15.

Witcover, Jules. *Marathon: The Pursuit of the Presidency, 1972–1976.* New York: Signet, 1977.

Index

CBS News, ix, 7, 19, 22, 28, 58, 66, 70, 88, 145, 228, 256–59, 278; and 1968 conventions, 6, 40, 44–55; and 1972 conventions, 79–83; and 1974 election, 89–91; and 1982 election, 216–20; and 1984 conventions, 234–36; and 1984 election, 237; and 1985 inaugural, 238; and 1986 election, 247

Center for First Amendment Studies, 273, 291, 310

Chavez, Caesar, 45, 64, 70, 299

Cheney, Dick: as congressman, 157, 195; as Ford's chief of staff, 98–100, 102, 112, 113, 352 (n. 4), 355 (n. 4); as vice president, 313, 318

Churchill, Winston, 16, 35, 77–78, 117

Clarence, Thomas, 277, 365, 366

Clement, Paul D., 309

Clinton, Bill, 106–11, 281, 282, 285, 293, 303, 308, 321, 330

Clinton, Hillary, 330

Columbus Day Parade, 214–16

Connally, John, 134, 155, 171, 178

Connor, Dennis, 293

Couric, Katie, 88, 90

Cronkite, Walter, 2, 22, 216, 235; and 1968 conventions; 46, 48–49, 52, 54–55; and 1972 election, 79, 80–83, 89, 91; and 1980 election, 178

Cross, Bob, 92–94, 114, 259

Cuomo, Mario, 215, 359 (n. 6)

D

Dahlgren, Virginia, 22, 24, 348 (n. 12)

Daley, Richard, 53–54

D'Amato, Alphonse, 210, 288

Davis, Angela, 68

Dawes, William, 9

Dawson, Mimi Weyforth, 143–44, 148–50, 284; as FCC commissioner, 189, 228, 363 (n. 3); and Packwood reelection campaign, 158–60, 163, 165, 168–69, 172–73, 175–78, 180–82, 357 (n. 1, chap. 10)

Debuck, Diane, 117

Democratic Convention: 1956, 47; 1960, 27; 1968, 6, 17, 52–53, 55, 64; 1976, 179; 1984, 215

Dennis, Patrick, 249

Dewey, Thomas E., 16, 100

Diefendorfer, Bill, 149, 242–43

Dirksen, Everett, 19

Dolan, Terry, 190

Dolan, Tony, 190

Dole, Bob, 287, 289, 361 (n. 10); and 1976 presidential campaign, 121, 155, 354 (n. 22); and 1988 presidential campaign, 259, 265–66; and 1992 presidential campaign, 281; and 1996 presidential campaign, 297–98, 303

Donaldson, Sam, 82, 259

Donnelly, Elaine, 232

Douglas, Michael, 38, 205, 263, 309

Doyle, Dennis, 63, 70, 86, 176, 191

Doyle, Jim, 27, 31, 32, 154

Dukakis, Michael, 261, 266–69, 364 (n. 2)

E

Eagleton, Thomas, 81–82

Eckart, Dennis, 269

Edberg, Stefan, 273

Eisenhower, Dwight, 50; and 1952 election, 19–20, 41; and 1964 Republican Convention, 35–36; as president, 34, 67, 292, 342

Ellis Island, 10–12, 211–14, 218, 221

Emerson, Ralph Waldo, 9

Erburu, Bob, 226

F

Fairness Doctrine, 218, 229, 232–33, 238, 241, 249–51, 363

Falstaff, Henry V., 90

Falwell, Jerry, 274, 314

Feinstein, Dianne, 308

Ferraro, Geraldine, 234–37

First Amendment, 16, 68, 197, 229, 235, 245, 251, 291, 306, 329; and academic freedom, 310, 320; and advertising, 239; and censorship, 275–76, 323; and